From Nuremberg to Nineveh

– war, peace and the making of modernity

Mark Turley

Copyright © Mark Turley 2008

The right of Mark Turley to be identified as the author of this work has been asserted in accordance with sections 77 and 78 of the Copyright, Designs and Patents Act 1988.

All rights reserved. No part of this publication may be reproduced, stored in or introduced into a retrieval system, or transmitted, in any form, or by any means without the prior written permission of the publisher.

This book is sold subject to the condition that it shall not, by way of trade or otherwise, be lent, resold, hired out, or otherwise circulated without the publisher's prior consent in any form of binding or cover other than that in which it is published and without a similar condition including this condition being imposed on the subsequent purchaser.

First published in Great Britain
by
Vandal Publications, London

ISBN 978-0-9559810-0-5

CIP catalogue record for this book is available from the British Library

Cover design by Anastasia

This one is for Uta and Lola.

The past and the future.

Contents

1. Introduction 9
2. And so it goes… 13
3. The Climate of the Time 15
4. The Legal Platform 21
5. Defendants? 31
6. The Indictment 35
7. A most terrible and convincing case 40
8. Der Dicke 45
9. The Loneliest Man in the World 61
10. Skinhead, skinhead! 67
11. The Penitent Man 75
12. I am Kaltenbrunner… 84
13. The Root of all Evil 102
14. Nazi Diplomacy 111
15. The Politics of Race 116
16. The Sailors 128
17. Befehl ist befehl 132
18. A Thousand Years of Guilt 139
19. The Pied Piper and the Voice of Radio Deutschland 148
20. A final word on the trial 155
21. Genocide at Nuremberg 162
22. Freedom, Democracy and 'The Conquering of Evil'. 174
23. An Unseen Tyrant? 183
24. The Conceits of Academia 187
References 189

From Nuremberg to Nineveh

Introduction

Pre-dating the earliest days of recorded history, going back to the oral traditions of the ancient tribes, the most abiding theme of human storytelling has been the battle between good and evil. The Hindu legend of Rama and Sita, Adam and Eve, Beowulf and Grendel, the list could stretch for volumes. This clear division of our experiences of the world appeals, it seems, to something simple within us. It offers comforting answers to our most troubling questions. It symbolises both our dealings with each other and that which we describe as 'conscience'. And it speaks of simple self-knowledge. After all, each of us is capable of kindness, compassion and sometimes cruelty. From folklore's witches and dragons, to Satan's army of demons, to the inscrutable Dr. Fu-Manchu or Darth Vader, we have used the motif of the monster, the fiend or the wicked villain and usually their ultimate defeat, to juxtapose that which we believe to be good and noble about our species.

The generation of people that grew up in the 1920s and 30s, during the fragile peace that followed the Great War, were perhaps more imbued with this notion than any that had gone before. The captivating, new medium of cinema raised them on a diet of weekly serials. One dimensional characters, physical action and cliffhanger endings provided the template. 'Horse operas' were big box office too – tales of the Wild West, of spreading the American way beyond existing frontiers, in which morality was so clearly defined as to be shown by the colour of a man's hat. Throughout their childhoods and adolescence this age-group received regular doses of celluloid, pseudo-virtue in digestible, two-hour chunks. The Italian Marxist, Antonio Gramsci, would have described this as creating a 'cultural hegemony'.[1]

Following in the trenchfoot bootsteps of their fathers, who endured hell in the quagmires of Verdun, Paschendale and the Somme, this new cohort of cannon-fodder reached young adulthood and found themselves embroiled in a vicious and attritional war. Their war, however, would be far worse. Worldwide, sixty to seventy million people would die in it. And wartime, of course, has always leant itself to the promotion of simple moral polemics. As observed by the Chinese general, Sun Tzu, in his legendary manual 'The Art of War', written in the first millennium BC, 'The Tao causes the people to be fully in accord with the ruler. Thus they will die with him and not fear danger...Warfare is the Tao of deception.'[2]

Upon winning the war, the leaders of this generation of westerners had then to set about winning the peace. Just as before, popular culture and cinema would be invaluable, (as would academia – history is, after all, just another form of story) and the huge raft of films and books made about World War Two since its end, with very few exceptions, have enforced the idea that it was a battle between the forces of darkness and the forces of light: Star Wars without the spaceships.

Considering how simplistic this narrative is, it has shown incredible longevity. With the passing of time and the healing of divisions and resentments, it would have been reasonable to expect a more balanced view to emerge. Yet even today, in the early 21st century, opinion polls asking for the 'most evil man in history' will invariably throw up Adolf Hitler and often Himmler, Goebbels and Eichmann in their top tens. Roose- velt, Truman and Churchill are never mentioned. The latter is still regarded by many in Britain as a hero, a symbol of national greatness. Not only that, but the abbreviation 'Nazi' has become synonymous with *evil*. And this is not just in the popular mind.

The much quoted political theorist Hannah Arendt, after observing the trial Of SS officer Adolf Eichmann in Jerusalem (1961-62) coined a famous description. He possessed, she said, the 'banality of evil.'[3] This has become an oft-repeated sound-bite, appearing in newspaper articles, book reviews and all things connected to the history of the time. He did not, Arendt declared, appear to be deranged or a psychopath. His demeanour in the dock convinced Arendt that he was merely a normal bureaucrat who had participated in the Nazi conspiracy in much the same way as a senior manager in any hierarchical organisation

---

[1] Gramsci identified hegemony as a tool of ideological control used to maintain the status-quo by ensuring that society could be dominated by one group.
[2] Sun Tzu, *The Art of War* (Running Press 2003) p.11-15
[3] Hannah Arendt, *Eichmann in Jerusalem, a Report on the Banality of Evil* (Penguin, 1994 new ed.)

would.

It is testament to the level of unreality with which that period of history has been regarded that such a bizarre comment could achieve such renown. It shows that even academics bought into this idea of Nazi *evil*, to the extent that Arendt believed it was comment-worthy (she wrote an entire book about it) that Eichmann did not display outward signs of it.

This demonstrated that on several levels our image-hungry culture has made a childish connection between an ideology – National Socialism – and a mythical, religious notion – *evil*. This may have been expedient once, when we needed to rouse the boys to take up arms for the cause, but that time has long passed. Yet for various reasons, many of them political, this connection has persisted into the present day. Over the last thirty years, the majority of serious books on the subject have made little attempt to take a more adult view. Titles have included; *Adolf Hitler, Evil Mastermind of the Holocaust* (Jacobs-Altman), *The Evil that Men do, the Rise of the Nazis* (Rubin), *Heydrich, the Face of Nazi Evil* (Drederichs), *Explaining Hitler, the Search for the Origins of his Evil* (Rosenbaum), *Hitler, the Pathology of Evil* (Victor), *The Logic of Evil, Social Origins of the Nazi Party* (Brusleigh), *Mirroring Evil, Nazi Imagery in Recent Art* (Kleebatt), *Hitler's Bureaucrats, the Nazi Security Police and the Banality of Evil* (Lozowick), *Leap to Life, Triumph over Nazi Evil* (Rebhun), *Soldiers of Evil, Commandants of Nazi Concentration Camps* (Segev), *Nuremberg, Evil on Trial* (Owen) and many, many more.

This book sprang from a simple premise, that in the real world, the one that exists outside of Hollywood and comic-books and blood-and-guts horror novels, there is no such thing as *evil*. There may be evil acts, but not evil entities. It also sprang from a question – how can so many supposedly intelligent people, university professors, published historians and researchers, buy into such a silly idea?

Invariably when considering these issues, we are led on a path toward the Holocaust, the result of the escalating anti-Jewish policies of the Nazis during the thirties and early forties, in which it is said that six million Jews (perhaps as many as eleven million people altogether) were singled out and deliberately exterminated, roughly half in huge homicidal gas chambers. Beyond that, however, and sometimes it is difficult to see beyond that, we are faced with a very clear issue. And it is to do with how we, in the modern world, perceive the things that happen to us. On examination, we see that some events become iconic.

Everyone remembers, so we are told, where they were when Neil Armstrong descended the ladder and walked on the moon. The shootings of John F. Kennedy or John Lennon, Martin Luther King's 'I have a dream' speech, the finding of Elvis Presley, cold on his toilet, full of burgers and barbiturates, all occupy sacred places in our collective consciousness. They have been engineered into legend and became far greater through repeated recollection than they ever really were.

Even when this grab-bag method of memory is applied to the horrors of war, the knowledge it imparts is still delivered superficially, as snapshots – that howling, Vietnamese girl, naked before a Napalm sky, the Hiroshima mushroom cloud, the bodies at Belsen. We use them like stock-photos, to be wheeled out whenever a bit of pathos is desired – look here's that important thing that's common to all of us – isn't it poignant/amazing/terrible?

But none of this, obviously, bears any relation to genuine memory. These images are only simplistic visualisations of things too complex and problematic to show in a photo or a ten second movie clip. These 'memories', in so far as they exist, have been manufactured for us.

The event primarily discussed within these pages does not have iconic status. Unlike the visceral images of World War Two, The Nuremberg Trial receives relatively little coverage. It wouldn't make such a good snapshot, you see. But in the pages that follow it will be demonstrated that it was an event so fundamental in creating the world we live in now, that every global citizen should examine it. It was arguably the defining event of the last hundred years – we still live in its shadow. And like a great deal of things that happen during or as a result of war, it has been so obscured by propaganda that few understand its true meaning.

Defendants under guard in the dock at Nuremberg
Front row, left to right: Göring, Hess, von Ribbentrop and Keitel
Back row, left to right: Dönitz, Raeder, von Schirach and Sauckel

1

And so it goes…

…as time goes on I firmly believe it (the trial) will come to be recognised as one of the most important events in the history of the world.[4]

- US prosecutor Thomas Dodd

After six years of fighting, the like of which had never before been seen, a façade of peace was unfurled in 1945, ushered in by the surrender of a German nation reduced to rubble and the devastation of nuclear attack on Japan. In Britain, America and the Soviet Union, thoughts naturally turned to what to do with the erstwhile enemy. Pre-planned pieces fell into place and on November 21st, in a courthouse in the Middle Franconian region of Bavaria, a portly, middle-aged lawyer stood and began to talk. His words were slow, heavy with gravitas and chosen with measured confidence, expressing the importance of rea- son and responsibility; the moral imperatives of law. His address lasted for an entire day and even now, from Berlin, to New York, to Jerusalem, it finds resonance in the ears of the world.

So began The Trial of the Major War Criminals before the International Military Tribunal (IMT), popularly now known as the 'Trial of the Century'. Set in the impressively renovated *Justizpalast* (Palace of Justice) on *Fürtherstrasse* 22 in Nuremberg, it was to be the world's first truly international legal hear- ing. Not only did the prosecution team consist of French, British, American and Russian lawyers but two hundred and fifty members of the world's press sat above the proceedings in a gallery. A company of twelve interpreters were on hand to translate. They chattered into microphones as the lawyer spoke.

Nuremberg was a trial of many firsts. Among them was the now common practice of simultaneous translation, which involved listening in one language and relaying the meaning instantly in another. Members of the courtroom were provided with headsets with five channels that provided English, French, Russian and German versions of whatever language was being spoken. Listeners simply had to pick the channel appropriate to their needs at any given time.

The deliverer of this marathon monologue was Allied chief prosecutor, Robert Houghwout Jackson, originally from Frewsburg, New York, considered by contemporaries to be one of the finest legal minds of his generation and still regarded in some circles today as the greatest Supreme Court Justice of the 20th Century. Over his left shoulder, as he so eloquently spoke from the lectern sat Hermann Göring, Rudolf Hess and Julius Streicher, along with the rest of the most culpable surviving members of the Third Reich. With Hitler, Himmler and Goebbels dead, the victorious Allies had selected twenty-four Germans to stand trial in this, the first and most important of their tribunals. Three of them, Martin Bormann, Robert Ley and Gustav Krupp von Bohlen und Halbach were unavailable, due to (possible) disappearance, sui- cide and terminal ill-health respectively. Of the twenty-one remaining defendants charged, eleven would be sentenced to death, three received life sentences, two received twenty years, one fifteen and one ten. The other three defendants, Hjalmar Schacht, Franz von Papen and Hans Fritzsche were acquitted, al- though all of them were immediately retried and convicted in Germany, receiving sentences of various lengths.

Jackson opened by saying:

> 'That four great nations, flushed with victory and stung with injury stay the hand of venge- ance and voluntarily submit their captive enemies to the judgment of the law is one of the most significant tributes that power has ever paid to reason.'[5]

---

[4] Christopher J Dodd, *Letters From Nuremberg*, (Crown 2007) p.308
[5] Nuremberg Trial Proceedings, Vol.2, 2nd day, Wednesday, 21st November 1945, p. 98-102

Yet not everyone agreed with this noble oratory. Even as the trial was beginning it had stirred considerable controversy. Mr Jackson's predecessor as US Supreme Court Associate Justice (and shortly to become Chief Justice) Harlan Fiske-Stone remarked at the time:

> 'Jackson is away conducting his high-grade lynching party in Nuremberg. I don't mind what he does to the Nazis, but I hate to see the pretense that he is running a court and proceeding according to common law. This is a little too sanctimonious a fraud to meet my old-fashioned ideas.'[6]

Stone's was not a lone voice, either. Speaking in 1947, Congressman John Rankin of Mississippi commented on the ongoing legal proceedings in Nuremburg by saying:

> 'As a representative of the American people I desire to say that what is taking place in Nuremberg, Germany, is a disgrace to the United States...'[7]

Another congressman, Lawrence H. Smith of Wisconsin, expressed a similar view, declaring in 1949:

> 'The Nuremberg trials are so repugnant to the Anglo-Saxon principles of justice that we must forever be ashamed of that page in our history ... The Nuremberg farce represents a revenge policy at its worst.'[8]

It is difficult therefore, for the modern-day analyst to know what to believe. On the one hand, the founding ethos of the United Nations was partially built at the trial and with it the basis of the modern world order. More controversially, the cornerstones of evidence for the Holocaust were laid at Nuremberg. If then the trial really was some sort of lynching party and nothing more, is it reasonable to doubt its conclusions? And where exactly does that line of thinking lead?

On the other, perhaps it is possible that even if such a description were accurate, lynching parties may be justifiable if those being lynched deserve it. Did the criminality of the Nazi regime mean that the end justified the means? Was the tribunal, as Justice Jackson would have had the world believe, a triumph of justice over anger and a benchmark in international conflict resolution? Or was it a kangaroo court, a shadow-play of the war itself, in which victors attacked a defeated and defenceless enemy, using verbal, legal and ideological ammunition rather than the real thing? Finally and most importantly, why does any of this matter?

These questions will be answered over the course of the pages which follow. Initially, the circumstances, practices and judgments of that first great trial at Nuremburg will be examined, in order to give a contemporary verdict on it. That will be followed by a discussion of the implications of this for a world treading a precipitous path across the cliffs of the 21st Century.

---

[6] Harlan Fiske Stone, *Pillar of the Law*, Alpheus T. Mason, (Viking, 1956)
[7] W. Bosch, *Judgment on Nuremberg* (University of North Carolina Press 1971), p. 83.
[8] Congressional Record, Appendix, Vol. 95, Sec. 14, (June 15, 1949), p. A 3741

2

The Climate of the Time

'Be on your guard. When you deal with Germans you must be on your guard. We were taken in by them after the last war: many of us swallowed their story about the "cruel" Treaty of Versailles...many of us believed their talk about disarmament and the sincerity of their desire for peace. And so we let ourselves in for this war, which has been a good deal bigger than the last. There are signs that German leaders are already making plans for a Third World War. That must be prevented at all costs.'[9]

- Instructions for British Servicemen in Germany, 1944

It is assumed that most readers already have a passing knowledge of World War Two and Nazi Germany. Who hasn't, in this era of Spielberg blockbusters, the History Channel and the instigation in 2001 of an annual Holocaust memorial day? This book will not therefore rehearse the story of Hitler's rise to power, his various laws and edicts, the European political chess-match that followed the Treaty of Versailles or the eventual outbreak of hostilities. Neither will it expend much space on military tactics and manoeuvres. There exist many other books, written by eminently qualified individuals, in which accounts of all of these may be found. All that needs to be made clear at this point is that the trial was instigated at the end of six years of total war, in which soldiers from every continent had fought and perhaps as many as seventy million people, nearly two-thirds of whom were civilians, had lost their lives.[10]

During the course of such bitter conflict, it is to be expected that deep enmities are forged and it is undeniable that prior to Nuremburg there existed a powerful and openly expressed loathing of Germany, its regime and even in some cases its people, among the Allied leaders. With at least one of the figures involved, this hatred owed its genesis to the First World War and had continued, uninterrupted until the beginning of the Second. At a private lunch in 1936, soon-to-be Prime Minister, Winston Churchill, in conversation with General Robert E Wood, remarked tersely that, "Germany is getting too strong. We've got to smash her." Speaking in 1940, when considering the possibilities of bombing targets in Germany, Churchill stated that military targets should take priority over killing German civilians, as he considered it to be a case of "business before pleasure". In 1941 he similarly declared, "There are less than 70 million malignant Huns – some of whom are curable and others killable!"[11]

Further to that, and of more direct relevance, it has emerged, through previously secret papers released in 2006 from the British War Cabinet in London, that as early as January 1942 the issue of the punishment of Nazi leaders had been discussed.[12] At that point, it seems Churchill had simply advocated immediate execution, without trial, apparently preferring the electric chair method, with the use of an Act of Attainder[13] to bypass the inevitable legal obstacles.

It needs to be borne in mind when considering these statements, that although at the time there were rumours of some civilian and prisoner-of-war atrocities in Western Russia, there was, at that point, not much credence given to the idea of a genocidal programme against the Jews, which was first raised by Anthony Eden in the House of Commons in December of that year. Neither was there any real belief in gas chambers or even much concern over concentration camp conditions, the first documentary evidence of which appeared in the Witold Pilecki and Vrba/Wetzler escapee reports of August 1943 and April 1944 respectively. It can be safely assumed therefore that Churchill's desire to see German leaders summarily executed regard-

---

[9] *Instructions for British Servicemen in Germany, 1944* (Bodleian Library, University of Oxford, 2007, first published by the Foreign Office, 1944) p.32-33
[10] Estimates actually vary between 50 and 75 million World War Two casualties. John Ellis provides a number of around 55 million, Martin Gilbert about 60. 72 million is suggested through collation of a large number of sources here: *Second Source-List and Detailed Death Tolls for the Twentieth Century Hemoclysm* http://users.erols.com/mwhite28/warstat1.htm#Second
[11] Nicholson Baker *Human Smoke* (Simon and Schuster 2008) p.241 & 314
[12] John Crossland *Churchill: Execute Hitler Without Trial* The Sunday Times, January 1, 2006. http://www.timesonline.co.uk/tol/news/uk/article784041.ece
[13] An Act of Attainder is a piece of legislature declaring a person or group of persons guilty of a crime and punishing them without trial.

less of legality, had nothing to do with the treatment of Jews or other civilians and was due, in fact, to practical expediency.

Churchill was also instrumental in establishing the Moscow Declaration of October 1943, by which time allegations of German barbarity *were* being made. The final section of the document, entitled 'Statement on Atrocities' was signed by the US President, Franklin D. Roosevelt, Churchill and the Soviet Premier, Joseph Stalin, a man to whom such things were not an unfamiliar subject. They noted the 'evidence of atrocities, massacres and cold-blooded mass executions which are being perpetrated by Hitlerite forces in many of the countries they have overrun and from which they are now being steadily expelled.' As evidence for this, various reports were produced which were later collated into a volume entitled 'Soviet Government Statements on Nazi Atrocities' which will be discussed later. The delegates determined that Germans would be sent back to the countries where they had committed their crimes and 'judged on the spot by the peoples whom they have outraged'.[14]

At the conference at the Russian embassy in Tehran in November/December 1943, Stalin brought the hard-line Russian perspective to bear among post war Allied plans, by suggesting that between 50,000 and 100,000 of Germany's highest ranking officers be rounded up after the war and shot. Despite his own, earlier statements, Churchill was disgusted at the callousness of the idea, (presumably he had smaller numbers in mind) replying, 'I would rather be taken out in the garden and shot myself than sully my own and my country's reputation with such infamy.' Despite, or maybe because of Churchill's annoyance, Roosevelt tried to lighten the tone by jokingly suggesting a compromise of 49,000. It is claimed that Churchill stormed from the room in temper at this point.[15]

However, the conference finished with the signing of the Declaration of the Three Powers on December 1st 1943 which stated their intent to pursue victory over Germany, while looking forward to the war's end and the peace that would follow by saying, 'We shall seek the cooperation and active participation of all nations, large and small, whose peoples in heart and mind are dedicated, as are our own peoples, to the elimination of tyranny and slavery, oppression and intolerance. We will welcome them, as they may choose to come, into a world family of Democratic Nations.'[16]

As this global embrace of democracy, freedom and tolerance was being imagined in Tehran, simultane- ously spawning the twin embryos of the UN and a culture that would later be called political correctness, the American Secretary of the Treasury, Henry Morgenthau Jr. was busy drawing up plans for Germany's postwar fate. The view in Allied circles at the time was that the instigation of war was to be characterised as only Germany's fault, as had been the case with World War One and that Hitler had to be viewed as the natural successor to Kaiser Wilhelm and Otto von Bismarck in the line of Prusso-German megalomaniacs. Morgenthau, the son of a successful Jewish real estate broker, who had been a leading figure in establishing the US War Refugee Board in January 1944, which allowed 200,000 European Jews free entry to the US to escape from persecution[17], grasped the nettle of this rather jaundiced view more readily than most. The 'Morgenthau Plan' he devised, in tandem with Harry Dexter White,[18] was an object lesson in vindictiveness and was fiercely criticised by many commentators, most notably from within his own cabinet by Henry Stimson, who viewed it as counter-productively malicious. It is easy to see why.

Morgenthau's draconian proposal was to reduce Germany's threat capacity by having the nation broken up, partitioned into separate states, stripped of heavy industry and forced to permanently return to an agrarian economy. One cannot help but recall David Lloyd-George's cry of 'Squeeze Germany until the pips squeak!' from the end of World War One. This vision of a Third-World style Germany of impoverished peasants was ratified by President Roosevelt and then agreed to by Churchill at the Second Quebec Conference on Sep-

---

[14] The Moscow Conference, 1943. http://www.yale.edu/lawweb/avalon/wwii/moscow.htm
[15] Winston S Churchill, *'Closing the Ring', volume 5 of 'The History of the Second World War'* (Penguin, 1954) p.330 and Elliot Roosevelt, 'As He Saw It' (Duell, Sloan and Pierce, 1946) p.190
[16] The Tehran Conference http://www.yale.edu/lawweb/avalon/wwii/tehran.htm
[17] Penkower, Monty Noam. *'Jewish Organizations and the Creation of the U.S. War Refugee Board.'* Annals of the American Academy of Political and Social Science 1980 (450): 122-139. ISSN 0002-7162
[18] White was also one of the chief architects of the Bretton Woods Conference of July 1944, at which the postwar American economic-globalisation strategy was devised. This strategy, the results of which are still with us today, supplanted economic nationalism such as that operated by Nazi Germany and eliminated Imperial Trade Preferences, which were the cornerstones of the economic power of the British Empire.

tember 16th 1944.[19] Roosevelt's reasons for supporting the plan in the face of vociferous opposition are unclear but it is not unreasonable to conclude that the plan simply matched his personal inclinations, as in an August 26th, 1944 letter to Queen Wilhelmina of the Netherlands, he had written: 'There are two schools of thought, those who would be altruistic in regard to the Germans, hoping by loving kindness to make them Christians again – and those who would adopt a much "tougher" attitude. Most decidedly I belong to the latter school, for though I am not bloodthirsty, I want the Germans to know that this time at least they have definitely lost the war.'[20]

Roosevelt's personal antipathy to the German people is further evidenced in his dealings with those around him, as shown by comments made during a meeting with Morgenthau. 'We have got to be tough with Germany and I mean the German people not just the Nazis,' he had said. 'We either have to castrate the German people or you have got to treat them in such a manner so they can't just go on reproducing people who want to continue the way they have in the past.'[21] The view of Morgenthau as German-hater supreme and the driving force, perhaps even originator behind post-war anti-German policy must therefore be tempered. It would seem that Roosevelt possessed vicious anti-German feelings which he expressed in the most extreme terms and it is probable that Morgenthau was mirroring his boss' views rather than influencing them.

Churchill's agreement to the plan seems to have been more reluctant, having initially resisted the proposals before being convinced, at least in some part, by Lord Cherwell, his personal assistant. Cherwell is a man described as possessing a 'pathological hatred for Nazi Germany'. In addition it is alleged that a 'medieval desire for revenge was a part of his character.'[22] Morgenthau himself described Cherwell as 'helpful' in the discussions[23] and Churchill eventually agreed, saying, 'At first I was violently opposed to the idea. But the President and Mr Morgenthau – from whom we had much to ask – were so insistent that in the end we agreed to consider it.'[24]

A fly quickly appeared in the Allied ointment, however. Some details of the plan were leaked. The news reached Germany, where the Reich minister for propaganda, Josef Goebbels, used it to stir up his flagging citizens. Forewarned of the fate that awaited them after capitulation, the *Wehrmacht* (regular army) and their reinforcements from the *Volksturmman* (Home Guard) and the *Hitler Jugend* (Hitler Youth) found extra determination to fight to the bitter end. It also helped to rouse the abject and demoralised civilian population. Conditions under Allied bombing raids and wartime privations may have been tough, but were nothing compared to that which Roosevelt, Churchill and Morgenthau had in mind. In some ways therefore the plan had become self-defeating. Recognising this, Roosevelt publicly backed away from it, yet despite this negativity, Morgenthau's vision remained on the table.

Eventually, The Morgenthau Plan was enforced. On May 10th, 1945, President Harry S. Truman signed the US occupation directive JCS 1067[25]. The directive was recognised by Morgenthau himself as being his plan in disguise[26] and was effective for two years, forbidding German economic re-development, except in the agricultural sector. Production of oil, rubber, ships and aircraft were strictly prohibited. This was implemented while the Soviets looted public and private property and busily dismantled all the undestroyed German heavy industry they could lay their hands on, transporting it back to the USSR, 'down to the last bolt and screw.'[27]

The machinations of Roosevelt (by that time deceased), Morgenthau and their associates did not go unnoticed. While JCS 1067 was enforced in Germany (and right in the middle of the IMT hearing), on February

---

[19] John L. Chase *The Development of the Morgenthau Plan Through the Quebec Conference* The Journal of Politics, Vol. 16, No. 2 (May, 1954), pp. 324-359
[20] Eleanor Roosevelt *The Roosevelt Letters, volume III: 1928 – 1945*, (George Harrap, 1952).
[21] John Morton Blum, *From the Morgenthau Diaries: Years of War, 1941 – 1945* (Houghton-Mifflin, 1967) p.342
[22] John W. Wheeler-Bennett and Anthony Nicholls, *The Semblance of Peace* (WW Norton 1974), p. 179.
[23] Blum, p.373
[24] Churchill, *The Tide of Victory*, (Penguin 1954), pp. 138 – 139.
[25] JCS 1067 was created from a synthesis of The Morgenthau Plan and suggestions made by the American State and War departments.
[26] Michael R. Beschloss, *The Conquerors: Roosevelt, Truman and the Destruction of Hitler's Germany, 1941 – 1945*, (Simon & Schuster 2002) p. 233
[27] From a statement made by Göring at the trial. Nuremberg Trial Proceedings, Vol. 9, 82nd day, Friday 15th March 1946, p.349

5th 1946, Senator Homer E. Capeheart made the following statement before the United States Congress:

'The fact can no longer be suppressed, namely, the fact that it has been and continues to be, the deliberate policy of a confidential and conspiratorial clique within the policy-making circles of this government to draw and quarter a nation now reduced to abject misery. In this process this clique, like a pack of hyenas struggling over the bloody entrails of a corpse, and inspired by a sadistic and fanatical hatred, are determined to destroy the German nation and the German people, no matter what the consequences...For nine months now this administration has been carrying on a deliberate policy of mass starvation without any distinction between the innocent and the helpless and guilty alike.

'The first issue has been and continues to be purely humanitarian. This vicious clique...have betrayed the GIs who have suffered and died, and they continue to betray the American GIs who have to continue their dirty work for them.

'The second issue that is involved is the effect this tragedy in Germany has already had on the other European countries. Those who have been responsible for this deliberate destruction of the German state and this criminal mass starvation of the German people have been so zealous in their hatred that all other interests and concerns have been subordinated to this one obsession of revenge. In order to accomplish this, it mattered not if the liberated countries in Europe suffered and starved. To this point this clique of conspirators have addressed themselves: Germany is to be destroyed. What happens to other countries of Europe in the process is of secondary importance.'[28]

Capeheart was not only referring to JCS 1067 here, but allegations of a wider policy of mass starvation, theft and brutality. This has been referred to by other authors, such as Alfred Maurice de Zayas and Giles McDonagh[29], who recount a post-war occupied Germany where deliberate deprivation, rape, torture and murder were commonplace.

Adding to the voices of disapproval, Lewis Douglas, chief advisor to General Lucius Clay, US High Commissioner, also attacked JCS 1067 and its creators, saying that it was: 'assembled by economic idiots. It makes no sense to forbid the most skilled workers in Europe from producing as much as they can in a continent that is desperately short of everything.'[30]

Yet the directive remained, enforced in Germany by a team of US Treasury officials, led by Bernard Bernnstein, who became dubbed The Morgenthau Boys. They stayed until July 1947, when JCS 1067 was replaced by a new directive, JCS 1779 which instead stressed that: 'an orderly, prosperous Europe requires the economic contributions of a stable and productive Germany'. In reality this was little more than a thinly veiled expression of concern at the widening influence of the Soviet Union, whom the USA and Britain feared would have free reign in Central Europe if Germany was kept in a state of weakness. This U-turn signalled the end for the Morgenthau Boys who promptly resigned.[31]

Prior to its eventual demise, another staunch supporter of the Morgenthau Plan had been Dwight Eisenhower, at that time Supreme Commander of the Allied forces in Europe and future President of the United States. His role was not merely that of an approving bystander however. He had actually been responsible for appointing the Morgenthau Boys and made several statements which left little doubt as to his feelings towards the German nation.

'In my personal reactions, as the months of conflict wore on, I grew constantly more bitter against the Germans.' he wrote in his 1948 memoirs. With reference to his duty to send letters of condolence to the families of deceased soldiers, he continued, 'I know of no more effective means of developing an undying hatred of those responsible for aggressive war than to assume the obligation of attemption to express sympathy to families bereaved by it.'[32]

---

[28] Ralph Franklin Keeling, *Gruesome Harvest: The Allies Postwar War Against the German People*, (Institute of American Economics, Chicago 1947), p. 75-76
[29] Giles McDonagh, *After the Reich, The Brutal History of the Allied Occupation*, (Basic books, 2007)
[30] Robert Murphy, *Diplomat Among Warriors*, (Collins, 1964) p. 251
[31] Vladimir Petrov, *Money and conquest; allied occupation currencies in World War II*. (John Hopkins Press, 1967) p. 228-229
[32] Eisenhower, Dwight D. *Crusade in Europe* (1948, reprinted Main Street Books; September 1, 1990)

Eisenhower, who was himself Pennsylvania Dutch[33], seemed particularly concerned with the plight of Dutch civilians formerly trapped behind German lines: 'I am done trifling with them (the Germans) and while I have held my hand for fear of intensifying Dutch suffering, if the German doesn't play the game absolutely, I intend really to punish him when I can turn my attentions in that direction.'[34]

Further to these statements are the allegations of deliberate and callous denial of basic human rights to German POWs in the Eisenhower-controlled camps of post-war Germany. The allegations were most starkly made in the Canadian author James Bacque's now notorious work, 'Other Losses' in which he claimed to have uncovered 'the shocking truth behind the mass deaths of disarmed German soldiers and civilians under General Eisenhower's command.' Bacque alleged that Eisenhower had changed the status of the POWs to DEF (disarmed enemy forces) in order to circumvent the Geneva Convention which laid down strict rules regarding how prisoners of war should be treated. The book's dramatic conclusion – that upwards of half a million German soldiers died[35] as a result of a deliberate policy of dehydration, starvation and denial of medical assistance made for shocking reading and enabled the book to become a bestseller in Germany, but has now been somewhat discredited. Stephen Ambrose, a historian who has spent the better part of his career writing about Eisenhower, dismissed Bacque's work as 'worse than worthless.'[36] Yet in saying that, he did not dispute that German POWs had suffered terribly from exposure and starvation and many had died in the camps, he only disputed the numbers of deaths and Eisenhower's motives for changing their status, claiming it to be a simple case of resource allocation. In Ambrose's later work, a book written in response to Bacque (a collaboration with Gunther Bischoff) he even seemed to corroborate Bacque's claims of American vindictiveness by quoting General Clay as saying 'I feel the Germans should suffer from hunger and from cold, as I believe such suffering is necessary to make them realize the consequences of the war which they caused.'[37]

Despite this, it is hard to believe that Eisenhower would have allowed his antipathy towards Germans to express itself through mass murder, but the fact that this mistreatment happened, whatever its motive, in camps under American command, at the same time as the Morgenthau influenced directive JCS 1067 prevented Germany from making any small steps to recovery and the Red Army rampaged through the Eastern territories raping, torturing and murdering, is further indication of the climate of the time.

Eisenhower possibly summed it all up himself when confronted with the embarrassment of German POWs being transported from one of his camps to another in sealed boxcars and dying of suffocation on the journey. 'I loathe having to apologise to Germans,' he said, 'but this time I shall have no recourse.'[38]

It is clear then that in the period surrounding the Trial of the Century, the four most powerful political and military Allied leaders were making statements and forming policies which are abhorrent to modern sensibilities. It is impossible to envisage a modern, Western Head of State suggesting that we castrate our enemies. Anyone who spoke of 'undying hatred' of another nation, permanently crippling their economy, or starving surrendered soldiers would be venomously rounded upon by the modern media. It is simply unthinkable that an American commander as prominent in the world today as Eisenhower was then, would express thoughts such as the one quoted above – the ensuing outcry would see said commander removed from his job and prosecuted. And this point is not being made in order to criticise General Eisenhower – it is always an exercise in futility to judge the actions of any historical figure with the morality of the present, but this is the key to understanding Nuremberg's origins. Such sentiment at the time was acceptable, even normal. Being anti-German to the point of outright racism was expected, given the circumstances. Hence the willingness to play along with the vindictiveness of JCS 1067, hence talk of 'summary executions' and 'judging Germans on the spot' and hence blind eyes turned to the disgraceful excesses of the occupying forces. And it was from this climate of hatred and vengeance that the Nuremberg trials were conceived.

That legal proceedings ever emerged at all from such a climate is, on one level, as Justice Jackson de-

---

[33] The 'Dutch' in 'Pennsylvania Dutch' is, in fact, a corruption of '*Deutsch*'. The population were originally of German heritage and spoke a low *Rheinisch* dialect, still used by the Amish populations of the area.
[34] Personal Letter from Eisenhower to Marshall, April 27 1945, from the Eisenhower Library, Abilene
[35] Bacque, James, *Other Losses*, (Prima) 1991. p.187
[36] Ambrose, Steven, *Ike and the Disappearing Atrocities* New York Times Book Review, Feb. 24, 1991
[37] Steven Ambrose and Gunther Bischoff, *Eisenhower and the German POWs, Facts against Falsehood* (Louisiana State University Press, 1993) from the introduction, p.1-25 – Ambrose only claims between 56,000 – 78,000 German POW deaths to have occurred, about 1percent of all German POWs.
[38] Eisenhower letter to Marshall, March 18, 1945. RG 383.6/10 NARS Washington

scribed, a 'tribute to reason'. A spate of out-of-hand shootings would have surprised no-one. But that does not expunge the lingering doubt that the proceedings at Nuremburg would have been tainted by these attitudes. Is it reasonable to believe that the resentments of the victorious nations receded as the trial began, replaced only by the rationality and scrupulousness of law? Yet, at the same time, it needs to be borne in mind that postulating that such resentments affected the proceedings at Nuremberg, to the point of making them unsound, is worthless without examining those proceedings and determining to what extent they were actually affected. For that reason, during the course of the following chapter, the precedent-setting international law created for Nuremberg will be examined, ripples of which still affect us today. The Guantanamo Bay Trials, begun in August 2008, the first American War Crimes Tribunals since World War Two have reused much of the law piloted at Nuremberg. Through this examination, the real, rather than the stated aims of the trial will be assessed.

Quite simply, was it an attempt to judge, or to punish?

3

The Legal Platform

'Laws are like sausages. It is better not to see them being made.'

- Otto von Bismarck

To understand the platform of law on which Nuremberg was built, it is necessary to take a few steps backwards to trace its development. The three major conferences of World War Two (Tehran, Yalta and Potsdam) saw the steady refinement of Allied attitudes towards Germany into specific policies. By the time of the Yalta summit, from February 4th to February 11th 1945, it had been agreed between Stalin, Churchill and Roosevelt to make the unconditional surrender of Germany a priority. After the war, Germany would be split into four zones, with a similar partition of Berlin. Germany would also undergo demilitarization, decartelization and the policy which more than any other encapsulated the zeitgeist, denazification.[39]

Before the 'big three' managed to meet again, Roosevelt died and was replaced by Truman. During the course of the conference at Potsdam (July 17th – August 2nd) a general election in Britain removed Churchill from office and replaced him with Labour's Clement Atlee.

The desired unconditional surrender was obtained on May 8th (VE day) and attention at the meeting turned to the establishment of the post-war order. At Potsdam 'democratisation' was added to the list of processes to be applied to the new Germany. It was further agreed, in line with pre-war Polish proposals, to move the German Eastern border westwards to the 'Oder-Neisse' line, reducing the nation's size by twenty five percent.[40] Attached to that decision was a controversial footnote – it involved the deportation of all Germans living beyond the newly created eastern border, thus creating a massive wave of refugees. More than twelve million ethnic Germans were expelled from their ancestral homes during this time, many of them were held in concentration camps on the way and 2.1 million died before reaching Germany.[41] The treatment of these people at the hands of the victorious powers is a truly shameful page of twentieth century European history and is seldom discussed, but is tangential to this topic and so will not be relayed here.

In connection with the decision above, all German annexations in Europe made during the thirties were to be instantly reversed, without recourse to the opinions, positive or negative, of those living in such areas. This included the Sudetenland, Alsace-Lorraine, Austria and the westernmost parts of Poland where German speakers and ethnic Germans were in the majority. It was also at Potsdam that the transition from summary execution to trial was finalised, with the agreement to prosecute those deemed to be war criminals through a court of law.

Movement on this last decision was swift and on August 8th the London Charter of the International Military Tribunal (sometimes just called the Nuremberg Charter) was signed, which designated the crimes indictable under its authority. These crimes were assembled under the general banner of concepts which had existed since the Hague Conventions of 1899 and 1907 but the problem for the Allies, was that having decided that Nazi Germany was solely responsible for the outbreak of war and that they would accept lurid Soviet and Polish reports of atrocities, as well as those of the major Jewish/Zionist organisations *a priori,* the scope of Nazi crimes far exceeded the limits of pre-existing international legislation. They appeared to describe 'a guilt that was beyond crime.'[42] The signatories to the London Charter therefore classified four new categories of crime. The definitions of these were somewhat vague and overlap to a large degree, beginning with the

---

[39] United States Department of State *Foreign relations of the United States. Conferences at Malta and Yalta, 1945* Washington, D.C.: U.S. Government Printing Office, 1945 lxxviii http://digicoll.library.wisc.edu/cgi-bin/FRUS/FRUS-idx?id=FRUS.FRUS1945
[40] The territories east of the new border comprised East Prussia, Silesia, West Prussia, and two thirds of Pomerania. These areas were mainly agricultural, with the exception of Upper Silesia which was the second largest centre of German heavy industry.
[41] De Zayas, Alfred-Maurice *A Terrible Revenge, the ethnic cleansing of the East European Germans* (St Martins Press 1994)
[42] *Hannah Arendt – Karl Jaspers Correspondence 1926-1969*, quoted in Douglas, p.39

master charge of 'Conspiracy or the Common Plan' and then three charges which formed part of this conspiracy, namely: War Crimes, Crimes against Peace and Crimes against Humanity. Such a quick recodification of international law took place because it had been undergoing a behind-the-scenes process of development for some time. The central concept, the conspiracy charge, which essentially made the whole trial hang together was not, as is commonly stated, an invention of Jackson, but owed its genesis to Colonel Murray Bernays of the Special Projects Branch.

Bernays had become involved in preparations for Nuremberg as a direct result of Henry Stimson's horror at learning of the severity of the Morgenthau Plan in 1944. Stimson had engaged Assistant Secretary of War, John McCloy to investigate alternatives to Morgenthau's proposals and McCloy in turn deferred the task to the SPB.[43] In this way, the documents ended up on Bernays' desk.

A scholar of Jewish Lithuanian extraction, Bernays' life epitomised the early twentieth century ideal of the American dream. Having emigrated to the USA at the age of 6, in 1900, he made a meteoric rise from humble childhood to graduation from Harvard Law School and marriage to Sigmund Freud's niece, Hertha Bernays, whose name he adopted. Upon receiving the order and analysing the list of Nazi crimes, which ranged from civilian atrocities to war tactics to elements of their domestic and economic policies, he cogitated for days and eventually came to this conclusion:

> 'The crimes and atrocities were not single or unconnected but were the inevitable outcome of the basic criminal conspiracy of the Nazi party. This conspiracy, based on the Nazi doctrine of racism and totalitarianism, involved murder, terrorism and the destruction of peaceful populations in violations of the laws of war.'

In this way, Bernays felt they would be able to kill several birds with one stone. It wasn't only specific criminals who would be tried, but Nazism itself. He continued, 'Therefore the thing to do is to try the organisations along with the Nazi leaders on the conspiracy charge and having convicted the organisations, the conviction could serve as prima facie proof of the guilt of any of their members.'[44] This piece of legal ingenuity was adopted, almost word for word, by Jackson in drafting the Nuremberg Charter. And it remained the driving force behind the trial until the end.

Such a process, with men like Bernays and ultimately Jackson adapting international law to meet their own ends, naturally led to accusations that Nuremberg simply created law to suit itself. The most notable of these criticisms came from Associate US Supreme Court Justice, William Douglas, who alleged:

> 'The Allies were guilty of substituting power for principle at Nuremberg. I thought at the time and still think that the Nuremberg trials were unprincipled. Law was created *ex post facto* (after the fact)[45] to suit the passion and clamour of the time.'[46]

Such an argument also formed the defence counsels' opening statement at the trial. Others believe that as the basis of the law had existed since 1899 and the Nuremberg charter simply represented a development of it, the *ex post facto* criticism did not apply. Indeed, in response to Douglas' criticisms some modern historians have contended that:

> 'the argument of *ex post facto* and *nullem crimen sine lege* (no crime without law) was raised as a defence during the tribunals'. Legal scholars and jurists agreed this violated general legal conventions but believed that the 'overriding principle' of justice allowed for the prosecution to proceed.

---

[43] Joseph E Persico, *Nuremberg Infamy on Trial*, (Penguin 1994), p.15 and Robert E Conot, *Justice at Nuremberg*, (Carrol & Graf 1983) p.10
[44] The Bernays Papers, Box 1, Bernays to wife, June 10th, 1945, quoted in Conot, p.12
[45] *Ex post facto* is Latin for 'after the fact' and refers to laws being adopted which make an act illegal retrospectively, or increasing a penalty after a crime has been committed. Such laws are prohibited by most nations (including the USA, the UK and Germany) and are now prohibited by Article 7 of the European Charter for Human Rights. Despite this, *ex post facto* charges have recently been used to prosecute defendants at the Guantanamo Bay trials of 2008.
[46], H. K. Thompson, Jr. and Henry Strutz, *'Dönitz at Nuremberg: A Reappraisal'* (Torrance, 1983)

Justice required the punishment of these men as the Nuremberg defendants…'[47]

In other words, Nuremberg operated on an illegal basis, yet the situation was so extreme that this was necessary. Such a position, common within pre-existing Nuremberg analysis, is horribly unsound as it ignores the basic principle of 'innocent until proven guilty'. To say that a man's crimes are so awful that justice requires he be tried, regardless of the legality of doing so, is a classic circular argument. It is the law that will prosecute him. If that law is, in itself, unlawful then there can be no basis for prosecution. It also suggests that what was taking place was not really a trial at all. If guilt was presupposed, why bother with the legal process? Was it simply window dressing? It would seem that enacting Churchill's initial plans would have sufficed and saved everyone involved a lot of time and effort.

When the issue of the suitability of the charges is considered, as outlined in the Nuremberg charter, careful questions must therefore be formulated. There is little point in asking if the charges were legal. Officially, the answer is yes, but only in the sense that Jackson *et al* had made them so. A more pertinent question is to ask whether, considering the circumstances, the charges were appropriate. Bearing in mind what is now the established historical record, it is very difficult to question the legitimacy of the War Crimes or Crimes against Humanity charges, even if the Humanity charge can be viewed as *ex post facto*. What should be remembered in that regard is that the legal principle of *ex post facto* is designed to protect individuals from being charged with an act which they could not have known at the time was criminal. To provide a simplistic example, an individual carrying a toy gun at a shopping centre could not be tried if his national government passed a law six months later outlawing the carrying of toy guns in public. CCTV footage of him holding the offending item filmed half a year prior to the passing of the law could not incriminate him, as he would not have been aware at the time that his actions were illegal. To apply this to our subject, it simply cannot be claimed that the Nazis were ignorant of the illegality of all of their actions at the time they were carried out. Aggressive war making *is* blurry, as shall shortly be discussed, but to suggest that citizens of an advanced European nation would not have known that forcing millions of people from their homes to be used as slave labour, while cold-bloodedly murdering others would be against any normal rule of law would be to suggest the absurd. Therefore, without at this stage going into the accuracy or otherwise of the accepted historical record, (which to some degree depends on the evidence presented at the trial and how it was handled, which will be examined shortly), it is unreasonable to claim *ex post facto* as a defence on these charges. On this basis therefore the War Crimes and Crimes against Humanity charges (counts three and four) are seen to have been appropriate. There was clearly a case to answer there.

However, the situation with count two, Crimes against Peace (planning or waging a war of aggression), is much harder to delineate. This is crucial because contrary to popular belief, it was this charge, that Germany's aggression had sent the world spinning into conflict, on which the lion's share of the prosecution was placed. The civilian atrocities were very much a secondary issue, as shall be demonstrated later. The problem here is that in almost all cases it can be very difficult to determine whether particular acts of war are aggressive or defensive in nature. Invariably, a little of both is usually true. Although it was not Austria, Poland, Czechoslovakia, Belgium, the Netherlands, Denmark, Yugoslavia, Greece or Russia that invaded Germany during the thirties and early forties, but rather vice-versa, the causes of these individual events cannot be explained solely in terms of German aggression.

The venerated British historian AJP Taylor, for example, argued that Hitler was governed primarily by opportunism and improvisation and sought not to wage aggressive war but merely to defend his nation's interests. 'The Austrian affair was underway,' he wrote. 'It had not been launched by Hitler. It was sprung on him by surprise and he took a chance as always.'[48]

Inevitably, discussion on this point reverts to the debate over who started World War Two, the full version of which begins somewhere in the 19th century, takes in the Anglo-French entente of 1904 (and the motivations for it), progresses through to World War One and the Treaty of Versailles, with its infamous 'War Guilt Clause', then busies itself with German expansionism after the European power game of the 1920s and 30s. This is an immense subject in its own right and will only receive brief lip-service here.

Immediately after the surrender, mainstream historical opinion collected around the 'it was Hitler's fault'

---

[47] Ginsburgs, George & Kudriavtes, *The Nuremberg trial and international law*. (Martin Nijhoff 1990) p. 53&54
[48] AJP Taylor *Origins of the Second World War* (Simon & Schuster 1961), p.142

view. Hitler was portrayed as a ravenous lunatic who wanted war at all costs and forced the unwilling Allies into conflict. Such opinions prevailed, unchallenged throughout the post war period. The (thoroughly denazified) German historian Joachim Fest gave a supreme example of this kind of reasoning when he wrote:

> '...the world felt itself challenged to the limit by the so-called *Kristallnacht*... and the swallowing up of Czechoslovakia, by the spectacle of Hitler tearing up the Munich agreement before the ink was dry. As though intoxicated, alternately pursuing his actions and being dragged along by them, seeking refuge in rhetorical delirium before the masses and with his judgment clouded by emotional exultation, Hitler diligently arranged the preconditions for the catastrophe.'[49]

German aggression and Hitler's mental instability were thus blamed almost exclusively for the outbreak of global hostilities, particularly in breaking the Munich agreement by invading Poland. Such a view would obviously validate the Nuremberg charge. An attempt to outline all the arguments and counter arguments relating to this position will not be made here, but it should be pointed out that current historical opinion on the matter is quite evenly split. Richard Overy summed this up by saying, 'While some see a clear intention on his (Hitler's) part to launch wars of aggression, based on the ideas of racial struggle and world empire expressed in Hitler's writing and speeches, others emphasise the importance of functional explanations: Nazi leaders were forced into war through fear of domestic unrest and economic crisis...'[50] He goes on to say that, 'By concentrating on Germany we are in danger of forgetting that wars do not take place in a vacuum... German statesmen reacted to problems and stimuli over which they had no control...It must not be forgotten that war in 1939 was declared by Britain and France on Germany and not the other way round.'[51] He also states that 'France and Britain had complex interests and motives for war'[52] and: 'The Polish issue gave a moral gloss to what was in fact a decision about when was the best time to fight for Britain and France.'[53]

It is worth noting at this point that Britain had a chance to sign an agreement with the Soviet Union in August 1939, which would probably have prevented World War Two from happening, by completing the encirclement of Germany which had been so decisive in World War One. Had such an agreement been made, Germany would have been in no position to fight, yet Britain decided to send a junior representative to the meeting, who lacked the authority to sign anything, which the Russians rightly perceived as an insult, thus scuppering any chance of the deal being struck. This seems like an extraordinary faux pas for the British Government to have made at such a sensitive time, unless of course it was part of a carefully judged ploy to bring about war on their terms, at the moment they wanted it.

There are therefore many complexities and pitfalls with attempting to charge anyone with 'aggressive war' and for a substantial proportion of modern day analysts, 'German aggression' just does not cut it as an adequate explanation for what happened between 1935 and 1939. International politics and diplomacy entwine into too complicated a web to pick out simplistic accusations of that nature.

Even for those who maintain the very arguable position that German aggression was more marked than that of the Allies, there remains the question of moral equivalence. Why punish Germany for incidents of aggression when it was and always had been (and remains) a key component of international relations? Even if you assert that it is an unwelcome one and that treaties and conventions were in place to limit it, which Germany acted in defiance of, can we not also accuse the Allies of similar behaviour?

The United States, for example, with its lend-lease practices, its shoot-on-sight policy with its armed Atlantic convoys and embargoes against Japan in the Pacific[54] was acting aggressively for some time before it officially entered the war. A clear and specific example of this exists in 'the Greer incident' on September 4th 1941, in which the USS Greer, a Wickes class destroyer, fired on a German U-boat which was responding to an attack from a British plane. This took place three months before the USA officially entered the conflict and was in direct contravention of the Hague convention, article one of which states, 'The Contracting Pow-

---

[49] Joachim C. Fest, *The Face of the Third Reich*, (Pelican, English translation 1972 – first published in German 1963) p.86
[50] RJ Overy *The Origins of the Second World war* 2nd ed, (Longman, 1998) p.1
[51] ibid p.2
[52] ibid
[53] ibid p.69
[54] Harry Elmer Barnes, ed., *Perpetual War for Perpetual Peace: A Critical Examination of the Foreign Policy of Franklin D. Roosevelt and Its Aftermath* (1953) and Jonathan G. Utley, *Going to War with Japan, 1937 – 1941* (1985)

ers recognize that hostilities between themselves must not commence without previous and explicit warning, in the form either of a reasoned declaration of war or of an ultimatum with conditional declaration of war.'[55]

This act of undisclosed war was also in contravention of the London Charter, which Jackson helped to draw up. Equally, the United States' decision to transfer fifty of their destroyers to Great Britain, as part of the 'Destroyers for Bases Agreement' in 1940[56], could also be seen as an act of aggression, or maybe even conspiracy. There exist many other such examples related to actions of all the prosecuting powers, some of which will be listed shortly. Could therefore the Germans on trial not simply have defended themselves by pointing out how their enemies had committed qualitatively similar acts? No, for reasons to be explained below, the defence of *tu quoque* (you too)[57] was denied to Nuremberg defendants. The aggressive war charge (Crimes against Peace) is therefore the one that most criticism can be levelled at and it appears unsound largely because the Allies were attempting to convict Nazis for things they had done themselves.

Count One, the Conspiracy or Common Plan is also difficult to defend on grounds of logic. A brief examination of a section from the indictment, which will be looked at in more detail later, specifically the part relating to Göring, says that he was indicted on this count because, 'He promoted the accession to power of the Nazi conspirators and the consolidation of their control over Germany...'[58] From a rational viewpoint, it seems rather moot to take the man who was Commander in Chief of the German Armed Forces (*Reichsmarschall*), Head of the Luftwaffe and Minister of the Economy, (for a time he was second in command to Hitler and would have become Führer had Hitler died) and charge him with such an offence. *Of course* he conspired to obtain and consolidate Nazi power. A trial was not required to prove that. The question surely, is why is that a crime? As a member of a political organisation, such ambitions go with the territory. It's rather like accusing a professional footballer of conspiring to win the cup.

Its only criminality can lie in the fact that the state he conspired to establish committed criminal acts. Yet the purpose of the trial was supposedly to prove this. Evidence regarding Nazi crimes had not yet been assessed by a court of law. On this basis the conspiracy charge is seen to be a stark example of putting the cart before the horse. The formulation of the charge required that the guilt of the defendants be assumed before it was proven. It is unsurprising that it was this part of the charter which eventually gave the judges and prosecutors the most trouble.

The Nuremberg Charter, drafted by Jackson, Robert Falco (France), and Iona Nikitchenko (Russia) was a document of thirty articles and essentially set out the basis on which the trial would operate. Jackson has already been discussed and will feature prominently throughout this book. Nikitchenko, whose final role was that of judge at Nuremberg, came to London with a dubious reputation, having presided over several of Stalin's famous show trials during the purges of the late thirties. Again, he will be discussed later, but his pre-trial attitude is neatly summarised by the following statement, 'We are dealing here with the chief war criminals who have already been convicted and whose conviction has been already announced by both the Moscow and Crimea declarations by the heads of the (Allied) governments ... The whole idea is to secure quick and just punishment for the crime.'[59] Falco, on the other hand, was a vastly experienced and well thought of French judge but is viewed as something of a minor figure among the three. He became the alternate French judge at the tribunal.

In summary, it is worth emphasising, at this early stage, that the Charter which formed the very basis of law on which the Nuremberg trial would operate, was conceived by a Jewish/Lithuanian American immigrant, (in itself not remarkable, but bearing in mind the nature of some of the accusations against the defendants, hardly a recipe for objectivity) then drawn up by the United States chief prosecutor, before being ratified by a Russian judge who saw his role only in terms of meting out punishment to already guilty Nazis. This combination of subjective personalities does not inspire much confidence that the foundation of law they built would be even. It must therefore be asked whether this lop-sidedness demonstrated itself in the charter they drafted. As it is important to our subject that a clear understanding of the charter is gained, se-

---

[55] *Laws of War : Opening of Hostilities (Hague III); October 18, 1907*

[56] Hague, Arnold. *Destroyers for Great Britain: A History of 50 Town Class Ships Transferred from the United States to Great Britain in 1940.* (Annapolis MD: Naval Institute Press, 1990.)

[57] *Tu quoque* is Latin for 'you too' and in legal parlance means that a defendant can defend themselves on a charge because their accuser has done the same thing.

[58] *Nuremberg Trial proceedings Volume One.* Indictment, Appendix A.

[59] Whitney R. Harris, *Tyranny on Trial: The Evidence at Nuremberg* (SMU Press, 1954, p. 16-17.)

lected articles are quoted on the following pages.

Article 1. In pursuance of the Agreement signed on the 8th day of August 1945 by the Government of the United States of America, the Provisional Government of the French Republic, the Government of the United Kingdom of Great Britain and Northern Ireland and the Government of the Union of So- viet Socialist Republics, there shall be established an International Military Tribunal (hereinafter called 'the Tribunal'') for the just and prompt trial and punishment of the major war criminals of the European Axis.

Article 3. Neither the Tribunal, its members nor their alternates can be challenged by the prosecution, or by the Defendants or their Counsel. Each Signatory may replace its members of the Tribunal or his alternate for reasons of health or for other good reasons, except that no replacement may take place during a Trial, other than by an alternate.

Article 6. The Tribunal established by the Agreement referred to in Article 1 hereof for the trial and punishment of the major war criminals of the European Axis countries shall have the power to try and punish persons who, acting in the interests of the European Axis countries, whether as individuals or as members of organizations, committed any of the following crimes.

The following acts, or any of them, are crimes coming within the jurisdiction of the Tribunal for which there shall be individual responsibility:

(a) CRIMES AGAINST PEACE: namely, planning, preparation, initiation or waging of a war of aggression, or a war in violation of international treaties, agreements or assurances, or participation in a common plan or conspiracy for the accomplishment of any of the foregoing;

(b) WAR CRIMES: namely, violations of the laws or customs of war. Such violations shall include, but not be limited to, murder, ill-treatment or deportation to slave labor or for any other purpose of civilian population of or in occupied territory, murder or ill-treatment of prisoners of war or persons on the seas, killing of hostages, plunder of public or private property, wanton destruction of cities, towns or villages, or devastation not justified by military necessity;

(c) CRIMES AGAINST HUMANITY: namely, murder, extermination, enslavement, deportation, and other inhumane acts committed against any civilian population, before or during the war; or persecutions on political, racial or religious grounds in execution of or in connection with any crime within the jurisdiction of the Tribunal, whether or not in violation of the domestic law of the country where perpetrated.

Leaders, organizers, instigators and accomplices participating in the formulation or execution of a common plan or conspiracy to commit any of the foregoing crimes are responsible for all acts performed by any persons in execution of such plan.

Article 8. The fact that the Defendant acted pursuant to order of his Government or of a superior shall not free him from responsibility, but may be considered in mitigation of punishment if the Tribunal determines that justice so requires.

Article 16. In order to ensure fair trial for the Defendants, the following procedure shall be followed: **(a)** The indictment shall include full particulars specifying in detail the charges against the Defendants. A copy of the indictment and of all the documents lodged with the Indictment, translated into a language which he understands, shall be furnished to the Defendant at reasonable time before the Trial.
(b) During any preliminary examination or trial of a Defendant he will have the right to give any explanation relevant to the charges made against him.
(c) A preliminary examination of a Defendant and his Trial shall be conducted in, or translated into, a language which the Defendant understands.

(d) A Defendant shall have the right to conduct his own defence before the Tribunal or to have the assistance of Counsel.

(e) A Defendant shall have the right through himself or through his Counsel to present evidence at the Trial in support of his defence, and to cross-examine any witness called by the Prosecution.

It is made clear via several repetitions during the document that the purpose of the tribunal is to punish the 'war criminals of the Axis' powers only. It is this that effectively removed the *tu quoque* defence. This is particularly important when reviewing article six, in which the charges were defined. It becomes clear that the United States was clearly culpable of the 'Crimes against Peace' charge, due to their actions in violation of the Hague convention. Ironically, at the very time the charter was being drawn up and Nuremberg Law was being created, the United States would also have been indictable under the War Crimes charge which spoke of 'murder or ill treatment of prisoners of war'. Without the cushion provided by articles one and six, General Eisenhower may well have found himself with some uncomfortable questions to answer regarding conditions in the *Rheinwiesenlager* (POW camps on the Rhine). Further to that, the Soviet Union were in direct *ex post facto* violation of the Crimes against Peace charge having attacked Finland in December 1939, for which they were expelled from the League of Nations. Undeterred, the Red Army had then invaded Lithuania, Latvia and Estonia a few months later, swallowing them, against the wishes of their peoples, into their nation. This aggression on the part of the Soviet Union was recognised by the other members of the tribunal, who agreed simply to ignore it. A letter, written by Jackson, was attached at the end of the Nuremberg Indictments document and contains this extract:

'In the Indictment of German War Criminals signed today, reference is made to Estonia, Latvia, Lithuania, and certain other territories as being within the area of the USSR. This language is proposed by Russia and is accepted to avoid the delay which would be occasioned by insistence on an alteration in the text. The Indictment is signed subject to this reservation and understanding: I have no authority either to admit or to challenge on behalf of the United States of America, Soviet claims to sovereignty over such territories. Nothing, therefore, in this Indictment is to be construed as a recognition by the United States of such sovereignty or as indicating any attitude, either on the part of the United States or on the part of the undersigned toward any claim to recognition of such sovereignty.'[60]

It is clear that Jackson felt uneasy over the situation, otherwise such a caveat would not need to have been added. It is also worthy of note that he stated that the wording in the indictment was chosen by the Soviets and that the other members of the tribunal opted not to argue, to save time. This gives an indication of the behind-the-scenes workings of Nuremberg, where international power plays and tactics were still present between the representatives of the victorious powers, but temporarily subsumed in the effort to attain a common goal. Remember that within two or three years, Russia and not Germany would be the great enemy.

The United States were equally culpable on the same count, having occupied Greenland and Iceland (both neutral countries) during the war. Britain does not escape either, having jointly (with the Soviet Union) invaded Iran, another neutral country, in August 1941.[61] Similarly, just as the tribunal was beginning, France was flaunting the Nuremberg charge of War Crimes by employing thousands of German prisoners of war as forced labourers.[62]

From a more general point of view, it is particularly interesting that the War Crimes description focuses on treatment of POWs, civilians and even mentions some aspects of war at sea but avoids any mention of aerial bombing.[63] Was this an oversight on the part of Jackson et al? Or could it be that in regard to that particular War Crime (and it *was* defined as such by the first Hague convention of 1899, with its quaint con-

---

[60] Nuremberg Trial Proceedings Volume One, *Letter of reservation by the United States Prosecutor in regard to wording of the indictment.*
[61] J. McMillan, *Five Men at Nuremberg* Harrap (1985), pp. 245, 414.
[62] C.FitzGibbon, *Denazification* (W. W. Norton, 1969), pp. 71-72
[63] The first paragraph of Count One of the indictment talked of 'the indiscriminate destruction of cities, towns and villages and devastation not justified by military necessity.' However the specifications of this general charge in Count Three made no reference to aerial bombardment. Neither did the relevant paragraph of indictment appendix A, describing Göring's crimes.

demnation of 'bombing from balloons')[64] the Allies completely outdid their enemies? One wonders if the surviving residents of Hamburg, Dresden, Hiroshima and Nagasaki may have raised an eyebrow to learn that what happened to their civilian populations did not constitute a 'war crime' whereas a much smaller-scale yet qualitatively similar tragedy at Rotterdam (which was listed on the trial indictment, but not the judgment) initially did, simply because it was conducted by the Luftwaffe and not the US or British air forces.

Finally, it is worth returning briefly to the charter to look at three of the most controversial of its articles, namely those that relate to evidence, in particular which evidence could be presented and accepted by the IMT. Much has been made of these articles by those seeking to criticise the Nuremberg process.

> **Article 19.** The Tribunal shall not be bound by technical rules of evidence. It shall adopt and apply to the greatest possible extent expeditious and non-technical procedure, and shall admit any evidence which it deems to be of probative value.
>
> **Article 20.** The Tribunal may require to be informed of the nature of any evidence before it is entered so that it may rule upon the relevance thereof.
>
> **Article 21.** The Tribunal shall not require proof of facts of common knowledge but shall take judicial notice[65] thereof. It shall also take judicial notice of official governmental documents and reports of the United Nations, including the acts and documents of the committees set up in the various allied countries for the investigation of war crimes, and of records and findings of military or other Tribunals of any of the United Nations.[66]

To anyone new to the subject of Nuremberg or law in general, article nineteen appears to be a damning indictment of the way the tribunal was run. To assert that the court will run without technical rules of evidence seems an insane statement. Article twenty-one, which states that the tribunal shall not require proof of facts of common knowledge, is similarly alarming to read. Such a perspective is common in previously existing literature that seeks to discredit Nuremberg. Mark Weber, of the 'Institute for Historical Review' said, in relation to articles nineteen, twenty and twenty-one, that 'on the basis of these articles, the Tribunal accepted as valid the most dubious evidence.'[67] However such views are usually based on a simple misconception of what role technical rules of evidence play in normal court proceedings. The situation is not nearly as straightforward as it seems.

Put simply, rules of evidence determine which testimony, documents and exhibits can be submitted for consideration by the court and the weight such evidence is given in determining a question of fact.[68] The United States Federal Court has quite strict rules of evidence, for example stating that, 'a witness may not testify to a matter unless evidence is introduced sufficient to support a finding that the witness has personal knowledge of the matter' or 'hearsay is not admissible as evidence.'[69] However, although it is a firm legal tradition to have technical rules for evidence in the USA or Canada, the same is not true for continental Europe, where both the French and the German legal systems, for example, have operated for many years without them. As many of the lawyers working at Nuremberg (and two of the three who wrote the London Charter) were European, the lack of technical rules was probably nothing more than a courtesy to them, rather than any sort of indication that the court would accept wild accusations. Indeed, Jackson himself seemed to say as much when he wrote,

---

[64] *Laws of War – Prohibiting Launching of Projectiles and Explosives from Balloons (Hague, IV); July 29, 1899* http://www.yale.edu/lawweb/avalon/lawofwar/hague994.htm
[65] Judicial notice is a rule of evidence which allows a 'fact' to be accepted as such by the court if it thought to be so well known that it is a waste of time to examine it.
[66] Charter articles reproduced from *The Avalon Project : Charter of the International Military Tribunal* http://www.yale.edu/lawweb/avalon/imt/proc/imtconst.htm#art2
[67] Mark Weber, *The Nuremburg Trials and the Holocaust*, Institute for Historical Review, http://www.ihr.org/jhr/v12/v12p167_Webera.html
[68] The Legal Information Institute http://www.law.cornell.edu/donors/solicit.php?http_referer=/rules/fre/rules.htm
[69] ibid

'The rules of evidence that should govern the tribunal might have caused serious disagreement if we had insisted on our own. Continental lawyers regard our common-law rules of evidence with ab- horrence...We settled, therefore, upon one simple rule: that the tribunal shall admit any evidence which it deems to have probative value. While this vested considerable discretion in the tribunal, it had the merit of making admission of evidence turn on the value of what was proffered rather than upon compliance with some formal rule of evidence.'[70]

On face value there is therefore nothing wrong with article nineteen of the charter. It is perfectly in order as a basis for law, even if it makes for strange reading for the uninitiated. The only issue it does raise, of course, as Jackson admits above, is that it places great discretion in the hands of the judges. In what would have already been a highly pressured environment, this would levy even more responsibility on the shoulders of those in that position. It remains to be seen whether they discharged such weighty duties honourably.

Article twenty is often used to support the claim, famously made by the defendant Joachim von Ribbentrop (German Minister for Foreign affairs – sentenced to death), that:

'the defence had no fair chance to defend... Our prepared application for the submission of evidence was not allowed ... Without good cause being shown, half of the 300 documents which the defence prepared were not admitted. Witnesses and affidavits were only admitted after the prosecution had been heard; most of them were rejected... Correspondence between Hitler and Chamberlain, re- ports by ambassadors and diplomatic minutes, etc., were rejected. Only the prosecution, not the de- fence, had access to German and foreign archives. The prosecution only searched for incriminating documents and their use was biased. It knowingly concealed exonerating documents and withheld them from the defence.'[71]

However, the article in question could also simply be seen as a means by which the judges could limit the amount of evidence being brought to bear to a manageable amount. If a more laissez-faire approach to the presentation of evidence had been taken, the trial could conceivably have stretched on for years, therefore negating the opportunity for the swift justice the Allies so desired.

Article twenty-one is another that easily arouses suspicion, by stating that without proof, judicial notice would be taken of facts of common knowledge. It also states that Allied reports into the alleged Nazi of- fences will be accepted by the court. Bearing in mind that we already have Allied judges and Allied prosecu- tors, it is not hard to see why the production of evidence by the Allies and the high status accorded such evi- dence by the court would be the cause of much consternation. But, as with the issue of technical rules of evi- dence, allowing facts of common knowledge is not unusual practice for a court. The modern US Federal Court, for example, also accepts evidence on such a basis.[72] Once again, whether this rule was a hindrance to justice at Nuremberg will only be clarified when the trial proceedings and judgements are examined. If the court, for example, accepted gassings, mass-shootings or other atrocities as facts of common knowledge, without further reliable proof, then in retrospect, the Nazis convicted of Crimes against Humanity would seem to have been very hard done by. If however, corroborative evidence was presented and subjected to cross examination and judicial evaluation prior to being accepted, in order to support the claims, there could be little cause for complaint, assuming that said evidence was of value.

In evaluation of the basis of law that was developed for Nuremberg, there was therefore not much written which had a necessarily corrupt interpretation or that is directly indicative of a vindictive, lopsided trial, other than article three of the charter, which stated that neither the tribunal itself nor its associates could be chal- lenged by the prosecution or the defence. But this, in conjunction with the repeated statement in articles one and six, that the purpose of the trials was to punish the war criminals of the Axis only, would seem to display what could reasonably be described as a flaw (and hysterically described as many things.) In the search for quick judgement, Jackson tipped the scales too far in the Allies' favour. If international law was being cre-

---

[70] Robert H Jackson, *Nuremberg In Retrospect: Legal Answer To International Lawlessness* American Bar Association Journal. 35 ABAJ 813 (1949).
[71] W. Maser, *Nuremberg, a Nation on Trial,* (Scribner 1979), p. 199.
[72] The Legal Information Institute http://www.law.cornell.edu/rules/fre/rules.htm#Rule101

ated by the London Charter, the normal spirit of justice would demand it be equally administered to all. To make a set of rules which are only forcibly applied to those who have just lost a war, by those who have just won it, is as clear cut an example of victor's justice as could hope to be found. However, other criticisms of the charter are broadly unfounded or at least debatable and can only be properly evaluated in the light of an examination of the indictments, transcripts and judgements.

With no small degree of controversy therefore, Jackson had managed to complete his first major task. The legal platform had been built.

4

Defendants?

Having cleared the first set of hurdles, Jackson's next priority was to get hold of some Nazis to put on the stand. Rough lists of potential war criminals had been drawn up several years before, by all the Allied leaders, which had gradually congealed into some sort of accepted idea. Unfortunately, events had overtaken that accepted idea and the top end of the list had become shapeless. Hitler and Goebbels were dead. Heinrich Himmler was caught and arrested, at Bremervörde, in Northern Germany, apparently attempting to make his way to Switzerland. However he too quickly committed suicide in custody. Before moving on, it should probably be mentioned that there is a degree of controversy over Himmler's death. It has been alleged by some historians and in particular Martin Allen that Himmler had been involved in negotiations with the British government for some time regarding a possible collaborative move against the USSR (there is further evidence for this in Hitler's last political testament) and that he was actually murdered by his captors to prevent him from revealing the nature of the negotiations. Regardless, this meant that the three most wanted and infamous Nazis were unavailable.

Bernays set to work on a new list, the first draft of which contained 125 names. This was soon pared down to less than half that number. In Mondorf, Luxembourg, the Palace Hotel was converted into a deten- tion centre and given the rather lame codename 'Ashcan' (a 1940s American synonym for rubbish bin). Hermann Göring, officially the number-two man to Hitler, eventually arrived at Mondorf at the end of May, having surrendered to an American infantry division in the Austrian Alps on May 7th. He was held first at a castle in Kitzbühel, then moved to Augsburg for interrogation, before transfer to Mondorf.[73] Despite his longstanding position as *Reichsmarschall*, after Hitler's suicide and with crushing defeat an absolute cer- tainty, the poisoned chalice of German Führership had actually not been passed to Göring, due to a last min- ute falling-out with Hitler, but to Admiral Karl Dönitz, an unswerving and old fashioned military man who

had impressed Hitler in his position as head of the *Kriegsmarine* (Navy). Dönitz set up government in Flensburg, with Albert Speer appointed as Minister in charge of Economics and Production,[74] and other appointments made regarding post-war Germany's military and education system.

At the surrender meeting, Dönitz sent General Alfred Jodl to negotiate with the Allies, not to affect the terms of the surrender, which he knew he had no power to do, but simply to delay the inevitable for as long as possible. It was felt that by doing so, German soldiers would be able to make their way west to surrender to the British and the Americans, whom they expected better treatment from than the Russians who had already swallowed up the East. Jodl performed the task admirably and was presented with a medal by Dönitz upon his return.

However the Flensburg government was short lived, lasting a mere three weeks. On the 23rd May, Lowell W. Rooks, Eisenhower's personal representative (Eisenhower himself simply refused to engage in dialogue with Germans, hence his absence from the surrender also), addressed Dönitz and his cabinet at their headquarters.

'Gentlemen,' he said. 'I am empowered by the Supreme Allied Commander to inform you that as of this moment, the Flensburg government is dissolved.'[75] He then produced a list which relayed who would be taken to Mondorf pending trial for War Crimes. As well as Dönitz, General Alfred Jodl, Field Marshall Willhelm Keitel, Alfred Rosenberg and Albert Speer were taken from the Flensburg area to prison. Others followed quickly.

Foreign Minister Von Ribbentrop was found at a Hamburg apartment. Fritz Sauckel, who had helped direct the foreign forced labour program, was located hiding in a cave, of all places. The 'Jew Baiter' Julius

---

[73] Conot, p.31
[74] Persico, p.29
[75] Persico, p.30

Streicher was arrested at his farmhouse.[76] Hans Frank, the 'Butcher of Cracow' was located in a makeshift office in Schliersee.[77] Hans Fritzsche, the radio presenter and Admiral Erich Raeder (along with Raeder's wife) were captured by the Russians and sent first to Moscow for interrogation, then later to Mondorf.[78] Rudolf Hess had been in Britain since 1941 and was flown over for the trial. Robert Ley, leader of the German Labour Front and implementer of the *'Kraft durch Freude'* ('Strength through Joy') programme, was arrested in his pyjamas by American troops at a mountain retreat near the Austrian border, using an assumed identity.[79]

Others, who made little attempt to hide, were simply rounded up from their homes or places of work, or, like Baldur von Schirach (leader of the Hitler Youth) turned themselves in. Still others fled to other continents, in particular South America, where Argentina offered political asylum to those being pursued and refused to deport them. This process of rounding up Nazi war criminals was to continue for several decades, with each trial (the IMT was the first of many) throwing up new possibilities for indictment. Every time a witness was called and a name was mentioned, that name was added to a list of potential future defendants. Eugene Davidson stated that through this process: 'each trial set off a chain of trials.'[80] As the first and strongest link in the chain, the IMT had to set a powerful precedent.

Altogether, some fifty-two leading Nazis were assembled at Mondorf[81], of whom twelve appeared as defendants before the IMT and many of the rest as witnesses. During their stay there and after they were moved to the prison wing at the Palace of Justice, stories began circulating regarding the mistreatment of prisoners in Allied hands. Admiral Raeder's wife, for example was held by the Russians, mostly in a prison just out- side Berlin, without charge. Frau Göring and her young daughter were similarly treated by the Western Allies, as were the wives of Baldur von Schirach and Walter Funk.[82] Upon arrest Hans Frank was forced to 'run the gauntlet' of a seventy foot long line of American GIs raining blows upon him with their fists and feet. This ordeal led him to attempt suicide in his cell.[83] Julius Streicher was repeatedly beaten and spat on by black GIs after his arrest.[84] He was also subjected to psychological torture – one night guards projected the shadow of a hangman's noose onto the wall of his cell using a piece of string and a spotlight then woke him to confront it, laughing at his screams.[85] Ernst Kaltenbrunner, the SS officer, was hospitalised for cerebral haemorrhaging whilst at Nuremberg, most likely caused by blows to the head.[86] Albert Speer, although not brutalised himself, reported in his memoirs that while being held briefly at the interrogation camp of Oberürsel near Frankfurt, prior to transfer to Nuremberg, he sat in his cell listening to 'the rough shouts of American guards' to which prisoners responded with 'anxious replies and screams.'[87] Hjalmar Schacht, who was also detained at Oberürsel for a time, described it as having the worst conditions he had experienced, German or Allied.[88] When one considers that Schacht spent the last year of the war in three concentration camps, ultimately a prisoner in Dachau during its final, epidemic-ravaged months, the depth of the statement's meaning becomes clear. Rudolf Höss, the Auschwitz commandant, not a defendant at the IMT, but a key witness, wrote in his autobiography:

'I was maltreated by the Field Security Police... At my first interrogation, evidence was obtained by beating me. I do not know what is in the record, although I signed it. Alcohol and the whip were too much for me. The whip was my own, which by chance had got into my wife's luggage. It had hardly ever touched my horse, far less the prisoners. Nevertheless, one of my interrogators was con-

---

[76] Conot, p.34
[77] Persico, p.26
[78] Davidson, p.30
[79] Tusa, p.40
[80] Davidson, p.28
[81] Tusa, p.42
[82] Davidson, p.30
[83] Persico, p.19
[84] Davidson, p.51
[85] Persico, p.150
[86] The official cause of Kaltenbrunner's injuries was 'stress'.
[87] Albert Speer, *Inside the Third Reich*, (Book Club Associates London, 1971) p.507
[88] Overy, *Interrogations*, p.66

vinced that I had perpetually used it for flogging the prisoners. After some days I was taken to Minden-on-the-Weser, the main interrogation center in the British Zone. There I received further rough treatment at the hands of the English public prosecutor, a major.'[89]

There remains too an air of suspicion surrounding the death of Robert Ley, who ingeniously managed to commit suicide in his tiny cell by strangling himself against the toilet pipe with a towel, while under constant surveillance. Further doubts can therefore be cast on the Nuremberg process because of these occurrences. Although not part of the trial itself, the gathering of defendants and their incarceration and interrogation prior to the hearing form an important part of the whole. It has been alleged by some historians, such as David Irving and Rupert Butler that this mistreatment went further than army grunts releasing pent-up antagonism on their captives. Irving, in his book 'The Last Battle' described how Konrad Morgen, the former SS judge advocate and another important IMT witness, refused to give 'perjured testimony' to the effect that Ilse Koch ('the Bitch of Buchenwald') had fashioned lampshades from the skin of murdered inmates. Morgen claimed that as a result, 'the Americans almost killed me...They threatened to turn me over to the Russians or French or Poles.'[90]

Rupert Butler, in his book 'Legions of Death' discussed the Höss affidavit presented at the trial (to be discussed in detail later) and how Bernard Clarke, of the British War Crimes Group stated that 'it took three days (of torture) to get a coherent declaration out of him.'[91] Such allegations raise the bar from the simple incidents of mistreatment which so often happen when enemy captures enemy, (witness the recent abuses of Iraqi POWs by coalition soldiers) to being evidence of a wholly corrupt legal process, in which false evidence was obtained by physical coercion. Much anti Nuremberg literature plays upon these ideas very heavily. Mark Weber of the Institute for Historical Review stated, 'Allied prosecutors used torture to help prove their case at Nuremberg...'[92] Weber cited Butler among the sources he used to make this statement. Unfortunately, both Butler and Irving have now been somewhat discredited, Irving very publicly, after the Lipstadt trial, during which the judge described him as: 'a racist, an anti-Semite, a Holocaust denier and a falsifier of history.' While according to Jamie McCarthy of the 'Nizkor' anti-Holocaust denial website, 'The potboiler, Rupert Butler's "Legions of Death", is clearly not written with historical accuracy in mind.'[93]

However, there has been some small concession from mainstream history, as in a 1993 article in Vanity Fair, the eminent historian Christopher Browning explained Butler's work by stating that Höss was 'a very weak and confused witness.'[94] Yet clearly, if that were the case, doubt would also have to be cast over the content of Höss' testimony, which will be discussed at length later. It is not acceptable to dismiss some of what Höss' says for this reason, yet accept other parts as objective truth. Regardless of the above, the fact remains that many Nuremberg inmates were abused physically. Whether or not it was done systematically, to extract false testimony, it happened and is not a feature of legal process that many would see as serving the cause of justice.

Once moved from Mondorf (or in the case of Hess, the UK) to Nuremberg, the prisoners were kept in complete isolation. The Americans took the unprecedented decision to ban all German military insignia and to declare that they no longer acknowledged German military rank. This enabled them to circumvent the Geneva Convention, under which solitary confinement was forbidden.[95] The prisoners were allowed out of their cells for half an hour's exercise a day, which involved walking around in twos or threes, in a circle, in the yard, in silence and in single file. They were allowed to use primitive washing facilities twice a week. The food, cooked by German POWs, was adequate, amounting to about 1800 calories a day.[96] On reflection, this Spartan regime may have caused more problems for the Allied prosecutors than it solved. Many of the prisoners lost weight and were weaned off alcohol and cigarette habits. Göring, for example, lost nearly five stones between his capture and the beginning of the trial, entering the dock at a nimble ten stones and thirteen

---

[89] Rudolf Hoess, *Commandant of Auschwitz*, (Phoenix Press, 2000) p.174. Höss was ordered to write this book by his captors.
[90] David Irving, *Nuremberg, The Last Battle*, (Focal Point Publications 1997) p.223
[91] Rupert Butler, *Legions of Death*. (Hamlyn, 1983) p.235
[92] Mark Weber, The Nuremberg Trials and the Holocaust, http://www.ihr.org/jhr/v12/v12p167_Webera.html
[93] http://www.nizkor.org/ftp.cgi/people/h/ftp.py?people/h/hoess.rudolf.ferdinand/on-torture
[94] Christopher Hitchens *Whose History Is It?* Vanity Fair, Dec 1993.
[95] Davidson, p.21
[96] Conot, p.35

pounds.[97] He was also free of the morphine dependence that had plagued him since 1923. It is unlikely he would have managed quite such an emphatic appearance before the court without this enforced detox.

After several months of interrogation, isolation and indignity, on October 6th, 1945, twenty-one men were indicted personally by Airey Neave, a British war hero[98] appointed by the tribunal to carry out various official tasks. Neave admitted to having a sleepless night prior to performing this duty. He recalled, 'Why was I, who survived the defence of Calais and the flight from Colditz so *bouleverse* (upset)?' He answered this rather self-aggrandising question by saying, 'It was the fear of these monsters in the Nuremberg jail. How should I react when I came face to face with them?'[99]

A fear of monsters? When Neave arrived in Göring's cell, the former *Reichsmarschall* stood and offered him the bed to sit on (there was no chair). Neave read his statement, handed him the indictment and Göring quietly said, 'So it has come.'[100]

---

[97] Davidson, p.59. 5 stones equates to 70 pounds or roughly 32 kilos.
[98] Airey Neave was a wartime organizer of MI9 and the first Englishman to escape from Colditz.
[99] Neave, p.58
[100] ibid, p.73

5

The Indictment

Below is a table of defendants at the IMT and the charges for which they were indicted.

- • – indicted
- G – indicted and subsequently found guilty

Name	Count 1 Conspiracy	Count 2 Crimes against Peace	Count 3 War Crimes	Count 4 Crimes against Humanity
Göring	G	G	G	G
Ribbentrop	G	G	G	G
Hess	G	G	•	•
Kaltenbrunner	•		G	G
Rosenberg	G	G	G	G
Frank	•		G	G
Bormann	•		G	G
Frick	•	G	G	G
Ley	•		•	•
Sauckel	•	G	G	G
Speer	•	•	G	G
Funk	•	G	G	G
Schacht	•	•		
Krupp	•	•	•	•
von Neurath	G	G	G	G
von Schirach	•			G
Seyss-Inquart	•	G	G	G
Jodl	G	G	G	G
Raeder	G	G	G	
Keitel	G	G	G	G
Streicher	•			G
Dönitz	•	G	G	
Fritzsche	•		•	•

[101]

In addition to the above, certain Nazi organisations were indicted as 'criminal' by the IMT, thereby making membership of them a criminal offence also. These organisations were *Die Reichsregierung* (The Reich cabinet, Hitler's Ministers), *Des Korps der Politischen Leiter der Nationalsozialistischen Deutschen Arbeiterpartei* (The Leadership Corps of the Nazi Party), *Die Schutstaffeln* (the SS), *Die Geheime Staatspolizei* (the State Police, or Gestapo), *Die Sturmabteilung* (The SA or brownshirts) and *Die Oberkommando den Wehrmacht* (the High Command of the German Armed Forces).[102] This led to some strange decisions as to who to place on the stand.

---

[101] Table of indictments constructed using information from *The Avalon Project : Indictment : Appendix A*, http://www.yale.edu/lawweb/avalon/imt/proc/counta.htm
[102] ibid, *appendix B*

The first observation that can be made when viewing the indictments in this sort of format is that the only charge common to all defendants was that of Conspiracy and that ultimately only seven defendants were convicted of it. The conspiracy charge was very much Jackson's baby. As stated in the previous chapter, he hadn't conceived it, but had nurtured it and put it at the centre of the Nuremberg case. During the early meetings, he was forced to defend it against vigorous opposition from Maxwell-Fyfe (British prosecutor) among others. Jackson felt that he would be able to assemble enough documentary evidence to make a case that showed that the outbreak of World War Two and its resultant seventy million deaths were all part of a Nazi master plan. This, essentially, would demonstrate the inherent evil of the Nazi regime and incriminate those associated with it. Maxwell-Fyfe thought this was too woolly and fanciful a concept to work in a court of law. How could you possibly prove that all these Nazi actions since the early days of the party, through to the years of government, were part of some grand design? Surely the picture was more complex? Outside influences had to be looked at, individual policies and politicians examined. How could you prove who was in on the conspiracy and who was ignorant? How far down the party hierarchy would it reach? According to Ann and John Tusa, the British delegation thought that the conspiracy charge 'was too vague, too grandiose to be effective.'[103] The French and Russians had similar misgivings, believing it was more appropriate to concentrate on the actual commission of criminal acts rather than people conspiring to do so. But Jackson was an ambitious man (he was being tipped for high political office at this time, having made the short list for running-mate for Roosevelt in the 1940 election)[104] and he made it stick. What is of particular interest here is that this overall conspiracy or master plan became the prevailing view of an entire branch of history. Intentionalist historians, like Lucy Davidowicz, have long maintained that the Nazis committed their crimes as part of a Führer-initiated scheme, born in the earliest days of the Nazi Party which was eventually implemented by party officials and underlings, thereby implicating all of them.

The seeds for the development of this interpretation were sown immediately. In an article published on the day the last indictments were served by Neave, October 19th, 1945, The New York Times said the defendants had been charged with 'participation in the bloodiest, blackest plot against peace and humanity that has ever stained history's pages.'[105] How well such an idea was proven during the trial and moreover how far it was accepted by the judges after the evidence was heard, is something to be discussed later.

The second observation is that to anyone other than those with a special interest in the history of Nazi Germany and who have read extensively on this subject before, at least half the defendants are unknowns. This is due largely to the criminalisation of Nazi organisations. Leaving to one side Göring, Hess, von Ribbentrop, Dönitz, Raeder, Keitel and Jodl, we have such luminaries as Julius Streicher, who was well known, but was essentially a newspaper publisher. Did the production of his gutter tabloid *Der Stürmer* really qualify him to be a Major War Criminal, worthy of being tried alongside leading political and military figures? The answer is clearly 'no', but he was there because he had been side by side with Hitler from the early days and was therefore implicated in the conspiracy (also because he was *Gauleiter* (Governor) of Franconia for a time and therefore was a member of the leadership corps). Gustav Krupp von Bohlen und Halbach was an industrialist and a patriot who actually publicly opposed the Nazis until 1933, when they became the government, at which point he began to support them as his patriotic duty. Also, as his company manufactured arms, it made sense to be on good terms with the government, whoever they were, as they were in a position to send a lot of business his way. Indeed, his company became the major manufacturer of steel and weapons to support German rearmament. It cannot be claimed that his record was spotless – during the war he did make use of slave labour presented to him by the Reich, for example, as many German factories and farms did.[106] Clearly he was implicated to some degree in some of the charges, but was he a Major War Criminal?

Hans Fritzsche (who was eventually acquitted) spent most of his pre-Nuremberg life as a newsreader and radio presenter, before taking up a second-tier position under Goebbels in the Ministry for Propaganda. As Goebbels could not be tried, the Russians decided to put Fritzsche in the dock instead. It is particularly odd to

---

[103] Tusa, A&J, *The Nuremberg Trial*, (MacMillan 1983) p.83
[104] Persico, p.10
[105] *Drexel Sprecher, 92, US Prosecutor at Nuremberg, dies*, Douglas Martin, NY Times, May 8th 2006, http://www.nytimes.com/2006/05/08/us/08sprecher.html?ex=1304740800&en=c3e6f67d25cb228a&ei=5090&partner=rssuserland&emc=rss
[106] Gall, Lothar: *Krupp. Der Aufstieg eines Industrieimperiums*, (Berlin 2000)

note that the Allies deemed men such as these to be 'Major War Criminals' whereas Rudolf Höss, for example, the commandant of Auschwitz whom the victorious powers eventually judged to have presided over the deaths of three million Jews[107], was not. Robert Conot explains this by saying that the IMT was, 'a case in which the charges were prepared and the defendants chosen before the facts had been more than cursorily investigated.'[108]

It is also interesting that of the eighteen indictments which involve count four, Crimes against Humanity, only one mentions concentration camps (that of Kaltenbrunner, senior SS figure) and only three specifically mention persecution of the Jews (Fritzsche, Streicher, Schirach). And two of these are solely related to the issue of anti-Semitic propaganda, *not* physical persecution. The other fourteen are vaguely worded and say things like 'a wide variety of crimes against persons and property'[109] or 'the abuse of human beings for labour.'[110] To the modern eye, it seems peculiar that the great crime for which the Nazis are so infamous, the Jewish Holocaust, with its gas chambers, corpse-pits and huge open pyres of burning bodies, was only faintly alluded to by the prosecution at this stage and then in non-specific terms. The majority of indictments were, in fact, centred around the conspiracy to wage and participate in aggressive war. Was this due to the Allies not wishing to highlight Holocaust atrocities, for some reason? That seems unlikely, given the climate of the time and the avowed intention of the charter to 'punish Axis war criminals'. The emphasis of such a heinous crime would surely have facilitated the process. Some, like Norman Finkelstein, have controversially argued that our view of the importance of the Holocaust has changed over time due to political reasons and that contemporarily it was viewed as a peripheral issue. Others still, even more controversially and outside of mainstream history, have argued that the Holocaust has since been exaggerated or even partially invented by special interest groups and that the Nuremberg prosecutors were only the beginning of that process of exaggeration and invention. These sensitive issues will be discussed in more detail in chapter twenty. Regardless of when or why The Holocaust became such a dominant socio-political and cultural focus, and the reasons be- hind its late emergence, it was clearly not the major concern of Jackson et al at Nuremberg.

After the indictment was drawn up, formalities were commenced, firstly involving documents being delivered to the defendants by Allied staff on the 19th August. These letters informed defendants of the charges for which they would stand trial and of their right to legal counsel. A list of potential lawyers, (all German) were delivered with the letter, so that the defendants could select their own representation. In accordance with the stipulation of the IMT, notices informing the German population of the indictments were placed in thousands of locations around the now Soviet, American, British and French controlled zones. Details of the indictments were also played at regular intervals on German radio.

Between the delivery of documents to the defendants and the commencement of courtroom proceedings, there were several issues to be ironed out. The first of these was the condition of Gustav Krupp von Bohlen und Halbach, who was bedridden, incapable of speech and incontinent following a severe stroke and an incurable condition called 'progressive arteriosclerotic softening of the brain'.[111] His lawyer, one Theodor Klefisch, wrote to the tribunal asking that proceedings against him be postponed until such time as his health allowed him to stand trial. The lawyer provided two medical examination certificates confirming Krupp's condition. For confirmation, the IMT sent their own team of six doctors to Krupp's house, all of whom confirmed that Krupp's condition was genuine and that he was in no fit state to attend court. They also confirmed that it was unlikely he ever would be. This posed the IMT with a dilemma. Should they agree to postpone Krupp's case until such time as he should be fit for trial, they would really be agreeing to 'quash all proceedings.'[112] None of the member states deemed that to be an appropriate course of action, bearing in mind the Krupp Company's role in rearming Germany during the thirties and using slave labour in 1944. Jackson, on behalf of the USA respectfully opposed the application, recommending that Krupp's son, Alfried

---

[107] In the IMT judgement document, they repeated the claim from the Höss affidavit that 2.5 million Jews had been exterminated in gas chambers at Auschwitz and a further half a million had died of natural causes. Mainstream history no longer maintains these figures. http://elsinore.cis.yale.edu/lawweb/avalon/imt/proc/judwarcr.htm#persecution
[108] Robert E. Conot, Justice at Nuremberg, (Carroll & Graf 1983) p.28
[109] from Göring's indictment
[110] from Ley's indictment
[111] IMT Vol.1. *Doctor's certificate provided by Karl Gersdorf MD, District Doctor, Werfen, Salzburg.*
[112] ibid *'Answer of the United States prosecution to the application on behalf of defendant von Bohlen'*

who had taken over the company as a result of his father's ill-health in 1943, be tried instead.[113] The Soviet Union, France and Great Britain all opposed this. Jackson was disappointed and responded by writing, 'The United States respectfully submits that no greater disservice to the future peace of the world could be done than to excuse the entire Krupp family and the armament enterprise from this Trial in which aggressive war making is sought to be condemned.'[114]

The British chief prosecutor, Hartley Shawcross responded by suggesting that Krupp senior be tried in absentia. France, in the form of prosecutor Dubost, initially agreed with Shawcross and then wrote a second statement siding with Jackson. This was enough to carry Jackson's motion and a document indicting Alfried Krupp in his father's place was signed by the French, American and Soviet prosecutors on the 16th November.[115]

There followed a series of applications and responses between the defence and the prosecutors/judges. Firstly, Julius Streicher's lawyer applied for the hearing to be postponed, on the grounds that he had been given insufficient time to prepare his case and did not have access to the prosecution documents held by the court.[116] The motion was overruled by Judge Geoffrey Lawrence (Great Britain), the president of the hearing.[117]

Some psychological examinations were then called for, firstly by Colonel Yuri Pokrovsky, the chief Soviet prosecutor, who requested an examination of Streicher on the grounds that 'Streicher declared quite unexpectedly that he "had been holding the viewpoint of Zionism."' Hilariously, Pokrovsky saw this outburst as evidence of insanity. It clearly had not occurred to him that both Nazis and Zionists[118] had wanted the Jews out of Germany, albeit for different reasons. There was obvious potential for common ground. Indeed, Pokrovsky's opinion is in direct conflict with modern writers, such as Lenny Brenner, who describes 'exposing the Zionist role in the Hitler era' as 'required of historians'[119]. It is also worth noting that in contrast to Jackson or Shawcross, Pokrovsky seemed happy to mention what has become known as the Holocaust, referring to Jews being 'tortured and murdered as a direct result of propaganda.'[120] With regard to Streicher, it is probable that although he was indicted on the conspiracy charge too, his role as a propagandist led his case to rest more on count four than the other defendants.

Streicher was declared psychologically sound and fit to face trial. Hess' lawyer then proposed a motion to have his client examined. The IMT rejected that motion, but then proposed their own. Hess was examined and deemed well, despite suffering from 'hysteria characterized in part by loss of memory.'[121]

The final notable activity before the trial began took the form of the Motion adopted by all Defence Counsel,[122] in which they objected to the entire Nuremberg process on the grounds that law had been created *ex post facto* and that the trial violated the principle of *Nulla Poena Sine Lege* (no penalty without law). The collected counsels for the defence requested an independent body, authoritative in international law to rule on the legality of the Nuremberg charges and the trial procedure. It is assumed they had some sub-unit of the newly formed United Nations in mind, although it is doubtful that the organisation, created essentially by Churchill and Roosevelt during their various World War Two conferences, would have had a great deal of sympathy to their cause. The IMT rejected the motion on the grounds that it was in contravention of article three of their charter, namely, 'Neither the Tribunal, its members nor their alternates can be challenged by the

---

[113] ibid.
[114] ibid
[115] ibid *'Motion of the committee of Chief Prosecutors to amend the indictment by adding the name of Alfried Krupp von Bohlen as a defendant.'* Although the motion was carried, there was not enough time to prepare a case against Alfried Kupp and he did not appear before the IMT. He was later tried in an American-run court in Germany and convicted for use of forced labour, then subsequently retried and exonerated.
[116] ibid. *Motion on behalf of defendant Streicher for postponement of the trial as to him*
[117] ibid *Memorandum of the United States Prosecution on the motion on behalf of defendant Streicher*
[118] Zionism was the political movement aimed at establishing a homeland for the Jewish people in Palestine. It was very active in Europe and the United States from the end of the 19th century onwards, with several large and ultimately influential organisations campaigning for it. Largest of these was the World Jewish Congress. As they neared their goal, in the 20s, 30s and 40s, part of the efforts of these organisations was to encourage European Jews to emigrate to Palestine.
[119] Lenny Brenner, *51 Documents, Zionist Collaboration with the Nazis*, (Barricade 2002), p.326
[120] ibid *Motion of the Soviet Prosecution for a psychological examination of the defendant Streicher.*
[121] ibid *Report of Commission to examine defendant Hess*
[122] ibid *Motion Adopted by all Defence Counsel*

prosecution, or by the Defendants or their Counsel.'

Again, it is difficult to defend the morality of a legal process which creates its own adaptation of international law, determines selectively who it will be applied to and then declares its new, adapted laws unchallengeable, simply by its own authority. Finding justification for this is the real dilemma facing the pro-Nuremberg analyst. The argument that the Nazis 'deserved it' is simply unsatisfactory. It opens up a minefield of potential issues for the future that such a precedent would create. In the modern era, post World War Two, who would determine who deserved this sort of treatment? Who would determine who was acting aggressively? Who would determine who could be indicted for their war crimes? Most importantly, on all these matters, who would be the arbiters? It would seem to be related solely to the possession of power. And this appears to be the basis on which Nuremberg worked.

By the time the defence counsels' application had been summarily rebuffed, there was nothing left to do other than begin.

6

'A most terrible and convincing case'

The hearing before the IMT began on Thursday 15th November 1945, with a series of preliminary discussions. These conferences between the prosecution, defence and bench are of little interest to anyone other than those fascinated with the finer points of technical legal matters. The only item of general historical concern regarded the defendant Martin Bormann who, at the end of the war, had tried to escape the Soviet advance by fleeing Berlin in a tank. The Soviets captured the tank at the River Spree and threw hand grenades into it. Of several survivors taken and interrogated, two said Bormann had been killed but one thought he had only been injured. The IMT therefore decided to try him in absentia on the off chance that he was still alive.[123] This spawned a generation of absurd sightings and stories, culminating with a film of the Sex Pistols playing football with him, in full Nazi regalia, on Copacabana beach in 1979.[124]

The trial proper began on Tuesday 20th November with the reading of the indictments. These were of a more detailed nature than the general indictment written before the trial and laid out the specific charges against each defendant and the Nazi organisations which the IMT had deemed to be criminal. Pleas were entered on the second day – all defendants pleaded not guilty, some with a degree of righteous indignation, like General Alfred Jodl, Chief of the *Oberkommando den Wehrmacht's* Operations Division (later found guilty on all four counts and sentenced to death, then posthumously exonerated by a German court in 1953) who said, 'Not guilty. For what I have done or had to do, I have a pure conscience before God, before history and my people.' Contrastingly, when asked to enter his plea, Rudolf Hess stood and simply said '*Nein*' (no), to laughter from the press gallery. The president of the court interpreted this as meaning 'not guilty'.[125]

The rest of the day was mainly taken up with Jackson's address, in which he reiterated much of what had been said during the indictments and talked passionately about the duties of the assembly. Of the men in the dock, he said:

> 'They have so identified themselves with the philosophies they conceived and with the forces they directed that any tenderness to them is a victory and an encouragement to all the evils which are attached to their names. Civilization can afford no compromise with the social forces which would gain renewed strength if we deal ambiguously or indecisively with the men in whom those forces now precariously survive.'

Despite this rather polemical description, he went on to assure the court that, 'we (the prosecution) will give you undeniable proofs of incredible events' and stated that, 'we (the tribunal) must never forget that the record on which we judge these defendants today is the record on which history will judge us tomorrow. To pass these defendants a poisoned chalice is to put it to our own lips as well...'[126]

A thorough analysis of Jackson's prolonged soliloquy would require a book-length project of its own, but contained within the sections quoted above, the essence of its contradiction can be seen. On the one hand he spoke of the defendants in terms of 'evils' which still 'precariously survive' within them, urging the court 'not to compromise' or 'deal ambiguously'. On the other he continued his vaunted rhetoric on matters of justice, honour and principle. One could say, that in doing the former he was merely performing his role as chief prosecutor, yet the fact that Jackson was more than this at Nuremberg, that he drafted the London charter and had virtually written the trial rule-book himself (with Bernays' help), gives the analyst some cause for concern. Again, it raises the issue of objectivity. Could the Allies really be enemy, then victor, then judge, jury

---

[123] ibid. *Nuremberg Trial Proceedings Vol. 2 – Third Preliminary Hearing*
[124] The Sex Pistols, *The Great Rock and Roll Swindle*, (Warner Bros/Virgin video) 1982
[125] Nuremberg Trial Proceedings, Vol. 2, 2nd day, Wednesday 21st November 1945, p.96
[126] *Nuremberg Trial Proceedings Vol. 2, 2nd day, Wednesday 21st November 1945, p.100*

and executioner and be expected to fulfil these roles without bias? Jackson clearly thought so, despite having some misgivings. He summed up what would become the Nuremberg debate years before it began, by saying:

> 'Less than 8 months ago nearly all our witnesses and documents were in enemy hands. The law had not been codified, no procedures had been established, no tribunal was in existence, no usable courthouse stood here, none of the hundreds of tons of official German documents had been examined, no prosecuting staff had been assembled, nearly all of the present defendants were at large, and the four prosecuting powers had not yet joined in common cause to try them. I should be the last to deny that the case may well suffer from incomplete researches and quite likely will not be the example of professional work which any of the prosecuting nations would normally wish to sponsor.'

He then countered this tentatively negative view of his creation by continuing:

> 'It is, however, a completely adequate case to the judgment we shall ask you to render, and its full development we shall be obliged to leave to historians... Unfortunately, the nature of these crimes is such that both prosecution and judgment must be by victor nations over vanquished foes. The worldwide scope of the aggressions carried out by these men has left but few real neutrals. Either the victors must judge the vanquished or we must leave the defeated to judge themselves. After the First World War, we learned the futility of the latter course. The former high station of these defendants, the notoriety of their acts, and the adaptability of their conduct to provoke retaliation make it hard to distinguish between the demand for a just and measured retribution, and the unthinking cry for vengeance which arises from the anguish of war. It is our task, so far as humanly possible, to draw the line between the two.'[127]

Here, Jackson was fudging one issue, the lack of neutrals – it would have been relatively easy to set up such a tribunal, the Swiss, for example, would have been a decent starting point.[128] He was also referring to the legal process which occurred at the end of the First World War, when the victorious powers decided to try Kaiser Wilhelm II and his accomplices for war guilt. The initial idea was to have the Kaiser tried in a court of one of the victorious nations, but the Dutch, who held him, refused to surrender him to the Allies, because 'the political adversaries of the Kaiser would be both judge and prosecution in the case' and also 'an impartial judgement without prejudice was unlikely,' going on to add that 'the development of a new law cannot start with an injustice.'[129] Trials were therefore allowed to take place at the German Supreme Court, where of the 901 defendants, 888 were acquitted. The Allied powers wanted no repeat of this after World War Two. According to Eugene Davidson, 'This time it would be brought home to the Germans that war, aggressive war, is a crime, that they had been not only the victims but the participants in a criminal regime, a criminal conspiracy planted in the Prussian-German soil of militarism.'[130]

'The Prussian-German soil of militarism' – it was a convenient concept for the Allies. Otto von Bismarck, Kaiser Wilhelm, Adolf Hitler, all fruits of the same bush, all created by some sort of innate desire to dominate and attack that was simply part of their society, part of their people, maybe even some sort of genetic determinant. Yet to modern eyes it appears to be little more than a risible Colonel Klink caricature. Even if those individuals were militaristic, would such a description be applicable only to the Germans? Prior to and during the time about which this book is concerned, Britain had used industrial might and superior naval power to forcibly conquer a quarter of the world. Yet this did not, at that stage, attract the same kind of condemnation. The French had also made aggressive gains in territory throughout Africa, Asia and across the

---

[127] ibid.
[128] There are issues regarding the Swiss. Although they were officially a neutral country, the controversy surrounding 'Nazi gold' stored in Swiss banks tarnished their image somewhat. The point remains though that if objectivity was really desired, somebody, with more neutrality than Britain, USA, France and the USSR (if necessary even a coalition of 'minor' neutral nations) could have been engaged for the legal process.
[129] Hans Heinrich Jeschek, *Die Verantwortlichkeit der Staatsorgane nach dem Voelkerstrafrecht* (Bonn: Ludwig Roehrscheid Verlag 1952) quoted in Davidson, p.4
[130] Eugene Davidson, *The Trial of the Germans* (University of Missouri Press) p.4

Indian, Pacific and Caribbean oceans. America had relatively recently annexed California and other parts of Mexico. Historically many, many nations, too numerous to list, but including other European powers and former powers such as Russia, Spain, Holland and Portugal had all been more warlike and expansionist than Germany. Yet Germany alone was consistently described as an aggressor, an invader and a hot-bed of militarism.

A possible explanation is that, in the eyes of the victors, expansionism was acceptable, provided those being conquered were not also European. Could it be that tribes of Apache, Zulu and Arawak were fair game, while the French or the Poles were not? It's quite plausible. Modern ideals of racial equality and non-exploitation of the developing world were yet to become fashionable, although Robert Jackson, who as a young lawyer had defended a poor black man accused of murder by white farmers in Missouri, would be instrumental in making them so. But the suspicion remains that this may have had more to do with the other major powers seeing off the dangerous newcomer in the race for global domination, rather than being any sort of rational assessment of national character.

The Prosecution began on the 22nd November, with a long and frankly tedious presentation from Colonel Robert Storey regarding the methods of collating and presenting documents which would be used. The first real evidence of the trial was presented on day three, in the form of a chart, which the American prosecutor Ralph G. Albrecht explained. The chart showed the pyramidal structure of the Nazi state, with the Führer at the top, the *Gauleiter* (regional governors) underneath, leading down to the *Kreisleiter* (district leaders), the *Ortsgruppen leiter* (village or locality leaders), the *Zellenleiter* (in charge of a small area within a village or locality) and finally the *Blockleiter* who often were in charge of an area little bigger than that which housed two dozen families. Albrecht stated that it was through this system that the Nazi conspiracy functioned and he spoke in terms of the *Weltanschauung* (ideology or world view) which this structure promoted. Realistically, what he demonstrated was that the Nazi state worked on several levels, via a chain of command, which was not in any way unusual. Similar hierarchies can be seen all over the world, in nation-states of all forms. The attempt to criminalise the Nazis for having such a structure and claiming it as evidence of a conspiracy seems strange at best, misguided at worst. Yet Albrecht made a point of highlighting some features of the chart which provided clues as to why he had placed importance upon it. 'The Führer at the top of our chart is the supreme and the only leader in the Nazi hierarchy...the *Gauleiter* and the *Kreisleiter*, to cite two examples, charged with a particular duty by the Fuehrer, could call on these organisations (the SS and the SA) for assistance in carrying out their tasks. These sinister implications of the use of this power will become more apparent as the Prosecution's case develops...'[131]

In other words, Nazi officials at different levels could call on various forms of security forces to assist them if they felt it necessary. Again, it's not the most staggering of accusations. One wonders whether the Soviet representatives on the prosecutors table saw anything familiar in Albrecht's exposition.

Albrecht then went on to talk at length about Hitler's assumption of absolute power via *Das Ermächtigungsgesetz* (The Enabling Law) which gave him complete control over Germany's legislation and established him as a dictator. He then pointed out exactly where the various defendants fitted onto the chart in order to implicate them as a part of Count One, The Common Plan or Conspiracy. That the men on trial were members of the Nazi state was obvious and it is accepted that for the benefit of the court some form of evidence had to be presented to confirm this, (hence the chart). However the underlying implication throughout this part of Albrecht's presentation seemed to be that the Nazi state was inherently illegitimate because it was a dictatorship and not a democracy. Therefore membership of it constituted an illegal action. This appears a rather presumptious standpoint. On what authority had repressentative democracy been determined as the only acceptable form of government? Why was the *Führer Prinzip* (Leadership Principle) inherently worse than a constitutional monarchy like the UK, or a republic like the USA? Is it not a matter for nations to determine their form of government internally? And if not, how could the Soviet Union, at that time operating as a Communist dictatorship, try Germany for operating as a Nazi dictatorship? This was the first appearance at the IMT of this point, which is of some importance. It is a theme to which this book will return later.

Albrecht's summary of Nazi bureaucracy met with early criticism from Rudolf Dix, the defence counsel for Schacht and Otto Nelte, who represented Field Marshall Keitel. The latter pointed out that the Reich Defence Council, which Albrecht had devoted considerable time to describing, had never actually existed. Nei-

---

[131] Nuremberg Trial Proceedings Volume 2, 3rd day, Thursday, 22 November 1945, p.161

ther had the Secret Cabinet Council which Albrecht had also included in his presentation. Both had simply been suggestions made at cabinet meetings, which never came into fruition. At this early stage, on the morning of the fourth day of the trial, this raised issues, for the first time, regarding the Allied use of German documents – whether they fully understood what they were looking at and whether the quality of their translation was up to the task of providing evidence for a trial which would shape the future of the world. The baton on this point was picked up by Dix who said, 'We have now been able to see, in part, the briefs and documents which were introduced in court yesterday. In that connection we have established that some of the documents submitted by the Prosecution yesterday were not quoted in their entirety, nor were they presented in substance...'[132] Such complaints from the defence team would become a regular feature of the trial.

Setting another precedent for the courtroom events of the next eleven months, Judge Lawrence, as the tribunal President, ruled that the 'documents are admissible, but the defendants can prove at a later stage any matters which are relevant to the documents. It is not necessary for the defendants to make objections at this stage.'[133] This meant that the prosecution was able to put forward its case, insubstantial presentation, selective quotations and all, and have it carried by the worldwide media, virtually without dissenting voices, for the entire four months it took them to perform it. This period saw evidence presented by all four Allied powers, films shown of Nazi aggression, concentration camps and atrocities as well as the calling of witnesses. The eyewitnesses largely told gruesome horror stories, like Severina Shmaglevskaya, who described how babies at Auschwitz were removed from their mothers at birth. 'In the name of all the women of Europe who became mothers in concentration camps, I would like to ask German mothers, where are our children now?' she said, before going on to describe how Jewish babies were thrown alive into crematorium furnaces. 'The children were thrown in alive,' she said. 'Their cries could be heard all over the camp.'[134] She was followed on the stand by Samuel Rajzman, a member of the prisoner labour unit at the Treblinka camp, who related the story of the gas chambers there and how women had their heads shaved so the hair 'could be used in the manufacture of mattresses for German women.'[135] He went on to state that at Treblinka they killed 'from ten to twelve thousand persons daily'[136] before going on to relate a tale of pregnant woman being forced to give birth in front of SS guards and her own mother, also a camp inmate. 'When the baby was born,' he said, 'the SS asked the grandmother who they should kill first. The grandmother begged to be killed. But, of course, they did the opposite; the newborn baby was killed first, then the child's mother, and finally the grandmother.' Incredibly, Rajzman concluded by also describing babies being thrown alive into furnaces, as though this act of unspeakable barbarity were some sort of Nazi camp policy in Poland. It would have been an interesting point for the defence counsel to pursue – that this apparently individual act of sheer, brutal callousness should be committed by entirely different people at entirely different camps. Did it perhaps suggest collusion on the part of the witnesses? Had they been fed this line by someone? Were they simply repeating a rumour they had heard or had they actually seen this happen? Unfortunately we will never know the answers to these sorts of questions.

Such testimony had huge emotional impact upon the members of the court and the only chance for the defence to negate that would have been to show it to be exaggerated, or even false, through cross examination. However, as cross examination was not part of the German trial process, the German lawyers were completely inexperienced and, to a man, inept at it.[137] Neither of the witnesses mentioned above were asked *any* questions by the defence lawyers and when they did chance their arm, the results were often comical. Telford Taylor, the American prosecutor, recalled: 'Dr Otto Nelte, for Keitel, made the usual beginner's mistake of asking long, complex questions which did not pin the witness down...Nelte did his client little good...Dr Sauter, for Ribbentrop asked even longer questions and made absolutely no headway with the witness...he made himself ridiculous...'[138] Judge Biddle also wrote, in his notes: 'As usual the cross-examination emphasizes the prosecution's case' and 'counsel for SS asks stupid questions...counsel for Gestapo – cross examination only underscores evidence...Babel for the SS as usual makes a fool of himself',

---

[132] Nuremberg Trial Proceedings Volume 2, 4th day, Friday, 23rd November 1945, p.203
[133] ibid
[134] Nuremberg Trial Proceedings, Vol.8, 69th day, Wednesday, 27th February 1946, p.316
[135] ibid, p.325
[136] ibid, p.327 this figure is no longer maintained by history.
[137] Taylor, p.190
[138] ibid

etc.[139]

The result was that such testimonies went entirely unchallenged. That is not to suggest that any of these witnesses were liars, but rather that eyewitness testimony is a form of evidence usually riddled with inaccuracies. The human capacity for projection of events they have only heard about or had suggested to them as being their own experience and relating them as such, coupled with the tendency to exaggerate or confuse details of events that occur at times of high stress is well known. Part of the purpose of cross examination is to help the court determine what, *precisely*, can be regarded as fact within a witness statement, bearing in mind human fallibility and what may simply be hearsay or even a mistaken interpretation placed on something they did see. This purpose was simply not served by defence counsels at the IMT because of their unfamiliarity with the version of the law they were being asked to practice.

By the time the prosecution had finished, they had covered everything from aggressive war, to anti-Semitism, to the Euthanasia programme, Operation Barbarossa (the invasion of Russia), the *Einsatzgruppen* (SS squads working in occupied territory in Eastern Europe), slave labour, the *Endlösung* (Final Solution) and the abominations committed in the name of medicine. The court was reeling with the grisliness of it all and the media delighted in taking away gory detail after gory detail for their front pages. At this stage of the trial, before any of the defendants had even been called to the stand, Judge Birkett described the proceedings thus far as 'a most terrible and convincing case of complete horror and inhumanity…'[140]

It was going to take something extraordinary to hold back the tide.

---

[139] Conot, p.319
[140] ibid

7

Der Dicke

'War is like a football game, whoever loses gives his opponent his hand and everything is forgotten.' [141]

Hermann Göring

Of all the Nazi leaders of World War Two, Hermann Göring probably received the most ridicule. Although a highly decorated and much revered World War One flier – he took over Manfred von Richthofen's famous squadron after the Red Baron was killed in combat – by the 1930s he had become a portly, rosy-cheeked, bon vivant, with a penchant for fine art and a dependence on morphine. It is said that he frequently received guests at his *Karinhall* estate just outside Berlin, sloshed on French wine and decked up in a bejewelled toga and face-paint. He was famously lampooned as 'Minister Herring' in Charlie Chaplin's 1940 film, 'The Great Dictator'. Perhaps it is because of these things that the Allies so underestimated him. The performance he mustered at Nuremberg clearly came as something of a surprise.

Göring descended from a family of high bourgeoisie bordering on aristocracy. His father, Heinrich Göring, was the first Governor-General of German South West Africa (known as Namibia today). After World War One, in which he was one of the foremost fighter pilots of his generation[142], clocking up twenty-two confirmed kills, he tried various jobs, before joining the Nazi party in 1922. Hitler took an immediate liking to him and appointed him leader of the *Stürmabteilung* (SA or 'Brownshirts'). This was the first of many positions that Göring would fulfil within the party and future government. By the time war began in 1939, he was *Reichsmarschall*, (Supreme Commander of German Armed Forces) and Minister for the Economy, having already been commander of the Luftwaffe since 1935. Shortly after the outbreak of war he was

---

[141] Immediately after his arrest and before his imprisonment in 'Ashcan', the Americans threw a party for Göring at a castle in Kitzbühel. A US general asked for a picture of him as a souvenir. Göring agreed and wrote this message on the photograph. Conot, p.31

[142] Göring had a reputation as a chivalrous warrior. The Danish pilot, Captain Krause-Jensen, who flew for the French, described how his machine gun jammed during a dogfight with Göring. He beat his fist against the weapon in desperation. When Göring saw this, he banked his machine, saluted and flew off. (Neave, p.67)

appointed as the Führer's successor.

His exalted position in the Nazi hierarchy saw him indicted on all four counts and he was unique among the defendants in that he had been a prominent, ever present figure in the Nazi movement, from its beginnings in the early twenties until its final days in 1945. There was a feeling among many Nuremberg bystanders that Göring was the big one and the success or failure of the entire IMT procedure rested, to a large degree, on his case.

As the prisoners were assembled at 'Ashcan' and then Nuremberg, Göring assumed the position of leader of the accused, after winning a verbal duel with Dönitz. In his prison diaries, the psychologist Gustave M Gilbert reported that during an early meeting Göring had claimed that he would advise all his fellow defendants to restrict their defence to a simple utterance of 'Kiss my arse!' He explained this truculent attitude by saying, 'As far as the trial is concerned, it's a cut and dried political affair and I am prepared for the consequences.' When asked by Gilbert what those consequences might be, he replied, 'I know I shall hang.'[143]

As the trial approached however, it seemed his attitude changed and he began to view the proceedings as an opportunity, a final chance to send a defiant message to the German people. Gilbert, whose role as psychologist was masked in professional neutrality, but who in reality worked closely with the prosecution, reported on this to the Allied team and they steeled themselves for what they felt would be the biggest challenge to their success.

When things got underway, particularly as the prosecution picked its way through the opening week's accusations of Nazi aggression and expansionism, most of the defendants united behind what Gilbert described as 'Göring's front'.[144] Of particular amusement was the Americans' description of the 1938 Anschluss (un- ion) with Austria as being an act of aggressive war. Although Anschluss had been outlawed by the Treaty of Versailles and was therefore, strictly speaking, an illegal move under international law, it was hardly an act of belligerence. The reality had seen German soldiers greeted from the Austrian border by cheering crowds. As they passed through towns, local women and children placed garlands of flowers on their guns, which were not fired once in anger. If the Anschluss were, as the Allies claimed, an invasion, it was the most welcome and celebrated invasion of all time.[145] Those being invaded largely wanted to be.

During recess, Göring loudly pointed this out to the other defendants. 'Didn't the Austrians pave the Führer's way from the German border to Vienna with flowers? Who had ever seen such joy?'[146] His words were met with smiles and universal agreement. Von Schirach later commented that he thought he 'would die' (with laughter) when the evidence had been presented. But this Göring-led solidarity would soon crumble.

A week after Jackson had delivered his opening soliloquy, on the afternoon of November 29th, 1945, Sydney Alderman, associate trial counsel, prepared the Tribunal for the presentation of the prosecution's most dramatic piece of evidence. 'At this point it is planned by our staff to show a motion picture, and it will take some few minutes to make the physical arrangements in the courtroom, so that if the Court should feel like recessing, those arrangements could be made.' he said.

After the recess, the members resumed their places with a projector in place before them. Thomas Dodd, a member of the American prosecutorial team, described the purpose of the screening. '...this film which we offer represents in a brief and unforgettable form an explanation of what the words 'concentration camp' imply.'[147] This constituted another first for Nuremberg. Although motion pictures had been submitted in some form as trial evidence as early as 1915, there exist no records of any court prior to the IMT using film of atrocities as proof of criminal wrongdoing.[148]

It was the showing of this movie, which had been produced by Lieutenant Colonel George Stevens, one of Hollywood's leading pre-war directors, which broke some of the prisoners' resistance. It must be remembered that this was an era in which people were not yet hardened to the gruesome moving image. Film, as a relatively new medium, possessed awesome power. It is for this reason that the prosecution decided to use it, rather than just presenting eyewitness testimony and documents. It would give visceral impact to their case.

---

[143] Gilbert p.13
[144] Gilbert, p.54
[145] Shortly after the Nazi 'invasion' a referendum showed that 99.73% of Austrians were in favour of it.
[146] Persico, p.143
[147] Nuremberg Trial Proceedings, Vol. 2, 8th day, 29th November 1945, p.431
[148] Douglas, Lawrence, *Film as witness: screening 'Nazi Concentration Camps' before the Nuremberg Tribunal*. (Yale Law Journal, November 1995) p.449-481

The movie picked its way through scenes of malnourished and typhus-racked corpses at Dachau, Belsen, Mauthausen and Buchenwald, to the *greuelpropaganda*[149] images of items made from human skin and the shrunken head which was allegedly made from a Polish inmate. At Mauthausen, in Austria, an American inmate was interviewed who stated that executions were carried out by the SS using methods of shooting, beating, exposure and pushing prisoners off a 'hundred foot cliff'.[150] At Buchenwald, one of the Allied team held what appeared to be a hammer up to the camera, while it was explained that it was 'one of the weapons used by the SS guards.' A simple wooden kennel was shown at the Armstadt camp, as the narrator melodramatically intoned that it housed a 'savage guard dog', as if that were anything unusual for a prison. Buildings with no particular defining features were shown from the outside only and described as being centres for medical experiments or torture houses. Other scenes showed several camps where the Allied soldiers located graveyards, then dug up corpses to take pictures of them, before forcing local civilians from surrounding villages to come to the camp to re-inter them. In one, now infamous case, at Belsen, the British dug ditches and pushed hideous hillocks of bodies into them with a bulldozer. A clip from a camp near Leipzig showed the usual array of mangled corpses, while the narrator explained that a couple of hundred prisoners were herded into a barn and the barn was set on fire by the SS. It was alleged that at the Hadamar 'concentration camp', (in reality it wasn't a concentration camp at all, but a sanatorium, implicated in the T4 Euthanasia programme prior to 1941) prisoners were killed by gas chamber and by giving them overdoses of morphine.[151]

At least two of the men in the dock (Frank and Funk) were moved to tears by the scenes. Several others bowed their heads. Airey Neave, working for the prosecution, commented on the film in his personal record of the trial by saying, 'Those ghastly piles of naked, moon-white corpses would not soon be forgotten…It was there that we discovered the truth.' He also stated that the film provoked 'worldwide loathing for the leading Nazis.'[152]

By any analysis, the film provided a turning point for the trial. But it ought to be made absolutely clear at this stage that despite popular perception, it provided no substantial evidence for gas vans or gas chambers or any other apparatus of genocide. It stated that death by gassing occurred at Hadamar (without offering any form of visual supporting evidence) and devoted several minutes to showing the gas chamber at Dachau (the *brausebad* or shower/bath room). During the course of this exposition, the narrator described the dummy showerheads, the pipes for introducing and venting the gas and a valve for regulating pressure, although it should be noted there is nothing about any of the items shown which proves them to be what they were being described as. One wonders why the Allied soldiers in the film did not detach one of the showerheads, for example, to demonstrate to the camera that it was a dummy, or attempt to provide some sort of evidence that the pipes shown were gas pipes and not water pipes. Some might accuse the poser of such questions of being unnecessarily cynical, but when it is borne in mind that the historical consensus no longer alleges that gassings actually took place at Dachau, the sense of mystery deepens. Recent visitors to the camp museum could enter and view the *Brausebad* in which there was a mounted placard which read 'Gas chamber – disguised as a shower room – never used as a gas chamber.' Yet Lieutenant Stevens and his team clearly believed it was used and stated so in their movie, describing at length the entire process, showing the towels and the soap that inmates would be given to trick them into co-operating. Why this belief should have changed over time is somewhat suspicious.[153] The evidence cannot have changed. The American liberators of Dachau found

---

[149] This is German for 'atrocity propaganda'. Most of the ghoulish concentration camp exhibits are now viewed suspiciously by objective analysts. It has been pointed out that the shrunken head, for example, supposedly of a murdered Pole, has distinctly non-European features and long hair, whereas all camp inmates had their heads shaved.

[150] The 'cliff' here refers to a part of the quarry at Mauthausen where many inmates were put to work. It is corroborated by the testimony of Hollriegel, an SS guard at the camp who appeared in the early stages of the trial. Nuremberg Trial Proceedings, Vol. 4. 27th day, Friday, 4th January 1946, p.387

[151] The film can be viewed on a variety of websites. For example,
http://www.archive.org/search.php?query=subject%3A%22Concentration%20Camp%22
where they state that the copy was dubbed from a video copy at the National Archives in College Park, Maryland. National Archives Identifiers: ARC: 43452 NAIL: 238.2

[152] Neave, p.6

[153] The idea of Dachau as an extermination centre was corroborated at the IMT by the testimony of Dr Franz Blaha whose affidavit stated that, 'Many executions by gas or shooting or injections took place right in the camp. The gas chamber was completed in 1944, and I was called by Dr Rascher to examine the first victims…' Nuremberg Trial Proceedings, Vol. 5, 32nd

what they found. Yet in 1945 it was stated by them, in the form of this film, that Dachau had a functioning gas chamber and operated, to some extent as a death camp, whereas today that is no longer held to be true by the majority.[154]

At the time, such was the power of the images that the court was literally stunned by them. No-one at the IMT (except for Rudolf Hess, momentarily) dared to challenge what had been shown on the screen.

In general, the film showed appalling scenes of death and disease, with large numbers of emaciated corpses and shuffling, half-dead survivors. With a hard head, however, when one looks past the sheer horror of it all, there would seem to be a highly rational alternative explanation to the one provided. One wonders, in fact, what the Allies had expected to find, as they overran a nation which had been suffering from naval blockade and devastating aerial bombardment, while fighting a war on two fronts for the previous four years. German infrastructure had been destroyed, roads, railways and communication systems all severely disrupted. Clearly, in such a scenario, getting hold of medical or food supplies would be difficult, moving them around doubly so. There were cases of hunger and deprivation aplenty among the regular German population. It would therefore be logical to expect prisoners in camps to be the worst off, as they would be the last to receive any scraps of scarce resources which could be found and delivered. This is not a pleasant fact and does not concur with liberal ideals of humanitarianism, but in reality is how most nations would have operated under the circumstances. Supplies would go to troops first, the regular population second and prisoners last, if at all. Was it not probable that the emaciated, dysentery and typhus racked inmates (dead and alive) owed their plight to the prevailing conditions, more so than Nazi barbarism, or an extermination plan? And why was this alternative explanation not considered by the prosecutors? Further to that, it should also be emphasised that no scene in the film depicted any of the camps in Poland which are now cited as being the

'death camps'[155]. In spite of this, in the broader, historical context, it has since been used as proof of the Jewish Holocaust, most notably at the trial of Adolf Eichmann, in 1961. On that level it must also be categorically stated that there is nothing in any scene of the film to identify any of the victims in it as Jewish (for example by the wearing of stars). That is not to say that none of the prisoners in the film were Jewish, they could have been, but the scenes could just as easily be showing German political prisoners, Russians, Poles or other Europeans and this second view was, in fact, what was stated by the narrator. In the voiceover that accompanied the pictures, Jews were mentioned only once, in reference to the Ohrdruf camp. This was during the course of an hour. It is reasonable therefore to conclude that the film-maker and the prosecutors at Nuremberg did not intend the movie to be viewed with the modern Holocaust interpretation, but rather as simple, piecemeal evidence of Nazi criminality.[156]

Probably the most important comment to make, before applying this to Göring, is that this sort of evidence was really of little value to the court. Although one can understand the prosecution's desire to break up the monotonous conveyor of documents, the showing of this kind of film did not fit within the context of such an important trial. The evidence presented in the movie was of the sort known as 'prejudicial' within the legal profession. There was little in the way of fact to be established from it. The only real facts to be gleaned were that Nazi Germany operated a camp system and that by the time the camps were liberated, in 1945, conditions were awful and many people had died in them. It served, however, to have an emotional effect on those who saw it, including the world's newspapermen and it is probable that was, in fact, the intention behind it.

After the day's proceedings had finished, Gilbert waited until the evening to go to the cells of various prisoners to gauge their reaction. The scenes had clearly affected all of them. They were forced to abandon any remaining idealism and to realise the abominable horrors of the conflict they had been involved in. Worse still, they now had to accept the effects of the shocking conditions that had prevailed within their arena of responsibility. Fritzsche was particularly moved, saying, 'No power on heaven and earth will erase

---

day, Friday 11th January 1946, p.176 Several other testimonies of the period made the same allegation, yet it seems that mainstream history has now determined this evidence to be inaccurate.
[154] Raul Hilberg classified Dachau as a 'concentration camp', not a 'death camp'. *The Destruction*, p.1320
[155] According to Martin Broszat of the *Institut für Zeitgeschichte* in Munich – Auschwitz, Belzec, Chelmno, Majdanek, Sobibor & Treblinka were the 'death camps' – in other words camps where extermination of prisoners was the primary function. (Die Zeit, 19th August, 1960, p.16). This view was also taken by Raul Hilberg and most modern Holocaust historians.
[156] see note

this shame from my country.'[157] Wilhelm Frick expressed incomprehension and bewilderment. General Jodl was disgusted by the movie and said that had he known of such things, 'he would not have tolerated it for a single day.'[158] Göring was in a state of near-depression. He knew that the film had destroyed the morale of his colleagues.

His mood had not been helped either by a reacquaintance he had made in court that morning. Robert Kempner had worked under Göring at The Prussian Ministry for the Interior and Göring had fired him, in 1933, for several reasons, including the fact that he was part Jewish. Kempner delighted in approaching Göring in the dock and reminding him of his final words the day he had sacked him. 'Get out of my sight,' he had said. 'I never want to see you again.' 'Well, here I am,' Kempner crowed, before moving away to take his seat at the prosecution table. After spending a short time in a concentration camp, he had fled Germany after the passing of the Nuremberg laws and was now a US citizen on Jackson's staff.[159]

Göring was the first of the defendants to be called and finally took the stand in March. By this point, as a result of Gilbert's regular reports to Jackson and the other prosecutors, a plan was devised to undermine the standing of the former *Reichsmarschall* among the defendants. He was forced to eat lunch and exercise in isolation, while Albert Speer, the architect and armaments minister, who will be discussed shortly and whom the Allied staff had decided could be influential in their favour, ate with a group of three others, including Funk and von Schirach who were believed to be swaying.[160] Gilbert himself described the purpose of this as being 'to let Speer and Fritzsche wean the other two away from Göring's influence and to give even von Schirach a chance to declare that Hitler had betrayed German Youth and that racial policy was Germany's catastrophe.'[161] Göring was allegedly 'furious' at the new arrangements.[162]

The plan initially seemed to have the desired effect, Gilbert noting in his diary on February 19th that 'the Göring tyranny is at an end'[163] and bragging to Speer that he had defeated 'the attempts of Göring to obstruct justice.'[164] Von Schirach reportedly stated during this time that, 'Göring is a big man, but he belongs to an outworn medieval, tradition…I am thinking of the future of German youth.'[165]

Göring's case began, on March 8th, with the calling of General Karl Bodenschatz, his former adjutant. Gilbert, who seldom wrote anything that painted Göring (or most of the other defendants) in anything other than an entirely negative light described the former *Reichsmarschall* as being so nervous that his hands were trembling as his attorney, Dr Stahmer, began the defence.[166] The crumbling of 'Göring's Front' seemed complete after Bodenschatz had finished testifying. He was not renowned for his mental agility and although able to keep pace with Stahmer's gentle prodding, Jackson tore him to pieces in the cross examination, a fact which was met with delight by several of the defendants, to Gilbert's pleasure. Whilst at lunch, Jodl laughed and commented that Bodenschatz 'sure didn't help Göring's case any', going on to tell Gilbert that 'your man Jackson is a clever prosecutor.'[167] Gilbert reported Schacht to be 'brimming over with joy' at the morning's proceedings, exclaiming, 'The fat one is sure taking a beating so far!' He then went on to join Jodl in lauding Justice Jackson, whom he described as a 'brilliant cross examiner.'[168]

Göring's own response was interesting, knowing, with the benefit of hindsight, what would transpire. He expressed pity at Bodenschatz' humiliation, describing him as 'loyal' and 'only wanting to say a good word for his chief'. With typical bravado he then issued a battle cry: 'Wait until Jackson starts on me. He won't have any nervous Bodenschatz to deal with.' Whether he meant the comment sincerely at the time or not (Gilbert seemed to doubt it, describing him talking 'nervously' and as having 'trembling fingers')[169] it was a

---

[157] Persico, p.144
[158] ibid, p.145
[159] ibid, p.142
[160] Gilbert, p.155
[161] ibid, p.158
[162] ibid, p.159
[163] ibid, p.161
[164] ibid, p.160
[165] Taylor, Telford, *The Anatomy of the Nuremberg Trials*, (Bloomsbury 1993), p.423
[166] Gilbert, p.185
[167] Gilbert, p.186
[168] ibid
[169] ibid

prescient appraisal of what was to come.

After Bodenschatz' humbling at the hands of Jackson, the next witness to be called was Erhard Milch, who in 1933 had taken up the position of Luftwaffe *Generalfeldmarschall*, which placed him just below Göring in the command chain of the German air force, despite not being a flier. For most of the war, Milch was a member of the Central Planning Board, organised by Albert Speer, which handled the distribution of raw materials between the military and civilian sectors.[170] Milch's questioning by Stahmer, for the defence, was brief. According to Telford Taylor, 'its value was negligible.'[171] Milch only managed to state that Göring was essentially opposed to war, that the Luftwaffe was a defensive, rather than offensive organisation and that neither he nor Göring knew of concentration camp atrocities. The wisdom of Stahmer calling Milch as a witness was soon called into question, as after a flurry of questions from other defence counsels, Jackson stood to tear into him with the same easy zeal with which he had humiliated Bodenschatz. After four hours of cross examination, which among other things demonstrated via documentary evidence that Milch had ordered Russian prisoners of war to be executed, (his signed order said that he 'wanted them hanged in the factory for the others to see'[172]) despite stating under oath moments before that he hadn't, the *Generalfeldmarschall* left the stand 'utterly discredited.'[173]

There followed short and unremarkable testimonies from Colonel Bernd von Brauchitsch, (Göring's chief wartime adjutant), Paul Koerner (another member of the Central Planning Board) and another *Generalfeldmarschall*, Albert Kesselring, whose testimony mostly concerned the Luftwaffe's bombing activities, which did not form part of the indictment and so was largely a waste of time. In summation of Göring's case that far, Telford Taylor stated that the witnesses 'had said little to help Göring'[174] and the feeling around the court was that Jackson was proving to be a formidable opponent for anyone. That was, until the afternoon of March 13th, when Minister Herring himself left the dock and took up his position in the witness box.

Göring's interrogation by Stahmer lasted for two and a half days. In practice, it was not an interrogation at all, but a series of loose, open-ended questions which allowed the former *Reichsmarschall* to speak at length on a variety of issues. Stahmer's fourth question, for example, was 'tell the Tribunal when and under what circumstances you came to know Hitler'[175] Göring's response was an uninterrupted ten minute speech.

It would be easy, given such circumstances, to presume that Göring was being self-indulgent and irritating the members of the Tribunal, but at this early stage, they were content to give him free rein.

This was possibly due to the fact that in relation to some of the charges against him, he seemed happy to incriminate himself. Later on during Göring's first day in the witness box, Stahmer had been asking a series of questions relating to Hitler's accession to the position of Chancellor, prior to declaring himself *Führer* of Germany. In other words, as the prosecution would have seen it, Stahmer was asking Göring to delineate his role in Count One, the conspiracy to consolidate the Nazi dictatorship. Göring replied proudly, 'I have done everything which was at all within my personal power to strengthen the National Socialist movement…When I look back, I believe I have not failed to do anything to consolidate our power to such an extent that it would not have to yield to the chances of the political game or to violent actions, but which would rather…lead the Reich and lead it – as we hoped – to a great development.'[176]

Göring's willingness to admit guilt in terms of his senior role in the conspiracy was partly due to fatalism – he firmly believed that he would be executed (as shown by his early discussions with Gilbert and corroborated by his assistant counsel, Werner Boss, who said, 'He is certain he is going to be hanged, but he has said he will die like a man'[177]) and therefore had nothing to lose. It was also due to practicality. Such a leading figure within Nazi Germany stood no chance of being pronounced innocent of conspiracy, so there was little point denying it. However there is also a sense that he wanted his last moments of fame (or infamy) to mean something. That he did not want to be remembered as *der Dicke*, Fatty Hermann. It is also true that by openly admitting his actions in contravention of Count One, he wanted to show the shallowness of the charge, that

---

[170] Taylor, p.323
[171] ibid
[172] ibid, p.324
[173] ibid
[174] Taylor, p.328
[175] Nuremberg Trial Proceedings Vol.9, 80th day, Wednesday 13th March 1946. p.235
[176] ibid p.253
[177] Tusa, p.275

he had done nothing that anybody in his position, in any nation would not have done.

Göring's two days of defence questioning ended with a final oration on the international laws of which he had fallen foul. It was a vigorous and rousing speech and Göring finished by saying, '…at this point I should like to say the same words which one of our greatest, most important, and toughest opponents, the British Prime Minister, Winston Churchill, used: In the struggle for life and death there is in the end no legality.'[178]

The judge immediately adjourned with murmurs of approval echoing around the courtroom. One of the Russian prosecutors was overheard to say, 'the pig will long be remembered for this speech.'[179] Telford Taylor described Göring as 'lucid and impressive'[180], going on to state that 'his explanation of how and why things happened during the rise of Nazism and the life of the Third Reich was interesting and at times fascinating.' Judge Birkett joined in the plaudits, saying 'Göring reveals himself as a very able man who perceives the intent of every question almost as soon as it is uttered.'[181]

Göring's erstwhile opponents within his own ranks also seemed impressed. Speer said, 'Seeing him so serious and stripped of his diamonds and decorations, making a final defence before a tribunal, after all the power, pomp and bombast, it was really gripping!'[182] Von Papen remarked, 'That is the Göring of the early days.' Schacht commented that everything Göring said was right and Fritzsche said he had described the early years of the party exactly as it was. Von Schirach was emotional and said that his heart had been in his mouth while Göring spoke. Dönitz too was impressed, saying, 'Biddle is really paying attention. You can see that he really wants to hear the other side of the story.'[183]

Despite the best efforts of Gilbert, it seemed that the Göring front was in danger of reforming, but the general feeling persisted that up to that point things had been easy for him – he had after all, only been questioned by his own lawyer. After another day's questioning by the other defence lawyers, March 18th saw him again take to the stand, this time to be confronted by Jackson. It seemed at this stage that the whole Göring case was poised. The prosecution had got the better of all of Göring's defence witnesses but the man himself had so far provided the star turn of the trial. Jackson, who assumed responsibility for the lion's share of the cross examination, could tip the balance.

Jackson began his interrogation with a question that was almost rhetorical in nature. 'You are perhaps aware that you are the only living man who can expound to us the true purposes of the Nazi Party and the inner workings of its leadership?' he said.

Göring settled his frame against the back of the chair. 'I am perfectly aware of that.' His reply was calm and confident.[184] It was a significant mistake on Jackson's part to begin in this way. He had started by inviting Göring to expound. And Göring hardly needed such an invitation. It is important to bear this in mind as their tussle is examined in more detail. Jackson would later justify this by stating in his memoirs that it had been his intention to appeal firstly to Göring's ego, to flatter him and get him to reveal his criminality by inducing him 'to display his Nazi attitudes.'[185] If that was indeed his intention, rather than simply being a retrospective attempt to save face, it backfired badly. The initial exchanges between the two were similar in character to those between Göring and Stahmer several days before, with Jackson asking a question, intended to unsettle or agitate Göring and Göring answering it candidly and with certainty.

Jackson – 'You, from the very beginning, together with those who were associated with you, intended to overthrow and later did overthrow, the Weimar Republic?'

Göring – 'That was, as far as I am concerned, my firm intention'

Jackson – 'And, upon coming to power, you immediately abolished parliamentary government in Germany?'

Göring – 'We found it to be no longer necessary…'

Jackson – 'You established the Leadership Principle, which you have described as a system under

---

[178] Nuremberg Trial Proceedings, Vol. 9, 82nd day, Friday 15th March 1946 p.363
[179] Time Magazine, *Stiff Ears*, 25th March 1946 http://www.time.com/time/magazine/article/0,9171,888136,00.html
[180] Taylor, p.329
[181] ibid, p.330
[182] Gilbert, p.194
[183] ibid, p.197-8
[184] Nuremberg Trial Proceedings, Volume 9, 84th day, Monday 18th March 1946, p.416
[185] Taylor, p.335

which authority existed only at the top, and is passed downwards and is imposed on the people below; is that correct?'

Göring – 'In order to avoid any misunderstanding, I should like once more to explain the idea briefly, as I understand it...In the Leadership Principle (*Führer Prinzip*) we sought to reverse the direction, that is, the authority existed at the top and passed downwards, while the responsibility began at the bottom and passed upwards.'

Jackson – 'In other words, you did not believe in and did not permit government, as we call it, by consent of the governed, in which the people, through their representatives, were the source of power and authority?'

Göring – 'That is not entirely correct. We repeatedly called on the people to express unequivocally and clearly what they thought of our system, only it was in a different way from that previously adopted and from the system in practice in other countries. We chose the way of a so-called plebiscite. We also took the point of view that even a government founded on the Leadership Principle could maintain itself only if it was based in some way on the confidence of the people. If it no longer had such confidence, then it would have to rule with bayonets, and the Führer was always of the opinion that that was impossible in the long run – to rule against the will of the people.'[186]

And so it went on. Jackson questioned Göring for three days, interrupted temporarily by the calling of Birger Dahlerus, a Swedish businessman and close friend of Göring's who had tried to prevent the outbreak of war via diplomatic contacts in both Britain and Germany. In that time Jackson covered the Leadership principle, the abolition of political opposition, the concentration camps, the attack against the Soviet Union, the Reichstag fire, the Röhm purge, the Treaty of Versailles, the Anschluss, the Four-year plan and eventually finished up with the treatment of the Jews. At every turn Göring parried Jackson's lunges with ease, either nonchalantly answering questions in the positive, or directly disagreeing with Jackson's assumptions. When adopting the latter strategy, it seemed to completely nonplus Jackson, who had little or no response. According to Telford Taylor, 'Jackson was unable or unwilling to confute Göring's objections and his handling of the questions soon created the impression that the defendant was dialectically superior to the prosecutor.'[187] Albert Speer would later summarise Göring's approach while speaking to Gilbert, in his cell. '...when Jackson cross-examines Göring, you can see that they just represent two entirely opposite worlds – they don't even understand each other. Jackson asks him if he didn't help plan the invasion of Holland and Belgium and Norway, expecting Göring to defend himself against a criminal accusation, but instead Göring says, "Why yes, of course, it took place thus and so ..." as if it is the most natural thing in the world to invade a neutral country if it suits your strategy.'[188]

It was clear to all but the most subjective observers that Jackson could not handle his man. As question after question was met with increasingly confident responses, the façade of Jackson's professional exterior began to slip. The first signs of real cracks in the plaster appeared when Jackson was quizzing Göring about the operation of the concentration camps.

Jackson – 'Was it also necessary, in operating this system, that you must not have persons entitled to public trials in independent courts? And you immediately issued an order that your political police would not be subject to court review or to court orders, did you not?'

It needs to be recalled at this stage that Jackson had initially asked Göring to 'expound' on the innermost workings of Nazi Germany. The question seemed relatively open ended and Göring reasonably answered with an explanation.

Göring – 'You must differentiate between the two categories; those who had committed some act of treason against the new state, or those who, might be proved to have committed such an act, were naturally turned over to the courts. The others, however, of whom one might expect such acts, but

---

[186] Nuremberg Trial Proceedings, Vol. 9, 84th day, 18th March 1946, p.417
[187] Taylor, p.336
[188] Gilbert, p.211

who had not yet committed them, were taken into protective custody, and these were the people who were taken to concentration camps. I am now speaking of what happened at the beginning. Later things changed a great deal. Likewise, if for political reasons – to answer your question – someone was taken into protective custody, that is, purely for reasons of state, this could not be reviewed or stopped by any court. Later, when some people were also taken into protective custody for non-political reasons, people who had opposed the system in some other way, I once, as Prussian Prime Minister and Reich Minister of the Interior, I remember...'

Jackson apparently did not like the direction the answer was taking and interrupted the defendant.

Jackson – 'Let's omit that. I have not asked for that. If you will just answer my question, we shall save a great deal of time. Your counsel will be permitted to bring out any explanations you want to make. You did prohibit all court review and considered it necessary to prohibit court review of the causes for taking people into what you called protective custody?'
Göring – 'That I answered very clearly, but I should like to make an explanation in connection with my answer.'
Jackson – 'Your counsel will see to that. Now, the concentration camps and the protective custody...'

Having denied Göring the right to offer his explanation and being in the process of attempting to move on, Jackson now found it was his turn to be interrupted, by the President of the court, Judge Geoffrey Lawrence.

The President – 'Mr Justice Jackson, the Tribunal thinks the witness ought to be allowed to make what explanation he thinks right in answer to this question.'[189]

So Jackson was forced to back-pedal and allow Göring to explain, which he of course did, articulately and at length. Jackson then resumed his questioning but was clearly 'internally seething.'[190] This was, however, only the tip of the iceberg, Göring so rattled Jackson that soon he would have him completely lose his cool in open court. On the 19th March, in the afternoon session, Jackson began a line of questioning intended to show that Göring had conspired to militarise the Rhineland months in advance, in direct defiance of the Treaty of Versailles.

Jackson – 'You testified that the movement into the Rhineland had not been planned in advance.'
Göring – 'Only a short time in advance, I emphasized.'
Jackson – 'How long?'
Göring – 'As far as I recall, at the most 2 to 3 weeks.'
Jackson – 'Now, I call your attention to the minutes of the 10th meeting of the Working Committee of the Reich Defence Council, Document Number EC-405 toward the end of that document, the discussion on 6th month, 26th day of 1935, which reads as follows ...'

Jackson was attempting here to pull exactly the same manoeuvre which had worked so well on Milch – eliciting a statement from a witness and then immediately introducing a document to contradict it. Unfortunately for him, this time it completely blew up in his face. Göring leafed through the sheaf of papers he had been given, found the correct section and read it. When he had finished he looked up with a quizzical expression.

Göring – 'Oh, no, here you have made a great mistake. The original phrase – and this alone is the point in question – is: 'c) Preparation for the clearing of the Rhine.' It is a purely technical preparation that has nothing at all to do with the liberation of the Rhineland....'

Jackson pursued it with another question but it emerged that Göring was quite correct. The original document had been mistranslated and only discussed the clearing of civil river traffic from the Rhine in the event of

---

[189] Nuremberg Trial Proceedings, Vol.9, 84th day, 18th March 1946, p.420
[190] Taylor, p.337

war. It had nothing to do with military occupation of the Rhineland whatsoever. Embarrassed and desperate, Jackson blurted out:

> **Jackson** – 'You mean the preparations were not military preparations?'
> **Göring** – 'Those were general preparations for mobilization, such as every country makes, and not for the purpose of the occupation of the Rhineland.'
> **Jackson** – 'But were of a character which had to be kept entirely secret from foreign powers?'
> **Göring** – 'I do not think I can recall reading beforehand the publication of the mobilization preparations of the United States.'

Göring's tone, dismissive and bordering on sarcasm, infuriated Jackson, whose inability to corner his witness at any stage during the previous two days of dialogue caused him to erupt with frustration, delivering the following outburst.

> **Jackson** – 'Well, I respectfully submit to the Tribunal that this witness is not being responsive, and has not been in his examination, and that it is perfectly futile to spend our time if we cannot have responsive answers to our questions. We can strike these things out. I do not want to spend time doing that, but this witness, it seems to me, is adopting, and has adopted, in the witness box and in the dock, an arrogant and contemptuous attitude toward the Tribunal which is giving him the trial which he never gave a living soul, nor dead ones either. I respectfully submit that the witness be instructed to make notes, if he wishes, of his explanations, but that he be required to answer my questions and reserve his explanations for his counsel to bring out.'[191]

A rumble of concern, disapproval and shock rose up around the courtroom. Jackson had been shouting, un- able to control his temper. Judge Lawrence decided it was time to adjourn. That night, Jackson offered to quit. He went to Judge Biddle's office, complained that he was being unsupported by the bench and said, 'I had better resign and go home.'[192] He was persuaded to stay. The following morning, Jackson clearly had not recovered from the setbacks of the previous day and began by repeating the last of the exchange he had with Göring in an attempt to get Lawrence to agree to some sort of limitation on Göring's responses. Lawrence again denied Jackson, saying 'surely it is making too much of a sentence the witness said...Every country keeps certain things secret.'[193] As a result, the deflated Jackson's remaining questions lacked vigour or purpose, he asked Göring about *Kristallnacht* and the Jews (the Jewish question was discussed here in terms of loss of rights, property, ghettoes and camps but not in terms of extermination or genocide), some actions by the Luftwaffe and Göring's collection of looted foreign art, but made little headway. He was, according to Telford Taylor, 'defeated and bitter.'[194]

First hand views of the Göring – Jackson duel were nearly unanimous in their verdicts. As well as Taylor, the British Alternate Judge, Norman Birkett, saw the exchange as an unmitigated victory for Göring. 'The cross-examination had not proceeded more than ten minutes' he wrote, in his diary, 'before it was seen that he (Göring) was the complete master of Justice Jackson.'[195] In his report to the British Foreign Office, Patrick Dean (Assistant Under-Secretary to the Foreign Secretary) wrote, 'Justice Jackson...was very disappointing and unimpressive...Göring indulged in much Nazi propaganda and showed everything in a favourable light for himself.'[196]

Airey Neave described Göring's stand as an 'extraordinary performance'[197] and went on to state that Jackson was 'ill prepared for this contest.'[198] By way of summary he stated that, 'it was the complex person-

---

[191] Nuremberg Trial Proceedings, Vol 9, 85th day, 19th March 1946, p.507
[192] Persico, p.279
[193] ibid, 86th day, 20th March 1946, p.508
[194] Taylor, p.339
[195] ibid, p.341
[196] ibid, p.337
[197] Neave, p.282
[198] ibid, p.283

ality of Göring...which led to the defeat of Jackson.'[199] Judge Biddle wrote to his wife, Katherine that Jackson had been, 'beaten, full of a sense of failure,'[200] that his cross-examination had been 'futile and weak'[201]. He also claimed that Jackson had made a 'silly speech' (referring to his complaint about Göring's answers).[202] According to Ann and John Tusa: 'several newspapers commented on the sustained note of (Göring's) sweet reasonableness...' and 'Jackson had failed to extract a single admission which had not already been obtained in direct evidence...'[203] Janet Flanner, who wrote for the New Yorker stated that 'Jackson cut a poor figure...' and that he 'teetered like a country lawyer...' while Göring had shown 'one of the best brains of the period of history when good brains are rare.'[204] Rebecca West, in the same magazine wrote that '...Mr Justice Jackson could not cross-examine Göring at all well, because he had a transatlantic prepossession that a rogue who held high office would be a solemn and not a jolly rogue, and was disconcerted by his impudence.'[205] In a similar piece, a reporter for Life magazine wrote, 'Göring obviously enjoyed himself as he kept the court spellbound for days,'[206] while the legendary American journalist, Walter Cronkite, in his memoir 'A Reporter's Life' wrote, 'Jackson was totally unnerved by Göring's almost jovial impudence. To Göring's insouciance he could respond only with bluster and a posture reminiscent of the country lawyer he once had been.'[207]

It was, it seems, by all accounts, success for Göring and catastrophe for Jackson. All accounts that is, except one. Gustave Gilbert was the only first-hand observer of Göring's questioning by Jackson not to see it in these kinds of terms. Reading the page of his diary which concerns these events, his personal tendency to criticise the defendants (especially Göring) and over-emphasise the Jewish angle becomes clear. His entry for March 20th, written after Jackson had finished his cross-examination, reads as follows: 'A nip and tuck duel between Göring and prosecutor Jackson. In spite of Göring's evasive tactics, it was established that Göring was responsible for supporting anti-Semitic decrees. In spite of his claim to being a moderating force in the Jewish question, he had to admit to taking over Jewish businesses and property...levying a fine of a billion marks on the Jewish population, ordering Himmler and Heydrich to settle the elimination of the Jews from German economic life...He had then turned to the destruction of Jewish property...'[208]

Either Gilbert had been sleeping throughout the first two and half days of questions, which had nothing to do with Jews or the 'Jewish question' or he simply did not see them as being worth mentioning. How on earth Gilbert managed to view Jackson's humiliation before Göring as a 'nip and tuck duel' is further testament to his subjectivity. Telford Taylor himself commented on this bizarre bit of reportage, stating that 'it is remarkable that Gilbert's diary describes only Jackson's questions on Göring's anti-Semitic decrees and makes no mention of the general criticism of his cross examination...'[209] Taylor postulated that Gilbert may have advised Jackson on tactics and was therefore too embarrassed to record the outcome of his advice in his book. It appears that Taylor is being kind to Gilbert here because the diary is not simply guilty of omission on this episode, but actually of misrepresentation.

Following up on that point, it is interesting that the prison psychiatrist, Leon Goldensohn (another Jewish American) commented that Gilbert's relationship with Göring was 'rather strained'[210]. Telford Taylor, one of the American prosecutors, also stated in his personal record of the trials that Gilbert had never liked any of the defendants and 'pictured them as weaklings more than they deserved.'[211] This presents us with something

---

[199] ibid, p.284
[200] Persico, p.284
[201] ibid, p.280
[202] Tusa, p.282
[203] ibid, p.278 &280
[204] Persico, p.270
[205] Taylor, p.343
[206] Conot, p.346
[207] Dodd, p.30
[208] Gilbert, p.205
[209] Taylor, p.342, the comment appears in a footnote at the bottom of the page.
[210] Goldensohn, Leon, *The Nuremberg Interviews* (Pimlico 2006), p.119
[211] Taylor, p.600. Taylor here is referring specifically to the time just after the defendants had received their sentences (which in many cases meant death.) The fact that Gilbert was so quick to pour scorn on the prisoners at such a time is quite revealing, especially bearing in mind that as a psychologist he should have been fully aware of the mental and emotional stresses of the situation.

of a problem. Gilbert's *Nuremberg Diary* is rightly regarded as one of the most important primary sources regarding the IMT as he was the man who spent more time with the defendants than any other. For this reason he is frequently quoted in Conot, Davidson, Overy and most other secondary works written on this subject. Yet despite his supposedly dispassionate role as a psychologist, he, as an American, who held frequent meetings with the prosecution team, even helping to devise strategies to undermine the defendants, was clearly not objective. What's more, as a Jewish American, (of Austrian descent) one has to wonder, bearing in mind the nature of some of the accusations against the men in the dock, whether objectivity on his part was ever possible. When one also considers the fact that the only other member of court staff assigned to have regular contact with and to make evaluations of the prisoners was also a Jewish American (Goldensohn), one has to question whether any consideration toward objectivity was ever given. Did the IMT, in the form of Jackson et al really want to receive unbiased, balanced reports of these men, or only that which would assist in incriminating them? It is yet another issue brought forth by the Allied-run tribunal scenario and raises important questions about the written history of Nuremberg. If the documents available to historians are only those generated by the prosecution, or written by those associated with the prosecution, like Gilbert's diary, or Goldensohn's interviews, are we not guilty of projecting an entirely one sided view?

Göring's testimony continued for a further two days, firstly with questions from the British prosecutor, Maxwell-Fyfe, then from the Russian, Rudenko. Fyfe picked his subjects intelligently, and cross-examined with more skill than Jackson. He went straight onto the offensive, questioning Göring on the shootings of British airmen who had escaped from the prison at Stalag-Luft III. For the first time since he had taken the stand, Göring was removed from his comfort zone. Suddenly the impeccable memory for document and de- tail he had shown against Jackson disappeared and he began claiming to be unable to remember details or names.

Fyfe – 'Can you tell us the date at which he (General Korten) made this communication to you?'
Göring – 'No, I cannot tell you that exactly...'
Fyfe – 'Who was the first to tell you about it? Was it your chief of staff who told you about the shootings? Do you mean that someone else had told you about the shooting?'
Göring – 'I cannot say exactly now whether I heard about the shooting from the chief of staff, or from other sources...'
Fyfe – '...Now, these shootings of these officers went on from the 25th of March to the 13th of April; do you know that?'
Göring – 'I do not know that exactly.'[212]

However, despite his clever point of attack and deftness of questioning, Fyfe was only able to rattle Göring and cause him to become evasive. He couldn't pin him down. He was able to show that Göring was responsible for having the escaped prisoners rounded up but, according to Taylor, 'Fyfe's evidence fell short of establishing Göring's complicity in the murders,'[213] the responsibility for which seemed instead to fall on Himmler, who had received his orders directly from Hitler. Taylor's verdict on this part of Fyfe's cross examination was that 'the prosecution established no basis for a criminal charge against Göring on this affair.'[214]

This does not mean that Fyfe's efforts were seen as failure, however. On the contrary, Fyfe demonstrated that a man in control of his documents (which Jackson had not been) and of dextrous enough mind to compete with Göring in open court (which Jackson had not been) was more than capable of getting under his skin. Unlike Jackson, Fyfe also introduced evidence regarding what is today called the Holocaust – firstly in the form of Document D-729 which discussed methods employed by the *Einsatzgruppen*, the mobile squads of SS who performed anti-civilian actions throughout Eastern Europe. The document, a transcript of a conversation Göring had with Mussolini in Venice, in 1942, read as follows:

'The Reich Marshal then described Germany's method in fighting the partisans. To begin with, all

---
[212] Nuremberg Trial Proceedings, Vol 9, 86th day, 20th March 1946, p.573
[213] Taylor, p.344
[214] ibid

livestock and foodstuffs were taken away from the areas concerned, so as to deny the partisans all sources of supply. Men and women were taken away to labour camps, the children to children's camps, and the villages burned down. It was by the use of these methods that the railways in the vast wooded areas of Bialowiza had been safeguarded. Whenever attacks occurred, the entire male population of the villages were lined up on one side and the women on the other. The women were told that all the men would be shot, unless they – the women – pointed out which men did not belong to the village. In order to save their men, the women always pointed out the non-residents. Germany had found that, generally speaking, it was not easy to get soldiers to carry out such measures. Members of the Party discharged this task much more harshly and efficiently. For the same reason, armies trained ideologically, such as the German – or the Russian – fought better than others. The SS, the nucleus of the old Party fighters, who have personal ties with the Führer and who form a special elite, confirm this principle.'

It should be noted here that the document does not present the now accepted view of *Einsatzgruppen* activities as being Jews selectively rounded up and shot, although it does contain some similarities. Indeed, there is nothing in the document that demonstrates the *Einsatzgruppen* were at all focused on exterminating Jews, but rather presents them as being involved in weeding out partisan fighters (many of whom may well have been Jews, for obvious reasons) from the villages in occupied territory. Essentially it describes a form of guerrilla war, similar to that which the USA found itself enmeshed in Vietnam or the coalition forces have recently encountered in Iraq. It should also be noted that certainly in the first of those two modern parallels, the method of dealing with the problem of non-uniformed partisans was exactly the same. In the sense that the document was presented at the IMT, Göring did not see the need to deny it or offer an alternative interpretation (despite the fact that he repeatedly denied all knowledge of what is now called the Holocaust.) After reading it, Fyfe asked, 'Now is that a correct description?' And Göring replied, 'Yes, certainly.'[215]

A few minutes later and Fyfe mentioned, during the course of another question that four million people had been killed at Auschwitz.[216]

Göring – 'This I have heard as a statement here, but I consider it in no way proved – that figure, I mean.'

Fyfe – 'If you do not consider it proved, let me remind you of the affidavit of Hoettl, who was Deputy Group Leader of the Foreign Section, of the Security Section of Amt IV of the RSHA. He says that approximately 4,000,000 Jews have been killed in the concentration camps, while an additional 2,000,000 met death in other ways…are you telling this Tribunal that a Minister with your power in the Reich could remain ignorant that that was going on?'

Göring – 'This I maintain, and the reason for this is that these things were kept secret from me. I might add that in my opinion not even the Führer knew the extent of what was going on. This is also explained by the fact that Himmler kept all these matters very secret. We were never given figures or any other details.'[217]

The Hoettl affidavit will be discussed more thoroughly in chapter twenty, but for now it will suffice to point out that it was not an official policy document or a letter containing an extermination order, but simply a recollection of a conversation that Hoettl had with Adolf Eichmann in August 1944. Hoettl attributed statements to Eichmann in which Eichmann recalled a conversation he had previously had with Himmler concerning the deaths of six million civilians. It seems that this piece of hearsay was solely enough (at this stage – Höss, the Auschwitz commandant had not yet testified), without presenting the witness for cross-examination, to convince the court of the four million death toll.

Fyfe then went on to harangue Göring using some other pieces of Holocaust evidence.

---

[215] Nuremberg Trial Proceedings, Vol. 9, 87th day, 21st March 1946, p.608
[216] ibid, p.610. This figure is no longer accepted by anyone. The Auschwitz museum now states that 1.5 million people died there, 'mainly Jews'.
[217] ibid

Fyfe – 'You told Mr Justice Jackson yesterday that there were various representatives in Eastern territories, and you have seen the films of the concentration camps, haven't you, since this Trial started? You knew that there were millions of garments, millions of shoes, 20,952 kilograms of gold wedding rings, 35 wagons of furs – all that stuff which these people who were exterminated at Maidanek or Auschwitz left behind them. Did nobody ever tell you, under the development of the Four Year Plan, or anyone else, that they were getting all these amounts of human material? Do you remember we heard from the Polish Jewish gentleman, who gave evidence, that all he got back from his family, of his wife and mother and daughter, I think, were their identity cards? His work was to gather up clothes. He told us that so thorough were the henchmen of your friend Himmler that it took 5 minutes extra to kill the women because they had to have their hair cut off as it was to be used for making mattresses. Was nothing ever told you about this accretion to German material, which came from the effects of these people who were murdered?'[218]
Göring – 'No and how can you imagine this ...?'

It seems that Göring did not deem it necessary to his own defence to point out that finding shoes, clothes, gold and other personal items does not, in itself, prove that the owners of those items are dead. It simply proves that the items were confiscated, which in itself would be a nasty enough crime, but obviously falls short of genocide. Fyfe on the other hand, seemed happy to connect the dots and state that such evidence showed that the people to whom they belonged were exterminated, as if the entire matter had already been resolved beyond reasonable doubt. Nonetheless, Fyfe persisted and was about to elicit one of the three key moments of the trial in regard to the Holocaust question.

Fyfe – '...Do you still say neither Hitler nor you knew of the policy to exterminate the Jews?'
Göring – 'As far as Hitler is concerned, I have said I do not think so. As far as I am concerned, I have said that I did not know, even approximately, to what extent these things were taking place.'
Fyfe – 'You did not know to what degree, but you knew there was a policy that aimed at the extermination of the Jews?'
Göring – 'No, a policy of emigration, not liquidation of the Jews. I knew only that there had been isolated cases of such perpetrations.'[219]

Fascinatingly, rather than asking Göring to explain what he meant by his last remark, what 'isolated cases' he was referring to and what exactly had happened in those cases, Fyfe chose to end his cross examination there. As a result we shall never really know what Göring knew about this issue.
In general however, Fyfe did a good job of putting the former *Reichsmarschall* on the back foot and was only guilty of a few mistakes, the most notable being that his claims regarding numbers of Nazi victims kept changing. He began by quoting Hoettl and the six-million figure mentioned above. A few questions later he said, 'something like ten million people have been done to death in cold blood, apart from those killed in battle.'[220] And a few questions after that he stated, 'I am not asking about details; I am asking about the murder of four or five million people.'[221] It would seem to be reasonable to wonder where these figures were coming from and whether there was any particular reason why they might be changing. A critical evaluation might conclude that Fyfe was either making it up as he went along, or that the prosecution were so confused over the major claims that they did not yet have their facts straight. Was the four or five million meant to be Jewish camp deaths, the six million the total Jewish deaths and the ten million the total including non-Jews? That would seem to be a reasonable guess, as Fyfe himself did not make it clear, yet those figures would all be considered inaccurate by modern Holocaust historians, the most eminent of whom, Raul Hilberg, in his seminal 'The Destruction of the European Jews' put the overall Jewish total at 5.1 million, of whom 2.9 mil-

---

[218] ibid, p.611
[219] ibid, p.618
[220] ibid, p.610
[221] ibid, p.614

lion died in camps and 2.2 million of other causes.²²² It would appear that there is good reason therefore to doubt the quality of evidence that the prosecution was using on this particular issue. Their figures would not have been revised by history otherwise. Besides, like the situation with the Stalag Luft questioning, Fyfe was unable to elicit anything from Göring to add to that which had already been established, in the court's eyes, by other evidence.

There remained the small matter of Göring's interrogation by Rudenko, for the Soviet Union, but again, this was uneventful compared to the Jackson fiasco and yielded little. There was barely concealed hostility between the two men and much of the questioning revolved around Germany's plans to attack the western Russian territories and their eventual breaking of the Nazi/Soviet pact by doing so. Again nothing was demonstrated that hadn't already been proven, as far as the tribunal was concerned, by documents and the cross examination became a verbal duel between two men who represented fierce historical enemies.

Rudenko – '…In that case, you considered the annexation of those regions a step to come later…?'
Göring – 'Not in principle. As an old hunter, I acted according to the principle of not dividing the bear's skin before the bear was shot.'
Rudenko – 'I understand. And the bear's skin should be divided only when the territories were seized completely, is that correct?'
Göring – 'Just what to do with the skin could be decided definitely only after the bear was shot.'
Rudenko – 'Luckily, this did not happen.'
Göring – 'Luckily for you.'²²³

It was all good, knockabout stuff, continuing in the same vein for a couple of hours before Rudenko turned his attentions from the aggressive war charge and onto Crimes against Humanity.

Rudenko – 'Please tell me, do you know about Himmler's directives given in 1941 about the extermination of thirty million Slavs? You heard about it from the witness Von dem Bach-Zelewski here in court. Do you remember that?'
Göring – 'Yes. First of all it was not an order but a speech. Secondly, it was an assertion by Ze-
lewski. And thirdly, in all speeches that Himmler made to subordinate leaders, he insisted on the strictest secrecy. In other words, this is a statement from a witness about what he had heard, and not an order. Consequently, I have no knowledge of this nonsense.'²²⁴

Göring was quite right. Rudenko's question represented another attempt by the prosecution to support an atrocity claim by introducing what amounted to nothing more than a piece of hearsay as evidence. The difference between this and the evidence mentioned by Fyfe is that the court did not seem to give this any further credence. A plan to exterminate thirty million Slavs, unlike the Jewish genocide, did not appear on the final judgment – but it was introduced to the IMT in much the same way, with a qualitatively similar witness statement presented as proof.

This was practically the end of Göring's testimony. The French prosecutor waived his right to cross-examine and Stahmer asked a few more questions for the defence and then it was over. Twelve days had elapsed since the Göring case had begun.

The feeling among the prosecution was that the whole thing represented an opportunity lost, particularly the bulk of the cross examination as handled by Jackson. Although there was enough documentary evidence to convict Göring on that basis alone, the decision to hold the trial in the first place was founded on the idea that they could be seen to be delivering justice. In Göring's case this task had now been made harder. It was felt they would have to convict him in spite of his performance in court rather than because of it. Judge Birkett saw this as greatly reducing the IMTs effectiveness, 'the trial from now on is really outside the control of the tribunal,' he wrote, reflecting on Göring's time on the stand 'and in the long months ahead the

---

[222] Raul Hilberg, *The Destruction of the European Jews*, (3ʳᵈ ed, Yale 2003) p.1320
[223] Nuremberg Trial Proceedings, Vol. 9, 87ᵗʰ day, 21ˢᵗ March 1946, p.627
[224] ibid, p.644

prestige of the trial will steadily diminish.'[225]

Others, like Telford Taylor, saw this as an overstatement of Göring's importance to the prosecution. There were, after all, twenty-two defendants with a mountain of documentary evidence against them, yet the fear that the trial could provide a public platform for the resurgence of National Socialism persisted, with Birkett stating that it might 'restore German belief in their leaders.'[226]

After conferring, the judges therefore agreed to prevent other defendants speaking at length as Göring had done. During the afternoon session of March 23rd, before the case of Rudolf Hess began, Lawrence made the following statement to the court.

> 'The Tribunal has allowed the Defendant Goering, who has given evidence first of the defendants and who has proclaimed himself to be responsible as the second leader of Nazi Germany, to give his evidence without any interruption whatever, and he has covered the whole history of the Nazi regime from its inception to the defeat of Germany. The Tribunal does not propose to allow any of the other defendants to go over the same ground in their evidence except insofar as it is necessary for their own defence.'

It can therefore be safely concluded that Göring's case had a profound effect on the tribunal. The matter of time was one issue. If all the defendants were allowed to elucidate as Göring had, the trial could stretch on for years, an issue repeatedly emphasised by Jackson.[227] The matter of propaganda was another, mentioned privately by Birkett and publicly, in open court via a conversation between Lawrence and defence counsel Rudolf Dix on 22nd March. Placing limitations on the defendants' answers may have helped to serve these peripheral goals, but whether they helped more generally in the pursuit of justice is an issue which will be discussed later.

At the deliberation meetings to establish the court's judgement in September, the findings on Göring's guilt were arrived at without complication. Judge Rowe stated, 'Göring was often, indeed almost always the moving force, second only to his leader...He was the prime conspirator. He was the leading war aggressor. He was the director of the slave labour program and the creator of the oppressive program against the Jews and other races.'[228]

Rowe's colleagues unanimously agreed with him and it was decided to put Göring to death. Göring responded to his fate, which he had been resigned to since before the trial began, by saying 'I'm glad it's not a life sentence, because those who are sentenced to life imprisonment never become martyrs.'[229] After sentencing, as he was being led back to his cell, he bumped into Fritzsche (who had been found not guilty) in the corridor. Göring was in shackles, as all the convicted men were, but his guard allowed him to shake hands as well as was possible. With no recourse to his own recently announced fate, Göring said, 'Very glad you've been acquitted. We had a bit of a bad conscience as far as you are concerned.'[230] He bade the former radio presenter goodbye and was led away. Later on he was to proclaim: 'In fifty or sixty years there will be statues of Hermann Göring all over Germany, little statues, maybe, but one in every German home.'[231]

As is now common knowledge, Göring escaped the noose by managing to take a cyanide capsule in his cell. How he obtained the poison is a mystery, with the most popular explanation being that he was assisted by prison officer Lieutenant 'Tex' Wheelis who befriended him during the trial. Although fertile ground for conspiracy theory, it's a trivial issue and of no great consequence.

Along with the other eleven men to receive a death sentence, the former *Reichsmarschall's* ashes were thrown into the *Conwentzbach*, near Munich, which flows into the Isar River. As yet, sixty-two years on, not one statue of Hermann Göring has been erected anywhere in Germany.

---

[225] Taylor, p.341
[226] ibid
[227] Jackson often began his interjections in court with 'in the interests of time' or similar phrases.
[228] Conot, p.486
[229] Gilbert, p.434
[230] Taylor, p.600
[231] Fest, p.129

8

The Loneliest Man in the World[232]

Rudolf Hess

This chapter deals with an incredible story. Like so many other aspects of this book, it is a story which in itself could stretch to several hundred pages. Taken at face value, it is also a story that could read like some sort of Boy's Own adventure fantasy (although ultimately rather a tragic one). And like all great stories from the past, it contains almost as much mystery as history.

When Rudolf Hess died, in 1987, Whitney Harris, the American prosecutor, wrote, 'With his death, Hitler's tyranny ended.'[233] News pictures that night relayed striking images. They showed some shots of Hess when young; beetle-browed and intense, as above, mostly standing by Hitler's side, then cut to more recent footage of a frail, old man wandering in a garden. When the camera homed in to a facial close-up, an incredible withering was displayed. It was wastage beyond that of mere age. Skin sat against bones like folded tissue paper. The face belonged to a man who been in solitary confinement for nearly fifty years.

Rudolf Hess was born in Alexandria, Egypt in 1894. He was the son of Fritz Hess, a wealthy import and export merchant who had inherited the family business, Hess & Co from his father, a self made man. He had an unremarkable childhood and like so many of his future Nazi colleagues found both himself and a sense of purpose during the First World War. He began in the artillery, swiftly moving into the infantry where he fought both at Ypres and the Somme, winning the Iron Cross, second class, in April 1915. He continued to see active service throughout the hellish battlefields of Belgium and France and in May 1916 fought at Verdun, which he described in a rather sensitive, well written poem as 'a savage fire' which 'howled like a su-

---

[232] chapter title borrowed from Eugene K. Dick, *The Loneliest Man in the World, The Inside story of the Thirty Year Imprisonment of Rudolf Hess* (Secker & Warburg 1974)
[233] Dodd, p.361

pernatural hurricane in which individual blows were scarcely heard.'[234]

In June of 1916 he was wounded and sent to hospital. Upon release he was promoted to platoon leader. In July he was wounded again and then almost killed in August when shot beneath the left shoulder during a battle with Russian infantry. Luckily, the bullet passed clean through his body with no damage to the heart or spine. After another period of convalescence he joined the Flying Corps in October 1916 and saw out the rest of the war in active aerial combat as a fighter pilot. This was regarded as the most dangerous military job of the era, with the average life expectancy of a flyer reckoned to be six weeks after taking off for their first mission.[235] When looking at the totality of his service record, it is not therefore an excessive use of superlatives to describe the fact that Hess survived the war as miraculous.

Like many others, Hess viewed the armistice and the fleeing of the Kaiser with shame. All the hard work, all the sacrifice, all the loss of young life had been for nothing. As his squadron was dissolved in 1918, his thoughts were summarised by his commander, a garrulous, athletic and enormously brave pilot by the name of Hermann Göring. 'Gentlemen' he had said, 'our time will come again!'[236]

The immediate postwar career of Hess was similar to several other Nazis. He joined the Freikorps in 1919 and became a National Socialist after hearing Hitler speak in 1920. The turning point of his life occurred three years later when he was imprisoned with Hitler in the Landesberg jail following the Munich Beer Hall Putsch. There he took down the dictated text of Hitler's turgid and repetitive autobiography/political, ideological manifesto, 'Mein Kampf' a work he later would claim partial credit for, writing in a letter to his wife that the book contained many of his own ideas.[237] As a result of this he formed a very close bond with Hitler and after release took on a series of roles, beginning with being Hitler's private secretary from 1925-32, then becoming Deputy Leader of the Party, then Minister without Portfolio in 1933. In 1938 he became Secretary of the Cabinet Council and in 1939 a member of the Council for Reich Defence, at which point he was declared successor to Hitler and Göring. He kept this position until 1941, when his politi- cal and executive career came to an abrupt end.

Hess was therefore clearly indictable under Count One, as a member of the Nazi Leadership Corps. His role in the upper echelons of the German military implicated him to some extent him in Counts Two and Three, although it is now known that he had little authority in these areas as Hitler did not trust his ability with military tactics and logistics. One would have thought that the ending of his political career in 1941 would have seen him less likely to be implicated in the Holocaust and other civilian atrocities, the bulk of which occurred under the umbrella of Operation Barbarossa, and possibly not therefore charged with Count Four. However the Allied prosecutors clearly felt that someone as high in the Nazi hierarchy as Hess must have been culpable on all levels, as he was indicted on all four counts. But before looking at this in more depth and examining the trial and judgement as it applied to Hess, there is a gap to be filled in his story.

The reason why Hess' career ended when it did and what happened to him between then and 1945 is probably the most intriguing event to come out of the entirety of World War Two. To cut to the chase – on the 10th of May 1941, Rudolf Hess climbed into a twin-engine Messerschmitt, Bf 110 fighter plane at Augsburg airfield and took off, alone. He flew north-west to Norway, then turned west, passing over the North Sea, through airspace covered by British radar and protected by British air defences, before parachuting out of the plane and landing in a field near Eaglesham Village, about three miles outside of Glasgow. Upon land- ing, wearing a Luftwaffe uniform and carrying an attaché case containing homeopathic medicines and sev- eral reams of notes, he was taken into custody, where he gave a false name, calling himself 'Alfred Horn,' then asked to be allowed to see the Duke of Hamilton.[238] Eventually he did see Hamilton, who was woken and told of the arrival of a German flier at about midnight, yet remarkably made no effort to meet him until the following day.

Hess and Hamilton had met before, at the Berlin Olympics of 1936 and Hess told him that he had arrived to broker a peace deal between Britain and Germany. The general gist was that Britain would be allowed to

---

[234] A translation of the poem 'Before Verdun' by Rudolf Hess, is reproduced in Peter Padfield, *Hess: The Fuhrer's Disciple*, (Macmillan 1991) p. 8
[235] Statistic taken from website 'A Century of Flight' http://www.century-of-flight.net/Aviation%20history/airplane%20at%20war/splash.htm
[236] Padfield, p.11
[237] Davidson, p.110
[238] Padfield, p.205

keep her empire if Germany could be left to control Europe. America would then not need to enter the war and Germany could turn full attention to the threat posed by Russia.

Such a proposal, coming from the deputy Führer, on a solo mission into the heart of enemy territory, was utterly unprecedented. It was an act of such enormity and strangeness that it is sometimes difficult to believe that it really happened. Sir Jock Colville, Churchill's private secretary, wrote in his diary: 'the occupant of the Nazi plane was Rudolf Hess. There never has been such a fantastic occurrence.'[239] Unfortunately for Hess, Churchill showed little interest in his mission or peace plans (perhaps because they involved him leaving office) and ordered him to be detained immediately as a prisoner of war. He wrote a note to Anthony Eden, the foreign secretary which said: 'This man like other Nazi leaders is potentially a war criminal and he and his confederates may well be declared outlaws at the end of the war…in the meanwhile he should be strictly isolated in a convenient house…he should not have any contact with the outside world., or visitors…he should see no newspapers and hear no wireless…'[240]

To return briefly to a point made near the beginning of this book, it is worth noting that Churchill is using terms such as these early in 1941. Fully four years before the war would end, he was already anticipating that leading Nazis would be seen as criminals. Remember that this is two years before the earliest, unconfirmed reports of the Holocaust had filtered through, eight months even before the Wannsee Conference had taken place and a month before Operation Barbarossa began. It is abundantly clear that in reality, the civilian atrocities which have been so repeatedly emphasised by modern history served only as garnish, added at a later date – they were *not* the crimes for which the Allies primarily wished to try the Nazis. The only crime Nazis could have been guilty of by that point was the planning and waging of aggressive war.

The official reaction, from both Britain and Germany, was that Hess had lost his mind. Hitler called his cabinet together at the Berghof and explained that 'insanity ran in Hess' family'[241] He issued a communiqué stating that Hess had 'a disease which had been becoming worse for years', that he 'showed signs of mental disturbance' and was 'a victim of hallucinations'.[242] Such a conclusion was supported by the fact that Hess was examined frequently by his British captors who initially declared him sane, as recorded by parliamentary private secretary Harold Nicolson, 'he is reported to be perfectly sane and…in good health.'[243] But they soon changed their minds and declared him a 'schizophrenic personality with hysterical overlay.' By 1943 he was also allegedly suffering from bouts of amnesia.[244]

One might reasonably have expected the Ministry of Information to have spun an interesting tale around this incident. It would appear to have been ripe with potential for British propaganda, but they chose, for rea- sons unknown, not to capitalise upon it. Lord Cadogan even went as far as to suggest that Churchill release a statement saying that Hess had turned traitor and defected to the UK, yet Churchill ignored this advice and the statement he eventually made, which said that Hess was unhinged and had flown to the UK independently, without the knowledge of Hitler or anyone else, was virtually identical to the equivalent German statement written by Goebbels.[245]

There are many ideas and theories concerning the Hess incident, ranging from bizarre Hitlerite plans, to Secret Service plots and covert contact with members of the British Royal Family. It is well known that there was a peace movement in the UK at the time and that Lord Hamilton was connected to it. It is also well known that members of the House of Windsor supported it. Hess' co-defendant Fritzsche mentioned that the flying ace Ernst Udet had stated it was technically impossible to land a Bf 110 in Britain under the conditions in which Hess undertook his mission. Udet believed that Hess must have landed in the channel and been res- cued.[246] This book will not seek to further explore this issue other than by saying that it seems clear that there

is far more to the story than meets the eye. We will not know for sure until 2017, when the Hess file is finally opened after seventy five years of Top Secret classification. The mere fact that the papers concerning the Hess incident have been classified for so long indicates the presence of a sensitive sub-plot. Perhaps, for

---

[239] ibid, p.218
[240] ibid, p.228
[241] Davidson, p.117
[242] Padfield, p.229
[243] ibid, p235
[244] Davidson, p.118
[245] Padfield, p.235
[246] Gilbert, p.133

now, the best explanation is the one given by Hess himself, in a letter to his wife, Ilse.

'My coming to England in this way is, as I realise so unusual that nobody will easily understand it. I was confronted by a very hard decision. I do not think I could have arrived at my final choice unless I had continually kept before my eyes the vision of an endless line of children's coffins, with weeping mothers behind them, both English and German...'[247]

Other leading Nazis saw Hess' peace attempt as utterly foolish. Göring was 'hardly able to control his own scorn.' At Nuremberg, Von Papen, von Neurath, Schacht and Funk expressed disgust and desperation at the details of Hess' adventure.[248]

So, his seemingly reckless mission a failure, Hess found himself first held in the Tower of London, then imprisoned in Mytchett Place, a manor house near Aldershot, where he was well looked after, although kept largely alone. He developed certain paranoid delusions during this time, as perhaps is only natural, becoming convinced that his guards would poison him. Whilst in captivity he attempted suicide three times, first by hurling himself over a banister at the top of a staircase, secondly by stabbing himself in the chest and late in the war by going on hunger-strike. His bouts of amnesia increased in frequency and duration. There were fears among the Allies that he might be declared unfit to face trial and have to be sent for medical care in Switzerland rather than to Nuremberg, (there were also suspicions that he was faking it for exactly that reason), but a medical panel appointed by the four victorious powers declared him well enough to participate in the proceedings.

Hess' first noticeable contribution to the trial came after the showing of the film of the Nazi concentration camps described in the previous chapter. It is reported that most of the defendants seemed deeply moved by the pictures, going pale, covering their eyes, murmuring 'horrible' or even, in the case of Walther Funk and Hans Frick, openly crying. Hess, on the other hand, never turned his gaze from the screen, did not appear to falter and said in an audible, clear, normal voice, 'I don't believe it,' at which point Göring turned to him and told him to be quiet.[249]

Later, as the hearing began in earnest, Hess stirred the already confusing mix of plots and sub-plots by making this opening statement to the tribunal, '...Henceforth my memory will again respond to the outside world. The reasons for simulating loss of memory were of a tactical nature...' He went on to briefly state that he did not view the tribunal as competent or recognize its authority.[250] Gilbert (the prison psychologist) concurred with Leon Goldensohn (the prison psychiatrist) that Hess did indeed suffer from some mental issues, due to the stresses of being incarcerated in Britain, but that he deliberately exaggerated them when it suited him.

Despite his self-announced recovery, Hess' involvement at Nuremberg is difficult to analyse because he managed to remain a peripheral figure throughout the trial. Along with Göring, he was the most senior Nazi figure in the dock yet he said less than virtually any other defendant. Even when his own case was being heard, he did not take the stand, his lawyer choosing not to question him due to concerns over his mental state.[251] There is therefore no testimony and cross-examination of Hess to read and from which to draw conclusions.

The case against him was presented by Lieutenant Colonel Griffiths-Jones on the 8th January. Jones made his way through a series of decrees and state actions performed by Hess during his various official assignments and then moved on to his flight to his England, which he outlined as being part of the conspiracy to wage aggressive war, by saying, 'his humanitarian reasons for coming, which sounded so well on the 10th or between the 10th and 15th of May, took on quite a different light when barely a little more than a month later Germany attacked the Soviet Union... One cannot help remembering an exact parallel between this business and that which took place before Germany attacked Poland, when every effort was made to keep England out of the war and so let her fight her battle on one front only. Here the same thing appears to be happening.'[252]

In other words, Jones was alleging that Hess' flight was little other than an attempt to create favourable

---

[247] Hess, Ilse *'Prisoner of Peace'* (Bloomfield 1954)
[248] Gilbert, p.133
[249] Padfield, p311
[250] Nuremberg Trial Proceedings Vol. 2 , 9th Day, Friday 30th November 1945
[251] Padfield, p 313
[252] Nuremberg Trial Proceedings, Vol. 7, 53rd day, Thursday, 7th February 1946, p.142

conditions for Barbarossa, which like all other events of the war, was being characterised solely as an act of pre-meditated German aggression. It should perhaps be remembered here that in adopting such a position, the prosecutor was contradicting the official line given by his own government, but even if Jones' analysis were accurate, there would have been nothing particularly criminal about Hess' actions as he described them. Germany was at war with many nations and although officially allied by treaty, the mutual hostility between Communist Russia and Nazi Germany was openly known. Not only that, but for several months Russia had been performing aggressive mobilisations along the German front, in line with the Zhukov proposal published on May 15th 1941. There are several historians (in particular Maser and Suvorov), who see the launching of Barbarossa as a pre-emptive strike against Soviet plans to invade central Europe rather than merely an unwarranted Nazi attack. Regardless of any of the above however, it would have been perfectly valid for Germany to broker a peace deal with one nation, while remaining at war or launching war upon others. The matter as it applied to the Hess case only really concerned the relationship between Germany and Britain. Jones' point of argument is therefore seen to be very weak.

Throughout the majority of the proceedings, which stretched for eleven months, Hess simply sat reading or chatting with those around him, frequently laughing or grinning. He virtually never used the headphones provided to listen in to the simultaneous translations, amazingly not even when the verdicts were announced and sentences passed. According to Gilbert, Hess left the court proclaiming not to know what was to happen to him.[253]

His only real moment of involvement came near the end of the trial, on the 31st August 1946, when the defendants were allowed to stand and make a brief statement in order to finalise their defence. With a few exceptions, most declared their own innocence in the face of Nazi crimes, without denying the crimes themselves, stating that they had no knowledge of what was happening and even in some cases apportioning sole blame to Hitler or Himmler. The majority of the defendants were weary and beaten by that stage and their orations were apathetic. Typically, Hess did not follow this trend.

He began by comparing the IMT to the show trials of Stalinist Russia, although he did not refer to them by name, saying that, 'In the years 1936 to 1938 political trials were taking place in one of these countries. These were characterised by the fact that the defendants accused themselves in an astonishing way. For example, they cited great numbers of crimes which they had committed or which they claimed to have committed.' He went on to point out how some of his fellow accused in Nuremberg had behaved in ways consistent with those entangled within such pseudo-legal process.

Particularly when bearing in mind the involvement of Nikitchenko and Rudenko and the criticisms of Nuremberg that were already being made, this was a point that potentially had some mileage, but Hess managed to turn what started as an intriguing comment on the psychology and thought-processes of the accused in such circumstances into some kind of third-rate sci-fi skit by going on to talk about people with 'strange eyes' coming to visit him in his cell and alluding to a hypnotic power that had attacked the minds of him and his fellow defendants.[254] He rambled on in such fashion for about twenty minutes, at which point the judge interjected and asked him to stop.

When the verdicts were given, the judges pronounced Hess guilty on counts one and two, but innocent on counts three and four. At the deliberation meeting the Russian contingent, in typical style, argued forcibly for a death sentence but were outvoted. They remained highly suspicious of Hess' time in Britain and did not understand why he had not been executed by Churchill's government. Their refusal to condone Hess' sentence was officially recorded in the judgment and announced before the court after the sentences had been read. Hess partially concurred with the Soviets. 'Why don't they let me die?'[255] Hess asked his cell guard, later that evening, after learning of the verdict. He and the other Nazis sentenced to prison were taken to Spandau, in the British sector of West Berlin. The prisoners were largely kept apart and denied permission to speak to each other when brought together for exercise or work detail. During his time in Spandau, Hess' weight dropped to under nine stone. His paranoid delusions continued, as did his bouts of amnesia. The debate over whether these were real or feigned in order to try to secure an early release continued.

Outside of the subject of this book, but of general interest, there are various other controversies associ-

---

[253] Padfield, p.316
[254] Nuremberg Trial Proceedings, Vol. 22, 216th day, Saturday 31st August 1946
[255] Anders, *Im Nürnberger Irrgarten*, quoted in Fest, p.297.

ated with Hess which refuse to go away. There is a rumour, for example, allegedly started by Richard Arnold-Baker, an MI6 officer who spent many hours questioning Hess during his imprisonment, that the man kept captive at Spandau was not actually Hess at all. This rumour has developed into a belief that Hess really was executed at Churchill's behest and the man who was flown to Nuremberg and subsequently gaoled was a double.[256] Such hypothesising strays from the realms of what is regarded as history and becomes something else. (There is another theory that Hess was eventually murdered, as opposed to committing suicide.) Regardless of such tales, Spandau became a sort of Mecca to neo-Nazis who would parade around outside and hold noisy demonstrations there up until Hess' death. One wonders what Hess must have thought as he sat in his cell, listening to the clamour of their boots and chanting.

Perhaps it is the mark of the magnitude of a figure's life when these kinds of myths and rituals build up around them. Perhaps it signifies that for whatever reason, their life has transcended normality. And perhaps it is only then that for better or for worse, they can truly be considered legendary.

In the final analysis, we must ask whether Hess' treatment at the hands of the IMT can be viewed as fair. It is the feeling of this author that it can not, although at the present time we are not in possession of all the facts – perhaps the opening of the Hess file in 2017 will change things. Although he was Hitler's right hand man and clearly devoted to the Führer, whom he described as 'the greatest son whom my people has brought forth in its thousand year history,'[257] ultimately he flew to Britain, as far as we presently know, risking his own life to try to cease hostilities. The idea of convicting such a fellow of Crimes against Peace seems slightly at odds with logic. The issue of how he received such a heavy sentence, when from 1941 onwards he was imprisoned and playing no further part in the war or the government of his nation is also somewhat difficult to square. Winston Churchill himself concurred with such a view, writing, 'I am glad not to be responsible for the way in which Hess has been and is being treated. Whatever may be the moral guilt of a German who stood near to Hitler, Hess had, in my view, atoned for this by his completely devoted and frantic deed of lunatic benevolence. He came to us of his own free will, and, though without authority, had something of the quality of an envoy. He was a medical and not a criminal case, and should be so regarded.'[258]

Nevertheless, after an early life packed with more action than the average novelist could invent, Hess died aged 92 in Spandau, completely alone, the last of the others having been released twenty years previously.

---

[256] David Southwell and Sean Twist, *The Conspiracy Files*, (Carlton Books, 1999)
[257] Nuremberg Trial Proceedings, Vol. 22, 216th day, Saturday 31st August 1946
[258] Winston S. Churchill, *The Second World War, Volume 3, The Grand Alliance*, (Penguin 1950) p.55

9

Skinhead, skinhead!

Julius Streicher

If hating the Jews was the Nazis greatest crime, then Julius Streicher was the greatest criminal of them all. His first recorded reaction to the indictment (as noted by prison psychologist, Gilbert), was that the trial was 'a triumph of World Jewry.'[259] He retained this viewpoint until death.

He is one of only five Nuremberg defendants to get a chapter to himself in this book, for two reasons. Firstly, despite history's misgivings regarding his unabashed anti-Semitism - a belief-system he openly subscribed to, voiced and never retreated from, even when faced with a noose - he was a controversial and colourful character. There exist many lurid tales about his sexual habits, fiery outbursts and shady financial dealings. Such scandalised views were contemporarily expressed by Justice Jackson, who described him as a 'vulgarian' and Airey Neave, who applied to Streicher the soubriquet 'the Beast of Nuremberg'[260]. Such opinions have since been frequently repeated by historians like Robert Conot who, described Streicher as 'venomous' and a 'sexually obsessed sadist'[261]. How much these thumbnail portraits owe to scholarly historical enquiry and how much to cartoonish representations of Nazi evil, twinned with a desire to defame the arch Jew-baiter is open to debate, but what cannot be denied is that the Streicher story is intriguing.

---

[259] Gilbert, p.6
[260] This title appears as a caption next to a picture of Streicher in the illustrations section in the middle of Neave's book – Neave also describes Frank as 'the Butcher of Poland', Von Papen as the 'Silver Fox' and Schacht as the 'Irascible Banker'. He seemed to enjoy inventing nicknames for the defendants.
[261] Conot, p.382

The other, perhaps more pertinent reason, is that of the twenty-two men sentenced by the IMT (bearing in mind that Bormann was tried in absentia) he was the only one who was judged guilty purely on the count of Crimes against Humanity. Implication in the development of what we now call the Holocaust, by spreading anti-Semitic propaganda via *Der Stürmer*, his newspaper, was enough to see him sentenced to death.

Prior to the trial beginning, in one of his initial psychological examinations,[262] Streicher explained his anti-Semitism to Gilbert, saying, 'I am the only one in the world who clearly saw the Jewish menace as a historical problem. I didn't become anti-Semitic because of any personal mistreatment or a grudge – not at all – I was *called* to it! My realization of the Jewish menace came from the Talmud itself...'[263] As his case was heard, he was to offer further exposition of his views.

On an interpersonal level, at Nuremberg, Streicher did himself few favours. He upset the sensitivities of the guards assigned to watch him by exercising naked in his cell.[264] (A habit which added to his 'pervert' image, although public nudity is commonplace and perfectly normal in Germany and the countries of Scandinavia, it is probable that Streicher saw nothing wrong in what he was doing). Several of the other defendants bore grudges against him from pre-trial times and he found himself an outcast, even among the Germans. The only one who talked to him was Ley, who promptly committed suicide. His shaved head and famously belligerent manner (highly evocative of a youth sub-culture which would flourish twenty years later in the UK) may have created the right image as a soldier and Nazi governor, but made a poor impression on the prosecutors and judges. From the outset he had to be frequently reminded by the judge to stay on-topic, as he had a tendency to answer each question with a story. After the experience with Göring, the tribunal was not prepared to tolerate this and eventually restricted the length of his responses.

The tone for his testimony was set within the first five minutes, as Streicher made a statement in which he attacked his own lawyer, Dr Hanns Marx, saying that he had not been conducting his defence in the way that he wished. Marx responded by declaring that he hadn't really wanted the case in the first place and asking the judge for permission to stand down. 'When I was asked to take over Herr Streicher's defence, I naturally had grave misgivings...' he said. 'I am aware that at this stage of the proceedings it would be very difficult for me to follow the matter to its logical conclusion and ask to be relieved of this task of defence...and for that reason I feel bound to ask the Court to decide whether in these circumstances I am to continue to defend my client.'[265]

Judge Lawrence declared that the case needed to proceed and so it did, as it began, with Streicher, in his own inimitable way, attempting to defend himself and with his attorney seeming most of the time as if he were questioning for the prosecution. It seems there were press reports written at the time which accused Marx of being an anti-Semite for having accepted Streicher's case. Marx clearly wished to disprove these accusations by being hard on his client in his questioning, which may have served that purpose, but did little to advance the defence.

Julius Streicher had grown up one of nine children and became a schoolteacher as a young man. He had fought with distinction in World War One, rising to the rank of lieutenant and receiving the Iron Cross First Class. He had actually formed his own political movement, a section of the *Schutz und Trutz Bund* (The Defensive and Offensive Alliance) in Nuremberg, after the war, which in many ways mirrored the embryonic National Socialist party in Munich. Like Hitler, his talent for public speaking became apparent quickly and he garnered much support. Indeed, his organisation had more members than the Nazis until the point when the two groups merged in 1921.[266] This occurred after Streicher went to see Hitler speak at the Munich *Bürgerbräukeller* (beer hall), an event he later described as though it were some divine epiphany. 'Adolf Hitler was speaking there,' he said. 'I had only heard his name. I had never seen the man before. And there I sat, an unknown among unknowns. I saw this man shortly before midnight, after he had spoken for 3 hours, drenched in perspiration, radiant. My neighbor said he thought he saw a halo around his head; and I, Gentlemen, experienced something which transcended the commonplace.'[267]

---

[262] Streicher scored the lowest of any defendant on the IQ test, getting only 106, barely above average. Gilbert p.31

[263] Gilbert, p10 (The 'Talmud' Streicher is referring to here is an ancient holy book of Judaism)

[264] Owen, James, Nuremberg, *Evil on Trial*, (Headline 2006) p.216

[265] Nuremberg Trial Proceedings Vol. 12.115th day. Friday, 26 April 1946, p.306

[266] Conot, p.381

[267] Nuremberg Trial Proceedings Vol. 12.115th day. Friday, 26 April 1946, p.308

So impressed was he with Hitler's oratory that he approached him and offered his own burgeoning movement as an addition to the National Socialist one. Hitler accepted, more than doubling the Nazi membership in one stroke. Later, Streicher was to participate in the 'Munich Beer Hall Putsch' of 1923, in which the Nazis attempted to seize power, initially of Munich, but ultimately of Bavaria and the whole of Germany. Streicher's role in this established him within Hitler's circle of trust.

After Hitler's release from prison, in 1925, Streicher was made *Gauleiter* of Franconia. Initially this was merely a role of public speaking and administration. Bearing in mind that at that stage the Nazis were just a small political party among many other small political parties, Streicher was simply the party co-ordinator for the area. That changed in 1933 when the Nazis were elected. Streicher then became a deputy to the Reichstag and his role of *Gauleiter* assumed greater significance. He kept this role until 1940, when, for various reasons, including escalating allegations of corruption, he lost his position of favour with Hitler and was given leave of absence. At this time he was also banned from public speaking and so went to live quietly on his farm-estate, (continuing his newspaper on a decreasing scale) where he stayed until 1945 when he was arrested by the Allies. It is worth noting then, that like Hess, Streicher's political career and most pertinently, the part of it in which he actually wielded some executive power, coincided with such relevant events as the passing of the Nuremberg laws in 1935 and The Night of the Broken Glass in 1938, but not with the Final Solution or the vast majority of World War Two, by which point he was a complete outsider of the regime.

Unlike Hess, the court clearly viewed his case in terms such as these, as he was never indicted on counts two and three and acquitted on Count One, participation in the Conspiracy or Common Plan. This was also because the nature of the charge, as it was applied to all defendants, changed before the final judgements were made. The conspiracy charge was eventually limited by the judges to only apply to the waging of aggressive war - an important point, to be analysed in chapter nineteen. Streicher's role as *Gauleiter* clearly did not implicate him in this and they were left with no choice other than to clear him. However, it was Streicher's activities as writer, editor and publisher of the now infamous *Der Stürmer* (The Attacker) newspaper, for which he was best known and primarily charged.

Der Stürmer began as little more than a pamphlet in 1923, with a tiny circulation around Nuremberg. By 1927 it had developed a readership of approximately 27,000, eventually reaching a peak of nearly half a million in 1935 before tailing off again. The motto of the newspaper, printed at the bottom of every leader-page was the slogan, *'Die Juden sind unser Unglück!'* (The Jews are our misfortune!).

It is problematic, in today's terms, to properly describe the content of *Der Stürmer*. In some ways it was a typical gutter tabloid, full of invective and hysterical editorial, using short sentences and simple vocabulary. In others it sank lower than that, with its blatant racism, but also in the credibility of some of its stories, which must have stretched the credulity of all but the most gullible of readers. However, it was undeniably political. It may have been polemical, alarmist and guilty of muck-raking to discredit the enemy but those whom it sought to attack (other than the Jewish population in general) were political figures; mayors, industrialists and foreign heads of state. One could not see a modern tabloid with such a focus achieving much success.

Demographically, however, its readership was typical tabloid. This was demonstrated most aptly by examining the relationship of the paper to some of the other defendants. Hermann Göring, who saw himself as a sort of Wilhelmian gentleman-flier, had banned the paper in all departments under his jurisdiction. Bearing in mind Göring's numerous official roles, this amounted to a great deal of departments. Similarly, Baldur von Schirach banned *Der Stürmer* in all Hitler Youth hostels and education centres, deeming it to be unsuitable for the young Nazis under his command. On the other hand, Robert Ley, the leader of the German Labour Front, was an avid supporter and did his utmost to promote the paper to the road-layers, farmhands and factory workers for whom he became such a figurehead. This discrepancy is not coincidental.

However, just as it is today, it is very difficult to gauge the real influence of the paper. To use a comparison, Britain's current biggest selling tabloid, 'The Sun' is read daily by over three million people[268], is perceived to have a working class readership and is assumed by popular opinion and it seems, also by the paper's staff[269] to play some sort of role in shaping national attitudes, but it is impossible to quantify this. To

---

[268] Its average circulation figures in July and August 2007 were 3,158,045 per day. (ABC Data)
[269] Who can forget the headline that appeared two days after John Major's 1992 election victory, 'It Was The Sun Wot Won It!'

what extent people internalise media output of any kind is an enormous debate in its own right, on which there is no clear consensus. Streicher may have been read by many people, but how much did he influence them? Did the readers of *Der Stürmer* buy it for a cheap laugh at the Jews' expense or to be told what to think? In reality, it seemed self-evident that the paper would have helped to arouse anti-Semitic feelings among working class Germans, but was it possible to link this to anti-Semitic violence? Streicher was forced to address the issue of his role in inciting racial hatred during his cross-examination but asserted that he 'did not intend to advocate or inflame but to enlighten.'[270] Few believed this, but due to the nature of his 'crime', it was difficult to provide any sort of real proof to the contrary.

Streicher was asked many questions, by both his defence counsel and the prosecution about the escalation of anti-Jewish activity that led up to the alleged exterminations that took place in Eastern Europe from 1942 onwards (while *Der Stürmer* was still being published). The idea seemed to be that if it could be proven that Streicher was supportive of the events, perhaps even complicit in them, then a causal link from the newspaper to them could be demonstrated.

When questioned, by Marx about the original Nazi plan for solving the 'Jewish Problem', he had said, 'Before 1933, therefore, the solution of the Jewish problem was not a topic of discussion. I never heard Adolf Hitler mention it; and there is no one here of whom I could say I ever heard him say one word about it.'[271]

Clearly Hitler had considered the issue before, as it featured heavily in 'Mein Kampf', written in 1923-4, but Streicher's assertion that it was not a priority until 1933 is quite believable. Before then Nazi efforts would have centred on obtaining power. There was little point composing solutions to a problem they were not in a position to solve. Streicher went on to admit freely that he participated in the organisation of the boycott of Jewish shops and goods on the 1st April 1933 and accepted partial responsibility for the development of the Nuremberg laws in 1935, reaffirming before the court that:

> 'I have written that any further mixture of German blood with Jewish blood must be avoided. I have written such articles again and again; and in my articles I have repeatedly emphasized the fact that the Jews should serve as an example to every race, for they created a racial law for themselves – the law of Moses, which says, 'If you come into a foreign land you shall not take unto yourself foreign women.' And that, Gentlemen, is of tremendous importance in judging the Nuremberg Laws. These laws of the Jews were taken as a model for these laws...That was the beginning of Jewry which, because it introduced these racial laws, has survived throughout the centuries, while all other races and civilizations have perished.'[272]

He was then chastised by his own lawyer for making a 'digression'. This was followed by another question, in which Marx asked him,

'Were you of the opinion that the 1935 legislation represented the final solution of the Jewish question by the State?'

Streicher replied, 'With reservations, yes. I was convinced that if the Party program was carried out, the Jewish question would be solved...But I believed that another international solution would still be found, and that some day discussions would take place between the various states with regard to the demands made by Zionism. These demands aimed at a Jewish state.' [273] This tied in with Streicher's pro-Zionist statements made prior to trial, which the Soviet prosecutor, Pokrovsky took as evidence of insanity. It is now widely known that many Nazis supported the Zionist movement as being fellow Nationalists with mutually convenient aims.

Marx then broached the subject of physical persecution of the Jews, in particular the events of *Kristallnacht*. Specifically he asked whether Streicher had helped to incite it.

Streicher replied, '...it is my conviction that the contents of *Der Stürmer* as such were not incitation. During the whole 20 years I never wrote in this connection, 'Burn Jewish houses down; beat them to death.'

---

[270] Nuremberg Trial Proceedings, Vol. 12, 116th day, Monday 29th April 1946, p.317
[271] Nuremberg Trial Proceedings Vol. 12, 115th day, Friday, 26 April 1946, p.311
[272] ibid, p.314
[273] ibid, p.315

Never once did such an incitement appear in *Der Stürmer*.'[274]
He went on to state, with reference to the Holocaust:

> '...I wish to state that I had no opportunity...to learn what was actually going on. I first heard of the mass murders and mass killings at Mondorf when I was in prison (awaiting trial). But I am stating here that if I had been told that 2 or 3 million people had been killed, then I would not have believed it. I would not have believed that it was technically possible to kill so many people; and on the basis of the entire attitude and psychology of the Führer, as I knew it, I would not have believed that mass killings, to the extent to which they have taken place, could have taken place.'[275]

Marx then asked about Hitler's order to kill the Jews. It needs to be borne in mind here that historians have never produced or been able to prove that there was such an order and much of the debate between 'functionalist' and 'intentionalist'[276] Holocaust historians revolves around this point. Indeed, many of the former camp, including, among others, Raul Hilberg,[277] do not believe that there was a single Hitler order. Streicher stated that, 'I therefore answer your question by saying that the Führer could not be influenced.' Tellingly, he continued by saying that the order must have been given on Hitler's initiative alone, because the fact 'becomes clear from his will.'[278]

Streicher's entire stance on the extermination issue is fascinating.[279] As stated previously, Streicher was alone on his farm, under Gestapo guard, outside of the regime during the implementation of the Holocaust and he repeatedly stated under oath that he found it difficult to believe that such a thing happened. 'I do not know, and again I would not have believed it.' He said. 'To this day I do not believe that 5 million were killed. I consider it technically impossible that that could have happened. I do not believe it. I have not received proof of that up until now.'[280] Yet despite his incredulity, never did he actually deny that exterminations, as ordered by Hitler, happened. What apparently convinced him of the reality of the Holocaust were the contents of Hitler's will. Perplexingly, however, the document in question mentions nothing of exterminations or a *Führerbefehl* to initiate them. The will makes a vague reference to something unpleasant, stating of the war that Jews were 'the real criminal' and going on to say that 'not only would millions of grown men suffer death, and not only hundreds of thousands of women and children be burnt and bombed to death in the towns, without the real criminal having to atone for this guilt, even if by more humane means.'[281] This vague statement of malicious intent could refer to extermination, possibly, but could also refer to a number of other things (deportation, slavery, loss of property etc). As Hitler dictated the document hours before committing suicide, he would have had no reason to be reticent. Additionally, if he wanted to cover-up his racially motivated genocide, then he would not have mentioned it at all. The fact that he did allude to something, without specifying what, tends to lead to the conclusion that he was probably not referring to physical extermination.

Streicher's position therefore appears rather odd and he indicated this himself by also saying, 'I declare that whoever got to know the Führer's deepest emotions and his soul, as I have personally, and then later had to learn from his testament that he, in full possession of his faculties, consciously gave the order for mass extermination, is confronted with a riddle.'[282]

Marx also posed Streicher many questions regarding his publications, both in regard to *Der Stürmer* and

---

[274] Nuremberg Trial Proceedings, Vol. 12, 116th day, Monday 29th April 1946, p.319
[275] ibid, p.321
[276] 'Intentionalism' is a school of thought which holds that the Holocaust was directed from the top layer of the Nazi state, was the direct result of a Hitler order and had its origins in the Nazi world view, possibly being conceived as early as when *Mein Kampf* was written. 'Functionalism' holds that the Holocaust happened in a piecemeal fashion as a reaction to pressures from within and outside the Reich and often involves the belief that there was no Hitler order given for it. (see note 276)
[277] In *The Destruction of the European Jews*, Hilberg stated that 'In the final analysis, the destruction of the Jews was not so much a product of laws and commands as it was a matter of spirit, of shared comprehension, of consonance and synchronization.' p.55
[278] Nuremberg Trial Proceedings, Vol. 12, 116th day, Monday 29th April 1946, p.323
[279] von Schirach adopted exactly the same stance on the issue.
[280] Nuremberg Trial Proceedings, Vol. 12, 116th day, Monday 29th April 1946, p.373
[281] *Hitler's Political Will*, Web Genocide Documentation Centre, University of the West of England, http://www.ess.uwe.ac.uk/documents/poltest.htm
[282] Nuremberg Trial Proceedings Vol. 12, 116th day, Monday, 29 April 1946, p.368

the anti-Semitic children's books his publishing house produced. At one point Marx asked about a 'special issue' of the newspaper which included a particularly lurid feature about alleged Jewish ritual murders. Streicher responded to his attorney by saying, 'I should like to ask my counsel to express no judgment as to what I have written; to question me, but not to express judgment. The Prosecution are going to do that.'[283] He went on to explain that his sources for the story came from:

> 'a reference made to a book written in Greek by a former Rabbi who had been converted to Christianity. There was reference made to a publication of a high clergymen of Milan, a book which has appeared in Germany for the last 50 years. Not even under the democratic government did Jews raise objections to that book. That ritual murder issue refers to court files which are located in Rome, it refers to files which are in Court. There are pictures in it which show that in 23 cases the Church itself has dealt with this question. The Church has canonized 23 non-Jews killed by ritual murder. Pictures of sculptures, that is, of stone monuments were shown as illustrations; everywhere the source was pointed out; even a case in England was mentioned, and one in Kiev, Russia. But in this connection I should like to say, as I said to a Jewish officer here, that we never wanted to assert that all Jewry was ready now to commit ritual murders. But it is a fact that within Jewry there exists a sect which engaged in these murders, and has done so up until the present.'[284]

Jackson intervened angrily at this point to protest against Streicher's explanation, stating that he was making 'charges against the Jewish people' and requesting that Streicher be 'returned to his cell' and held 'in contempt of court.'[285] Marx, however assured the court that he was finished with that particular line of questioning and the case moved on.

A few questions later and the prosecution began their cross-examination, led by Lieutenant Colonel, Griffiths-Jones; Junior Counsel for the United Kingdom. Griffiths-Jones picked up where Marx had left off, reading from an article in *Der Stürmer* which stated, 'The Jewish problem is not yet solved, nor will it be solved when one day the last Jew will have left Germany. Only when world Jewry has been annihilated, (*vernichtet*) will it have been solved.'

Streicher explained this extract by saying, 'If that is how you understand 'annihilation' (*vernichtung*). That was written by my chief editor at the time. He says that the Jewish problem will not yet be solved when the last Jew will have left Germany. And when he suddenly says that only when world Jewry has been annihilated will it be solved, then he certainly may have meant that the power of world Jewry should be annihilated. But my Party comrade Holz did not think of mass killing or the possibility of mass killing.'

Griffith – Jones – 'The German word used there is '*vernichtet*,' is it not? Look at your copy. '*Vernichtet*' that means 'to annihilate.'

Streicher – 'Today when you look back, you could interpret it like that, but not at that time.'[286]

Here, within Streicher's case, we are confronted with a microcosm of many of the issues that comprise what has come to be known as Holocaust Denial today. Not just in *Der Stürmer*, but in many Nazi documents and speeches, we find words such as *vernichtung*, *ausrottung* and *liquidierung* (to annihilate/destroy, to uproot/exterminate and to liquidate) being used in relation to the Jews. Streicher claimed that such extreme language was used metaphorically and either meant their removal from German territory or the destruction of their political and economic power, rather than their physical being. He also stated that such extremity of language was being used in response to equivalently virulent anti-German propaganda. In particular he referenced the little-known work 'Germany must Perish!' by American/Jewish author Theodore Kauffmann which advocated the compulsory sterilization of all Germans, due to the 'inbred lust of the German nation for

---

[283] ibid, p.335
[284] ibid, p.336
[285] ibid
[286] ibid, p.356

conquest and mass murder.'[287]

From the detachment of the present day, it does seem to be a flawed argument to suggest that on the one hand the Nazis were doing their utmost to exterminate the Jewish race while keeping it secret from the world and on the other, to suggest that Streicher was writing about these ongoing exterminations openly in his newspaper. Both can not be true. Either the Nazis were doing this and were happy to publicise it or Streicher was, as he claimed, writing metaphorically. It does not appear however that such a simple logical defence occurred either to Streicher or his lawyer.

Griffiths Jones continued to produce extracts from *Der Stürmer*, some of which contained very strongly worded sections such as, 'There must be a punitive expedition against the Jews in Russia...The Jews in Russia must be killed. They must be utterly exterminated.'

Such material is difficult to interpret in anything other than one way, although as will be demonstrated in later chapters, the situation regarding the Jews of Russia was slightly different to that of Jews in general, as far as the Nazis were concerned. After that quotation, Dr Marx spoke up with an objection.

'A number of extracts from *Der Stürmer* have been mentioned here which have been put before me for the first time.' he said, returning to the standard refrain of defence lawyers throughout the trial. 'Some of them are articles which have not been written by the defendant personally. Some are signed by Hiemer, and some by Holz, who was particularly radical in his manner of writing, and passages are being quoted which are perhaps taken out of context.'[288]

As publisher of *Der Stürmer*, Streicher accepted responsibility for its content, yet certain sub-editors were able to include items without his approval. The question here was whether it was just to condemn him for inciting hatred through extremity of language in articles he had not personally written. Legally, as editor-in-chief, it had to be acknowledged, if it could be shown that the paper did include incitement, the burden of guilt was his.

As the questioning continued, Streicher admitted reading about reported exterminations in the *Israelitisches Wochenblatt*, a Jewish newspaper he used to gather up to date information about those he opposed but he stated that he did not believe the reports and felt they were simple propaganda. (It should probably be pointed out that British intelligence thought exactly the same thing at the time.) As Griffiths-Jones' questioning continued and more and more extracts of *Der Stürmer* were produced, it became clear that it was on this matter that the prosecution case rested. Did Streicher know about the nature of the Final Solu- tion as the prosecution defined it and could it therefore be shown that he was partly responsible for its escala- tion via his publications?

It was a very difficult point to prove and such wooliness formed the central dilemma for the judges when the hearing finished and their deliberation discussions turned to Streicher. Judge Biddle asserted that it was 'preposterous' to call Streicher a conspirator just because he was 'a little Jew baiter'.[289] An American aide pointed out that 'Streicher might be a beastly man, but he had never actually killed anyone himself.'[290] Maxwell-Fyfe, in a clear reference to what is now called the Holocaust, insisted that Streicher should be hanged as an 'accessory before the fact.'[291] Stewart, another American aide, with an obvious penchant for gridiron terminology wrote, 'a cheerleader never carries the ball nor calls a play, yet by his continual goading of the crowd to frenzied excitement he is a personality in his team's success.'[292] Eventually, when the vote was taken, Biddle's views were accounted for and it was unanimously agreed that Streicher be cleared on Count One but declared guilty of Crimes against Humanity. Applying the law of the court in its strictest sense they then controversially agreed to put Streicher to death. In much of the analysis of the IMT that has been written since then, it is this piece of sentencing that draws the most criticism. According to Ann and John Tusa,

'there is a suspicion that Streicher was not judged strictly by the law but on the physical and moral revulsion

---

[287] Theodore N. Kauffmann *'Germany Must Perish!'* (Newark, N.J., Argyle press 1941), p.1. Library of Congress Call No.: DD222.K3 The book was by no means a bestseller, however the extremity of its message is partly reflected in the statements of President Roosevelt referenced in chapter two. Many allege however that its importance was deliberately overplayed by Nazis like Streicher for propaganda purposes.
[288] Nuremberg Trial Proceedings Vol. 12, 116th day, Monday, 29 April 1946, p.358
[289] Tusa, Ann and John, *'The Nuremberg Trial'* (Macmillan 1983) p.457
[290] ibid
[291] ibid
[292] Conot, p487.

he evoked.'[293] Such suspicion may have sat comfortably within the spirit and ethos of 1945, but it does not conform to any sort of sense of justice that would be subscribed to today.

The verdict clearly affected Streicher, who spent the next fifteen days awaiting his end, anxious and troubled in his cell. It is reported that he would frequently wake up shouting during the night, usually something about the Jews or 'spending Christmas in Valhalla.' When the day of his execution arrived he regained his composure and defiance, battling with the guards who came to wake and dress him. On the scaffold, before the gallows, he simmered with contempt and anger, firstly refusing to give his name, then spitting at sergeant John C. Woods, the American executioner. 'The Bolsheviks will hang you one day!' He cried. As the noose was fastened around his neck he shouted 'Purim Festival 1946!'[294] This was a reference to the Jewish 'Purim' holy day, which celebrates the deliverance of the ancient Jews from Haman, a Persian noble who, according to scripture, had devised a plan 'to destroy, to kill, and to cause to perish, all Jews, both young and old, little children and women' (Esther 3:13). This biblical final solution had been prevented due to God's intervention, whereupon Haman and his sons were hanged. Seconds before his death, Streicher was therefore displaying not only a sound grasp of Jewish religious mythology, but also a keen sense of allegory. His final words, before the trapdoor opened, the rope snapping taut, were 'Heil Hitler!'

Unfortunately, that is not the end of the Streicher story. There is a great deal of mystery surrounding the details of his (and some of the other defendants') execution. Official accounts of the time state that it was performed cleanly, yet there is a body of evidence to suggest otherwise. An article written months afterwards in the US Army 'Stag' magazine claimed that Woods 'used a short rope that prevented instantaneous death from a broken neck, instead insuring a slow death by strangulation. He built the trap door too small so that their facial features would be mutilated during the fall.'[295] American journalist Kingsbury Smith, of the International News Service, one of the few to witness the executions first-hand, wrote that, 'The trap opened with a loud bang. Streicher went down kicking. When the rope snapped taut with the body swinging wildly, groans could be heard from within the concealed interior of the scaffold. Finally, the hangman, who had de- scended from the gallows platform, lifted the black canvas curtain and went inside. Something happened that put a stop to the groans and brought the rope to a standstill. After it was over I was not in the mood to ask what he did, but I assume that he grabbed the swinging body and pulled down on it. We were all of the opin- ion that Streicher had strangled.' Ann and John Tusa also state that it took fourteen minutes for Streicher to die because his execution was 'deliberately slow.'[296] Donald E. Wilkes Jr, a Professor of Law at the University of Georgia Law School found some justification for this by saying, 'It was a grim, pitiless scene. But for those who had sat through the horrors and tortures of the trial, who had learned of men dangled from butcher hooks, of women mutilated and children jammed into gas chambers, of mankind subjected to degradation, destruction, and terror, the scene conjured a vision of stark, almost biblical justice.'[297]

This chapter began by saying that if Jew-hating was the Nazis biggest crime, then Streicher was the biggest criminal. But of course, that wasn't their biggest crime. Hating anybody, even for irrational reasons, is not criminal. Killing people or enslaving them or torturing them is, but Streicher did not do those things. Publishing what we in the twenty-first century describe as 'hate-speech' might be, by some standards, although it has to be balanced with the right to freedom of expression. Therefore, bearing in mind that Streicher's offence was the production of a newspaper, regardless of one's views of its content, an execution of any kind and in particular a deliberately botched one, is not something too many advocates of justice would countenance.

Friedrich Nietzsche once wrote, 'He who fights with monsters should be careful lest he thereby becomes a monster. And if you gaze for long into an abyss, the abyss gazes also into you.'[298]

One looks at Streicher's demise with modern eyes and wonders.

---

[293] Tusa, A&J, p457
[294] Conot, p. 506
[295] Stag Magazine, (Vol. 3, No. 1, December 1946)
[296] Tusa, p.486
[297] Tom Zeller jr. *'the Nuremberg hangings, not so smooth either'* Jan 17, 2007 New York Times, The Lede Blog http://theledeblog.blogs.nytimes.com/tag/criminaljustice/2007/01/07
[298] Friedrich Nietzsche, *Beyond Good and Evil*, (Dover Publications 1997), p.52

10

The Penitent Man

Have mercy upon me... according to thy loving kindness, according to the multitude of thy tender mercies, blot out my transgression. Wash me thoroughly from my iniquity, and cleanse me from my sin, for I acknowl- edge my transgression, and my sin is ever before me.

- Psalm 51 (5-14)

Albert Speer

On November 17th, 1945, only three days before the trial would begin, Albert Speer, Hitler's architect and Minister of Armaments called out to the guard of his tiny cell at the *Justizpalast* and asked for some paper and a pen. The guard obliged and he wrote the following, in capital letters, seven words to a line, as per the prison regulations:

'I am in possession of certain information as to military and technical questions that should be made known to the right persons.' Speer then followed this opening gambit with a few sentences outlining his knowledge of the arms industry and crucially, the mistakes Germany had made in the offensive against the USSR. It was a clever tactic.

Speer, whose reputation had been built on being astute and resourceful, had correctly guessed that in the inevitable post-war power-play between the USA and the USSR, the Americans would find the prospect of such information valuable. More transparently, he then turned to the future. In the case of the eventuality that he be imprisoned, he wrote, 'I should not fall into Russian hands. My knowledge should stay on this side of the fence.' He took this further by extrapolating that should he be executed, all that he knew would be lost. He then posted a reminder of how readily he had complied with and even facilitated the information gather- ing of his captors since his arrest. 'I myself have during this period not only given every possible informa- tion, but further still calmly dispelled the objections of my former colleagues towards open information.'
When he had finished, he folded the paper over and marked it; 'for transmission to Justice Jackson.'[299]

---

[299] Sections from letter quoted in Overy, *Interrogations*, p.139 and Persico, p.121

It was the first overt manoeuvre in what turned out to be a successful defence strategy – despite his wartime position near the top of the German hierarchy and his unquestioned implication in some of the charges, he would avoid the hangman's noose. Speer would later become known as 'the good Nazi'[300] and 'the Nazi who said sorry.'[301]

Speer's attitude had impressed his captors from day one. As early as June '45, while still being held in Mondorf, he was described by a Foreign Office official as being 'the one German who has shown possibilities of affording us assistance and inspiration...he is head and shoulders above our other captives.'[302] Airey Neave reported that Speer possessed 'charm and apparent ingenuity'.[303] Douglas Kelley, the prison psychiatrist for the first month, prior to the appointment of Goldensohn, was completely convinced of Speer's innocence, describing him as 'extremely intelligent, sensitive, creative...boyish in nature and concerned only with his work.'[304] It would be a mistake however to believe that Speer adopted this persona upon arriving in gaol, simply to save his own life. He, among all the twenty-two, was the most penitent. He was also the one most prepared to criticise the Nazi regime and in particular, Hitler. But this was not simply a prison-cell affectation.

Berthold Konrad Hermann Albert Speer began life as an architect, having grown up in Mannheim in South-Western Germany. Like so many of the men in the dock at Nuremberg, Speer joined the party after hearing Hitler speak, at a gathering in Berlin, in 1930. So inspired was he that he signed himself up without allegedly knowing much about the Nazi programme. Before long he was working as a party architect, renovating the district headquarters in Berlin in 1932 and then the Propaganda ministry for Goebbels. Goebbels recommended him to Hitler, who engaged Speer on a commission to work on the Reich Chancellery. Hitler was so impressed with his work that he made him Nazi Chief Architect in 1934, at which point he was still only twenty nine years old. They developed an instant rapport and it is often said that Hitler saw in Speer something he had once aspired to be himself, an artist and a visionary[305] and their relationship has been occasionally described with almost romantic undertones.[306] Allegedly, a friend of Speer's, who witnessed Hitler's daily over-the-shoulder absorption in his planning and drawings said, 'Do you know what you are? You are Hitler's unrequited love.'[307]

Together they dreamt up extravagant plans for Germany's future. The Berlin of the 'Thousand Year Reich' was to have a stadium which seated nearly half a million people, a hall which could hold 150,000, complete with an 825 foot dome, a 400 foot high arch, (fifty times bigger than the Arc de Triomphe) and a giant statue of a woman, some forty-six feet higher than the Statue of Liberty.[308]

On February 8th 1942, Fritz Todt, the Minister of Armaments and Munitions was killed in a plane crash. The vacated job really should have gone to Göring, as head of the Four Year Plan, but Speer convinced Hitler that this would be a mistake. Hitler called the *Reichsmarschall* to see him and informed him that the position would be given to Speer.[309]

Speer's influence with the Führer was obviously growing and some felt that it had grown disproportionately to his standing. He seemed able to dictate goings-on even outside of his given sphere of influence. An official in the Wehrmacht Armaments Office wrote at the time that, 'Speer is the only one who today can say anything. He can interfere in any department. He already disregards all other departments. We must join the Speer organisation and pull together, otherwise Speer will go his own way.'[310]

---

[300] Van der Vat, Dan, *The Good Nazi, the life and lies of Albert Speer* (Houghton-Mifflin 1997)
[301] Title of a BBC documentary, first broadcast on the 2nd May 1996.
[302] PRO, FO 371/46778, Kirkpatrick to Eden, 21st June 1945, with additional notes by Cavendish-Bentnick, 24th June 1945. Quoted Overy, *Interrogations* p.136
[303] Neave, p.139
[304] Douglas M Kelley, *22 Cells in Nuremberg: A Psychiatrist Examines the Nazi Criminals* (New York 1947) p.193-194
[305] Conot, p.239 & Davidson, p.484
[306] This is quite common in descriptions of Hitler's relationships with those around him. He seemed to provoke feelings of awe and adulation, which he returned with some kind of affection. In Gilbert's diary and other sources most of the defendants, including Hess and Göring, are described as being latent homosexuals at some point.
[307] Conot, p.240
[308] ibid
[309] Persico, p.162
[310] Conot, p.241

Speer's impossible task, in his new position, was to re-equip the German military within four months. Hitler had bitten off more than he could chew with Barbarossa and the entry into the war of the USA. Production of planes and weaponry were low – output of consumer products had maintained its pre-war level (due to a specific Hitler order) and the British and American levels of war production both dwarfed that of Germany. If imminent defeat was to be avoided, a rapid turnaround was required. Speer attacked this issue by redrawing priorities. The construction of new *Autobahns* (motorways) was halted and money was directed instead toward refurbishing railways which provided direct transport to the fronts. Speer was also responsible for the creation of the Central Planning Board, under whose auspices decisions were made to coordinate civilian and military production.[311]

Such was Speer's success at this task that while infrastructure crumbled and whole areas of the country descended into chaos and destitution under the whip of the Allied bombing campaign, German military production rose every year between 1942 and 1945. It is not an overstatement to suggest that Speer was probably the single most important man to the German war-effort in those final years, a fact later recognised by the American General F. L. Anderson who said, 'Had I known what this man was achieving, I would have sent out the entire American Eighth Air Force to put him underground.'[312] But Speer's success, no matter how impressive, served only to put a gloss on and ultimately extend a desperate situation. By 1945, Germany was being pushed back on all sides and the nation was close to being permanently crippled. Hitler, descending into fatalism in his bunker and with the publication of the Morgenthau Plan playing on his mind, ordered a 'scorched earth' policy, meaning that all industrial capability, as well as agriculture and important infrastructure, like bridges, be destroyed in the face of the advancing enemy, to prevent them from using it to their advantage or, in the case of the Soviets, dismantling them for transport home. This tactic, supported by Göring, Goebbels, Himmler and Bormann was designed to prolong the war as long as possible, in the hope that some last-minute way of ending the conflict through diplomacy or negotiation could be found, meaning that the Third Reich would be able to continue in some diminished form. There was, in fact, a serious belief at this time that the western Allies could be convinced to join Germany in a collaborative move against the USSR, thus completely transforming the pattern and outcome of the war. Such was Hitler's determination to give the Nazi era a chance of continued existence, that those who opposed him on this matter (for example soldiers who refused to dynamite bridges) were frequently executed.[313]

Yet Speer was able, at this stage, to use his position of favour with Hitler to advance an alternative point of view. 'I believe in the future of the German people...' He wrote, in a letter to the Führer on March 29th 1945. 'I can however no longer believe in the success of our affairs if in these decisive months at the same time, and according to plan, we destroy the substance of our people. That is so great an injustice...What generations have built up we are not permitted to destroy...Your order of March 19th takes away the last industrial possibilities and knowledge of it will throw the population into the greatest despair...I ask you therefore not to complete this act of destruction against your people.' The letter ended with the words, 'May God protect Germany.'[314]

Incredibly, rather than having the SS dispatched to shoot Speer as a traitor, which would have been the most likely outcome had the letter come from anyone else, Hitler actually heeded the Armaments Minister's words, passing a new decree on March 30th in which he watered down the scorched earth policy to one whereby demolitions were only to be carried out under immediate threat of enemy capture. Other plants and installations need only be paralysed, in the hope that a future resurgent form of the Reich could make them operational again when necessary.

Speer's position on this issue was indicative of his (justifiably) bleak view of German prospects. He was unique among Hitler's inner circle in that he felt that complete and total defeat was a certainty and that the priority should not be on securing advantageous terms for the Nazi regime, but for the future of the nation and its population, whoever their government might be. Such was his conviction on this point and his belief that Hitler would drag Germany down with him, that he actually claimed to have planned an assassination attempt on the Führer in February. The plan involved introducing poison gas into the air vents of Hitler's

---

[311] ibid
[312] Albert Speer, *Inside the Third Reich* (Book Club Associates, London, 1971) p.500
[313] Davidson, p.489
[314] ibid

bunker. This story, told to his interrogators at Nuremberg and confirmed by Armaments Ministry official, Dietrich Stahl, with whom Speer had collaborated on the scheme, served further to create distance (in the minds of the Allies) between Speer and the other defendants, especially Göring. In addition to killing Hitler, Stahl also claimed they had devised another plot to ambush and shoot Himmler, Goebbels and Bormann outside the Chancellery in Berlin, which sounded particularly unfeasible.[315] Speer's abilities in certain areas may have been considerable, but he was no assassin. No attempt was ever made to bring either plan out of the realms of fantasy.[316]

After Hitler's suicide, Speer could see the writing on the wall more clearly than most. Despite this he resisted the temptation to flee and joined the Flensburg government under Dönitz, as Minister for Economics. Shortly after Germany's surrender, he found himself called upon by the United States Strategic Bombing Survey, who were attached to Eisenhower's staff. On May 17th, the Americans simply turned up at the Castle of Glücksburg, belonging to the Duke of Holstein, where Speer and his family were staying and asked to have a conversation with him. Speer later wrote that they 'discussed the mistakes and peculiarities of bomb- ings on both sides.' These talks were to go on for nearly a week. He was personally thanked by General Anderson for participating in the discussions.[317]

Speer was taken prisoner early in the morning of May 23rd, by the British. A Sergeant strode into his room at the castle, greeted him and announced that he was being arrested. In what could be perceived as a gentlemanly gesture, the soldier unbuckled his belt, (holster and pistol still attached) and laid it casually on the table, informing Speer that he would be left alone for a few minutes to pack his things. The soldier then left, to wait outside, with the gun still in the room.[318] Speer chose not to take the quick way out however and before long was aboard a cargo plane, with the other members of the Flensburg government, being taken to Mondorf.

Unlike other captives, Speer was only at Mondorf for two weeks before being transferred to the Chesnay Palace, near Versailles, where he was kept along with other leading technicians, scientists, agricultural and railroad specialists. They were later moved from there to Kransberg Castle, near Frankfurt, formerly belong- ing to Göring, where Speer saw some other familiar faces – Hjalmar Schacht (soon to be a co-defendant), Professor Ferdinand Porsche (the car designer) and the flight and rocket genius, Wernher von Braun.[319] Speer quickly realised the game that was being played at Kransberg and told the other members of his department being held there 'to place our experience in the technology of armaments at their (the Americans) disposal.'[320]

When Speer learned that he was to be taken to Nuremberg and tried as a 'Major War Criminal' he was comforted by one of his guards, who told him 'You'll soon be acquitted and the whole thing forgotten.' Speer also described being touched by the 'kindly and troubled expression in the eyes of the British colonel as he bade me goodbye.'[321] It must have been difficult to swallow, as the jeep transported him to the *Justizpalast*. Despite his willingness to co-operate and give the Allies what they wanted, he was still to stand trial for the most serious crimes imaginable. Neave was eventually to indict Speer on all four counts.

From the beginnings of his captivity then, Speer had been identified as a compliant and helpful Nazi, one who was prepared to make concessions to and compromise with those who now controlled his fate. This, coupled with his pre-surrender reputation for being his own man, the only one in the regime who could stand up to Hitler, made him the perfect candidate for Gilbert's anti-Göring game when he was brought to Nuremberg. Speer scored a middle ranking 128 on Gilbert's IQ test and does not feature a great deal in the opening

---

[315] Speer himself never mentioned this second plan, either during interrogation or in his later publications.
[316] Overy, *Interrogations*, p.132-133
[317] Speer, p.499
[318] ibid, p.500
[319] Von Braun's case is an interesting one. Due to his technical abilities and the value of his knowledge – he had already pioneered various forms of jet fighters and rockets – he was taken back to the USA, naturalised as a US citizen and eventually put to work at NASA, where he served as director of the Marshall Space Flight Centre. He was never charged with any war crimes, despite his extensive use of slave labour and the fact he had held the rank of *Sturmbannführer* in the SS. Today, von Braun is remembered as the father of the US space flight programme. He was awarded the American National Medal of Science in 1975.
[320] Speer, p.503
[321] ibid, p.506

pages of Gilbert's diary. He first comes to prominence when Gilbert is doing the rounds after the showing of the 'Nazi Concentration Camps' film. His reaction was representative of the position he took throughout the trial. 'Speer showed no outward emotional effects,' Gilbert wrote 'but said that he was all the more resolved to acknowledge a collective personal responsibility of the Party leadership and absolve German people of the guilt.'[322]

Speer's participation in the courtroom was similarly muted to begin with, as his case was one of the last to be heard. It was not until the questioning of SD Chief Otto Ohlendorf, who described participating in ac-tions against Jews as part of the *Einsatzgruppen* activities, that Speer made an impact. The impact he then made however, was considerable. Dr Kuboschok (counsel for the Reich Cabinet) stood in momentraily for Speer's attorney, who was not available for court that day.

Dr Kuboschok – Witness, is it known to you that the Defendant Speer, contrary to Hitler's orders, took measures to prevent the destruction of industrial and other installations?
Ohlendorf: Yes.
Dr Kuboschok: That these measures also extended beyond the interior of Germany to the then still-occupied area of Upper Silesia, *et alla*?
Ohlendorf: I believe that the date when I learned about this was so late that, although applicable to some small areas in the West, it no longer applied to any area in the East.
Dr Kuboschok: One more question which you might perhaps know about. Do you know that the Defendant Speer prepared an attempt on Hitler's life in the middle of February of this year?
Ohlendorf: No.[323]

Kubuschok's third question here sent the court into uproar. The defendants seemed not to believe what they had heard and 'looked at each other in bewilderment.'[324] When the court recessed, Göring charged across the dock to confront Speer and an angry quarrel resulted – later that night, in his cell, Göring commented, 'Damn that stupid fool, Speer! Did you see how he disgraced himself in court today? … How could he stoop so low as to do such a rotten thing to save his lousy neck!'[325]

Speer, on the other hand, realised the implications of his revelation. '…Well, the bomb exploded today.' He said, to Gilbert. '… it is going to be a little tough for me now,'[326] before going on to relate yet another of his fanciful schemes, in which he claimed to have planned to kidnap the ten party leaders, including Hitler, Himmler, Goebbels, Bormann, Keitel and Göring and carry them on a plane to England. It would seem that despite the pressures of high office and the weight of responsibility for maintaining production, during the final days of the war Speer managed to find plenty of time in which to engage his imagination.

From here, Gilbert saw the thin edge of a wedge that could be driven home for Allied advantage. Speer had already shown a willingness to fit in with the prosecution's agenda, rather than that of his co-defendants. One or two others, particularly Schacht, made similar noises. Gilbert's visits to Speer became more frequent and their chats seemed to take on a more informal air. Before long they had hatched their plan to undermine the 'Göring front', the idea having arisen from a conversation in Speer's cell, over the weekend of January 12th -13th. Speer had begun by remarking scornfully on the superficiality of the defendants' comradeship and the insincerity of their dealings with each other. He even used himself as an example. 'I visited Göring's birthday party, for instance, even when I was working furiously against him because of his reckless and ne-glectful policies.' He then extended this analysis to his former colleagues. 'It would be a good thing if they would drop their masks and let Germany see the rottenness of the whole system.'[327]

After brief agreement from Gilbert, Speer resumed by saying, 'You know it is not a very good idea to let the defendants eat and walk together. That is how Göring keeps whipping them into line. It would be much better if they weren't intimidated from saying what they feel, so that the people will be rid once and for all of

---

[322] Gilbert, p.47
[323] Nuremberg Trial Proceedings, Vol. 4, 26th day, Thursday 3rd January 1946, p.342
[324] Gilbert, p.102
[325] ibid, p.102-3
[326] ibid
[327] Gilbert, p.121

the last rotten remains of their illusions about National Socialism. There are Germans who have gone to America and become good democrats; why not here?'[328]

This pivotal passage from Gilbert's diary either demonstrates chicanery on Speer's part or staggering naivety. Did he really believe that disingenuousness and behind-the-scenes politicking were only to be found in the government of Nazi Germany? Did he really think that the statesman of the 'good democracies' behaved so differently? To anyone with the remotest knowledge of political behaviour in nations like the USA and the UK, where it is arguable that the democratic process leads to greater insincerity, due to the need to say what is publicly popular, even if it is not the intention to follow it through, this kind of reasoning would be laughable.[329] It is just not possible that a man who had worked as a national civil servant for over a decade (and was credited with being some sort of minor genius) could be so simple minded. What is surely displayed here is a carefully judged ploy from Speer – another manoeuvre in his attempt to ingratiate himself further with those who controlled his future by saying what he thought they wanted to hear.

Speer's idea of prisoner separation was soon put into practice, meaning the inmates lost the right to communicate during exercise periods and were split up at lunch. He expressed his satisfaction with the new regime to Gilbert,[330] even seeming to relish it, saying with regard to the lunch rooms, 'I see you put Funk and von Schirach with me and Fritzsche. Obviously we two will sooner or later win those two over to taking a forthright stand against Hitler.' Gilbert responded by suggesting he put Dönitz with them too, to which Speer reacted negatively, saying, '…I feel a little inhibited when Dönitz is around.'[331]

With new freedom to rehearse and promote his (and Gilbert's agenda), Speer began to feel comfortable. On the weekend of February 23rd, he said that he was now 'much freer to plan his defence,' and that he wanted to 'denounce Hitler and the whole Nazi State for the fraud that it was.'[332] After Göring's performance on the stand (which even Speer had to admit was impressive) he repeated himself. 'Let the whole damn Nazi system and all who participated in it, including myself, go down with the ignominy and disgrace it deserves.'[333] Later, however, after the testimonies of Von Ribbentrop and Keitel, Speer complained that his fellow defendants were doing too well. He felt that they were 'not being unmasked' and instead were making a 'graceful exit as loyal nationalists.' Gilbert stated that at this stage, Speer was concerned that 'his own line of attack would fall flat.'[334] This was to be Speer's last moment of hesitation. Later in the trial, both von Schirach and Raeder delivered testimony that was damaging to the Göring front and from that point on Speer recovered his self assurance.

Speer did not actually testify until the 19th June and like so many of the cases at the IMT, his began with a complaint from his defence counsel, Dr Hans Flachsner, who said, 'I am not in possession of all the interrogatories I sent out. I have only received part of them. I will use those replies which are at my disposal to the best of my ability in the examination of the defendant.'[335] Flachsner was not actually complaining about the practice of the tribunal here, but rather the culture that the trial had created. Many of the requests for information he had sent out to former colleagues or associates of Speer had been declined, mainly through the recipients' fear of then being indicted themselves, for future trials.[336] The basis of the case which he had planned to make was therefore no longer available to him. Faced with having to do the best he could regardless, Flachsner began with a series of questions aimed at getting Speer to describe his upbringing and early career as well as the nature of the work in which he was engaged by the party. Judge Lawrence became quickly bored by the questioning and began to interject, urging Flachsner to get to the point.

From the point of view of the law that had been created for Nuremberg, the issues surrounding Speer

---

[328] ibid
[329] The awareness of the importance of 'public image' to politicians has obviously grown exponentially with the development of the mass media, particularly television, but this does not mean it was not also a factor prior to television's ubiquitousness, when cinema newsreels and newspapers performed the same function. Also, on a basic level, the sort of intra-personal insincerity that Speer is describing is common to any organisation where people have to work together.
[330] Gilbert, p.155
[331] ibid, p.160
[332] ibid, p.166
[333] ibid, p.211
[334] ibid, p.240
[335] Nuremberg Trial Proceedings, Vol.16, 158th day, Wednesday 19th June 1946, p.428
[336] Conot, p.429

were not complicated. They hinged on his use of forced labour and he knew it. In his testimony and cross examination, he did not try to dodge the issue. He admitted that he had known that most of the workforce supplied to him had been brought to Germany against their will, but attempted mitigation by saying 'I had no influence on the method by which workers were recruited. If the workers were being brought to Germany against their will that means, as I see it, that they were obliged by law to work for Germany. Whether such laws were justified or not, that was a matter I did not check at the time. Besides, this was no concern of mine. On the other hand, by application of force and terror I understand police measures, such as raids and arrests, and so on. I did not approve of these violent measures...'[337]

Speer therefore described a scenario in which he did not govern or organise the recruitment of foreign workers (the total of whom under his authority was put at fourteen million), as this was Sauckel's job. But through his applying pressure to Sauckel for more labour, knowing that 'violent measures' were being used to obtain it, he was openly admitting his culpability under count three (section H – Conscription of Civilian Labour). Jackson's subsequent and gentle cross examination dealt mainly with counts three and four, giving further indication of where the prosecution felt Speer's case rested. At one point he asked 'You also knew the policy of the Nazi Party and the policy of the Government towards the Jews, did you not?' Speer's answer, in common with every other defendant at the trial was, 'I knew that the National Socialist Party was anti-Semitic, and I knew that the Jews were being evacuated from Germany.'[338]

In further questioning, Speer admitted that he 'had no objection' to the 'deportation of 100,000 Jews from Hungary for subterranean airplane factories.'[339] He also saw no objection to sending 'slackers' to concentration camps. However he denied knowing that concentration camps were places of mass murder, or deliberate starvation, saying that he knew they were 'tough places to be put' but 'but not to the extent which has been revealed in this Trial.'[340]

In keeping with the amicable exchange that characterised his cross examination, Jackson finished his questioning by helping Speer to summarise his own defence. With a question that clearly demonstrated the prosecution's positive disposition toward Speer, he asked, 'Well, your point is, I take it, that you as a member of the Government and a leader in this period of time acknowledge a responsibility for its large policies, but not for all the details that occurred in their execution. Is that a fair statement of your position?'

'Yes, indeed.' Speer replied.[341]

Speer's position as the 'nice Nazi' was largely undamaged, and arguably even boosted by his time on the stand. Judge Biddle described him as 'the most humane and decent of the defendants.' Maxwell-Fyfe said he was 'by far the most attractive personality among the defendants.'[342] Fyfe also reported in his autobiography that his wife was 'profoundly impressed by Speer's evidence and manner.'[343]

After his individual case had finished, Speer maintained his stance of opposition to Hitler, Nazism and everything he had once worked for right until the end. Never was this shown more clearly than when, during the closing statements of the trial, Lord Hartley Shawcross concluded the British prosecution by saying that 'each of the defendants is legally guilty' and so were 'the people of Germany...in large measure.' He finished his vindictive tirade with a quote he wrongly attributed to Goethe[344], saying of the German nation that 'some day fate would strike them because they betrayed themselves and did not want to be what they are. It is sad that they do not know the charm of truth; that mist, smoke and berserk immoderation are so dear to them; pathetic that they ingeniously submit to any mad scoundrel who appeals to their lowest instincts, who confirms them in their vices and teaches them to conceive nationalism as insolence and brutality.'

Shawcross followed this by saying, 'With what a voice of prophesy he spoke,' and then, gesturing toward the dock, 'for these are the mad scoundrels who did these very things.'[345]

This combination of anti-German rhetoric and pantomime polemicism angered the defendants, who had

---

[337] Nuremberg Trial Proceedings, Vol.16, 159th day, Thursday 20th June 1946, p.456
[338] Nuremberg Trial Proceedings, Vol.16, 160th day, Friday 21st June 1946, p.517
[339] ibid, p.519
[340] ibid, p.516
[341] ibid, p.562
[342] Taylor, p.454
[343] ibid
[344] The words were actually written by Thomas Mann, in his novel, *Lotte in Weimar* (1939)
[345] Nuremberg Trials Proceedings, Vol. 19, 188th day, Saturday 27th July, 1946 p.527

already been upset by Jackson's closing statement. 'Compared to him (Shawcross), even Jackson was a charming fellow,' said von Ribbentrop.[346] Göring said, 'It's just as if we hadn't made any defence at all.' Even Schacht said that 'both Jackson and Shawcross had made miserable speeches, so biased and unfair.'[347] Speer, of course, disagreed. Like a court minstrel, skipping and singing his master's favourite song, he told Gilbert he was 'delighted with the speech, after all the stupid nonsense of the defence attorneys, each one trying to make his client look like a helpless, innocent man.'[348]

Historians continue to debate whether Speer was genuine in his condemnation of the regime he had been a part of, as had been the popular view, or whether it was simply survival instinct. Telford Taylor felt that Speer developed this stance as a strategy. 'He came to the trial exceedingly well prepared,' he wrote. 'He had been interrogated unceasingly, not only by the prosecution, but also by a string of military, administrative, engineering and other visitors greedy for full information of the German war machine...Thoughtful defendants can often profit from the questions and reactions of their interrogators...this experience aided Speer in framing his strategy for the trial.'[349] Robert Conot stated that 'Speer proved himself to be the cleverest of the accused,' and that a former colleague of Speer's had described him as 'a masterful liar.'[350] Joachim Fest described Speer's position during the trial as an 'attempt to escape responsibility behind his role as a technocrat.'[351] Others went even further. Hugh R. Trevor Roper called Speer 'the real criminal of Nazi Germany,' because 'for ten years he sat at the very centre of political power but did nothing (to avert criminal actions).'[352]

With regard to sentencing, Airey Neave believed that Speer's case was 'not a question of guilt or innocence, but one of mitigation.'[353] And it seemed to be so regarded by the judges, who felt that Speer's implication in the slave labour charge was unquestioned. Documentary evidence had already proven his guilt on that count even before he had admitted to it on the stand. The French and British delegations were inclined towards leniency because of Speer's anti-Hitler activities and his willingness to co-operate. Biddle however, initially agreed with Nikitchenko who obviously wanted Speer hanged.[354] Something persuaded him to change his mind almost instantly and in the second discussion he joined the other western powers in favouring a prison sentence. As a result Speer was pronounced guilty of war crimes and crimes against humanity. He was given twenty years.

In subsequent analysis, there has been much disagreement over Speer's sentence. If Speer's case is compared to Streicher's, for example, we see that Speer was found guilty on two counts and Streicher only on one. Speer's culpability was based on action – he had actually run a state department which made heavy use of slave labour and therefore contributed to the mistreatment of millions of people. Streicher simply published a newspaper, read by hundreds of thousands. Yet Streicher was hanged, while Speer was released from prison in 1966 and went on to become a bestselling author and something of a celebrity, appearing on television and being interviewed by Playboy; a professional *nestbeschmutzer*[355]. Even more striking is the comparison made between the cases of Speer and Fritz Sauckel (Plenipotentiary for Labour, to be discussed later). Both were implicated in the slave labour charge – Sauckel for actually organising the round-ups and deportations, Speer for demanding them. In terms of the Nazi hierarchy, Speer operated as Sauckel's immediate superior. They worked in close partnership. Yet Speer lived and Sauckel hanged.

Airey Neave recognised this discrepancy. Interestingly, he saw it in terms of class bias, 'Why should Sauckel who procured foreign workers for the trial be the more guilty?' he wrote, 'I was struck by the contemptuous attitudes of many at Nuremberg to the proletarian Sauckel.'[356]

Richard Overy agreed with Neave. 'I think for many of the prosecution team,' he said, 'many of those

---

[346] Taylor, p.497
[347] Gilbert, p.423
[348] ibid, p.424
[349] Taylor, p.450
[350] Conot, p.433
[351] Fest, p.314
[352] Hugh Trevor-Roper, *Last Days of Hitler*. Quoted in Fest, p.313
[353] Neave, p.343
[354] The Soviets favoured death sentences for all the defendants, hence 'obviously'.
[355] This is a derogatory German word meaning 'denigrator of one's own country' or 'traitor'.
[356] Neave, p.344

who interrogated Speer and came into contact with him, they came away with a sense that here is somebody very much like us. He could have been the bureaucrat down the office. He could be the judicial official they were having lunch with, where it was very difficult to feel that way about many of the other people in the dock.' Similarly, the American prosecutor Whitney Harris said of Speer, '…if he had manifested any other attitude his sentence would have definitely been death. That's the mitigating factor – his willingness to recognize the evil of the regime…'[357]

In any analysis of the Trial of the Century, this again provides cause for concern. It would seem that the Tribunal and in particular, those who held the most weighty of its responsibilities, namely deciding on the fate of the defendants, allowed personal feelings and political morality to cloud their judgements. Sentencing was not based solely (as it should have been) on the crimes proven to have been committed, but also on quaint ideals of decency or impressions of the individual's character. The frequently stated fear of Birkett and Jackson, that the defendants might use Nuremberg as a launch-pad to reignite German faith in Nazism also played a part in the decision making process. It must be borne in mind that if the Nazi ideology had survived, in any meaningful form, post-Nuremberg, then the purposes of the post war German policy, as laid out by Potsdam (democratization, denazification etc) would not have been served. Nuremberg would have failed. It made sense, therefore, on that level, to ensure that all the unrepentant Nazis, the ones who had the potential to lead a resurgence, were gotten rid of, regardless of implication or guilt. Speer had offered many unequivocal assurances, since the first days of German surrender, that he did not fit that category. By removing himself as a threat to the American led, post-war order, he also removed the need for him to be killed.

For some, like Streicher and Sauckel, this unlawlike attitude to sentencing spelled disaster. But for one man, who for a long while had been Adolf Hitler's closest friend and confidante, yet had turned against him as the war was lost and then denounced him before the world, it meant redemption.

---

[357] Harris and Overy speaking on BBC TV – *Nuremberg, Nazis on Trial: Albert Speer*, first shown on BBC2 on the 25th September 2006, 9pm

11

I am Kaltenbrunner, the big, bad man…[358]

Ernst Kaltenbrunner

No defendant before the IMT personified the stereotype of Nazi evil as perfectly as Ernst Kaltenbrunner. Not only did he arrive with a fearsome reputation, based on an early career of dealing out beatings, tapping telephones and instigating riots[359] (it was even alleged that Himmler had been afraid of him)[360] but he looked the part too, being just under six feet six inches tall, with a lean, hollow face, riven with an ugly scar on the left cheek.[361] The prosecutor Thomas Dodd described him as 'a crummy-looking creature, really an evil-looking man.'[362] Rebecca West wrote in the New Yorker that he 'looked like a vicious horse.'[363] Leon Goldensohn, after his first meeting with the former SS *Obergruppenführer* noted his '…calmness and well-mannered attitudes' which he thought to be 'indicative of a capacity for harsh, ruthless action, if such would have been the possibility.'[364] His case was to provide several of the most pivotal and consequential moments of the entire trial.

---

[358] Goldensohn, p.140. This is Kaltenbrunner's sarcastic description of himself during one of his early chats with the psychiatrist.
[359] Persico, p.153
[360] On 13th April 1945, the chief of the foreign intelligence service, Schellenberg, asked Himmler to receive a representative of the Zionist organization, The World Jewish Congress, a Mr Storsch, from Stockholm and Himmler said, 'But how am I going to do that in regard to Kaltenbrunner? I shall then be completely at his mercy!' *(2990-PS). From Kaltenbrunner's indictment.*
[361] Kaltenbrunner said the scar had come from duelling, while a student. (He was known to be a top-quality fencer, so this is not out of the question). Although a rumour persisted that he had really picked it up in a drink driving incident. (He was also known to be a heavy drinker, so equally possible.)
[362] Dodd, p.284
[363] Taylor, p.360
[364] Goldensohn, p.139

Kaltenbrunner was the highest ranking, surviving member of the SS (*Schutzstaffel* – literally 'defensive staff'). His immediate superiors for most of his career, Heinrich Himmler and the man now known as the 'the architect of the Final Solution', Reinhard Heydrich, were both dead. Kaltenbrunner therefore was being tried as a substitute for his more infamous, erstwhile colleagues. This meant that more so than the other defendants, his case was not one of individual crimes, but one in which he would be held responsible for the criminality of his organisation. It was a heavy responsibility to bear as by the end of the war, he also presided over the Gestapo and the SD (*Sicherhietdienst*), giving him the longest rap-sheet of any defendant. The stack of Allied-gathered documentary evidence relevant to his case was huge – he was heavily implicated in War Crimes through the *Waffen SS* combat activities[365] and also for staffing the concentration camps and forming the *Einsatzgruppen*. Most of what has come to be known as the Holocaust was alleged to have occurred through areas officially under Kaltenbrunner's jurisdiction.

Ernst Kaltenbrunner was born into a family of lawyers in 1903 in Ried im Innkreis (near Linz in Austria). In 1921 he went to Graz University and studied Chemico-Technical sciences at the Institute of Technology. Later on, when his father became seriously ill and the possibility arose that he might have to take over the solicitor's practice, he studied law, graduating as a Doctor of Law and Political Science in 1926. Kaltenbrun- ner joined the Party in 1932, having been involved with other nationalist movements such as the Non-Partisan Movement for the Protection of the Austrian Homeland, for several years, during which he had been an outspoken advocate of Anschluss. Upon joining the party he was quickly pointed toward the SS where he became the *Gauredner* (district speaker) and *Rechtsberater* (legal consultant) of the SS division VIII. In 1934 he and other leading Austrian Nazis were arrested by the Dollfus regime and thrown into the Kaiserstein-bruch Concentration Camp. The following year he was arrested again for conspiracy against the government and served six months in prison. On March 12th 1938, as a reward for his assistance in the Anschluss, Hitler promoted him to *Brigadeführer*. By September of the same year he had been promoted again, to *Gruppenführer* and after the assasination of Heydrich, in June 1942, he was made chief of the RSHA (*Reichssicherheitshauptamt* – Reich Security Main Office). By the end of the war he was SS *Obergruppenführer* and General of the Police, Chief of the Security Police and the SD, his roles having grown in significance after the assassination attempt against Hitler in July 1944.[366] Unlike some of the other defendants therefore, Kaltenbrunner's indictment was entirely justified, without at this stage analysing any of the evidence presented. On the list of crimes that had been drawn up, Kaltenbrunner's various positions within the Nazi hierarchy placed him in the unenviable role of being more culpable than anyone.

Like Streicher, Kaltenbrunner's reputation was such that he found himself shunned by the other defendants. Men who saw themselves as respectable statesmen, or noble soldiers, did not wish to be associated with rabble rousers, thugs and semi-demonic special forces operatives. After being absent due to poor health at the beginning of the trial, Kaltenbrunner eventually entered the courtroom on December 10th. On arriving in the dock, he extended his hand to General Jodl, who did not take it. He greeted and was blanked by both Frank and Keitel. Even his own lawyer, Kurt Kauffman (a former Nazi himself) would not shake his hand.[367]

During the early stages of the trial, as the prosecution presented its evidence, several witnesses, either through affidavit or direct testimony were to provide statements relevant to Kaltenbrunner's case. Possibly the most significant was that provided by Dieter Wisliceny, a thirty-four year old SS officer attached to Adolf Eichmann's staff. He had been interrogated in Nuremberg on the 15th November 1945 by Lieutenant Colonel Brookhart of the United States, and had furnished the American with a signed affidavit[368] which detailed his knowledge of the 'Final Solution to the Jewish question'. On the 3rd January 1946, as the Allied lawyers were presenting their evidence, he was brought into court and questioned as a prosecution witness by Brookhart. Brookhart had obviously carefully pre-arranged the questions so as not to confuse his witness – Wisliceny's answers in court amounted, in large parts, to an almost verbatim repetition of what can be read in his affida-

---

[365] The SS were highly regarded as fighting men. German generals like Eberhard von Mackensen attested to their courage and effectiveness in combat. Their percentage of losses was considerably higher than that of the regular army, due to their use on particularly dangerous assignments. Davidson, p.315

[366] Kaltenbrunner's biographical details taken from Davidson, p.322, Persico p.153-4 and the beginning of Kaltenbrunner's own testimony, Nuremberg Trial Proceedings, Volume 11, 105th day, Thursday, 11th April 1946, p.232

[367] Persico, p.155

[368] The Wisliceny affidavit can be read on the University of the West of England's website, here: http://www.ess.uwe.ac.uk/genocide/Wisliceny.htm

vit.

He made several hugely influential statements during this testimony. When asked about the time periods involved in attempting to solve the Jewish question, he said, 'Until 1940 the general policy within the section was to settle the Jewish question in Germany and in areas occupied by Germany by means of a planned emigration. The second phase, after that date, was the concentration of all Jews, in Poland and in other territories occupied by Germany in the East, in ghettos. This period lasted approximately until the beginning of 1942. The third period was the so called 'final solution' of the Jewish question, that is, the planned extermination and destruction of the Jewish race; this period lasted until October 1944, when Himmler gave the order to stop their destruction.'[369]

Wisliceny then stated that he had been personally informed by Adolf Eichmann of the order from Himmler to exterminate the Jews:

> 'Eichmann told me he could show me this order in writing if it would soothe my conscience. He took a small volume of documents from his safe, turned over the pages, and showed me a letter from Himmler to the Chief of the Security Police and the SD. The gist of the letter was roughly as follows: The Führer had ordered the final solution of the Jewish question; the Chief of the Security Police and the SD and the Inspector of Concentration Camps were entrusted with carrying out this so-called final solution. All Jewish men and women who were able to work were to be temporarily exempted from the so-called final solution and used for work in the concentration camps. This letter was signed by Himmler himself. I could not possibly be mistaken since Himmler's signature was well known to me...'[370]

Wisliceny mentioned that at the time the order had been written, the RSHA had been run by Heydrich. Brookhart then asked him, 'Did the program under this order continue with equal force under Kaltenbrunner?' Wisliceny replied, 'Yes; there was no diminution or change of any kind.'[371] Wisliceny's response therefore directly identified Kaltenbrunner as the defendant with most responsibility for the Jewish genocide.

Beyond Kaltenbrunner's case, Wisliceny's testimony had a far reaching impact on the development of the wider historical record. He was the only Nazi to testify before the IMT to the existence of a written order, emanating from the tip of the Nazi state pyramid, to exterminate the Jews. Most importantly, not only did he claim to have knowledge of this order or to have heard about it, but to have actually seen and read it himself. Other aspects of his testimony were similarly consequential. Although much of what he said was hearsay, simply repetition of things Eichmann had allegedly told him, Wisliceny explained his first hand knowledge of the Jewish deportations from Hungary, Slovakia, Greece, Bulgaria and Croatia. He also provided estimates as to the numbers of deportees who were chosen for labour and those who were selected for the 'final solu- tion' although he would not necessarily have been in a position to know this directly from his duties and it must be assumed that this is something else told him by Eichmann. After his questioning by Brookhart, which served mainly to rehash his affidavit, Wisliceny's part in the trial was all but over. Of the German defence lawyers, only Babel, counsel for the SS took the opportunity to cross examine. What he did was barely worthy of the name. Babel asked five questions, of no consequence whatsoever, aimed solely at demonstrating that it would be possible for SS officers outside of Eichmann's department to be unaware of what was happening.

In addition to Wisliceny's testimony, similarly important evidence was provided by Otto Ohlendorf, who commanded the SS *Einsatzgruppen* unit D in the Ukraine (to be discussed in chapter 17) and Erich von dem Bach-Zelewski, an SS *Obergruppenführer* and General in the *Waffen* SS who, from 1942, controlled the anti-partisan war in the Eastern territories and was instrumental in crushing the uprising of the Warsaw ghetto. Bach-Zelewski is an interesting case to briefly examine. Like Wisliceny his testimony would be damning, however unlike Wisliceny, whose IMT testimony resulted in him being tried and executed in Czechoslovakia in 1948, Bach-Zelewski was never tried for any War Crimes, despite his admissions regarding his own in- volvement in anti-Semitic actions. There appears to be no firm explanation for this by mainstream history.

---

[369] Nuremberg Trial Proceedings, Vol 4, 26th day, Thursday 3rd January 1946, p.356
[370] ibid, p.357
[371] ibid p.359

Richard Overy skirted the issue and wrote that Bach-Zelewski 'succeeded in persuading his captors of his good faith,'[372] which seems highly implausible, bearing in mind what he admitted to on the stand. A far stronger probability would appear to be that the Allies struck some sort of testimony-for-clemency deal with him. Bach-Zelewski, in contradiction to statements made by other Nazis in court stated that 'The principal task of the *Einsatzgruppen* of the Sicherheitspolizei was the annihilation of the Jews, gypsies, and political commissars.' When asked to confirm that the *Einsatzgruppen* were not, in fact, anti-partisan units, he said, 'For anti-partisan activities formations of the Waffen-SS, of the Ordnungspolizei, and above all, of the Wehrmacht were used.'[373] Bach-Zelewski was then asked by the Russian prosecutor, Pokrovsky, about the *Einsatzgruppe* B unit working in and around Smolensk, despite the fact that they had not been under his control. When asked if he received reports of their activities he said 'Not directly, but I managed to see them.'[374] He went on to detail their excesses to the court. Despite his earlier demarcation of actions against partisans and actions against Jews, he also said, 'in individual partisan groups Jews did participate, in numbers corresponding to the size of the Jewish population.'[375] Towards the end of his testimony, in a line that so encapsulated the ethos of the tribunal that it reads as if it were scripted, he claimed to have realised that the civilian actions were the inevitable result of Nazi ideology. 'If for years, for decades, a doctrine is preached to the effect that the Slav race is an inferior race, that the Jews are not even human beings, then an explosion of this sort is inevitable.'[376]

The prosecution did not depend solely on the perpetrator testimonies of SS men, however. Extremely powerful evidence of *Einsatzgruppen* activities was also provided by a particular piece of eyewitness testimony, which has gone on to assume great importance, not just to the IMT but to history in general. It was presented on Wednesday January 2nd, during Colonel Robert Storey's prosecution of the Gestapo. An affidavit was read to the court which had been obtained from Hermann Friedrich Graebe, a builder employed by the Wehrmacht in a civilian capacity in the occupied Ukraine. The witness was not presented for cross examination, but his words have become legendary, finding their way into a broad range of Holocaust literature, including school text books.

'Armed Ukrainian militia drove the people off the trucks...All these people had the regulation yellow patches on the front and back of their clothes and thus could be recognised as Jews...men, women and children of all ages – had to undress upon the order of an SS man, who carried a dog or riding whip...Without screaming or weeping the people undressed, stood in family groups, kissed each other, said farewells and waited for a sign from another SS man, who stood near the pit, also with a whip in his hand. During the 15 minutes that I stood near the pit I heard no complaint or plea for mercy. I watched a family...An old woman with snow-white hair was holding the one-year old child in her arms and singing to it, tickling it. The child was cooing with delight...The father was holding the hand of a boy about ten years old and speaking to him softly; the boy was fighting his tears. The father pointed toward the sky, stroked his head and seemed to explain something to him...I walked around the mound and found myself confronted with a tremendous grave. People were closely wedged to- gether and lying on top of each other...I estimated that it already contained about 1000 people. I looked for the man who did the shooting. He was an SS man, who sat at the edge of the narrow end of the pit, his feet dangling into the pit. He had a tommy gun on his knees and was smoking a cigarette. The people, completely naked, went down some steps which were cut in the clay wall of the pit and clambered over the heads of the people lying to the place where the SS directed them. They lay down in front of the dead or injured people...Then I heard a series of shots...Blood was running from their necks...The next batch was approaching already. They went down into the pit, lined themselves up
against the previous victims and were shot....'[377]

---

[372] Overy, *Interrogations*, p.181
[373] Nuremberg Trial Proceedings, Vol.4, 28th day, 7th January 1946, p.476
[374] ibid, p.480
[375] ibid, p.486
[376] ibid, p.493 Interestingly, Eugene Davidson stated that Bach-Zelewski 'was not one of the most reliable witnesses' although he does not explain why. The comment appears in a footnote on p.565 of his book.
[377] Nuremberg Trial Proceedings, Vol. 1, p.236

Like the Höss affidavit to be discussed shortly, Graebe's evidence became a cornerstone of the Holocaust narrative. Whereas Höss provided the basic story, as it is still relayed today, of the gas chamber process, Graebe provided the narrative as it is still told regarding the *Einsatzgruppen*. Telford Taylor confirmed the affidavit's importance, stating that its influence is so great because 'few eyewitness accounts of the mass killings have come to light.'[378] Indeed, such was the impact of the document that it was referred to throughout the trial and reread, in its entirety by the chief British prosecutor, Sir Hartley Shawcross, during his closing address. He even returned to it right at the end, as he addressed the bench to conclude the entire British case.

> **Shawcross** – You will remember when you come to give your decision the story of Graebe, but not in vengeance-in a determination that these things shall not occur again. 'The father'-do you remember?- 'pointed to the sky, and seemed to say something to his boy.'
> **The President** – The Tribunal will adjourn.[379]

It was also explicitly referenced in the IMT judgement document, in the section on the persecution of the Jews. 'The massacres of Rowno and Dubno, of which the German engineer Graebe spoke, were examples of one method (of genocide)'[380] it read.

Despite the affidavit's fame and influence, however, one cannot help but feel that had Graebe been put on the stand and the defence given the opportunity to cross examine (and had the defence lawyers been more skilled in cross examination) they could have questioned from various angles. How was it, for example, from the witness' opinion, that blind panic and hysteria did not occur? How on earth did the Nazis manage to create such a response from their victims? If the individuals concerned knew they were about to die, which Graebe's testimony suggests, surely they would make a desperate last-ditch attempt at life, rather than line- up politely and await the end? It is arguable obviously, that as a builder, Graebe would have been unable to comment on these kinds of psychological issues, although a more detailed probing of exactly what he had seen may have helped to shed light upon them.

Possibly most important to try to discover would have been that if this, as alleged by the prosecution, was part of a secret plan to exterminate all the Jews of Europe, why were the SS happy to have a builder watching them carry out this task for fifteen minutes? In the affidavit he stated himself that he 'was surprised he was not ordered away.' Conceivably, an action involving the shooting of a gang of partisans would have beneficial effects if local spectators were allowed. It would send a powerful message and act as a deterrent to others considering resistance. But the mass execution of women and children and babies? There could be no possible value in allowing outsiders to watch.

Bearing in mind that establishing a more detailed picture of the mechanics of the operation was not achieved in court, the modern day analyst or reader finds themselves confronted with a glaring issue. Rather than simply presenting the facts as observed by the witness, as one would expect in a trial of such serious- ness, the affidavit contained overt appealing to emotion. The descriptions of the family, the baby 'cooing' and the father telling his son about heaven have been included purely to tug at the heart strings. They offer nothing to the court in terms of establishment of fact regarding what the *Einsatzgruppen* did. The thumbnail portrait of the mean Nazi gunman, nonchalantly shooting civilians (incredibly accurately - all shots resulted in victims bleeding from the neck) with a cigarette hanging from his mouth, like a bandit in a western, stirs a similar response. From a purely rational, legal point of view, this all seems rather contrived. As with the Concentration Camps film, there is therefore much about the Graebe affidavit that is prejudicial, as if the stirring of an emotional response and not the solid presentation of events was its intention.

Despite the prominent place it has been accorded in Holocaust history, this affidavit, like so many others, must be read with caution. Unlike Höss, or any of the other Germans from whom evidence was obtained at the interrogation centres like Oberürsel, Graebe was not coerced. He did not need to be. Hermann Graebe in fact had a long history of anti-Nazi activity and had actually been imprisoned by the Gestapo for about a month in 1934. Not only that, but immediately after the trial he was given an administrative job by the

---

[378] Taylor, p.246
[379] Nuremberg Trial Proceedings, Vol.19, 188th day, Saturday 27th July 1946, p.528
[380] The IMT Judgement, War Crimes and Crimes against Humanity, Persecution of the Jews http://elsinore.cis.yale.edu/lawweb/avalon/imt/proc/judwarcr.htm#persecution

American authorities in Frankfurt, during which time he testified or provided affidavits for another 147 trials involving Nazis, before taking American citizenship and migrating to San Francisco, where he lived until dying in 1986.[381] It would appear therefore that far from simply being an impartial bystander, Graebe had an agenda, bore a clear grudge and was eventually given American domicile in exchange for his obliging co-operation with the prosecutors. This does not mean that his evidence was completely invented, it certainly appears that actions very similar to the one described by Graebe did occur, but raises further issues regarding the court's failure to present him for cross examination despite their repeated emphasis of his affidavit.

The task facing Kaltenbrunner and his lawyer was therefore huge. Aside from the stack of evidence, of which witnesses were only a part - there was also a formidable raft of documents – Kaltenbrunner suffered from an image problem, not only in terms of his personal appearance (which was mitigated by his eloquence, according to Judge Birkett, he was 'a fluent speaker' who spoke 'with great animation.'[382]), but in relation to his organisation. *Meine ehre heisst treue* (My honour is loyalty) is truly a motto that has passed into dark legend.

The caricatures which are so often drawn of the SS are easy to understand. Partly they are due to the politicisation of the Holocaust, whereby a series of (often fairly unconnected) events have been moulded together into an ideological whole. Once this whole is simplistically accepted, then the evil of the SS, as its perpetrator, is taken for granted. However, there is more to it than that and in discussing this branch of Nazi security apparatus, it would not suffice to pin issues of perception solely on the chests of historians and post war writers. It is without question that Himmler and the other leaders *wanted* the SS to be frightening – with their strict entry policy based on racial purity and physical prowess, their black uniforms and special *totemkopf* (death's head) divisions who wore skull insignia on their caps, they positioned themselves, in the public consciousness, only a few steps away from having fangs and drinking blood. Even other Nazis doubted the morality of men associated with it, as evidenced by the other defendants and their frequent pejorative remarks about Himmler and Heydrich. As a tactic, a means to control the public and to intimidate their enemies, the PR had been calculated and effective, but when it came to the trial this macabre masquerade played right into the prosecution's hands.

Kaltenbrunner's testimony began on the 11th April with the usual questioning from his own counsel. Kauffman got him to briefly summarise his early life and career and the role he had played in the Anschluss. Interestingly, while Kaltenbrunner detailed his rise through the ranks of the SS, he indicated a separation between himself and other members of the regime along regional grounds. He seemed to view himself as an Austrian first and member of the Reich second. Describing a December 1942 meeting with Himmler at Berchtesgaden, in which he was asked to set up the RSHA, he stated that:

'I explained to Himmler on which essential points I differed with National Socialism as to the home policy of the Reich, the foreign policy, the ideology, and the violations of law by the Government themselves[383]…I declared to him, specifically, that the administration in the Reich was too centralized; that Austria was violently criticising that centralized system…I told him that the creation of a new German criminal law, the way it was attempted, was wrong, and that German criminal law was casuistic.[384] The Austrian criminal law…had proved to be the best…I explained to him that the concepts of protective custody and of concentration camps were not approved of in Austria, but that every man in Austria wanted to be tried before a court of law.'

During the course of this meeting, Kaltenbrunner also claimed that it was agreed between himself and Himmler that Heinrich Müller[385] would retain control of all imprisonment and execution matters, that Kaltenbrunner would only nominally be Müller's superior and that Müller would receive orders on these matters

---

[381] Taylor, p.245
[382] Taylor, p.362
[383] Nuremberg Trial Proceedings, Volume 11, 105th day, Thursday, 11th April 1946, p.237
[384] Casuistry is a method of case-based reasoning. It is the standard form of reasoning applied in common law, but is open to abuse and was highly unfashionable for a time.
[385] Müller is another interesting character, who disappeared in 1945, never to resurface. Some believe he died, others that he went into hiding in South America (like Eichmann), others still that he was picked up either by the Americans or the Soviets and used as a secret agent during the Cold War.

directly from Himmler, thereby bypassing Kaltenbrunner in the chain of command.

Kaltenbrunner's time in custody and experience through interrogation had clearly shown him on which points his case would hinge, as he then said, 'I explained to him that anti-Semitism in Austria had developed in a completely different way and also required a different handling...Any personal or physical persecution of Jews was completely unnecessary.'[386]

Very quickly, therefore Kaltenbrunner's own testimony had moved to the crux of the issue as it applied to him. 'I am stating here emphatically that the special assignments which had been given to Heydrich, such as, for instance, the assignment with regard to the final solution of the Jewish problem, were not only not known to me at the time but were not taken over by me... The directives were given by Himmler, but in State Police and Criminal Police matters, things were often done, as I found out very much later, in the name of the Chief of the Reich Security Main Office, that is, in my name, without my knowing of or seeing these orders when they were issued... The chiefs of the Gestapo office and the Criminal Police office sometimes carried out these orders from Himmler, as I said, in such a way that they also signed my name as Chief of the Reich Se- curity Main Office and, as I probably might have to state in detail later, they so continued routine habits which prevailed during Heydrich's time, who united all executive powers in his' hand and who could delegate the respective powers to Muller and Nebe. But I never had those powers from the beginning...'[387]

This proved to be the central plank of Kaltenbrunner's defence. As document after document was brought out bearing his signature, he was forced to repeat himself time and time again. Understandably however, despite his insistence that his lack of executive power had been agreed informally with Himmler since the beginning, his position before the court appeared untenable. There are shades, here, of Streicher's case, whereby the question arose of whether he could be held responsible for articles by other writers which appeared in his newspaper. Here, Kaltenbrunner was claiming that he had not known of orders that bore his name, passed by his office. (It is actually probable that he was telling the truth – the vast majority of the 'signatures' were simply Photostats or stamps, or even just his name typed at the bottom of the page. It is normal labour-saving practice for underlings in an organization of any size to add their superior's name, otherwise there would be little time for the boss to do anything other than sign things all day.) Unfortunately for Kaltenbrunner, due to the principle of command responsibility he *had* to be accountable for such orders, whether or not he had ratified them personally.

An example of Kaltenbrunner's attempt to evade these kinds of charges is given below:

Kaltenbrunner – I must say that not once in my whole life did I ever see or sign a single protective custody order...
Dr Kauffmann – You will admit that, naturally, this statement of yours is not very credible. It is a monstrosity that the office chief should not know that such orders were signed with his name. How do you explain this fact, a fact which appears from the documents which bear your signature?[388]

In answering this question, Kaltenbrunner was forced to rehash the story of his meeting with Himmler that he gave the earlier in his testimony. A few questions later and his defence counsel offered the following, scathing summary of Kaltenbrunner's position to the court.

Dr Kauffmann – So that, if I understand you rightly, I can summarize your attitude as follows: You want to say that you had no knowledge of the protective custody orders, that you had no authority to issue them, and that you did not sign them, but since these protective custody orders were issued within the Amt IV[389], you ought to have had knowledge of them. Is this summary correct or is it not?
Kaltenbrunner – It is correct.[390]

Kauffmann seemed to be making little effort to paint his client in a positive light and before long he had

---

[386] See note 341
[387] ibid, p.240
[388] ibid, p.242
[389] Amt IV means 'office 4'. It was the Gestapo head office, a subsection of the RSHA.
[390] ibid, p.243

moved to the matter of the *Einsatzgruppen*. Following the testimonies of Ohlendorf, Wisliceny and von dem Bach-Zelewski, this area alone would easily be enough to hang Kaltenbrunner.

Kauffmann – What do you have to say in answer to the question whether or not you knew of the existence and the significance of these *Einsatzgruppen*?
Kaltenbrunner: I had no idea of the existence of these *Einsatzkommandos* as described by Ohlen- dorf. Later on I heard that they existed, but this was many months later. With regard to this point I want to say the following: It is known to the Tribunal from Ohlendorf's testimony and from Hitler's and Himmler's decrees which have been discussed here that orders for the killing of people had been given. These *Einsatzkommandos* have never been reorganized during the time when I was in office. These *Einsatzkommandos* which had been active up to that time were also dissolved or had been put under different commands before I took over the office. I do not know whether the witness Ohlendorf has stated here just when he returned from his *Einsatzkommando*.[391]
Dr Kauffmann – Were these *Einsatzgruppen* the result of an order from Hitler or of an order from the Reich Security Main Office?
Kaltenbrunner – It can only be due to an order from Hitler.
Dr Kauffmann – You just said that in the course of time you heard about the existence and significance of these *Einsatzgruppen*. Can you say exactly on which date you gained that knowledge?
Kaltenbrunner – I assume that this was at the time when I had my first audience with Hitler, or it may have been on the following day when I reported to Himmler, in November 1943.
Dr Kauffmann – 1943?
Kaltenbrunner – Yes.
Dr Kauffmann – If you had knowledge at that time of the *Einsatzgruppen* and their significance, then the question arises what your attitude about them was and, in case you condemned them, what you did to have them abolished? Did you have a possibility to do so or did you not?
Kaltenbrunner – I said before that an *Einsatzkommando* was never set up under my direction or my orders. The existence and the previous activities of such *Einsatzkommandos* became known to me late in the fall of 1943 and I knew that I would have to resist this misuse of the men who were under the Reich Security Main Office...I talked to the Führer about the facts on the *Einsatzkommandos* which had become known to me; and not only about that, but also I had the first opportunity to approach him about the entire Jewish problem, and about the orders given, by him and by Himmler against the Jews which had also become known to me at that time... I should like only to add that the *Einsatzkommandos* no longer came into the picture, so far as I was concerned, because the entire personnel was committed to the anti-partisan fighting or rather to the Higher SS Police Leader, I believe, on exactly the same day when I entered my office in Berlin. I believe I can remember distinctly that Von dem Bach-Zelewski was appointed Chief of anti-partisan fighting on 30th January 1943. This may also be the reason for the fact that I did not see any reports from the *Einsatzkommandos* themselves.'[392]

These answers provide some important points. Remember that the modern Holocaust interpretation of events views the *Einsatzgruppen* as being murder squads (admitted to by Ohlendorf in his questioning) who rounded up Jews as part of the Final Solution. Kaltenbrunner's statement here could therefore be used, in one interpretation to demonstrate his knowledge of the Holocaust. Eugene Davidson stated that 'Kaltenbrunner admitted he had known of the Einsatz formations but said their excesses were Himmler's fault,'[393] claiming also that Kaltenbrunner believed 'the Jews should be exterminated.'[394] Although Kaltenbrunner did indeed seem to mention the *Einsatzgruppen* in regard to 'orders against the Jews', he explains at the end of the quoted section that the *Einsatzkommandos* did not report to him as the matter of 'anti-partisan fighting' did not come under his jurisdiction. Again therefore, we find this blurring of the nature of the *Einsatzgruppen*

---

[391] ibid, p.244
[392] ibid
[393] Davidson, p.323
[394] ibid, p.322

actions. It appears to be unclear from the evidence exactly what the purpose of the *Einsatzgruppen* were. This is an important issue to address. Simply put, anti-partisan warfare, even if it is conducted in a brutal and chaotic manner,[395] is not the same thing as rounding up Jews selectively and killing them for purely racial reasons. Kaltenbrunner seemed to be admitting to knowledge of the former (as did Göring during his testimony) and not the latter. Of course it is possible, perhaps even likely, that many partisan fighters in Eastern Europe were Jews, it is also likely, as appears to be the case, that there were times when such operatives exceeded the boundaries of their orders[396] and simply wiped out what they deemed to be 'partisan infested villages' rather than hunting down and executing the actual partisans, but this still does not equate with the version of events commonly repeated by historians.

After dealing with this major issue, in which the waters appeared somewhat muddy, a specific order was produced referring to the execution of, '12 or 15 American parachutists who were captured in 1945.'[397] Kaltenbrunner again attempted to avoid responsibility by claiming ignorance, but beneath that we are faced with the fact that although enough to convict the *Obergrüppenfuhrer* of murder, in the great scheme of Nuremberg atrocities, it was not a particularly significant charge.

Through the rather blunt questioning of Kauffmann, Kaltenbrunner then went on to describe different kinds of camps, such as Correctional Labour Camps where Germans or foreign workers who avoided work were sent. These camps offered brief sentences (a maximum of fifty-six days), intended to provide the short, sharp shock necessary to coax inmates into providing labour upon their release. This relatively benign accusation was again presented with an official RSHA order, with Kaltenbrunner's name on it (although it wasn't signed).[398]

Following that, Kaltenbrunner was questioned regarding something more sinister – an order, allegedly given by Himmler, in which 'Soviet Russian political commissars and Jewish soldiers were taken out of prisoner-of-war camps and transferred to concentration camps, to be shot.'[399] But for this more serious crime (with its Holocaust intimations) the evidence provided was again not an official RSHA order, bearing Kaltenbrunner's name, but an Allied-produced affidavit, signed by Kurt Lindow, the Director of Office for Criminal Affairs in the RSHA. Lindow however, despite clearly being available, having been held in custody to produce the statement, was not presented to the court for cross examination and therefore the possibility to probe further on the matter was denied.

It seemed at this stage that a clear pattern was emerging. Minor charges were being presented with genuine German documents from the RSHA office, serious ones with witness affidavits. Kauffman then proceeded to press Kaltenbrunner on the matter of concentration camps.

Dr Kauffmann – You are accused of establishing the Concentration Camp Mauthausen, that you visited this camp repeatedly. The witness Hollriegel, who testified here, said he had seen you in this camp. He also claims to have seen you inspecting the gas chambers while they were in operation. There is an affidavit of Zutter, who has already been mentioned today and who claims to have seen you at the Concentration Camp Mauthausen...
Kaltenbrunner – The testimony is wrong. I did not establish any concentration camps in Austria where I was until 1943. I did not establish a single concentration camp in the Reich from 1943 onwards...[400]
Dr Kauffmann – Did you not, as testified by Hollriegel, see the gas chambers in operation?
Kaltenbrunner – Never; neither while they were operating nor at any other time did I see a gas chamber.

---

[395] Bach-Zelewski testified that 'the lack of detailed directives resulted in a wild state of anarchy in all anti-partisan operations' Nuremberg Trial Proceedings, Vol.4, 28th day, 7th January 1946 p.478
[396] Bach-Zelewski also said that 'Since there were no definite orders and the lower commanders were forced to act independently, the operations varied according to the character of the officer in command and the quality of the troops. I am of the opinion that the operations often not only failed in their purpose but even overshot their mark.' ibid. In addition he said, with regard to the destruction of entire villages that those 'steps would be taken by a commander on his own initiative.' ibid, p.483
[397] Nuremberg Trial Proceedings, Volume 11, 105th day, Thursday, 11th April 1946, p.246
[398] ibid, p.250
[399] ibid
[400] ibid, p.268

Kauffmann then pushed Kaltenbrunner to restate his position on this matter, to which he replied, '...I already answered that I never saw a gas chamber, either in operation or at any other time. I did not know that they existed at Mauthausen and testimony to that effect is entirely wrong. I never set foot in the detention camp at Mauthausen-that is, the concentration camp proper. I was at Mauthausen, but in the labor camp, not in the detention camp.'[401]

Kaltenbrunner's straightforward denials regarding Mauthausen are now borne out by several mainstream historians[402], who no longer allege that gassing took place there. This, like the Dachau issue raised earlier, again draws question marks over Allied evidence gathering. Here, with regard to Mauthausen, they had obtained an affidavit from Hollriegel, a member of the 'inner service of the camp' stating that prisoners were executed there by shooting and gassing. Hollriegel then appeared on the stand and largely just answered *Jawohl* (yes, of course) to a series of questions put to him by Colonel John Amen, based on his affidavit. He was not cross-examined by any defence lawyers. However, despite the unclear evidence regarding the two camps at Mauthausen or the *Einsatzgruppen*, the case was about to take an intriguing turn, as the matter of Auschwitz arose.

Dr Kauffmann – Now, will you please answer this question with 'yes' or 'no': Had the concentration camp at Auschwitz been known to you as such?
Kaltenbrunner – No, I did not know about it until November of 1943.
Dr Kauffmann – Were you, simultaneously with learning of the camp's existence, informed of the significance of this camp, namely, that it was exclusively an extermination camp for Jews handed over by Eichmann?
Kaltenbrunner – No, it could not have been known to anybody as such...At any rate-and I think this must be emphasized-there was such a complete secrecy regarding what went on in Auschwitz, that the statements of not only the defendants but of anyone else who might be asked by the Americans, 'Do you know about it?' and answers in the negative must be believed.[403]

This question is interesting because again, it is suggesting a scenario not borne out by History. Auschwitz was in no way *exclusively* an extermination camp. It was divided into three sections and by far the largest part of the camp, known as Auschwitz-Monowitz, was a huge industrial complex, with factories of the Buna Rubber Company, IG Farben, the Krupp armament works and various other well known German industrial entities who used forced labour during the war. The current historical belief is that the exterminations happened in gas chambers at Auschwitz-Birkenau[404] (also known as Auschwitz Two), while Auschwitz One was a regular detention camp where some gassings may have occurred. Despite Auschwitz having been liberated by the Soviets, such information was not presented at this stage of the trial. Instead, we get this assertion by Kauffmann (who, we must remind ourselves again, was a defence lawyer) that it was *exclusively* an extermination camp. Such belief persisted for some time after the trial, as Auschwitz and the sites of the other 'death camps' sat behind the iron curtain in Poland and could not be inspected. The current version of the Auschwitz picture did not emerge clearly until the sixties and seventies with the work of historians like Hilberg, Reitlinger and Pressac (in the popular mind it is still not clear today).

The next piece of discussion between Kaltenbrunner and Kauffmann regarding Auschwitz was to produce, in terms of the Holocaust, what could arguably be described as the most telling moment of the whole eleven months of courtroom proceedings.

Dr Kauffmann – One further question to that. When did you hear, for the first time, that the camp at Auschwitz was an extermination camp?

---

[401] ibid, p.269
[402] Olga Wormser-Migot denies the existence of Mauthausen gas chambers in *Le Système Concentrationnaire Nazi*, (Presses Universitaires de France, 1968) p.543, In his book, *The History of the Holocaust*, (Franklin Watts 1982), Yehuda Bauer states that no gassings took place at Mauthausen (p.209) & Raul Hilberg, in *The Destruction of the European Jews*, classifies Mauthausen as a 'concentration camp', rather than a 'death camp'. p.1320
[403] Nuremberg Trial Proceedings, Volume 11, 105th day, Thursday, 11th April 1946, p.272
[404] As stated by Höss at the trial and repeated by Historians like Hilberg, p.942

Kaltenbrunner – Himmler told me that in 1944, in February or March. That is, he did not tell me, he admitted it.[405]

The importance of this moment in the conflict between 'denial' and 'memory' cannot be overstated. It was one of only two moments during the entire eleven months of the trial that one of the defendants admitted, during direct testimony, to knowledge of some form of deliberate extermination. In terms of discussion on the Holocaust and what exactly did or did not happen, it is a huge thorn in the side of negationists who would wish to allege that deliberate killing did not occur at all. Kaltenbrunner is not simply saying, as other defendants did, that he had no knowledge of such things. He is stating, specifically and while being questioned by his own (admittedly quite hostile) lawyer that exterminations occurred. The answer was not coaxed or tricked out of him or presented on an affidavit that may have been signed under duress. It was a straightforward question and a straightforward answer.

Conspiracy theorists may wish to present arguments regarding Kaltenbrunner's treatment while in prison. As mentioned previously there lingers a suspicion that his head injuries were not caused by stress, as alleged, but by beating. However, such arguments would be weak, as no matter how badly you treat someone in their cell, or the interrogation room, it is very difficult to guarantee what they will say in court, particularly when such statements are likely to incriminate themselves. What becomes clear from Kaltenbrunner's testimony is that he actually hoped to exonerate himself by showing that although he knew of such occurrences, they were not performed under his authority and were therefore outside of his control. If he was lying, a more straightforward defence would simply to have been to deny all knowledge.

In response to that, it could also be proposed that Kaltenbrunner's admission here was part of a strategy, pre-arranged with his lawyer. That perhaps it was felt that the stack of Allied produced affidavits were such that denial of the charge would not work and the only way to have a chance of avoiding the death penalty was to accept the claim, but attempt to distance himself from it. Yet, aside from the fact that there is no evi- dence for such an explanation, it seems extremely unlikely that a defendant would choose to admit to knowl- edge of exterminations, if they did not actually have any. A witness could conceivably be given an amnesty in exchange for such an admission, as probably happened with Bach-Zelewski but it is difficult to conceive how this would serve to mitigate guilt or lighten sentencing for a defendant, making his statement before spectators and the media. There is therefore no rational explanation other than that Kaltenbrunner was telling the truth.

Unfortunately, further questioning did not manage to yield information regarding details. Kaltenbrunner stated that he had asked Himmler about numbers but Himmler had told him that he did not know. (Kaltenbrunner also claimed that he did not believe Himmler on this point.) Nothing was said with regard to methods or scope. With this in mind, Kaltenbrunner's testimony, which it should be remembered is still a form of hearsay evidence, although damaging to 'deniers' cannot be said to support the dominant narrative regarding Auschwitz. He gives no support for any of the figures, from the Soviets' four million to the modern one-and- a-half and he gives no support to the claim of gas chambers, the instrument of death which is supposed to have made such high figures possible. However, the importance of Kaltenbrunner's case to description of the Holocaust did not finish there.

During the second day of Kaltenbrunner's examination by Kauffmann, he made a further statement regarding the 'Final Solution'.

Dr Kauffmann – It is natural to assume, if I place myself in the position of the Prosecution, that you must have had knowledge of the 'final solution' and of that idea, if you met Himmler frequently. I therefore ask you again: Did not Himmler at some time put to you clearly what this 'final solution' was?

Kaltenbrunner – No, not in this form. I said yesterday that on the basis of all information which accumulated during the summer and autumn of 1943, including reports from enemy broadcasts and foreign news, I came to the conviction that the statement regarding the destruction of Jews was true, and that, thus convinced, I immediately went to see Hitler, and the next day Himmler, and complained to

---

[405] Nuremberg Trial Proceedings, Volume 11, 105th day, Thursday, 11th April 1946, p.273

both of them saying that I could not for one single minute support any such action...[406]

This gives a clearer outline to what Kaltenbrunner had said the day before. It seems that he had inferred from various sources, including foregn media, who would obviously have been pumping out propaganda, that exterminations were taking place. He then sought clarification on this matter, at which point Himmler offered some kind of confirmation.

Shortly after this, the baton on the Kaltenbrunner case was picked up by the bullish American prosecutor Colonel John Harlan Amen. In reality there seemed to be little difference between his line of questioning and Kauffman's. Later Kaltenbrunner was to say to Maxwell-Fyfe, 'I saw your people holding their sides with laughter. Please extend my congratulations to them for finding me such a stupid attorney.'[407] Amen's only noticeable tactical difference to the defence counsel was that he produced many 'surprise' affidavits, most of them provided by former concentration camp internees. Kaltenbrunner pointed out, quite reasonably, that eliciting incriminating statements from former camp inmates was of little value as evidence. They would obviously make such statements against a man in Kaltenbrunner's position for revenge. One which did not conform to this model was that provided by Franz Zieries, the former commandant of Mauthausen, while he lay dying. However it was still obtained and recorded by a concentration camp internee, in fact one of Zieries' former captives. With regard to the Zieries statement, Kaltenbrunner, a lawyer himself said, 'it is new to me that the Prosecution were using internees from concentration camps for the interrogation of Ziereis, who had been shot in the stomach three times and was dying. I thought that such interrogations would have been carried out by a man who was legally trained and who would be in a position to attach the right value to such statements.'

To this very sensible criticism, Amen could only manage to reply, 'Well, perhaps, Defendant, if you were conducting the Prosecution, you would do it differently...'[408]

Just as in Kauffman's questioning then, atrocity claims were being presented via affidavits, which Amen read to the court. The standard of evidence produced in them was poor, by anyone's standards. In one of them, the witness had not even been able to identify Kaltenbrunner by name, but referred to him as 'the tall man', hardly sufficient description to form a positive identification. Kaltenbrunner and Kauffmann requested that the witnesses represented through affidavits be brought to the court for cross examination. None of them ever were.

Another telling moment arrived with Amen's questioning regarding semantics. As already discussed, one of the more troublesome issues regarding the documentary evidence of the Holocaust is that there are no official German documents which mention exterminations or homicidal gassing. Instead we have words like *Liquidierung* and *Ausrottung*, (to liquidate and to uproot) which are open to interpretation. Historians have long maintained that this was due to a Nazi policy of extreme secrecy regarding the Holocaust. Most infa- mous of these coded terms is *sonderbehandlung*, which translates as 'special treatment'. There exist many documents in which the term is used as an apparent euphemism for killing. However, before the IMT, Kaltenbrunner was about to provide an alternative interpretation.

Amen – Defendant, you have heard evidence at this Trial with respect to the meaning of the phrase 'special treatment,' have you not? Have you heard that in this courtroom?
Kaltenbrunner – The expression 'special treatment' has been used by my interrogators several times every day, yes.
Amen – You know what it means?
Kaltenbrunner – It can only be assumed, although I cannot give an accurate explanation, that this was a death sentence, not imposed by a public court but by an order of Himmler's.
Amen – Well, the Defendant Keitel testified that, I think, it was a matter of common knowledge. Have you not at all times known what was meant by 'special treatment'? 'Yes' or 'no,' please.
Kaltenbrunner – Yes. I have told you; an order from Himmler – I am referring to Hitler's order of 1941, therefore also an order from Hitler – that executions should be carried out without legal proce-

---

[406] Nuremberg Trial Proceedings, Volume 11, 106th day, Friday, 12th April 1946, p.205
[407] Persico, p.314
[408] ibid, p.331

dure.

Amen then produced an affidavit, which was intended to prove that Kaltenbrunner had been responsible for ordering the 'Special Treatment' of individuals from time to time, thereby hoping to implicate him further in the act of genocide.

> **Amen** – In regard to 'special treatment', I have the following knowledge: On occasion of meetings of the office chiefs, *Gruppenfuehrer* Muller frequently consulted Kaltenbrunner as to whether this or that case should be specially treated or if 'special treatment' was to be considered. The following is an example of how the conversation went: Muller: Case *Obergruppenfuehrer* B please, 'special treatment' or not? Kaltenbrunner: Yes, or submit it to the *Reichsfuehrer* SS for decision...Both Muller and Kaltenbrunner proposed in my presence 'special treatment' or submission to the *Reichsfuehrer* SS for approval of 'special treatment' for certain cases which I cannot specify in detail. I estimate that in approximately 50 percent of the cases special treatment was approved.
> Are the contents of that affidavit true or false, Defendant?
> **Kaltenbrunner** – The contents are not correct, when given the interpretation you are giving to the document. You will see immediately that the tragic expression 'special treatment' is given here an absolutely humorous turn. Do you know the meaning of *Winzerstube* in Godesberg, and of *Walsertraum* in the Walsertal, and their relation to the term '*Sonderbehandlung*'? *Walsertraum* is the smartest and most fashionable Alpine hotel of the whole German Reich, and the *Winzerstube* is a very famous hotel in Godesberg in which many international meetings were held. Especially qualified and distinguished personalities were accommodated there-I would mention M. Poncet and M. Herriot and many more. They had three times the normal ration for diplomats, which is nine times the ration of the ordinary German during the war. They were daily given a bottle of champagne. They were allowed to correspond freely with their families in France and to receive parcels. These internees were allowed to receive visits on several occasions; their wishes were cared for wherever they were. That is what is meant here by 'special treatment.'[409]

Amen did not attempt to challenge Kaltenbrunner's interpretation of the document, which the defendant followed up by requesting that the establishments he had mentioned be contacted in order to verify his claim. Indeed when looking at what Amen read, Kaltenbrunner's version makes far more sense. It is ridiculous to believe that in a genocidal policy involving millions of people, individual cases would be discussed and decided upon. Kaltenbrunner's testimony also demonstrated, therefore that there was more than one meaning to *sonderbehandlung* and as a result, the belief in Nazi code words and euphemisms becomes somewhat more complicated to justify.

Before leaving the case of Kaltenbrunner, which in terms of establishing guilt, was the most clear-cut of any defendant, there is one final, momentous issue to be discussed. Following Amen's string of surprise affidavits, he had one last rabbit to pull out of the hat. '...that concludes the cross-examination,' he said, 'except for one point. There is a witness named Höss, who is called on behalf of the defendant, and through whom I would like to introduce two exhibits. If he is not to be called, however, then I would like to introduce those exhibits through the defendant. So I am wondering whether we could obtain a definite statement as to whether or not the witness Höss is actually to be called by the Defence.'[410]

The witness he was referring to was none other than Rudolf Höss, the commandant of Auschwitz. As stated near the beginning of this book, it is remarkable that Höss was not himself a defendant before the IMT. The scope of the crimes described under his jurisdiction was staggering. Kauffmann's decision to call Höss, bearing in mind the outcome of the commandant's interrogations while in custody, (one of which Kauffmann had conducted himself) is somewhat perplexing. How did he think that this would achieve anything for the purposes of defence? It is likely that he felt that as the affidavit would be presented by Amen anyway, the only chance he had to disassociate his client from the claims was to question the witness in open court. If it could be shown that Kaltenbrunner had nothing to do with the goings on at Auschwitz, it might serve to miti-

---

[409] ibid, p.338
[410] Nuremberg Trial Proceedings, Volume 11, 107th day, Saturday, 13th April 1946, p.377

gate guilt. Still, the calling of such a witness was, as Telford Taylor described 'an extraordinary decision.'[411]

It was to have a catastrophic impact, not only on Kaltenbrunner's case, but on that of every defendant. Whitney Harris, the American prosecutor, said of Höss' questioning and affidavit, 'It was a crime of such enormity that after that evidence, the defendants pretty generally gave up.'[412] During Höss' time on the stand, the court would hear the atrocity story to end all atrocity stories.

At least here, with the presentation of Höss as a witness, the trend of witness affidavits without the chance of questioning was bucked. Yet Kauffmann's inept performance in all regards would not take advan- tage of this in any way (were it possible to do so.) Later, Sir David Maxwell-Fyfe and the other prosecutors stated that they over-estimated Kauffmann. He had not picked up the subtleties of the adversarial system and

'had only learnt prosecutorial techniques'.[413] As a defence lawyer in a trial of such magnitude, this was not ideal. He was clearly aware of what was to come, having interrogated Höss himself, several days previously, as his first comment showed.

'Witness, your statements will have far-reaching significance. You are perhaps the only one who can throw some light upon certain hidden aspects, and who can tell which people gave the orders for the destruction of European Jewry, and can further state how this order was carried out and to what degree the execution was kept a secret.'[414]

Within minutes of this starting point, Kauffmann elicited admissions from Höss that 'hundreds of thousands of human beings were sent to their death'[415] at Auschwitz, that there was secrecy surrounding the figures and that according to Adolf Eichmann 'who had the task of organizing and assembling these people... two million Jews...men, women and children'[416] had been killed.

Höss, who mainly let Kauffmann do the talking and like Hollriegel before him, simply responded 'yes' to his questions, went on to state that he had been given the order to begin this genocidal process in 1941 by Himmler and that it was a matter of top secrecy, even to the extent that *Gruppenführer* Richard Glücks, the inspector of Concentration Camps, did not know about it. (How on earth it would be possible for the inspectors of camps not to notice millions of people being killed, was not something Kauffmann saw fit to ask.) Höss, with admirable nobility, then implicated his wife in the conspiracy by stating that although this was a 'secret Reich matter' and he had 'promised upon his life to keep the utmost secrecy,' he told her about what was going on at the end of 1942.[417]

He briefly described the gassing process, now well known; the arrival of transports, the removal of belongings, the deception regarding showers/delousing, and stated it took between three to fifteen minutes for the victims to die, depending on numbers and the temperature in the gas chamber. Relevant here, he also stated that Himmler and Eichmann both attended the camp and witnessed gassing, but Kaltenbrunner did not.[418] Further to that, he also testified that he had actually only met Kaltenbrunner on one occasion during his entire life and that the administration of Concentration Camps had come under the control of the Main Economic and Administrative Office and not the RSHA run by the defendant. Once such replies had been given, Kauffmann stepped down, apparently happy to have elicited what he needed from Höss. After a few, bland exchanges with other defence lawyers, it was time for Amen to step up. Amen dutifully performed a preamble of several pointless questions, which achieved little other than getting Höss to repeat what had already been said, before doing what he really wanted to do, which was read the affidavit.

'I have been constantly associated with the administration of concentration camps since 1934, serv- ing at Dachau until 1938; then as Adjutant in Sachsenhausen from 1938 to 1 May 1940, when I was appointed Commandant of Auschwitz. I commanded Auschwitz until 1 December 1943, and estimate that at least 2,500,000 victims were executed and exterminated there by gassing and burning, and at

---

[411] Taylor, p.362
[412] Harris quoted on the BBC, *Nuremberg, Nazis on Trial, Herman Goering*, first shown on BBC2 on the 26th September 2006, 9pm
[413] Persico, p.314
[414] Nuremberg Trial Proceedings, Volume 11, 108th day, Monday, 15th April 1946, p.395
[415] ibid, p.396
[416] ibid
[417] ibid, p.398
[418] ibid, p.401

least another half million succumbed to starvation and disease making a total dead of about 3,000,000. This figure represents about 70 or 80 percent of all persons sent to Auschwitz as prisoners, the remainder having been selected and used for slave labor in the concentration camp industries; included among the executed and burned were approximately 20,000 Russian prisoners of war (previously screened out of prisoner-of-war cages by the Gestapo) who were delivered at Auschwitz in Wehrmacht transports operated by regular Wehrmacht officers and men. The remainder of the total number of victims included about 100,000 German Jews, and great Numbers of citizens, mostly Jewish, from Holland, France, Belgium, Poland, Hungary, Czechoslovakia, Greece, or other countries. We executed about 400,000 Hungarian Jews alone at Auschwitz in the summer of 1944.'[419]

At this point, Amen looked up from the document and said, 'That is all true, witness?' Höss replied, 'Yes, it is.' There was more to come, initially to do with administration and chain of command issues, then:

'Mass executions by gassing commenced during the summer of 1941 and continued until fall 1944. I personally supervised executions at Auschwitz until first of December 1943 and know by reason of my continued duties in the Inspectorate of Concentration Camps, WVHA, that these mass executions continued as stated above. All mass executions by gassing took place under the direct order, supervision, and responsibility of RSHA. I received all orders for carrying out these mass executions directly from RSHA.'[420]

At this point Amen again asked if the statements had all been true and Höss again replied, 'Yes, they are.'

'The 'final solution' of the Jewish question meant the complete extermination of all Jews in Europe. I was ordered to establish extermination facilities at Auschwitz in June 1941. At that time, there were already in the General Government three other extermination camps: Belzek, Treblinka, and Wolzek. These camps were under the Einsatzkommando of the Security Police and SD. I visited Treblinka to find out how they carried out their exterminations. The camp commandant at Treblinka told me that he had liquidated 80,000 in the course of onehalf year. He was principally concerned with liquidating all the Jews from the Warsaw Ghetto. He used monoxide gas, and I did not think that his methods were very efficient. So when I set up the extermination building at Auschwitz, I used Cyklon B. which was a crystallized prussic acid which we dropped into the death chamber from a small opening. It took from 3 to 15 minutes to kill the people in the death chamber, depending upon climatic conditions. We knew when the people were dead because their screaming stopped. We usu- ally waited about onehalf hour before we opened the doors and removed the bodies. After the bodies were removed our special Kommandos took off the rings and extracted the gold from the teeth of the corpses.'[421]

'Another improvement we made over Treblinka was that we built our gas chamber to accommodate 2,000 people at one time whereas at Treblinka their 10 gas chambers only accommodated 200 people each. The way we selected our victims was as follows: We had two SS doctors on duty at Auschwitz to examine the incoming transports of prisoners. The prisoners would be marched by one of the doctors who would make spot decisions as they walked by. Those who were fit for work were sent into the camp. Others were sent immediately to the extermination plants. Children of tender years were invariably exterminated since by reason of their youth they were unable to work. Still another improvement we made over Treblinka was that at Treblinka the victims almost always knew that they were to be exterminated and at Auschwitz we endeavored to fool the victims into thinking that they were to go through a delousing process. Of course, frequently they realized our true intentions and we sometimes had riots and difficulties due to that fact. Very frequently women would hide their children under the clothes, but of course when we found them we would send the children in to be exterminated. We were required to carry out these exterminations in secrecy but of course the foul

---

[419] ibid, p.414
[420] ibid, p.415
[421] ibid

and nauseating stench from the continuous burning of bodies permeated the entire area and all of the people living in the surrounding communities knew that exterminations were going on at Auschwitz.'

Finally, after completing his reading, Amen again asked, 'Now I ask you, witness, is everything which I have read to you true to your own knowledge?'

'Yes' replied Höss.

Amen ended his cross examination there. Kauffmann asked a few more pointless questions, aimed again at distancing Kaltenbrunner from the goings on[422], then Rudenko, for the Soviet Union asked to be allowed to cross examine the witness regarding 'the annihilation of millions of Soviet citizens.'[423] Apparently he intended to heap further atrocities upon those that had already been described, but he was disallowed from doing so by Judge Lawrence, in the interests of avoiding 'unreasonable delay'.

The position of the Höss appearance within Kaltenbrunner's case, within the broader scope of the entire trial and by extension, within History, is a strange one. It seemed primarily to offer powerful evidence regarding various details of the extermination story. Demarcation of the Holocaust evolved from his affidavit. In analysis, however, certain peculiarities need to be borne in mind. Before looking at these it should be explained that such peculiarities are preyed on heavily by those engaged in Holocaust Denial and that by including them in this discussion, this book may be left open to accusations of 'denial'. However it is important that such pecularities are made clear, if a balanced judgement of the Höss evidence is to be reached.

Although Höss was actually called by the defence, he was ostensibly a prosecution witness. The affidavit he had signed during interrogation (which Amen read) would have been presented at the trial whether he had been called or not. As such, Kauffmann's questioning could almost be seen as an opportunity to cross-examine, yet during his questioning of the witness, Kauffmann did not seek to challenge, in any way, the contents of his affidavit. The crimes as alleged (like the others presented before the IMT) were simply left to stand. Perhaps the sheer scale of the atrocities described was enough to dissuade Kauffmann from attempting to question them. As already noted, Kauffmann's only interest was in establishing that Kaltenbrunner was not implicated, but even this was a strategy born of folly, as Kaltenbrunner's position as head of the RSHA meant he was implicated purely by his role.

If Kauffmann had sought to cross-examine properly (officially, as the witness was Kauffmann's, the prosecutors were actually cross-examining), it would have been relatively easy to find weaknesses in Höss' evidence. Firstly, the figures quoted, of two and a half million deaths by gassing, three million altogether, seemed astronomically high. As the timeframe being discussed was from June 1941 to Autumn 1944, the period involved was approximately forty months. In order to execute that number of people in that time requires an *average* of around 2,500 victims per day. Is that really feasible? It would have been interesting, for the sake of the historical record, if nothing else, for the court to have established exactly how Höss coped with the logistical nightmare that such an operation must have entailed. Indeed, how did the German infrastructure, already overburdened with the workload of war, manage to accommodate these demands? Simply getting that number of people into the camp on a daily basis must have required huge numbers of transports. Was half of the German rail service turned over to this purpose?

Further to that point, it is also interesting that Höss stated that he received this order to turn Auschwitz into a death camp in June 1941. Yet, as is common knowledge, it is alleged that the decision to begin the 'Final Solution to the Jewish question' was made at the Wannsee Conference in January 1942. Either Höss got his dates wrong[424] (in which case the timeframe above shortens, increasing the average number of daily victims) or Himmler engaged Höss on the Final Solution even before Heydrich, the 'architect of the Final Solu-

---

[422] Kauffmann returned to this theme in his closing statement, saying: "Kaltenbrunner could not have any more influence on it (the Jewish question)...according to the statement of Höss, the only man left alive who is familiar with this question, it is established that only about 200 or 300 people knew of the dreadful order of Himmler's...on the basis of which more than 4 million people were exterminated..." Nuremberg Trial Proceedings, Vol.18, 174th day, Tuesday 9th July 1946, p.65. This has been the cause of some controversy, originally questioned by Raul Hilberg and recently in an article in *Der Spiegel* in which it was claimed that around 400,000 Germans must have been 'in the know'.
http://einestages.spiegel.de/static/topicalbumbackground/1564/_ich_zeite_ruhig_auf_die_saueglinge.html

[423] Nuremberg Trial Proceedings, Volume 11, 108th day, Monday, 15th April 1946 p.418

[424] Many prominent historians assert that Höss meant 1942, not 1941. Most notably Robert-Jan van Pelt, in *Anatomy of the Auschwitz Death Camp*, edited by Yisrael Gutman and Michael Berenbaum, (Indiana University Press 1994), p 213

tion' knew about it. There are other anomalies, too. Höss mentioned a camp called 'Wolzek', for example, which did not, in reality, exist.[425]

For the most striking point regarding the Höss affidavit, we must however return to numbers. As stated near the beginning of this chapter, it is very hard to believe that a Nazi on trial, like Kaltenbrunner, would admit to knowledge of extermination if he did not actually have such knowledge. Höss' testimony, which supported his affidavit, is therefore very difficult to dispute. Although he was not actually on trial at the IMT himself, Höss must have realised that he was making a very large rod for his own back by verifying this
statement in court.[426] It is therefore equally difficult to believe that he would have been perjuring and incriminating himself at the same time. However, the figures given by Höss in Nuremberg, which were repeated in the court's final judgement, were quickly abandoned by Historians. Hilberg, for example, wrote in 1961 that 'up to 1 million'[427] died at Auschwitz. The plaque erected by the camp museum originally stated four million victims, but was removed in 1989 and replaced with one which said '1.5 million, mainly Jews.' In short, Höss' claim of three million is believed by few, if any historians today. Clearly, this begs an obvious question – if the current historical narrative is correct, why on earth would the man exaggerate his own crimes?

In attempting to reach a balanced judgement on Höss therefore, we need to accept the fact that he said things which virtually nobody in the modern world believes about Auschwitz. We cannot therefore take his affidavit and statements at face value. The obvious answer to this problem is that the affidavit was, on the most part, sensationalised and that this, for common-sense reasons, was not Höss' doing. Even if Höss was, as asserted by historian Christopher Browning 'a very weak and confused witness'[428] one would have thought any mistakes he made in the statement would have had the effect of minimising his crimes, not worsening them.

Clearly, as already seen, upon his initial arrest by the British in 1945, he was beaten by interrogators and forced to sign something which did not equate to objective truth.[429] There is nothing that can be found to suggest this treatment was ever repeated, but it is probable that something was done to ensure Höss kept to the story. In connection to that, it does appear that during the initial process of search and capture, threats were made to his family. On arrival at Höss' house, a squad of six officers who were 'practiced in the more sophisticated techniques of sustained and merciless investigation' asked Frau Höss for her husband's whereabouts. At first she was reluctant to divulge them, so Bernard Clarke, a sergeant in the British War Crimes Group and leader of the squad, began to shout, 'If you don't tell us we'll turn you over to the Russians and they'll put you before a firing-squad. Your son will go to Siberia.' The same threat was also made directly to the children.[430] Bearing in mind the climate of the time, it is highly plausible that the same methods, which were prevalent within Allied interrogations and evidence gathering, would have been used on Höss himself. Certainly, this first statement was then used as the basis for his questioning and also, it seems, his answers, when he was re-arrested and interrogated at Nuremberg by American prosecutor Whitney Harris on the 1st and 2nd April 1946.

It is difficult therefore to reach a conclusion. Many people, who subscribe to high ideals of legal or moral standards would state that as soon as physical coercion or threats against family members are brought into the equation, evidence provided by the witness is worthless. Does that mean therefore that the whole Höss story should be stricken from the historical record? In pondering this question, we see that the fact that Kaltenbrunner admitted to hearing about exterminations at Auschwitz takes on even greater significance. Were it not for that, it might well be possible to present a highly plausible case suggesting that what was said about Auschwitz at Nuremberg was, in the light of all evidence presented, untrue. The fact that Kaltenbrunner in-

---

[425] ibid p.279 Van Pelt asserts that 'Wolzek' was, in fact, 'Sobibor'. However the explanation given to account for this is somewhat tortuous.
[426] Höss would later be tried himself and was hanged at Auschwitz on April 16th 1947.
[427] Hilberg, p.1320 Many others, such as Lucy Davidowicz and Franciszek Piper broadly agree with Hilberg's figure.
[428] See note 84
[429] This is verified in the Höss autobiography where he stated 'evidence was obtained by beating me, I do not know what was in the record although I signed it' (p.174) Intriguingly, footnote 1 at the bottom of that page states that this first, signed statement 'does not differ substantially from what he said at Nuremberg.'
[430] Butler, p. 235 Butler is not highly regarded as a source but he personally interviewed Bernard Clarke to obtain this information.

dependently corroborated the extermination claim, (while denying knowledge of gas chambers and saying nothing regarding numbers) suggests that what in fact happened, as would be expected within the prevailing climate, is that something with a kernel of truth was overstated and inflated for political and propaganda reasons. Three million gas chamber victims at Auschwitz couldn't help the Allies win the war, but might, in conjunction with the newspapers and movie-reels, be useful in winning the peace. They would be an incredibly effective tool in discrediting the former regime, which was necessary – but cleverly, this would also offer a rite of salvation for the conquered people, through denazification and denunciation of what went before.

In reality, through convergent claims, it is reasonable to state that the Kaltenbrunner case proved that some form of exterminations *had* happened at Auschwitz, but nothing more[431]. The upshot of all of this was that Kaltenbrunner was found guilty on counts three and four and sentenced to hang. Such an outcome had never really been in doubt from the start. Telford Taylor stated that all the 'judges were, from the beginning, voting for death by hanging.'[432]

Kaltenbrunner knew his number was up. He was the only defendant found guilty who did not bother to lodge an appeal. Such false hope would have been crueler than the wait, no doubt and as all appeals were uniformly denied at a meeting of the Allied Control Council, on October 16th, it proved to be a sensible option. On the gallows, steady and composed, Kaltenbrunner said, 'I served the German people and the fatherland with willing heart. I did my duty according to its laws. I am sorry that in her trying hour she was not led only by soldiers. I regret that crimes were committed in which I had no part. Good luck Germany.'[433]

---

[431] Himmler's admission that Auschwitz was an extermination camp may have referred to overwork and poor diet, for example.
[432] Taylor, p.561
[433] ibid, p.610

12

The Root of all Evil

'Endless money forms the sinews of war'
- Cicero, *Phillipics*

Hjalmar Schacht and Walter Funk

By far the most oddly named defendant at Nuremberg was Hjalmar Horace Greeley Schacht (above left), whose international upbringing (he was known, in Reich circles as 'The American') had shaped not only his appellation but also his outlook and career.[434]

Schacht was of semi-aristocratic background, of essentially Danish heritage and had been educated in Hamburg. He studied at universities in Germany and in Paris, and after receiving a doctor's degree, began a banking career. For thirteen years he was at the Dresdner Bank before taking over the management of a bank of his own. In 1923 he abandoned his private career and went into public service as Commissioner for German Currency (*Reichswaehrungskommissar*). Soon afterwards he became President of the Reichsbank, a position he was to hold twice.[435]

The tribunal charged him primarily with aiding in the economic re-development of Germany after Versailles and therefore her rearmament and aggression. The primary obstacle to making this charge stick was that despite his alleged role in the conspiracy, Schacht had never actually been a Nazi. His first appointment as head of the Reichsbank, in December 1923, had been during the days of the Weimar Republic when he had also helped to found the German Democratic Party. Later, under the Nazis, he was again to take charge of the Reichsbank and at Hitler's behest became Minister for Economics and Plenipotentiary General for the War Economy, during which time he used his financial acumen to disguise the inflation caused by rearming the Reich.[436]

It seems he lost confidence in Hitler after a time and was implicated in various attempted coups during the late thirties, at which point he resigned his Ministerial position (in 1937) and left the Reichsbank (in

---

[434] Schacht's family was of Danish descent, (his mother was a Baroness) but his father had spent a long period living in the USA.
[435] Nuremberg Trial Proceedings Vol.12, 117th day, Tuesday 30th April 1946, p.416
[436] Dodd, p.42

1939), becoming a Minister without Portfolio. His alleged involvement in the bomb plot against Hitler in 1944 saw him arrested and sent to Ravensbruck, Flossenburg and finally Dachau, where he was still an inmate when it was liberated by the Americans in April 1945. He scored the highest of any Nuremberg defendant on Gilbert's IQ test, (getting 143, making him officially a genius along with Seyss-Inquart, Göring and Dönitz)[437] and despite his non-membership of the party was indicted on Count One, the 'The Conspiracy' and count two 'War Crimes'.

Schacht's successor, both as minister and Reichsbank chief, Walther Funk had a case which on first examination appeared slightly more serious. Funk was of middle class Prussian origin and although he, like Schacht, had spent most of his career in finance and banking[438], he had ascended to Schacht's positions after his fall from grace and therefore had been in control of Germany's monetary affairs during the war years. In that time he had worked closely with Göring on the four-year plan and became a member of the Central Planning Board organized by Albert Speer. Unlike Schacht, Funk had joined the party in 1931. Due to his closer party ties and the importance of his state positions during the war, Funk found himself indicted on all four counts.

Schacht's case was, from the beginning, harder to prosecute than any other defendant, except possibly Fritzsche. He was described by Telford Taylor as 'the banker who had supported Hitler's accession to the chancellorship and directed the financing of rearmament'[439] but in comparison to soldiers or ministers accused of aggressive war making or implicated in Crimes against Humanity it was tough to really pin down the area in which his guilt lay. He was a financial man, of considerable ability, who had used that ability in the service of his country, at the request of two completely different governments.

This lack of clarity was reflected by the Allies themselves, as during the period when lists of potential defendants were being drawn up, prior to trial, Schacht was something of a late addition. He had not been considered at all until late 1944, when Clement Atlee suggested his (and von Papen's) inclusion.[440] During the initial meetings of the Allied committees, Jackson had then appointed Frank Shea, an attorney on the American staff, to handle the 'economic aspects of the case.' It was Shea who followed Atlee's lead. On July 12th 1945, Schacht, Funk, Sauckel, Speer and Krupp were pencilled in for appearance before the IMT. Shea's thinking was that the guilt of these men was that 'they had given Hitler the material means to rearm Germany, *with full knowledge* that Hitler planned to use these armaments to carry out his program of German aggrandizement by military conquest.'[441] In other words the strength of the case that Shea envisaged, hinged to a large degree on the idea of conspiracy. If it could be proven that these financial and industrial operatives had engaged in their otherwise normal activities because they endorsed and embraced a master-plan of conquest, then they too could be found guilty. On July 23rd, however, less than four months before the trial would begin, Shea stated that all he had as proof of this theory were 'a few monographs and scattered bits of evidence.'[442] Colonel Amen, another of the American prosecutors, was scathing of Shea's ideas, saying the purpose of the trial was to convict war criminals, not 'reform European economics.'[443] Colonel Storey agreed, saying that the economic case would 'make us all look silly.'[444] Despite such objections, Shea set to work and gathered enough evidence to build what he believed was a credible case. Yet two months later, on August 15th, the French prosecutor, Passant, argued against indicting Schacht, saying 'he is, I believe, in many ways an unpleasant and unreliable character. But…he is not a war criminal…his defence would be so strong that if it did not secure an acquittal, the authority of the Tribunal would be seriously reduced.'[445]

As would be expected, Schacht himself fully concurred with Passant's view. After first arriving at Nuremberg he said to his interrogator, a Lieutenant Nicholas Doman, 'Young man, do you know why I am here…I am here because Justice Jackson wants an innocent man among the defendants who can be acquitted

---

[437] Gilbert, p.31
[438] he had also had a brief spell as a journalist and for a time worked in the Ministry for Propaganda, but even this was a financial role.
[439] Taylor, p.25
[440] Taylor, p.30
[441] ibid, p.81
[442] ibid
[443] ibid
[444] ibid, p.82
[445] ibid, p.88

to prove this is a fair trial.'[446] Later he was to say to Gilbert, 'It was really stupid of the tribunal to indict me. I could have been their best witness myself!'[447]

Schacht then spent the majority of the proceedings putting as much distance between himself and the loyal Nazis, like Göring, as possible. According to Gilbert he was 'burning with indignation' after the showing of the Concentration Camps Film, saying 'how dare they make me sit there with those criminals and watch a film on concentration camp atrocities! They know that I was an enemy of Hitler and ended up in a concentration camp myself! It is unforgiveable!'[448] Such a stance seems entirely reasonable, especially as Dachau, where Scahcht had been held, was one of the camps featured in the film. The idea that he was 'an enemy of Hitler' became a kind of mantra of his during the trial. He seemed to think that if he repeated it often enough, he would be believed. His links to the assassination attempt supported this, but other evidence that was to come to light did not.

Schacht took the stand on the 30th April. His initial questioning by his attorney, Rudolf Dix, enabled him to state several times that he was a 'a private citizen and not interested in party politics.' He described himself as a patriot who was 'proud to belong to a nation which has given to the world men like Luther, Kant, Goethe, Beethoven, to mention only a few.'[449]

During the course of his testimony he admitted to using 'Mefo bills' to finance rearmament[450] but was to make many disparaging remarks about Hitler and the party, which aroused distaste among most of the defendants, who thought he had had been as swept along as anyone else in the early days, but was now trying to deny it. Raeder said, 'He is a terrible man, that Schacht, what he says is just not true.'[451] Von Schirach said he 'had no respect for him any more'[452] and even Speer, his anti-Göring ally, said that Schacht was being 'insincere about his hostility to the Nazi Party in the early years.'[453]

During cross-examination with Jackson, Scahcht was reminded of his various public appearances, speeches and statements in which he had voiced support for Hitler and the Party program. A photograph was produced of Schacht giving the Nazi salute.[454] (Backstage, in his cell, Von Schirach told Gilbert that Schacht had once attended a reception at the Reich Chancellery at which his wife wore a large, bejeweled swastika brooch.)[455] Faced with the stacking up of these inconvenient details against his claim to have opposed Nazism, Schacht made some sort of explanation himself by saying, 'I think you can be much more successful in leading a person if you do not tell him the truth than if you do tell him the truth.'[456] (Schacht was actually describing a financial issue he had approached Hitler about, but Jackson took it as being instructive of Schacht's 'philosophy'.) The general feeling in the court was that Schacht was engaging in spin.

Walther Funk arrived in Nuremberg in poor health, suffering from prostate and urethra problems.[457] His interrogators and guards saw him as a weak and pathetic figure. When Airey Neave served him his indictment, he cried,[458] causing Colonel Andrus, who was accompanying Neave to shout, 'Be a man, Funk. Listen to the Major!' Andrus later described how Funk looked 'incapable of running a gas station.'[459] Like several of the other defendants, there were allegations from various quarters that he was a homosexual.

Funk took the stand immediately after Schacht, on the third of May and his case took only four days. Owing to his medical condition and general demeanour, he made a meek presence in the witness box. During his defence questioning he adopted a similar position to Schacht – that he was simply a banker who had done his

---

[446] Persico, p.333
[447] Gilbert, p.294
[448] Gilbert, p.48
[449] Nuremberg Trial Proceedings Vol.12, 117th day, Tuesday 30th April 1946, p.425
[450] Nuremberg Trial Proceedings Vol.12, 118th day, Wednesday 1st May 1946, p.473
[451] Gilbert, p.311
[452] ibid, p.316
[453] ibid, p.314
[454] Nuremberg Trial Proceedings Vol.12, 119th day, Wednesday 2nd May 1946, p.564
[455] Gilbert, p.318
[456] ibid, p.596
[457] Overy, *Interrogations*, p.84
[458] Neave, p.124
[459] ibid

duty to his country. However in cross examination, Thomas Dodd, for the United States picked holes in him. (In a letter to his wife, Dodd described the cross-examination as 'successful' and said that Judge Birkett had told him it was 'one of the very best of the trial'.)[460] Dodd elicited from him an admission that while President of the Reichsbank, he had accepted deposits of gold from the SS, without asking where they came from. It has since been alleged that this was gold stolen from Jews and other concentration camp inmates and luridly that it involved gold extracted from the teeth of murdered Jews. However, on examining this claim, we revisit another of Nuremberg's major issues.

Originally, in one of his first interrogations with the previously mentioned Colonel Andrus, Funk 'haltingly explained that he had been personally responsible for having Jewish prisoners murdered so that gold could be taken from their teeth without trouble. He had it knocked out of their mouths while alive, but if they were dead, it was less bother...'[461]

This obscene act of inhumanity and brutality, conducted in accordance with preconceived ideas of Nazi evil was not however, confirmed by Funk during cross-examination. In fact, while he described in detail the numbers and weight of the gold bars kept in the vaults of the bank, when Dodd asked him about whether there were also 'jewels, cigarette cases, watches, and all that business?'[462] in other words items confiscated from deportees, he replied, 'Never.' But then qualified this with 'I was in the vaults at the most four or five times...'[463]

Faced with a short film that showed articles of the kind Dodd described being found by Allied soldiers investigating the Reichsbank vaults in 1945, Funk initially stated that they must have been articles deposited by individuals in safety deposit boxes, over which he had no control. As Dodd applied more pressure he backpedalled a little and said, 'now I see quite clearly what was not known to me until now, that the Reichsbank did the technical work of melting down gold articles.' Dodd, in keeping with Allied prosecution prac- tice throughout the trial, then produced an affidavit from Funk's former assistant, Emil Puhl, without present- ing the witness for cross examination, stating that Funk had accepted knowingly such articles from the occupied Eastern territories[464]. Funk refuted this affidavit absolutely.

Conclusions can clearly be drawn about the discrepancy between the evidence produced via interrogation and affidavit and what came out on the stand. Either Funk was committing perjury, or his case presents another example of witness statements and confessions not reflecting objective truth.

With the economic case, it is worthwhile to briefly look beyond the criminality or otherwise of the two defendants and examine it from a twenty-first century viewpoint. This is because economics operates as the driving force behind most world events. All history is driven by money and power and those two commodities tend to be inextricably linked. If we want to have a proper understanding of World War Two and Nazi Germany, we must look at its economic situation, particularly in regard to other nations. When we do that, however, we find further evidence of Nuremberg's inherent contradictions.

Just as when considering German foreign policy and aggression, it needs to be borne in mind that nation states do not exist and thrive or fail in isolation. Recent years have seen two major works contribute to a new understanding of the Nazi 'Economic Miracle'. The political economist Guido Giacomo Preparata put forward a thorough and compelling, radical analysis of the international, financial forces at work behind Hitler's Germany. Published by Pluto Press in 2005, his book, which provides truly revelatory insights, seems largely to have flown beneath the radar of popular consumption. By contrast, Adam Tooze, an Economic Historian of Cambridge University, published a work with Penguin in 2007, which covered much of the same ground as Preparata's, while conforming more to establishment expectations regarding the evil of the Nazi regime and their sole blame for the start of the war. It is symptomatic of the cronyism and blinkeredness of both aca- demia and the publishing industries that Preparata has been virtually ignored while Tooze's work has been met with a fanfare of adulation.

By the late nineteenth century, Preparata argues, the British Empire had sensed the weakening of its hold

---

[460] Dodd, p.300
[461] Andrus, *The Infamous at Nuremberg*, p.56, quoted in Neave, p.126
[462] Nuremberg Trial Proceedings Vol.13, 123rd day, Tuesday 7th May 1946, p.167
[463] ibid
[464] ibid, p.169

on the world and had already begun to assess its potential challengers. The formation of Germany, under Bismarck, in 1871 was a major cause of concern. A central Europe of balkanised, tiny, competing states (known as the European 'balance of power') would never threaten British pre-eminence. But a strong, unified Germany could come to dominate the continent. If, either through alliance or conquest, a strong Germany could forge links with Russia, the results for Britain could be catastrophic. Therefore by this time, it had already become a priority of British foreign policy to contain Russia in the East and prevent Germany from becoming too dominant. Britain's opposition to Wilhelmian Germany, resulting in the entente with the traditional enemy, France in 1904 and eventually causing World War One, had nothing to do with political or ethical disputes. It was simply a matter of keeping down a challenger for global supremacy. Preparata's argument is nicely corroborated by many sources and perhaps most neatly in contemporary documents by the American diplomat, George F Kennan who worked in both Germany and Russia:

> 'There was, to be sure, an effort on the Allied side, increasing as the war ran its course, to portray the contest as one of political ideology, as a struggle between democracy and autocracy. To this, I think, we Americans were particularly prone. The effort was, in retrospect, unconvincing. Wilhelmian Germany at its worst was much closer to Western parliamentarianism and to Western concepts of justice than was the Tsarist Russia whose collaboration the Western Allies so gladly accepted in the early stages of the war. The truth is that the war was being waged against Germany, not because of the ideology of her government but because of her national aspirations. The ideological issue was an afterthought.'[465]

Kennan went on make a comment that although focused on World War One, so beautifully mirrors the situation with regard to World War Two and Nuremberg that it is worth transcribing:

> 'But I wonder whether anyone can read today the literature emanating from the Western countries...without feeling that he is in the presence of a political hysteria so violent that the real outlines of right and wrong, in so far as they may ever have existed at all, are largely lost in the turmoil. In the bewilderment that accompanied this hysteria, two mistakes were made. First, the significance of the German problem was inflated out of all semblance of reality. The Germans were a problem in Europe – yes; but they were not as awful a problem as all this: their guilt for the outbreak of the war was not so great, their victory would not have been quite such a catastrophe, nor would so many problems be solved by their defeat. But an even more serious error was the failure to recognize the limitations of modern war generally as a means to an end – the failure to realize to what extent prolonged warfare in the industrial age, with its fearful expenditure of blood and substance, was bound to be self-defeating.'[466]

On April 9th 1924, as defeated Germany struggled to stay afloat in the whirlpool of war guilt and reparations, the Dawes Plan was announced, named after the American banker Charles G. Dawes. Germany was crippled by the debt imposed at Versialles (6.6 billion Marks) and stripped of the Ruhr, her major source of heavy industry. She looked vulnerable, on the verge of destitution. The newly created Weimar Republic, that short-lived, democratic sandwich filling, spread between the bread of Monarchy and Nazism, was on the brink and the realisation dawned on the UK and USA that Communism could very well take hold in Germany, potentially enabling a relationship with the USSR and the terrifying prospect of what Preparata refers to as the 'Eurasian Embrace,' a power base spanning Eastern and Central Europe. The territory occupied by such a union, from the borders of Finland to the cusp of Arabia, from the Alps to the Sea of Japan, would have the tactical significance, sea access and impenetrability that would have given it carte blanche to rule the world.[467] This had to be avoided at all costs.

Tooze does not extend his analysis as far back into 19th Century British Imperial strategy as Preparata,

---

[465] George F. Kennan *Russia And The West, Under Lenin and Stalin* (Signet, 1962) p.7
[466] ibid, p.9
[467] Guido Giacomo Preparata, *Conjuring Hitler, How Britain and America and Made the Third Reich*, (Pluto Press, 2005) p.8 -15

choosing instead to begin in the Weimar days and therefore is not able to reach the same depth in examining the root causes, but does hint at something approaching the same thing, by discussing, 'the threat posed to Germany, along with the rest of the European powers, by the emergence of the United States as the dominant global superpower.' He goes on to add, 'Hitler predicted already in the 1920s that the European powers had only a few years to organise themselves against this inevitability.'[468] In other words, the economic games being played in Europe after World War One were an extension of the global strategies of the major powers, in particular Britain and the United States, who were already wary by that time of the possible evolution of Germany and Russia.

This is therefore a point of utmost importance. In the early twenties, it was relevant to the interests of both the waning world power, Britain and the rising star, America to assist in Germany's recovery. They did not do this from concern for their former enemy or a desire to restore some 'balance' to Europe[469], but to pro- tect the solidity of the Anglo-American fortress against potential challenge from the East. This sort of think- ing continued through to World War Two and even into its aftermath, most famously alluded to by Winston Churchill in his 'Iron Curtain' speech at Fulton, Missouri in 1946.

The bottom line, as described by both Preparata and Tooze, is that Schacht would never have been able to achieve his successes if it had not been for the help of highly influential men in other countries, in particular Sir Montagu Norman, the governor of the Bank of England, about whose relationship with Schacht, his biog- rapher, Andrew Boyle wrote, 'Schacht was only a useful instrument, the means to a greater end, yet one so necessary that Norman went out of his way to cultivate him…'[470]

In order to assist Schacht, Norman engineered a massive attack on the French economy, through the American company Morgan and Co, run by JP Morgan, in March 1924, whereby Francs were bought and then dumped onto the exchanges. As a result the Franc plummeted in value and the French economy also ap- peared on the brink of catastrophe. Having created this crisis, Morgan and Co then also offered the solution – a $100 million credit note, with a six month term.

The Dawes Plan, with its system of restructured reparation payments and American loans was then ush- ered in as a 'system for stabilizing Germany's currency.'[471] Although it bore Dawes' name, Preparata states that it was, in fact, a concoction of Morgan and Norman.[472] Tooze, on the other hand, claims it to have been designed by Owen Young, the chairman of the American corporation, General Electric.[473] Regardless, with the means to revive Germany in place, Norman continued to threaten the French, stating that their loan would not be renewed unless they agreed to the transfer of power regarding the German debt from the Reparations Committee to an American bureaucrat called S. Parker Gilbert and the immediate evacuation of the Ruhr. France reluctantly agreed and it was this that kick-started Germany's rebirth, fending off the potential for a Communist upsurge and bringing the 'Golden Years' of 1924-29. It was also this essentially Brit- ish/American scheme that therefore paved the way to the first steps of breaking with Versailles.

The financial ties between Anglo/America and Germany went far beyond assistance with their post armi- stice problems, persisting, in many forms, all the way through to World War Two. The previously mentioned General Electric were closely allied with the German company AEG, for example. IG Farben[474] the leviathan of mid 20th Century German Corporations, enjoyed a long standing relationship with the American company Standard Oil, a link which was forged during IG's research into making artificial oil from coal. (In 1929, Standard paid IG $35 billion in oil stocks for the world rights to this process). The entities then engaged in a partial merger, with the formation of the American IG company in December 1929. The board of this com- pany included Edsel Ford (of Ford motors) and Paul Warburg, the Chairman of the Manhattan Bank.[475] Ger- man aggression or war production apparently did not concern such people at all, even after Hitler took

---

[468] Adam Tooze, *The Wages of Destruction* (Penguin, 2007) p.xxiv
[469] A favoured British term of the time was the European 'balance of power'. This was, of course, a euphemism for the main- tenance of British interests.
[470] Andrew Boyle, *Montagu Norman* (Cassell, London, 1967) p.171, quoted in Preparata, p.162
[471] Preparata, p.163
[472] ibid
[473] Tooze, p.5
[474] The IG stands for '*Interessen Gemeinschaft*', which means 'Community of Interests'. *Farben* means 'colours' and refers to the company's origins as a chemical dye manufacturer.
[475] Preparata, p.169

power.

'Standard Oil will keep its cartel with IG Farben alive, war or no war...A standard official said...Technology has to carry on...'[476]

Even allowing for the fact that the two nations associated with these companies ended up on opposite sides in a global conflict, while their co-operation continued, none of this would be *too* remarkable, were it not that IG was the major supplier to the Nazi government of such items as synthetic rubber, plastics, explosives, gunpowder and aeroplane fuel, all of which were obviously crucial to the German war effort. Even more noteworthy is the fact that IG had a major factory at Auschwitz Three (Monowitz). It seems not even this was enough to put off their American partners. In addition, IG's Leverkusen outfit had a thriving pesticide division. It manufactured one particularly popular and effective product which was sold via a distribution company called Degesch. The brand name of this product, now world famous, was 'Zyklon B'.[477]

It is worth further emphasising that IG Farben's Holocaust links have been heavily utilised by some historians as a means to defame the German nation. William Shirer, for example, in his lauded, bestselling work 'The Rise and Fall of the Third Reich', wrote, 'It is not without significance for an understanding of the Germans, even the most respectable Germans, under Hitler, that such a distinguished, internationally known firm as IG Farben, whose directors were honoured as being among the leading businessman of Germany, God-fearing men all, should deliberately choose this death camp as a suitable place for profitable operations.'[478]

By reading such critically and popularly acclaimed, blinkered drivel one gets a measure of the sheer depth of misinformation surrounding this subject. Would the author of the book draw the same conclusions about the God-fearing American businessman who co-operated with and funded *the Germans*? Is acknowledging the role of men across the Atlantic in the same enterprise significant for an understanding of *the Americans*?

Schacht was later to openly describe the corporate relationship between some of his nation's most prominent rearming industries and British and American interests. After Gilbert reminded him that he had played a key role in German rearmament, he said, 'But so did all the other powers. That is no crime...'[479] When the trial was over Schacht was reinterrogated for information on German industrialists to be indicted in the next trial. 'If you want to indict industrialists who helped to rearm Germany' he laughed, 'you will have to indict your own too. The Opel Werke, for instance, who did nothing but war production, were owned by General Motors.'[480]

Aside from such corporate entanglements, the German economy continued to receive assistance from the Western Allies, throughout the Nazi era. The Wall Street Crash of 1929, often referred to as the trigger required to induce popular support for Nazism among normal Germans, was caused by the short term loans being paid out to Germany. Not only that, but it was fully anticipated by many leading financiers. Tooze stated that 'this merry go round in which Germans borrowed money from the Americans to pay the British and the French who then paid the Americans raised anxiety on all sides.'[481] Speaking in 1926, the midst of the 'Golden Years,' the Swiss banker, Felix Somary had said, 'We now find ourselves in a provisional state of rest...the calm before the tempest. How can we Europeans cope with a power such as the United States...? The only way out is for America to keep on extending short-term credits. Never has an economic cycle initiated such hazardous conditions as the bailouts of Austria and Germany...this cheap money policy cannot but usher in a gargantuan stock market bubble...That will set off the collapse...'[482]

It is reasonable to assume that if interested parties in Switzerland could see the shadow of disaster, so could the Gods of world money, in the form of Norman and Morgan. Indeed, it seems the crash was actually instigated, to some extent, by Norman himself, when, as if in a game of poker, he raised the Bank of England base rate to 5.5 percent in Febrary 1929. New York called his bet and responded in August by going to 6 per-

---

[476] Sasuly, Richard. *IG Farben* (New York: Boni and Gear 1947) p.149 quoted in Preparata, p.169
[477] ibid: Zyklon B is an industrial pesticide with which it is alleged about one million Jews were killed in the Auschwitz gas chambers.
[478] Shirer, p.798
[479] Gilbert, p.317
[480] Gilbert, p.430
[481] Tooze, p.6
[482] Preparata, p.175

cent. So Norman raised it again, to 6.5 percent in September and suddenly, according to Dana Noyes, the Financial Editor of the New York Times, 'the great decline began'[483]. The world economy floundered as it laboured under the burden of debt borrowed during the boom years. Lenders called their money home and consequences were far reaching – America itself drifted into the Great Depression, which would drag on for a decade, but the result for fragile economies, like that of Germany, surviving on foreign money, was catastrophic.

It is a worthwhile exercise here to pause and consider why the Western powers were so averse to allowing Germany to collapse in the early twenties, but were happy to stand by, perhaps to even engineer it, in 1929-30. Could it be that by that time, in the form of National Socialism, there was a viable and stronger alternative to Communism on offer? By watching the German economy tumble over a cliff and sending bourgeois and working class Germans into a state of utter desperation, the path for Hitler's ascension was prepared and this was completely acceptable for Anglo-America, as they knew that a Nazi government would never forge a meaningful alliance with the Soviet Union. The threat of the 'Eurasian Embrace' was thus removed. Indeed, to ease the transition to National Socialism, reparations were duly cancelled at the Treaty of Lausanne in 1932. This enabled Hitler and Schacht to begin the economic miracle.

Once ensconced, however, there was still work for the Führer to do to repair the nation's financial footing. It was a barely kept secret at the time that Hitler was receiving money from abroad. In 1934, the Manchester Guardian's foreign correspondent wrote, 'Hitler had large funds at his disposal, not obtained entirely from German sources. He got his money from certain capitalist interests in foreign countries, who were attracted by his hostility to Soviet Russia...'[484]

In 1934 Schacht was reappointed as head of the Reichsbank, with the initial task of aiding Hitler in rid- ding the nation of unemployment. He would never have been able to complete this task, or his subsequent one of providing for rearmament, were it not for the continued assistance of British and American interests which actually increased during this time. In July 1934 the Anglo-German Transfer agreement was finalised, with which Germany was allowed to build up a trade surplus which could be converted to Sterling. On December 4th of the same year, the Bank of England advanced the Nazis a loan of $4million.

Even armaments companies were happy to lend Hitler a hand. The British arms manufacturer, Vickers-Armstrong had offered to sell tanks and armoured cars to the German military as early as 1932. The chairman of the company, Sir Herbert Lawrence, when asked to reassure shareholders that the company was not helping to rearm Germany, said, in 1934, 'I cannot give you assurance in definite terms, but I can tell you that nothing is done without the complete sanction and approval of our government'[485]

According to the American ambassador to Berlin, William Dodd, in 1936, 'More than a hundred American corporations have subsidiaries here (Germany) or have corporate understandings... Standard Oil has made $500 million a year helping the Germans make ersatz gas for war purposes...The International Harvester Company president told me their business here rose 33 percent a year...Even our airplanes people have secret arrangements with Krupp.' Mysteriously, he also added that these companies invested in the Reich, but 'could take nothing out.' He wondered why they should be doing this 'when their company gets nothing out of the country.'[486] According to Preparata, 'at the time of Pearl Harbour, American investment in Nazi Germany amounted to an estimated total of $475 million.'[487]

The truly intriguing question to ask about all of this is 'why?' What was the motive of these western investors and creditors? Cash motivated deals would be one thing. Unscrupulous capitalists would sell to the devil himself if it involved profit. But much of the Western Allies' investment in Nazi Germany was made without hope of repayment. Schacht himself, speaking while imprisoned at Nuremberg, confirmed this, saying 'we were in no position to trade...and the loans we got obviously could not be repaid...Worse still were the loans between the Dawes and the Young plans...those were just bad loans that we didn't want and couldn't repay.'[488] The fact was that by 1939, Germany had repaid less than ten percent of her outstanding

---

[483] ibid, p.180
[484] Preparata, p.199
[485] ibid, p.225
[486] ibid
[487] ibid, p.226
[488] Gilbert, p.96

debt.[489]

It seems that a rather disturbing reality emerges. From the end of the First World War, as with so much of the world, Germany's financial affairs were controlled by Western corporate money. However unlike the rest of the world, in Germany's case this appears to have happened in the pursuit of a long term strategy. The playing out of this strategy could only lead to major conflict but those who had devised and implemented it did not concern themselves with that, provided their goals were achieved. It would have been perfectly pos- sible for Britain and America to accomodate and negotiate with Germany within an alternative plan, but this would have allowed the Reich to reach a position where it may have threatened their supremacy.

Schacht and Hitler were therefore little more than pawns in a game. The Nazis' national aspirations suited Anglo/America, which was happy to nurture them to the point of war when they could be conveniently used as a stick to beat them with. However, full fruition of these national aspirations could never be allowed. The only concern of the western financial power base was to cement its place at the top seat of the world table for as long as possible, regardless of consequences or human cost and it was prepared to swallow a few losses to achieve this. Investing in Nazi Germany because of its opposition to Soviet Russia retained the European 'balance of power' that served this purpose so well. At the expense of seventy million lives, it kept the An- glo-American corporations at the head of that table. And they are still there, with a few new partners, with the same agenda today.

As the trial drew to a close, in his scornful and sarcastic closing statement, Jackson said of the men in- dicted on the economic case, 'The positions they held show that we have chosen defendants of self-evident responsibility...Where shall we look for those who mobilized the economy for total war, if we overlook Schacht...and Funk?'[490]

The best answer would have been; over your shoulder, Mr Jackson.

That's where.

It is to the tribunal's credit that Schacht was acquitted, although it is to the tribunal's discredit that he was ever indicted in the first place. (It also needs to be remembered that he was instantly re-arrested by German authorities and sentenced to eight years hard labour by a denazification court – no-one was really *innocent* at Nuremberg). Funk was given life in Spandau but was released due to ill health in 1957. He died in 1960. The British and American corporate interests who had worked with them, of course, continued to turn a profit behind the backs of the world.

---

[489] Preparata, p.224
[490] Nuremberg Trial Proceedings, Vol.19, 187th day, Friday 26th July 1946, p.425

13

Nazi Diplomacy

Joachim von Ribbentrop, Franz von Papen and Konstantin von Neurath

To those who have accepted the popular line on modern European history and still cling to the received wisdom that World War Two was caused by Nazi aggression and little else, the title of this chapter would appear to be some kind of oxymoron. What need could a nation hell-bent on war and global domination have for diplomacy? Yet the international relationships at play in the pre war years and even after the conflict's outbreak, were complicated and inter-dependent. Germany's dealings within the global community had to be addressed at Nuremberg, but could and would only ever be examined in a one-dimensional way.

From the outset, the whole subject was an awkward area for the Allies. Questions would have to be chosen carefully in order to avoid the wrong information being brought to light. Several issues had the potential to cause a good deal of embarrassment and put up obstacles to the achievement of the trial's goals. How could the Russians keep straight faces, for example, jointly prosecuting the Nazis for the invasion of Poland, when they had agreed, in the Ribbentrop/Molotov pact of August 24th 1939, to do exactly the same in tandem
with them? How could Britain and the United States jointly prosecute Germany for breaking the terms of the Treaty of Versailles when the Americans had never ratified the treaty in the first place and on June 18th 1935, the British had agreed with German ambassadors the Anglo-German Naval Agreement, which gave their full backing to the German navy to exceed the limits set out in Versailles? How could the British and French jointly prosecute Germany for initiating aggressive war against Norway when it was something of an open secret that they too had planned to invade and occupy Norway, for tactical advantage?

Within this most sensitive of areas, three men were to be tried. They eventually met very different fates. Joachim von Ribbentrop, Franz von Papen and Konstantin von Neurath had all held high ranking positions within the Reich foreign office. Von Ribbentrop and von Neurath, both of whom had spells as Minister for Foreign Affairs, were indicted on all four counts, due to their key roles within the Nazi state, going right up into the midst of the war. Von Papen was a slightly different case. He was never a Nazi, having been a member of the Catholic Centre Party, a dyed-in-the-wool Monarchist and fully paid up fellow of the *Deutschen Herrenklub* (The German Gentlemen's club.) He had a brief spell as president of the *Reichstag* during the final years of the Weimar republic and when Hitler was finally appointed Chancellor, on 30th January 1933, in a Nazi/Conservative coalition, it was on the agreement that von Papen be made vice Chancellor, a post he resigned in July 1934 after a dispute with Hitler.

Despite this and probably to maintain favour with Papen's conservative supporters, Hitler appointed Papen as ambassador to Austria, a role which saw him play a part in the Anschluss. From 1939 to 1944 he assumed the relatively inconsequential position of Ambassador to Turkey.[491] His distance from the party and position on the fringes of the regime during its latter years meant that von Papen was indicted only on counts one and two.

Ribbentrop was by far the best known of the three within Allied circles, having been appointed Ambassador to the United Kingdom between 1936-39, a position in which he did everything asked of him by the Führer yet created something of a poor impression. On one, famous occasion he was introduced to King George VI and instead of simply greeting him and shaking hands, as was expected, he clicked his heels and thrust out his arm in a Nazi salute.[492] On another occasion he answered an informal question at a semi-official luncheon in Mayfair with a forty-five minute anti-Semitic monologue. Despite his own well documented anti-semitic views, Winston Churchill appeared most unimpressed, as did the minor royals in attendance.[493] Those who knew him at home tended to concur with the negative appraisal. Göring described him as 'a parrot'[494] (referring to his tendency to repeat whatever line Hitler took on things), while Prince Otto von Bismarck, a descendant of the renowned chancellor, regarded him as 'such an imbecile as to be a freak of nature.'[495] Hitler however described him as 'a genius.'[496]

Although all three had the aristocratic 'von' within their names, Ribbentrop acquired his through circuitous means.[497] In reality he came from a middle-class officer's family. By contrast and in contradiction of National Socialism's petty-bourgeois sensibilities, both von Neurath and von Papen were genuine aristocracy. Neurath was a Swabian Baron, while Papen hailed from a family of minor Westphalian nobility.

The evidence relevant to their cases largely fitted within Counts One and Two and much of it was presented during early December when Alderman and Amen for the United States and Shawcross, for the United Kingdom took their turns on the floor. These presentations revolved largely around German expansionism of the 1930s and the eventual outbreak of war. As would be expected, they presented a purely one sided view. For example, in his presentation, Shawcross pointedly avoided mentioning the Anglo-German Naval Treaty, and rather glossed over Munich, at which the occupation of Czechoslovakia had been agreed to by the British government. He also completely ignored the Ribbentrop/Molotov, pact to invade and carve up Poland. With regard to Britain's planned invasion of Norway, he said, 'I do not propose to argue the question whether or not these allegations were true or false. That question is irrelevant to the issues before this court.'[498] And with that he self-consciously sidestepped all matters of controversy.

When it came to the presentation of evidence against each of the defendants separately, Sir David Maxwell Fyfe presented the case against Ribbentrop, which essentially proved to be a summary of German foreign policy throughout the late thirties, as one would have expected. He detailed, from a purely Allied perspective, the invasions of Austria, Czechoslovakia, Poland, the Low Countries, Denmark and Norway. As Fyfe made his way through the list of Nazi 'aggressions', a particularly interesting point was raised when he quoted from a speech made by Hitler, in Ribbentrop's presence, regarding military actions in South Eastern Europe, particularly around Greece and Yugoslavia. Fyfe said, 'I desire to quote from there: Generally speaking, it would be best to liquidate the pseudo neutrals one after the other. This is fairly easily done if one Axis partner protects the rear of the other, as the latter finishes off one of the uncertain neutrals. Italy may consider Yugoslavia such an uncertain neutral.' The document went on to discuss the power relationships between Germany, Italy and various other countries, suggesting that neutrals who may in fact be prone to supporting the Allies, should be overrun. What is interesting is the use of the word 'liquidate'. It is worth remembering that in relation to other issues, the words *ausrottung*, *vernichtung* and *liquidierung* were deemed to have purely genocidal meanings. Yet here, Hitler used one of them in a context that was clearly not genocidal. When he talked of the 'liquidation' of Yugoslavia, he did not mean the country and its people should be utterly annihilated, but military conquest and the dismantling and replacement of the Yugoslavian state. This is worth remembering for the next chapter, during which the defendant Rosenberg tried to explain some of the

---

[491] Papen's biographical and career details from Davidson, p.176-218 and Neave p.160-172
[492] Conot, p.51
[493] ibid
[494] Conot, p.53
[495] Conot, p.52
[496] Fest, p.265
[497] he had himself adopted by the widow of his father's brother, a general who had been knighted, Conot p.51 and Fest, p.271
[498] Nuremberg Trial Proceedings, Vol.3, 12th day, Tuesday 4th December 1945, p.131

various meanings of these contentious German words.

Ribbentrop took to the stand on the 28th March and his defence and cross examination was one of the longest, other than Göring's. Unfortunately, Ribbentrop was an insomniac who rarely slept before four a.m. and who had been taking large doses of sleeping pills prior to the trial.[499]. His appearance before the court was lethargic – his eyes were heavy lidded and underscored with dark circles, his voice thick and slow. Even the other defendants were irritated by it and Schacht took to doing impressions of him in the lunch room, to the amusement of those around him.[500] As in his life before, he seemed to leave everybody with a poor impression at Nuremberg. Airey Neave described him as 'slovenly' and 'a second rate opportunist.'[501] Leon Goldensohn thought he was 'quite an affected fellow'[502] His former colleagues all made derisory statements.

His tedious testimony and then cross examination by Fyfe, then Faure (France), Amen and Rudenko was almost a waste of the court's time. With regard to the defence of his case, the evidentiary situation was hopeless and as Foreign Minister of Germany in a court that held his nation responsible for the outbreak of war, there was enough to condemn him purely on that score.

With regard to the other charges his case was less clear cut, although history has not always recorded this. Eugene Davidson, in an uncharacteristically unbalanced passage stated that Ribbentrop was 'as strong an anti-Semite as Streicher' and 'was deeply involved in the extermination of the Jews and the importing of slave labour.'[503]

Davidson's analysis does not appear justified, although Ribbentrop's case did bring out several anti-Semitic claims against him. For example, Faure, the French prosecutor, produced an affidavit regarding the Jews of Denmark, which said, among other things, '...the Reich Foreign Minister, Ribbentrop, obviously knew Hitler's intention to exterminate the Jews in Europe.' Ribbentrop responded to this signed statement by saying, 'What is written in this document is pure fantasy. It is not true.'[504]

Faure then produced a letter, signed by Martin Luther who worked under Ribbentrop in the Ministry, which discussed a policy of evacuation and enforced emigration of Jews from Europe. Ribbentrop did not deny the contents of this document and said, 'It was the Führer's plan, at the time, to deport the Jews from Europe to North Africa, and Madagascar was also mentioned in this connection. He ordered me to approach various governments with a view to encouraging the emigration of the Jews, if possible, and to remove all Jews from important government posts...'[505] Later in the questioning he made a similar admission stating that the evacuation plans for Northern Africa, Madagascar and Palestine had been deemed inoperable and that 'the Fuehrer had ordered that the Jews of the occupied territories in Europe were to be transported to reservations in the East and resettled there. That I did know. The carrying out of these measures, however, was not my task as Minister for Foreign Affairs of the Foreign Office, but I did know that it was the Fuehrer's wish...'[506]

Further to this allegation, another document was brought before the court which said 'The Foreign Minister declared that the Jews were either to be exterminated or sent to concentration camps. There was no other solution.' Ribbentrop replied with, 'I definitely did not say it in those words... These are notes. I personally have never seen these notes before; otherwise I should have said at once that this is nonsense and liable to misconstruction. I did not see these notes before; I saw them for the first time in Nuremberg. I can say only one thing which may possibly have occurred. I might have said ... well yes, 'the Jews cannot be exterminated or beaten to death, so, please do something in order that the Fuehrer will be satisfied at long last, and centralize the Jews.' That was our aim, at that time at any rate. We did not want to render the situation more acute, but we were trying to do something in Hungary so that no other department could take the matter in hand... This solution should consist of two points. One was the removal of the Jews from important government positions and two, since there were so many Jews in Budapest, to centralize the Jews in certain quarters of Bu-

---

[499] Davidson, p.161 & Conot.p.53
[500] Gilbert, p.225
[501] Neave, p.84
[502] Goldensohn, p.184
[503] Davidson, p.161
[504] Nuremberg Trial Proceedings, Vol. 10, 97th day, Tuesday, 2nd April, 1946, p.397
[505] ibid
[506] ibid, p.407

dapest.'[507]

What this demonstrates, in contradiction of what historians like Davidson have had to say, is that Ribbentrop was not demonstrating that he was knee-deep in the Holocaust, as we understand it today. Clearly, he was admitting to Crimes against Humanity, in the sense of his open admissions regarding anti-Semitic decrees, deportation, evacuation and the establishment of ghettoes but, like others, time after time, he categorically denied knowing anything about an extermination plan for Jews or the alleged goings-on at Auschwitz and other camps.

Rudenko brought up the matter of slave labour, which Ribbentrop admitted to knowledge of, but denied responsibility for. He also stated that, 'According to what I heard, all these foreign workers are supposed to have been well treated in Germany. I think it is possible, of course, that other things might have happened, too; but on the whole, I believe that a good deal was done to treat these workers well.'[508]

There were other attempts to connect him to Crimes against Humanity, or War Crimes. Fyfe asked him 'Are you saying that you did not know that concentration camps were being carried on in an enormous scale?' Ribbentrop replied, 'No, I knew nothing about that.'[509] Fyfe followed that up, several questions later with, '…the German official of Auschwitz has sworn an affidavit that 4 million people were put to death in the camp. Are you telling the Tribunal that that happened without your knowing anything about it?' Ribbentrop again answered in the negative. 'That was entirely unknown to me.'[510]

Several more questions passed and Fyfe broached the now familiar subject of partisans. Ribbentrop was initially evasive, but then admitted, 'I am of the opinion that the partisans who attack the troops in the rear should be treated harshly. Yes, I am of that opinion, I believe everyone in the Army is of that opinion, and every politician.'[511] Fyfe then produced a document, detailing an ambassadorial conference between Germany and Italy, in which issues relating to the territory of Croatia were reviewed, in which Ribbentrop had stated 'These partisan gangs had to be exterminated, including men, women, and children, as their further existence imperilled the lives of German and Italian men, women, and children.'

Clearly, again, Ribbentrop had admitted to knowledge of and complicity in what constituted a Crime against Humanity, although yet again it was in connection with partisans, rather than being an anti-Jewish measure. But by now the die looked well and truly cast. Schacht commented to Gilbert that Ribbentrop had 'convicted himself already.'[512]

The presentation against von Papen was brief. It was handled by the British junior counsel, Major J. Harcourt Barrington. Within the scope of the entire trial it was a relatively inconsequential case and as shall be explained later, was summed up by Barrington's opening sentence, 'The Defendant Papen is charged primar- ily with the guilt of conspiracy.'[513] Later discussions among the judges regarding the conspiracy charge radi- cally altered its interpretation by the court and rendered von Papen's case a non-event.

Maxwell-Fyfe again picked up the baton for presentation against von Neurath, which in many ways was very similar to Ribbentrop's, von Neurath having preceded him as Foreign minister. Fyfe outlined his role in German foreign policy, his holding of the position of *Obergruppenführer* in the SS (this was an honorary position, also given to Ribbentrop, which von Neurath said he did not actually want)[514] and his role in the protectorate of Bohemia and Moravia, under which some of the Crimes Against Humanity were alleged to have been committed. Neurath's main plank of defence was that he was serving his country, not Nazism, a fact that was evidenced by his various diplomatic posts during the days of the Weimar Republic, culminating with his serving as foreign minister in the government of von Papen, prior to Hitler accession to power. Indeed, he had only joined the party in 1937 as a concession to Hitler's wishes. He was implicated in some minor crimes in the Czech regions that he governed in the last part of his career, largely centred around the 'Germanisation' of the citizens there and his appearance on the stand was affected by his state of mind,

---

[507] ibid, p.410
[508] ibid, p.440
[509] ibid, 96th day, Monday 1st April, 1946, p.386
[510] ibid, p.388
[511] ibid, p.390
[512] Gilbert, p.231
[513] Nuremberg Trial Proceedings, Vol. 6, 41st day, Wednesday 23rd January 1946, p.73
[514] Nuremberg Trial Proceedings, Vol 6, 41st day, Wednesday, 23rd January, 1946, p.98

which many conjectured was failing due to age.[515]

At the deliberation meetings, von Ribbentrop's case culminated with one of the swiftest judging decisions of the entire trial. As with Göring, there was no option. To exonerate the German foreign minister would be to admit that other nations had played a role in causing the war. That simply could not happen. All judges voted for guilt on all four counts and a sentence of death by hanging.[516]

After initial deliberations by the judges it was felt that von Papen's only guilt lay within Count One. However, they had meanwhile decided that count one could only apply to Crimes against Peace – the charges of conspiracy to commit War Crimes and Crimes against Humanity were deemed inoperable and dropped against all defendants. Papen was therefore acquitted on a tied vote, with the British and American judges voting not guilty and the Russian and French in favour of a prison sentence.

Von Neurath's case provided one of the strangest judgements. He was harshly pronounced guilty on all four counts, but then given only a prison sentence of fifteen years.

Contrary to all expectation, on the gallows, Joachim von Ribbentrop was one of the calmest and most resolute of the convicted men. His last words were 'God protect Germany. God have mercy on my soul. My last wish is that German unity be maintained, that understanding between East and West be realised and that there be peace in the world.'[517] Post war events could not have done more to ensure that his wishes were not granted.

Von Papen was rearrested after his release and sentenced to ten years hard labour. He appealed and was released after two years, published an autobiography and died in 1969. Von Neurath was held in Spandau until suffering a heart attack in 1953. He was released due to ill health and died soon afterwards.

---

[515] Conot, p.450
[516] Taylor, p.561
[517] Taylor, p.610

14

The Politics of Race

An invasion of armies can be resisted, but not an idea whose time has come.
- Victor Hugo, 'Histoire d'un crime'

Alfred Rosenberg and Wilhelm Frick

According to the 2008 edition of the Oxford English Dictionary, racism is 'the belief that all members of each race possess characteristics, abilities, or qualities specific to that race, especially so as to distinguish it as inferior or superior to another race or races…' There is no other word in the English language more capable of raising the heckles of the average social scientist.

An internet search for it, in November 2007, using one of the net's most popular search engines, yielded nearly thirty two million results and on brief perusal, the majority appeared to be vigorously decrying it, as a belief system. (There were also a few vigorously supporting it – passions run high on both sides). Modern workplaces, educational institutions and even leisure facilities all have equal opportunities statements in place to combat it. Hate speech, defamation and religious intolerance, all sub-categories of it, have now become illegal, in some form, in the UK. Racism, within early 21st Century western culture, is no longer a crime of action, whereby discrimination in the form of racially motivated violence or destruction of property, or even name-calling is punished. It has become a crime of ideology. To borrow from George Orwell – it could be described as a 'thought crime'. European Union legislation passed in April 2007, the latest in a long line of national and international initiatives, makes it criminal to 'incite hatred or violence against a group or a person based on colour, race, national or ethnic origin.'[518]

Of course, the issue with the passing of such laws is that somebody has to define what counts as 'incitement' and what does not. There is then the remarkably tricky issue of balancing this with the right to freedom of speech, which is guaranteed by both the EU and the UN charters. Rather than attempt to take responsibility for this themselves, the EU have decided that it is a matter to be adjudicated upon by individual, member states. Of tangential interest to our subject, they do suggest that Holocaust Denial ought to be punishable

---

[518] Reuters, 18th April, 2007. *EU to agree watered-down anti-racism law*
http://uk.reuters.com/article/topNews/idUKL1816833320070418?pageNumber=2

(without defining what, specifically, Holocaust Denial is).[519]

Many people, when looking for the origins of this furore, talk of the British Empire, of 'Coolies' and 'Kaffirs' and the Afro-American slave trade which goes with it. However, important as these things were in shaping our current attitudes, they did not occur immediately before a period of enormous intercontinental migration. Neither did they drag behind them so obvious a chariot of legislation and opinion. The anti-racist focus of the late twentieth century stems instead from Nuremberg.

The seeds of this focus were sown in the legal platform built before the trial. By the time the indictment was written, with its delineation of the four counts, 'race' was being overtly referred to. According to Michael Marrus, '…'crimes against humanity' was a distinct innovation of the Nuremberg Trial'[520] created by the United Nations War Crimes Commission, who defined them as, 'committed against any person…because of race, nationality, religious or political belief…'[521] This represented the first appearance of 'anti-racism' in international law. Marrus also states that at the London conference at which the Nuremberg charter was drafted, the American prosecution team understood such crimes 'to be integral to Nazism itself'[522] Interestingly, Jackson added that 'he had been specifically urged by émigré groups'[523] to prosecute these crimes. As a result, it could well be argued that it was Jackson et al who pioneered the changing of the status of racism, from a philosophy whose evidence one may examine and evaluate and choose to agree or disagree with, like any other, to a crime.

There can be no doubt that the belief in Teutonic supremacy was fundamental to the Nazi party programme, wrapped-up as it was with ideas of the *Herrenvolk* and *Lebensraum*.[524] In 'Mein Kampf', Hitler made many references to racial issues and made it clear that they sat at the very heart of everything National Socialism was about. For example, in a chapter titled 'Race and People', he wrote, '…whenever Aryans have mingled their blood with that of an inferior race the result has been the downfall of the people who were the standard bearers of a higher culture'[525] and '…it was the Aryan alone who founded a superior type of humanity…he (the Aryan) is the Prometheus of mankind, from whose shining brow the divine spark of genius has at all times flashed forth.'[526] Jews, on the other hand were described as 'especially cunning'[527], lacking in 'idealistic spirit'[528] and being involved in 'a systematic use of falsehood.'[529]

To some degree therefore, *every* man in the dock at Nuremberg, through his association with Hitler and the party (and in some cases this association was stronger than others) stood accused of subscribing to 'racism'. Yet despite the pervasiveness of *Rassenpolitik* (racial politics) within Nazism, three of the defendants were associated with it above all others. One, Julius Streicher, has already been discussed. The second was Alfred Rosenberg, a writer of more academic posture than Streicher whose work was eventually to reach a very wide audience. Rosenberg was author of many articles in the *Völkischer Beobachter* (the National So- cialist newspaper, which he also edited), as well as several full length works. In 1920 he published 'The Trail of the Jew in the Course of Time' and 'Immorality in the Talmud' followed by, 'The Crime of Freemasonry'(1921), 'The Morass or Plague in Russia' (1922), then, in 1923, 'The Protocols of the Elders of Zion and Jewish World Politics' (republished 1940) and lastly his most famous work, which went on to sell over a million copies 'The Myth of the Twentieth Century' (1930)[530], which was a kind of Aryanised view of world history, arguing for an abandonment of Christianity (which Rosenberg said 'was ennobled solely by the fact

---

[519] Holocaust Denial is already punishable by the national law of a number of countries, including Germany and Austria. Several (in)famous deniers, including Ernst Zündel, Germar Rudolf and David Irving (who is not, by normal definition, a denier but is popularly regarded as such) have recently fallen foul of these laws and found themselves imprisoned.
[520] Michael R. Marrus, The Nuremberg War Crimes Trial 1945-6, A Documentary History (Bedford Books 1997), p.185
[521] ibid, p.186
[522] ibid
[523] ibid
[524] *Herrenvolk* means 'superior people' or more commonly, 'master race'. The word almost has class connotations, rather than racial ones – Herren actually means 'Gentlemen'. But in the Nazi context it assumed a racial meaning. *Lebensraum* means 'living space' and refers to the desire to expand German territory to accommodate their population's needs.
[525] Adolf Hitler, *Mein Kampf*, (Jaico 1988) p.259
[526] ibid, p.262
[527] ibid, p.272
[528] ibid, p.274
[529] ibid, p.277
[530] Rosenberg's publishing history taken from Fest, p.252

that Germans had believed in it'[531]) and a revival of Nordic paganism, involving views on Atlantis and other mythological ideas.[532] Racial theory played a key part in his thesis. 'The essence of the contemporary world revolution lies in the awakening of the racial type' he wrote, 'not in Europe alone but on the whole planet. This awakening is the organic counter movement against the last chaotic remnants of liberal economic imperialism, whose objects of exploitation...have fallen into the snare of Bolshevik Marxism, in order to complete what democracy had begun, the extirpation of the racial and national consciousness.'[533] In the same book he also stated that 'Racial history is therefore natural history and the mysticism of the soul at one and the same time...the history of the religion of the blood...is the great world story...of heroes and thinkers...inventors and artists.'[534]

In some senses the book contained shades of Karl Marx, whose fundamental belief was that class conflict powered the 'motor of history'. Rosenberg subscribed also to the 'conflict' view, but saw the wheels being turned instead by inter-racial struggle. This should really be of no surprise to anyone as the far right movements in Europe at the time owed their origins to the crisis of Marxism in the 1880s. They had begun as offshoots of Marxist thinking. It was a struggle in which he felt there could only be one winner. 'Today a new faith is stirring' he declared, 'the faith that along with blood we are defending the divine nature of man as a whole. The belief...that Nordic blood represents the mystery which has replaced and overcome the old sacraments.'[535]

Taken as a whole, the book contained little in the way of fact. It was difficult therefore to challenge it. What he wrote could not be construed as falsification as it was purely interpretative. Beneath its racial theorising bubbled a kind of new-age spirituality and a rejection of aspects of the capitalist ethos. Opinion on his magnum opus was mixed. Goebbels described it as 'an ideological belch'[536] while Hitler, it seems, made comments both of approval and disdain. Some other academics heaped praise upon it, like the philosopher Alfred Baeumler (a fellow Nazi) who said of the book that its ideas were of such great scope, they were not easy to grasp, hence the miscomprehension of some critics.[537]

Rosenberg had grown up in Estonia, in an ethnically German household. He had left his homeland in 1918, to escape the advance of Bolshevism and emigrated to Paris where he tried to engineer an entry permit to live in the UK, but was refused. As a result he opted for his second choice and made the journey to Munich.[538] He joined the German Workers Party soon after, in its early days under the leadership of Anton Drexler[539], as member 625, several months before it changed its name to the NSDAP[540] His responsibilities grew along with the party and among Rosenberg's eventual official positions he held the wonderful title of Commisioner of the Führer for the Safeguarding of the National Socialist Philosophy. (For this reason and for the purposes of brevity, he is often simply referred to as the Party Philosopher.)

The third of this trio of thought criminals was Wilhelm Frick, Hitler's Minister of the Interior, who was to author the infamous 'Nuremberg Laws' which forbad the mixing of Germans and Jews. Despite this rather key role in the development of the state apparatus of Nazism, Frick is an often overlooked figure, a fact which is even more surprising when his pivotal role in the early parliamentary days of the Party is considered. He had a police background and was one of the first National Socialists to be elected to the Reichstag, in 1923. In 1927, Frick became the Nazis parliamentary leader and in 1929, a Nazi surge in voting popularity saw them form a coalition government in which Frick was the first ever Nazi Minister of Germany, becom- ing Minister of the Interior and Education in Thurungia. It was a position he eventually resigned in 1931, af- ter banning the playing of Jazz in the region and installing Nazis in charge of the local University and Acad-

---

[531] Neave, p.110
[532] Davidson, p.133
[533] Rosenberg, Alfred, 'The Myth of the Twentieth Century', p.479, quoted by Brudno in the prosecution case against Rosenberg, Nuremberg Trial Proceedings, Vol 5. 30th day, Wednesday 9th January, 1946, p.42
[534] quoted in Fest, p.253
[535] ibid, p.254
[536] Neave, p.110
[537] Davidson, p.133
[538] Davidson, p.128
[539] It was alleged by the American prosecutor, Brudno that Rosenberg had joined even before Hitler. Nuremberg Trial Proceedings, Vol 5. 30th day, Wednesday 9th January, 1946. p.41. Rosenberg himself denied this.
[540] Nuremberg Trial Proceedings, Vol. 11, 108th day, Monday 15th April 1946, p.446

emy of Arts. After Hitler's accession to the chancellorship, Frick was immediately appointed to the cabinet as National Minister of the Interior and in his first act in the role, proposed the Enabling Law that would give Hitler complete executive power. The Law was eventually passed on March 24th 1933.

At Hitler's request Frick passed his first anti-Semitic decree in February 1934, which involved the dismissal of Non-Aryan officials in government employ. (Depending on length of service, they did receive pay-offs and pensions.) Eugene Davidson nicely summarised the dominant view of history, which tends to see the passage of racial legislation under Hitler as a greasy slope, leading towards an inevitable horror, when he described this Act as 'the first legal step toward the Final Solution.'[541]

On September 15th 1935, Frick passed the now infamous Nuremberg Laws, which illegalised marriage and extra marital sex between Jews and Germans and also stated that only those of Aryan blood could be German citizens. Indeed, on the 13th December, during their presentation on the persecution of the Jews, the prosecution, in the form of Major William Walsh, detailed a whole series of decrees signed by Frick which were discriminatory, ranging from the measures described above, to those which denied Jews access to parts of certain cities, or those which denied them participation in certain professions, like finance, medicine and the media.

In addition to the above, in the early thirties, the SS and the Gestapo had both fallen generally under Frick's jurisdiction, but by 1936, as both grew and the influence of individuals like Himmler and Heydrich developed, they broke away. Frick did not, therefore control these organisations during the time when it was alleged they committed their worst excesses. However that is not to say that he wasn't implicated in mass murder at Nuremberg. As well as being committed to Nazi racial theory, he was also involved in the Nazis' development of another ideology which predated them, yet formed an integral part of their world view, Social Darwinism[542], which would find its practical embodiment in the T4 Euthanasia programme.[543]

Robert Kempner, the émigré prosecutor on Jackson's staff, took the responsibility of presenting the case against Frick. He stated that, 'One category of Frick's contribution to the planning of and preparation for aggressive war deserves special notice. This is the systematic killing of persons regarded as useless to the German war machine, such as the insane, the crippled, the aged and foreign labourers who were no longer able to work.'[544]

Clearly, to any rational observer or reader, the implementation of a Euthanasia programme for handicapped and diseased individuals has little or nothing to do with preparation for war, however, from the line that Kempner continued to take, we can develop an understanding of why the evidence was introduced in this way. He went on to describe the Hadamar sanatorium, mentioned before in relation to the 'Nazi Concentration Camps' film and the atrocities committed there, which Kempner evidenced with a letter written by the Bishop of Limburg, which said, 'Several times a week buses arrive in Hadamar with a considerable number of such victims. School children of the vicinity know this vehicle and say, 'There comes the murder box again.' After the arrival of the vehicle, the citizens of Hadamar watch the smoke rise out of the chimney and are tortured with the ever-present thought of the miserable victims, especially when repulsive odors annoy them, depending on the direction of the wind.'[545] Hadamar had been liberated by the Americans, hence its appearance in their film and the American prosecution had taken responsibility for the Conspiracy and to some extent the Aggressive War' charges. (The latter was really handled by the British, but the Americans stepped in from time to time.) Having unearthed Hadamar, the Americans had obviously decided to introduce it through their case, even though what they were alleging would have constituted a 'Crime against Human- ity' and not 'Conspiracy' or 'Crimes against Peace'. The Soviets, however, who had responsibility for presenting the 'Humanity' charge had a preference for presenting their own evidence. Rather than have it forgotten, the Americans obviously decided to have Kempner squeeze Hadamar into his presentation, despite the fact it did not necessarily fit.

---

[541] Davidson, p.268
[542] Social Darwinism is the idea that theories of evolution and natural selection can be used to understand human society, in particular the domination of some groups by others. Oddly it does not always equate to a co-option of Darwin's thesis – it is applied as a label, even to the work of those who predate Darwin such as Thomas Malthus. Other famous exponents include Francis Galton and one of Rosenberg's personal influences, Arthur de Gobineau.
[543] Frick's biographical and career details taken from Davidson, p.260-281, Neave p.127-132 and Maser 205-7.
[544] Nuremberg Trial Proceedings, Vol. 5, 35th day, Wednesday 16th January 1946, p.361
[545] ibid, p.363

This constituted the only real evidence presented at the IMT regarding the Euthanasia programme. (There was also a brief report written by the Czechoslovak War Crimes Commission). Even as Kempner introduced this scant evidence, there were questions raised about whether this had anything to do with the case that had been brought before them. Judge Lawrence himself asked at one point, 'is it clear that the trial relates to the killing of Polish and Russian nationals in nursing homes or institutions of that sort?' Kempner replied, 'it is absolutely clear.'[546]

Within the context of the whole trial, then, T4 was an incredibly minor issue, almost nothing more than a footnote. However as the current historical narrative has placed substantial importance upon it, citing it as the forerunner of the Holocaust, in which much of the later practices, including gas chambers[547], were first trialled, a short paragraph will be taken to describe its implementation.

On July 14th, 1933, 'The Law for the Prevention of Offspring with Hereditary Diseases' was passed, (it had been written by Frick) which provided for the compulsory sterilisation of those with genetic disorders. Clearly, such practice has some links with Nazi racial ideology, as the desire for a *herrenvolk* could only be achieved by eliminating what are usually referred to as 'useless eaters.' Nazi films and articles of the late thirties in fact characterised the disabled as being *Lebensunwertes Leben* 'lives unworthy of living.' 'Useless eaters' (*unnuetze fresser*) was far less common but has become a kind of catchphrase of historians. This was the first step toward the development of the Euthanasia programme, which eventually operated through six centres; Bernburg, Brandenburg, Grafeneck, Hadamar, Hartheim, and Sonnenstein. Selected individuals were brought to the centres and killed.[548]

There is much in the tales of the T4 centres that replicated itself in the later witness accounts of the Holocaust death camps. The pretence of delousing and showers, the crematoria and the smell of the smoke, the suspicions of the townsfolk nearby, who never quite knew what was happening, but always suspected, and this theme has been developed heavily by several historians, in particular Henry Friedlander, in his 'The Origins of Nazi Genocide: From Euthanasia to the Final Solution.' However, the fact remains that evidence for the T4 programme was almost totally collated and presented at later trials and it is therefore outside of the subject of this book. All that is relevant here is that as the Minister of the Interior until 1943, the defendant Frick stood accused of legislating the programme into existence and then aiding in its implementation.

Rosenberg took the stand on the afternoon of the 15th April. It was not a fortuitous date as far as the arguing of his case was concerned. The morning session of the same day had been taken up with testimony and affidavit of Rudolf Höss. The court had just heard, in graphic detail, what the apparent results of the Nazi Philosophy were and the world's media had already begun to publish the story of gas chambers and three million victims at Auschwitz. Nazi 'evil', more so than ever, was now an accepted fact. Rosenberg privately told Gilbert he regarded this timing as 'a dirty trick' by the tribunal, a point to which Gilbert was predictably unsympathetic.[549]

The testimony elicited from Rosenberg by his defence lawyer, Dr, Alfred Thoma was, according to Gil- bert, 'a merry-go round of abstruse historical rationalizations.'[550] In reality, Rosenberg seemed to be attempt- ing to defend himself on the same basis on which he was being attacked, which was, at least in part, ideologically. By glancing back to the beginning of the trial and Brudno's presentation of the case against Rosenberg, this paragraph is seen, '...the first phase of proof will deal with Rosenberg as official National Socialist ideologist. The proof which I will present will show the nature and scope of the ideological tenets he expounded, and the influence he exerted upon the unification of German thought, a unification which was an essential part of the conspirators' program...'[551] after presenting his proofs, Brudno summed up by saying, 'If the Tribunal is satisfied that Rosenberg's ideas formed the foundation for the National Socialist ideologi-

---

[546] ibid, p.364
[547] It is worth noting that like the camps, none of the Euthanasia centres had gas chambers when they were liberated. All of them were alleged to have been dismantled or destroyed, even in the sanatoria like Hadamar, which continued to operate right up until 1945.
[548] It is claimed that most of the centres had gas chambers and killed also with lethal injection. However, no evidence for either method was presented before the IMT.
[549] Gilbert, p.266
[550] Gilbert, p.267
[551] Nuremberg Trial Proceedings, Vol. 5, 30th day, Wednesday 9th January, 1946, p.42

cal movement, I will pass on.'[552] A quick scan of Rosenberg's section of the indictment also shows the ideological nature of the majority of his crimes. It states that 'He developed, disseminated, and exploited the doctrinal techniques of the Nazi conspirators... he promoted the accession to power of the Nazi conspirators and the consolidation of their control over Germany... he promoted the psychological preparations for war...'[553] Certainly on counts one and two at least (he was indicted on all four counts) his crimes were not deemed to be those of actions, but of thoughts and words. The prosecution had alleged that his ideology had been fundamental to the 'conspiracy'. Rosenberg therefore had to defend his ideas in order to defend himself properly.

When asked to provide justification for the party programme as it was outlined in 1920, he said, 'The technical revolution of the 19th Century had certain social and mental consequences. Industrialization and the clamor for profit dominated life and created the industrial state and the metropolis with all its backyards and estrangement from nature and history.'[554]

Through this answer, Rosenberg described an often forgotten side to National Socialism, the desire to reconnect with the soil on which the Reich had been built. Money and the pursuit of it was seen as decadent and unnatural (and this was something Nazis identified with Jews who dominated banking and finance). Rosenberg identified a yearning, within his writings, for the Reich to begin an era in which technology and industry and profit played their part, but were not pursued above all else. Community and nature should be revived and celebrated. These utopian, 'green' ideals of Nazism are often overlooked in the clamour to condemn it, yet need to be remembered in any balanced discussion. Rosenberg summarized this himself, saying 'many terrible things have been delivered during these three months by the Prosecution, but nothing has been said about National Socialism'[555]

He was attempting to show that contrary to the opinion of the prosecution, such things as had been evidenced before the court thus far were an aberration, not a symptom. Thoma then moved him on, encouraging him to explain his beliefs on the class system, to which Rosenberg said, 'the reactionary caste prejudice of privileged circles had worked to the detriment of the people' adding that 'the representation of national interests should not be based on privileges of certain classes'[556]

Again, the egalitarianism that the Nazis sought to promote, similar, in some ways to the Marxist doctrine, is not something popularly remembered. Hitler's championing of the *Volkswagen* (people's car), the construction of the *Autobahns* and the implementation of the *Kraft durch Freude* (strength through joy) programme are all examples of this. Despite the elucidation being provided by Rosenberg's responses, however Dodd, for the USA and Rudenko, for the Soviet Union began complaining about Thoma's approach of encouraging Rosenberg to explain his beliefs. Dodd interjected by saying, '...I should like to say that no one in the Prosecution has made any charge against this defendant for what he has thought. I think we are all, as a matter of principle, opposed to prosecuting any man for what he thinks. And I say with great respect that I feel very confident that is the attitude of this Tribunal.'[557]

It is strange, bearing in mind the nature of the case that was held against Rosenberg, as outlined by Brudno, that such objections should have been raised. Dodd seemed to be directly contradicting what Brudno had said earlier in the trial. How else was the party philosopher to defend himself, other than by explaining his philosophy? There were ripples here still spreading outward from the case of Göring, whereby the tribu- nal had decided to prevent other defendants from speaking at length, for fear that they would use the trial as a basis for propaganda. If Rosenberg were permitted to fully explain the original intentions of Nazism and show it in a positive light, the aim of 'denazification' might be hampered.

Despite repeated complaints and interruptions, Thoma defended his right to continue such questioning, yet was certainly affected, as he began to hurry Rosenberg, pressuring him to be brief. Later that day Rosenberg complained to Gilbert about the constant derailing of his answers. 'Well' he said, 'if they just want to make it a criminal trial, why don't the prosecution stick to criminal acts instead of attacking my ide-

---

[552] ibid, p.49
[553] Nuremberg Trial Proceedings Vol.1, *Indictment Appendix A*
[554] Nuremberg Trial Proceedings, Vol. 11, 108th day, Monday 15th April 1946, p.447
[555] ibid
[556] ibid, p.448
[557] ibid

ology?'[558]

It was a very reasonable criticism. However, unlike Streicher, for example, both he and Frick had to face the fact that they also had other things on their plates. As Minister for the Eastern Occupied Territories, Rosenberg had nominally had charge over the part of the Reich in which the worst of the indictment's atrocities were alleged to have occurred. The role was, however, meaningless. Hitler had no faith in Rosenberg as an active politician and ensured that he was effectively bypassed in the chain of command. His authority in the area had therefore amounted to nothing. Clearly, he had not personally rounded up civilians or pulled a trigger. But he would, because of his official position, be held responsible for such things.

After Dodd's objection, he was then asked by his lawyer, 'Then I should like to ask the defendant how he will answer the charge that National Socialism preached a master race.'

This, in many ways, was the crux of Rosenberg's case and the defendant recognized it himself, giving the following response:

'I know that this problem is the main point of the Indictment and I realize that at present, in view of the number of terrible incidents, conclusions are automatically drawn about the past and the reason for the origin of the so-called racial science. I believe, however, that it is of decisive importance in judging this problem to know exactly what we were concerned with. I have never heard the word 'master race' (*Herrenrasse*) as often as in this court room. To my knowledge, I did not mention or use it at all in my writings...I spoke only once of super humans as mentioned by Homer, and I found a quotation from a British author, who...said the Englishman who had conquered the world had proved himself as a creative superman (*Herrenmensch*). Then I found the word 'master race' in a writing of the American ethnologist, Madison Grant, and of the French ethnologist, Lapouge. I would like to admit, however...that the word 'superman' came to my attention particularly during my activ- ity as Minister in the East- and very unpleasantly-when used by a number of leaders of the admini- stration in the East. Perhaps when we come to the question of the East, I may return to this subject in detail... however, I was convinced that ethnology was, after all, not an invention of the National So- cialist movement, but a biological discovery, which was the conclusion of 400 years of European re- search. The laws of heredity discovered in the 1860's, and rediscovered several decades later, enable us to gain a deeper insight into history than many other earlier theories.'[559]

Although on the defensive, Rosenberg was again describing the reality. Racial biology, as a branch of science (or at least *credible* science) did not find its beginnings in Nazism, only its end. Rosenberg and others had simply developed the ideas of Lamarck[560], a contemporary of Darwin and applied them to humanity. Neither were they the first to do this.

Racial theory had emerged, like most philosophical ideas, from a process of steady progression. Many pre-20th Century works, such as Emmanuel Kant's '*A Critique of Pure Reason*' (1781) or Arthur Schopenhauer's '*Parerga and Paralipomena*' (1851) contained elements of what would later be called racial ideology. The latter, for example contained this section:

'The highest civilization and culture, apart from the ancient Hindus and Egyptians, are found exclusively among the white races; and even with many dark peoples, the ruling caste or race is fairer in colour than the rest and has, therefore, evidently immigrated, for example, the Brahmans, the Incas, and the rulers of the South Sea Islands. All this is due to the fact that necessity is the mother of invention because those tribes that emigrated early to the north, and there gradually became white, had to develop all their intellectual powers and invent and perfect all the arts in their struggle with need, want and misery, which in their many forms were brought about by the climate. This they had to do in order to make up for the parsimony of nature and out of it all came their high civilization.'[561]

---

[558] Gilbert, p.267
[559] ibid, p.450
[560] R. Gayre of Gayre, *Race and Nazi Racism and the Latter's Impact on Anthropology*, The Mankind Quarterly, Vol. XVIII, No. 4, (April-June 1978), pp. 293-303
[561] Arthur Schopenhauer *Parerga and Paralipomena*, (Oxford University Press 2001) Volume II, Section 92

French writers like Lapouge and Gobineau, the Englishman, Francis Galton and the American, Madison Grant all pre-empted the Nazis in their racial interpretation of human biology. In Germany, Wilhelm Marr was the first to argue, in 1879 that social issues related to the Jews (their domination of certain spheres, in particular the financial and their failure to integrate with wider society) may have been, at least partly, a mat- ter of biology and heredity.[562] This theme was later picked up on by Eugene Dühring and then Theodor Fritsch. In the modern world a similar theory has been proposed by Kevin B. MacDonald, professor of Psychology at California State University. The Nazis were simply the latest in a long line of people to subscribe to such ideas.

As a result of the historical record regarding Nazi Germany, however, the scientific study of race has been completely removed from the post-war global agenda and replaced with the platitude that 'race is only skin deep' or the simple falsehood that 'there is no such thing as race.' It is only in the last ten to fifteen years that theorists like Harvard professor Richard Hernnstein or the University of Western Ontario's J.P. Rushton[563] have begun to re-approach the subject and when they have done so, they have generally been met with a cacophony of condemnation. The ethos created by Nuremberg has seen to that. Even more recently, Leeds University Professor, Frank Ellis was suspended from teaching, in 2006, for suggesting racial disparities in intelligence. Nobel Prize winning DNA scientist, James Watson found himself lambasted in the media and barred from speaking at the London Science Museum for racial comments made to the Sunday Times in 2007.

Baldur von Schirach, a defendant to be discussed in a later chapter, ended his defence with the statement that 'he who still clings to racial politics after Auschwitz is a criminal.'[564] One wonders if he had any inkling that by saying that he would be summarising the social norms and policies of the Western world for at least the next sixty-five years. After Nuremberg, race would become the 'elephant in the closet' of the intellectual community.

Later on, Dodd was to pick up Rosenberg's cross examination. In keeping with his earlier statements he focused mainly on crimes of action rather than ideas, initially eliciting admissions from Rosenberg that in regard to Eastern Europe, he had ratified the slave labour programme. He then produced a letter from Bormann to Rosenberg, discussing treatment of the Slavs, which made some shocking suggestions. 'The Slavs are to work for us, in so far as we don't need them, they may die...Education is dangerous. It is enough if they can count up to 100... As for food, they don't get any more than is necessary. We are the masters, we come first.'[565] It needs to be pointed out here that these were not Bormann's actual words. After the document had first been read at the trial, during Lt Lambert's prosecution presentation on the 16th January, it finished with the comment 'We respectfully submit this as an accurate paraphrase and summary of the text of that document, Document R-36.'[566] Dodd, however neglected to mention this, leaving the impression that it was a complete transcript.

He then proceeded to try to to smear Rosenberg with Bormann's paraphrased words, by alleging that he had replied with a letter of agreement, 'And you had agreed with these-if I may use the term-shocking suggestions of Bormann? In your letter you had agreed with these shocking suggestions of Bormann? 'Yes' or 'no'?' Rosenberg replied to this by saying, 'I wrote an appeasing letter so that I could bring about a pause in the constant pressure under which I was kept, and I would like to anticipate and say that my activity, and the decrees which I issued after this letter, did not change in any way; but, on the contrary, decrees were issued setting up a school and a system and for the further continuation of health control....'[567]

Dodd then moved into other familiar territory, producing a memorandum of a conversation between Rosenberg and Hitler that took place on the 14th December 1941, in which a speech was planned in which Rosenberg was meant to talk of the *ausrottung* of the Jews. This word has been mentioned before and translates literally into English as 'uprooting', however it is commonly translated as 'exterminating'. (Further dis-

---

[562] Francis R. Nicosia, *The Emergence of Modern Antisemitism*, in *The Holocaust, Introductory Essays*, edited by David Scrase and Wolfgang Mieder (Center for Holocaust Studies, University of Vermont, 1996) p.29
[563] Hernnstein authored *'The Bell Curve'* (1994) and Rushton *'Race, Evolution and Behaviour'* (1995).
[564] Nuremberg Trial Proceedings, 138th day, Friday, 24th May, 1946, p.369
[565] Nuremberg Trial Proceedings, Vol. 11, 110th day, Wednesday 17th April 1946, p.542
[566] Nuremberg Trial Proceedings Vol.5, 35th day, Wednesday 16th January 1946, p.332
[567] Nuremberg Trial Proceedings, Vol. 11, 110th day, Wednesday 17th April 1946, p.545

cussion of this point can be found in chapter twenty, towards the end of this book.) Dodd offered to provide Rosenberg a dictionary to confirm that the word related to genocide and Rosenberg replied, 'I do not need a foreign dictionary in order to explain the various meanings '*ausrottung*' may have in the German language. One can exterminate an idea, an economic system, a social order, and as a final consequence, also a group of human beings, certainly. Those are the many possibilities which are contained in that word... It means 'to overcome' on one side and then it is to be used not with respect to individuals but rather to juridical entities, to certain historical traditions. On the other side this word has been used with respect to the German people and we have also not believed that in consequence thereof 60 millions of Germans would be shot.'[568]

Clearly unsatisfied with the explanation, Dodd tried to press the issue, by linking Rosenberg's conversation with Hitler with the recently evidenced goings-on at Auschwitz. 'I want to remind you that this speech of yours in which you use the term '*ausrottung*' was made about 6 months after Himmler told Höss, whom you heard on this witness stand, to start exterminating the Jews. That is a fact, is it not?'[569]

Rosenberg replied, 'No, that is not correct...'

When considering Dodd's attempt to link Rosenberg's words with Auschwitz, it needs to be borne in mind that the historical consensus on Höss is now that he got his dates wrong and that the time he received his orders from Himmler was, in fact, June 1942, five months after Wannsee. In this way we see that Rosenberg's conversation with Hitler took place roughly seven months before any such order was alleged to have been given, not as claimed by Dodd, six months after. With the benefit of historical hindsight, therefore, the point that Dodd was seeking to make completely falls apart.

Dodd then tried to pin Rosenberg down to another admission, by saying, 'Well, actually, the Jews were being exterminated in the Eastern Occupied Territories at that time and thereafter, weren't they?'[570] After a bit of verbal sparring, Rosenberg responded. 'Yes.' He said. 'I quoted a document on that yesterday. I have heard from a witness that a district commissioner is said to have participated in these things in Vilna, and I have heard from another witness that in other cities the report came through that the Police would carry it out...'

Several letters were then produced by Dodd, one of which contained the following, rather vague statement, 'Clarification of the Jewish question has most likely been achieved by now through verbal discussions. Economic considerations should on principle remain unconsidered in the settlement of the problem.' The letter was signed with an 'R' which Dodd suggested was Rosenberg's initial. After a time, Dr Thoma inter- jected to point out that it referred to the '*Reichskommisar*', who was an individual called Lohse.

Eventually, a letter was produced written by Kube, one of Rosenberg's subordinates, to Lohse. It would provide another key moment of the trial in considering the Holocaust narrative. It read:

'In all the clashes with partisans in White Ruthenia (Russia)[571] it has proved that Jewry, in the former Polish part'-and so on-'is the main exponent of the partisan movement. In consequence, the treatment of Jewry in White Ruthenia is mainly a matter of political concern.... In exhaustive discus- sions with the SS Brigadefuehrer Zenner and the exceedingly capable leader of the SD, SS Ober- sturmbannfuehrer Dr Strauch, it was ascertained that we have liquidated in the last 10 weeks about
55,000 Jews in White Ruthenia... Radical measures are imminent for Baranowicze and Hanzewitschi. In Baranowicze alone, approximately 10,000 Jews are still living in the city itself; of these, 9,000 Jews will be liquidated...I fully agree with the Commander of the SD in White Ruthenia, that we shall liq- uidate every shipment of Jews which is not ordered or announced by our superior offices, to prevent further disturbances in White Ruthenia.'[572]

This, like several other moments at the trial, provides serious problems for those who would wish to deny. Clearly, there is minimal scope for doubting the authenticity of the document. Negationists would perhaps try

---

[568] ibid, p.553
[569] ibid, p.554
[570] ibid, p.554
[571] White Ruthenia, also known as White Russia, was a 9th to 12th-century state that existed in the territories of modern-day Belarus, Ukraine, and part of western Russia and eastern Poland.
[572] ibid, p.559

to reason that if the Allies were prepared to abuse witnesses to gain signed affidavits, they would also be prepared to doctor or even completely fake documents to advance their case. However such desperate hypothesizing would be rendered redundant by Rosenberg's reaction. He did not deny that such activities had occurred. In fact he admitted that he knew of such occurrences before the document had even been read. He had also admitted earlier, when being questioned by Haensel, defence lawyer for the SS, that the treatment of the Jews had passed through three stages, the last of which could only be described as involving 'Crimes against Humanity.'[573]

The figures involved are shocking and neither did Rosenberg dispute them, although he did refute Dodd's statement that the document had been found in his office. Yet again, when applying a critical evaluation to the document, set within its supposed historical context, an interesting issue is raised. Contrary to the view of mainstream history, the version of events described by the letter does not suggest a planned genocide of the Jews for racial reasons, but a planned mobilisation against a civilian enemy, due to the merciless necessities of warfare. Put another way, the Jews of White Russia were not being killed just because they were Jews. They were being killed because so many of them were partisans. It was an action not of racism, but of cold, callous, ruthless expediency aimed at increasing the efficiency of the Wehrmacht in the region.

As an interpretation, (and it is the straightforward interpretation of the document, based on what it actually says) this makes far more sense than the standard Holocaust one. An often posed question to the unswerving purveyors of the dominant Holocaust narrative is why would the Nazis waste valuable manpower and ammunition shooting civilians for the sake of it? Were they so hate-filled and irrational that they were prepared to be profligate at such a time? Surely, rounding up and shooting Jews could be left until later, if their only motivation was to rid Europe of them. They were, after all, attempting to win a war and that would have to be their all-consuming goal, at the time. With the partisan interpretation, the motive becomes clear and such a question need not be asked. Jewish partisans were a hindrance to the progress of Barbarossa. Removing them increased the possibility of military success.

This is by no means an attempt to excuse such practice. Clearly, the deliberate killing of civilians is morally indefensible, to whomever and by whomever it occurs, but there is a difference between killing civilians for no reason other than their ethnicity and killing them because of a belief (even if it is an inaccurate one) that they pose a security threat to your forces. As stated previously, there are many occasions when the American and British military have acted in such a way (Vietnam and the Boer War for example). Generally speaking, however, we do not define the My Lai massacre or Kitchener's 'scorched earth' policy and concentration camps as acts of genocide. There are modern parallels too, with occurrences in Iraq and Afghanistan.

Unfortunately, when embroiled in combat with a guerrilla or partisan enemy, any normal morés or rules of war usually fly out of the window. The Wehrmacht and various SS units were no different to the forces of other nations in this respect. It is a nigh-on impossible situation for any army to deal with. Where they were different is in the numbers alleged to have been involved. The Nazis' civilian actions were of a greater scope than those that had gone before, or those that have happened since, however this fact needs to be balanced with the scale of the territory they were trying to take. Having determined that a successful invasion of Russia was necessary, rightly or wrongly, to win the war, they were faced with enormous tactical difficulties. The Russian Front of World War Two became the biggest theatre of war in human history. The size of the area and the nature of the campaign, as it was being waged, determined that if civilian actions were to take place they could only take place on a massive scale. Again, this is not an attempt to excuse what the Nazis did, but simply to demonstrate that the 'racial' basis of the crimes so emphasised in pre-existing history appears to be an over-simplification or even a distortion. Like any nation at war, German actions in the East were governed more by a sense of military necessity than anything else.

Furthermore, what is particularly interesting is that the version of events provided by this document, which Rosenberg seemed to accept, would corroborate, to a large extent, the versions that emerged through the statements on the stand of Göring and Kaltenbrunner. Unfortunately for Rosenberg, however, his admission of knowledge of the mass murder of civilians, regardless of whether such action had a racial or military motivation, utterly condemned him in the eyes of the court, despite the fact that by 1940, it had, according to Joachim Fest, 'long been evident that Rosenberg had little or no political influence and no voice in the real

---

[573] ibid, p.525

decisions.'[574] His position as Minister for the Eastern Occupied Regions was 'purely formal' and his powers in the role were 'pathetically limited'[575] but he still held it, until the 12th October, 1944, when he resigned, writing in his letter to Hitler that '…you no longer consider my services necessary.' And that, for the prosecutors, would be enough.

Frick's defence began on the 24th April and like Hess', is difficult to assess as he did not appear on the stand. His attorney, Dr Pannenbecker simply presented a series of documents intended to demonstrate his client's innocence in the face of the charges. He began by providing evidence of Hitler's contradictory statements regarding peace in Europe, therefore arguing that Frick, as Minister for the Interior, could not have known Hitler's intentions and therefore was not part of a conspiracy to wage aggressive war. As Frick had never had anything to do with foreign policy, this seemed reasonable.

He asserted, with evidence, that in his role as Reich Protector for Bohemia and Moravia, Frick had not been responsible for excesses that were alleged to have occurred in concentration camps there and that, in fact, he had passed several decrees aimed at improving camp conditions. Pannenbecker then tried to submit a witness affidavit from Gillhuber, an underling of Frick's, who accompanied him on various official trips and flights to support this point. Fascinatingly, President Lawrence initially tried to rule against the introduction of such evidence, saying, 'The Tribunal considers that it cannot entertain an affidavit…unless he is offered as a witness, in which case he may be cross-examined.'

This was the result of a misunderstanding, Lawrence thought that the affidavit being presented was from Frick himself, yet it gives us an interesting insight into courtroom objectivity, as by this stage of the trial the prosecution had introduced innumerable affidavits without presenting witnesses for cross examination. Surely, either such practice was acceptable, or it was not. Why the Allied-run tribunal should allow the Allied-run prosecution to introduce such evidence but attempt to dissuade the German defence from doing so, seems to lead to a rather pointed conclusion.

After the misunderstanding was cleared up, Pannenbecker read the affidavit, which stated in categorical terms that Frick had never visited Dachau and had nothing to do with goings-on there. Yet the pro-prosecution imbalance of the proceedings was re-emphasised as Jackson immediately complained, saying, 'Your Honor, the Prosecution makes objection to this because it is a character of evidence that there is no way of testing…'[576] Judge Lawrence decided to reject the item, stating that it may be allowed to be re-submitted at a later date. It never was.

Frick's case was concluded with the calling of Hans, Bernd Gisevius, another who worked under him in the Minstry of the Interior. Pannenbecker intended Gisevius' testimony to distance Frick from Police actions. Whether it achieved this is questionable. Gisevius, a confirmed enemy of Göring, instead spent most of his time on the stand adding to the *Reichsmarschall*'s prosecution case, denouncing Göring for building up the Gestapo and demonstrating that he had collaborated with Himmler over the 'Night of the Long Knives', in 1934, in which Ernst Röhm and others were murdered, as a means to keep control of the government. The list of misdemeanours went on – a marriage scandal, the Reichstag fire, smear campaigns and allegations of homosexuality against certain Nazi officials. It was as if the whole thing had been ripped from the pages of a particularly shabby tabloid and all of it, it seemed, revolved around Göring. Gilbert later wrote that 'Frick knew perfectly well that his witness was cooking Göring's goose and he didn't seem to mind a bit…Frick's attitude clearly betrayed a malicious satisfaction in getting back at Göring for helping Himmler to get power at Frick's expense.'[577]

Frick's case ended as Gisevius left the stand. It had been a brief and curious affair, in which the defendant's decision not to testify, coupled with his attorney's choice of evidence, meant that most of the more serious accusations against him, the formation of the Nuremberg Laws, for example, or his implication in the T4 Euthanasia programme[578], were simply not addressed.

---

[574] Fest, p.255
[575] Fest, p.261
[576] Nuremberg Trial Proceedings, Vol.12, 113th day, Wednesday 24th April, 1946, p.164
[577] Gilbert, p.295
[578] In reality the Euthanasia programme had been ushered in through the back door. Hitler had initiated it through Bouhler and Brandt. Frick had been completely bypassed. Yet his refusal to take to the stand to defend himself against the charges

At the judges' deliberation meetings, Rosenberg was discussed initially on September 2nd, without consensus on guilt or sentencing. As a result his case was left until the 10th for further analysis, when all agreed that he was guilty on all four counts. Stewart, the American aide who discussed everything in reference to American Football, (see Streicher's case) wrote, 'Rosenberg was one of the second string trying to squeeze his way into the huddle with the big boys.'[579] 'He had really made the grade in the action against the USSR' he continued. 'He was definitely one of the boys who made the plans.'[580] His involvement in the party from the earliest days, his closeness to Hitler and his official position in Eastern Europe did for him, more so than his writings, the importance of which the judges felt had been exaggerated.[581] Lawrence (UK) and Nikitchenko (USSR) voted for hanging, De Vabres (France) for life imprisonment. Biddle (USA) initially abstained, but the following morning he too voted for hanging. The decision was made.[582] Rosenberg was the only man to mount the gallows, on that morning of October 16th, 1946, who did not speak a word to those observing.[583] The party philosopher passed into the next world in silence.

Frick too caused disagreement among the judges. The Russians, who were nothing if not consistent, voted for guilt on all four charges and death by hanging, but others wavered, particularly on counts one and two. Eventually, again after reconvening on September 10th, the vote found Frick guilty on counts two, three and four. He was also sentenced to the noose.[584] Just before they pulled the hood over his head, he said, 'Let live the eternal Germany.'[585] Later, as their ashes were scattered, along with Streicher's, so, in a sense, were the ashes of racial theory. It is a field of research so synonymous with Nazi 'evil' that few have dared to touch it since. Yet the reality is that although men like Rosenberg and Frick were indicted in part for their racial ideas, their judgements and sentencing focused more on things they were alleged to have done, actions that had occurred in areas officially under their jurisdiction. Neither does it necessarily follow that their philosophies led to such actions. It appears that there is corroborative evidence from the trial to suggest that the *Einsatzgruppen* actions, at least, were motivated by a sense of military necessity, rather than simple racism.

The Nazis' racial actions (which were not just anti-Jewish, but anti-Slav, anti-Romany, in fact anti any non-aryan), have set the world against the study of race. Rather than examine the issue and attempt to determine, to what extent, it may actually be of value to us, we have chosen to pretend that it does not actually exist at all. According to JP Rushton, 'antiracists…engage in rhetoric to deny (racial) differences and suppress discoveries.'[586] He goes on to say that 'for scientific progress to be made, it is necessary to rise above both 'racist' and 'antiracist' ideology.'[587] Jared Diamond, a prolific and popular author of modern anthropology, described Rushton's ideas as 'monstrous.'

It needs to be remembered, as stated earlier in this chapter, that the study of race did not begin with the Nazis. Simply because the Nazis adopted it and the Nazis committed atrocities, it does not necessarily follow that studying race leads to committing atrocities. Atrocities, in one form or another, are committed by most nations from time to time. Yet because of its association with Nazi 'evil' we are presently in danger of legislating racial analysis out of the realm of legal discourse. It could well be argued, when examining the basis of Nazi racism, which stemmed largely from the ideas of Lamarck, yet broadly ignored the theories of Darwin and several others, that it was the disregard or miscomprehension of racial biology and not, as popularly held, the belief in it, which led to Nazi racial ideology. The pursuit of human understanding should not suffer because of the misdeeds of any nation. Science and politics do not have to mix in any prescribed way. If the study of the biological basis of race can contribute to a deeper understanding of ourselves and each other, then surely the time has come to examine it openly. If not, we are just perpetuating ignorance.

---

meant that the accusations, made by Kempner, for the prosecution, early in the trial, stuck with the judges, to some extent. Conot (p.390) states this 'had considerable effect on their verdict.'
[579] Conot, p.487
[580] ibid
[581] ibid
[582] Taylor, p.561
[583] ibid, p.610
[584] ibid, p.561
[585] ibid, p.610
[586] JP Rushton, *Race, Evolution and Behaviour, A Life History Perspective*, (Charles Darwin Research Institute, 1995) p.1
[587] ibid

15

The Sailors

...The Wehrmacht must be completely non-political and be composed only of servicemen who, in full realization of this necessity, refuse to take part in any activity of domestic politics... the Wehrmacht infuses into its servicemen a manly and warlike spirit; not the desire for war or even a war of revenge or a war of aggression, for to strive after that would certainly in the general opinion of all Germans be a crime, but the will to take up arms in the defence of the fatherland in its hour of need.[588]

- Grand Admiral Raeder, speaking in 1928

Admirals Karl Dönitz and Erich Raeder

The German military was represented at the trial by four men (excluding Göring). Obviously all answerable to the charge of aggressive war, beyond that their cases were divided into distinct pairs. The representatives of the Army, Field Marshall Wilhelm Keitel and General Alfried Jodl, had to contend with accusations of heinous War Crimes and Crimes against Humanity. The version of events, as it was emerging through the trial, implicated them heavily in counts three and four particularly in regard to their alleged collusion with the SS *Einsatzgruppen* in their civilian atrocities.

By contrast, the two naval men, Admirals Karl Dönitz and Erich Raeder had seen little evidence outside of Count Two which particularly impacted upon their cases. The Navy's innocence in the face of Nuremberg's more notorious charges was best summed up by Rudolf Hess, during a moment of jocularity in the dock before the afternoon session of April 17th. Dönitz overheard Göring advising Rosenberg before the latter's cross examination by Rudenko and found the impromptu coaching session amusing. 'That's right' Dönitz said, 'You handle it papa!' Göring laughed and retorted with 'Quiet, children, you stick to your U-boats,' at which point Hess piped up with 'yes, they cannot say you killed Jews with your U-boats!'[589]

Despite the indescribably poor taste, Hess' punch-line was an accurate summary of the prosecution's position on the *Kriegsmarine*. By their roles, Raeder and Dönitz were clearly detached from Count Four and therefore both defendants were indicted only on the first three charges. From the outset, then, this put them at an advantage. One must remember that although seemingly something of a secondary charge, count four alone was enough to put Streicher to death.

---

[588] Nuremberg Trial Proceedings, Vol.13, 130th day, Wednesday 15th May 1946, p.617
[589] Gilbert, p.274

The child of a Westphalian farming family, Karl Dönitz joined the Navy as a regular seaman in World War One. He rose to prominence as *Grossadmiral, Befehlshaber der Unterseeboote* (Grand Admiral, Commander of Submarines), during World War Two and in 1943 was appointed Commander-in-Chief of the German Navy, replacing his fellow defendant Raeder. His next and final promotion provided an unexpected twist to his career when he was appointed Führer of Germany in Hitler's political will. The twenty-three days in which he was in charge of the by-then non-existent Reich were an odd affair in which he set up headquarters in the small town of Flensburg and made laws and plans which affected no-one, as by that stage virtually the entire nation was under foreign rule.

From the very beginning there had been question-marks over whether it was in the best interests of the tribunal to indict Dönitz. The British admiralty had actually argued against it, saying, in August 1945, '…there is insufficient evidence to convict him or warrant him being tried.'[590] It was felt, by and large, that he had done little that Naval or submarine commanders of any nation had not done.

The presentation of evidence against him was handled by Colonel H.J. Phillimore who, aside from the naval charges, spent a considerable amount of time describing Dönitz as an ardent Nazi. In this regard, Phillimore talked about 'his fanatical adherence to Hitler and to the Party… his belief in the Nazi ideology with which he sought to indoctrinate the Navy and the German people.'[591] He supported this statement, intended to incriminate Dönitz under Count One, with various documents and extracts from speeches he had made, before moving on to Naval matters.

Of all the military accusations (and there were several, orders to fire on merchant seamen, attacking without warning and so on), the only allegation against him that seemed to carry any real weight was that he had broken a great naval taboo by failing to rescue survivors from torpedoed enemy ships and even ordering that they be machine-gunned in the water. Phillimore stated, after regaling the court with one such tale, '…There are hundreds of similar stories, stories of voyages for days in open boats in Atlantic gales, of men in the water clinging for hours to a raft and gradually dropping off one by one, of crews being machine-gunned as they tried to lower their boats or as they drifted away in them, of seamen being blown to pieces by shells and torpedoes and bombs.'[592]

Dönitz' case was remarkable for several reasons and not least because his lawyer, the intelligent and well presented Otto Kranzbühler, proved to be the only defence counsel to really make some kind of impact on the trial, even managing to curry favour with Judge Biddle.[593] He was a quick-witted and articulate man who refused, like many, to be cowed by Allied omnipotence. He insisted on calling Dönitz 'Grand Admiral', despite the refusal of the court to recognize German military rank and insisted too on sending his assistant, Commander Meckel, to London, to inspect captured U-boat diaries being held there. Thus armed, Kranzbühler turned his considerable skills towards mitigating the allegations.

It was brought to light that despite America's numerous violations of international law during 1941, when they repeatedly engaged German subs in the Atlantic, despite not yet having declared war, Hitler, desperate not to give the USA a reason to join the conflict, had directly ordered Raeder and Dönitz not to retaliate. Dönitz described this himself by saying, '…when the American destroyers in the summer of 1941 received orders to attack German submarines, that is, before war started, when they were still neutral and I was forbidden to fight back, I was then forced to forbid the submarines in this area to attack even British destroyers, in order to avoid having a submarine mistake an American for a British ship.'[594] Until 1942, therefore, there were few alleged war crimes committed by German U-boats at all. In fact it appeared that Dönitz had taken more than reasonable steps to ensure that his fleet conducted themselves properly. On September 5th 1939, for example, after sinking the British ship *Royal Sceptre*, the U-boat commanders had stood by while survivors were transferred to a steamer. In the same year, after an attack on a Greek ship, a German U-boat picked up the entire enemy crew from the water and took them to safety.[595] It was clear that U-boat attacks in the early stages of the war were conducted with as much chivalry as could be reasonably expected and had been

---

[590] Conot, p.413
[591] Nuremberg Trial Proceedings, Vol. 5,33rd day, Monday 14th January 1946, p.202
[592] ibid, p.212
[593] Conot, p.417
[594] Nuremberg Trial Proceedings Vol 13, Wednesday 8th May 1946, p.265
[595] Davidson, p.395

against Allied shipping and not personnel.

However, the 'total war' that was being waged from the skies and on land by both sides, would soon develop at sea. The turning point, for the German U-boat flotilla, was a clear one. On September 12th 1942, the HMS Laconia, a fully-loaded British troopship, was torpedoed 360 miles north of Ascension Island in the South Atlantic. Not only was it well-manned, with a crew of 750, but was carrying 1,800 Italian prisoners of war, 100 Polish guards and 80 civilians. The attack did for many of the prisoners and passengers, who were below deck, but still resulted in approximately 1,400 survivors in the water. Dönitz, upon being radioed by the U-boat commander, Hartenstein, suspended a nearby mission to send two more U-boats to assist in the rescue. In addition Hartenstein sent out an SOS message in English, promising safe passage to any ship responding.[596] There was however, no response from any Allied vessel.

What followed was a valiant rescue attempt in which 400 survivors were taken aboard the three U-boats and the rest strung along behind on life-rafts tethered to the U-boat sterns. Hartenstein covered his sub in a red-cross flag in order to dissuade enemy attack and this odd procession made slow progress across the surface towards Africa for four days.

On the 16th, however, they were spotted by a B-24 bomber and despite the red-cross flag and frantic hand-signalling from survivors in the life rafts, were attacked. The bomber made five separate runs, damaging Hartenstein's U-boat and destroying most of the life-rafts. Understandably, the U-boats, fearful for their own survival, cut loose the remaining survivors and abandoned the rescue. This incident convinced Dönitz that destruction of the enemy had to take precedence over humanitarianism. There was no sense in rescuing enemy sailors if it left his vessels vulnerable to attack. The war in which he was involved, it seemed, offered no reward for gallantry.[597]

After demonstrating that the German navy had only abandoned its naval etiquette under extreme provocation, Kranzbühler then turned to the matter of attacks on non-military vessels. He produced a report from the British admiralty, dated October 1st 1939 which stated, 'German submarines are pursuing a new strategy' and urging British merchant vessels to 'ram every German submarine.'[598]

As a result of this Hitler had passed a direct order to Dönitz on the 17th October which stated, 'Submarines are permitted immediate and full use of armed force against all merchant vessels recognizable with certainty of being enemy nationality, as in every case attempts to ram or other forms of active resistance may be expected…'[599]

Kranzbühler was also able to demonstrate that many British merchant ships had gun layers and gun crews and some even anti-aircraft guns and depth charges. The question of them being illegitimate military targets was therefore forcibly resolved.

Despite success on every major issue, the zenith of Kranzbühler's case was yet to come. With admirable cleverness and no small degree of cheek, he obtained an affidavit from Admiral Chester Nimitz of the United States in which the American openly admitted that during the course of the war in the Pacific, his submarines had neither given warning prior to attack nor rescued survivors. Kranzbühler read the affidavit, which took the form of a questionnaire, to the court.

Although the *tu quoque* defence was expressly disallowed by the Nuremberg Charter, this final trick of Kranzbühler's had the desired effect. There was no way that the American prosecution could convict Dönitz and save any sort of face. Unfortunately for Dönitz, however, there were also the British, the Russians and the French to deal with.

At the deliberation meeting on September 12th, Judge Biddle presented a memorandum written by Jim Rowe, an American Naval intelligence officer. Rowe's opinion was that Dönitz had not 'waged unrestricted submarine warfare contrary to international law'[600] and that he should be found not guilty. Biddle concurred wholeheartedly with his countryman and declared to the other judges that 'Germany waged a much cleaner war than we did' and urged for acquittal. However Judge Lawrence for the UK, from whom many sailors were sent to watery graves by German U-boats, argued, with a display of stubbornness and shallow reasoning

---

[596] Conot, p.411 & Maser, p.153-4
[597] ibid
[598] Nuremberg Trial Proceedings, Vol 13, 127th day, Saturday 11th May 1946, p.411
[599] ibid, p.412
[600] Taylor, p.567

worthy of a teenager, that Dönitz, 'was typically national socialist – harsh and inhumane.' Apparently happy to ignore all substance of Dönitz' case, he voted for guilt on Count Two and prison. It was perhaps Dönitz' twenty-three days as Führer which shaped this decision. The *evil* of the Nazi regime, which the tribunal sought to highlight, meant that a man who had led it, even if only briefly and spuriously, had to be guilty of something. The Russians (of course) and the French agreed, also urging for guilt on count three and the United States found themselves outvoted and in the embarrassing position of convicting Dönitz for crimes their own naval chief had admitted to via a document read in open court. It was agreed to give Dönitz a ten year sentence. Biddle tried to reconvene the discussion on September 26th, hoping to turn the other judges from their decision, but noted that little headway was made, 'since dinner is approaching.'[601]

In most ways the case of Erich Raeder paralleled that of Dönitz. If anything he appeared, on paper, slightly less accountable, having only commanded the Navy during the opening years of war when relatively few war crimes were alleged to have occurred. He was also far less committed to Nazism and Hitler. Having been in a position of Naval Authority from 1928 – 1943 he was accused by the tribunal of assisting in German rearmament, in defiance of Versailles and being a prime mover behind German aggression of the 1930s. The court played heavily on his role behind the invasion of Norway, despite knowing that the British had intended to do so in order to attack Germany and the Germans had only done so as a preventative measure. Elwyn-Jones, presenting the case against Raeder even had the temerity to refer to the invasion as a 'perfidious Nazi attack.'[602] In a wonderful act of self-mirroring, the tribunal skirted its way around this subject simply by referring to Shawcross' skirting around of the same subject during the early days of the trial, 'Raeder defends his actions on the ground it was a move to forestall the British. It is not necessary again to discuss this defence, which the Tribunal have heretofore treated in some detail, concluding that Germany's invasion of Norway and Denmark was aggressive war.'[603] The reality was that the tribunal had not treated the matter in detail at all. It had been mentioned twice and both times simply dismissed out of hand in a matter of seconds.

Like most of the German officer corps, there is no doubt that Raeder viewed the Versailles Treaty as a great dishonour.[604] He had skilfully negotiated his way around it and had been the key figure in re-establishing German naval capability at the request of his government. But he was an opponent of Hitler on many issues – he had vigorously argued against launching Barbarossa, for example, in which he saw little chance of success. Göring, he saw as a competitor. Both wanted funding for their rearmament programmes and the Luftwaffe seemed favoured, which he resented. His primary 'crime', therefore in the eyes of the tribunal should surely have been mitigated by his lack of involvement in politics and the fact that Versailles had been viewed as dead in the water by most nations before Germany started to break its terms.[605] On the most serious issue, that of treatment of enemy sailors after attack, he was cleared, as was Dönitz. His harsh treatment at the hands of the judges came then as something of a surprise. Raeder was pronounced guilty on all three counts and given life. (The Russians had argued for death). He appealed against his sentence and asked for it to be commuted to death, 'by way of mercy', but was refused.[606] Like several other defendants given custodial sentences, Raeder did not complete his term and was released due to ill health in 1955. He published an autobiography in 1957 and died in 1960.

This means that those looking for an encapsulation of the way in which Nuremberg ignored the spirit of justice, need only have looked inside Spandau prison, during the late forties and early fifties, where one would have found two disciplined and proud naval men whose practices had been no worse and arguably better than their erstwhile enemies. Of course, their enemies were not in prison.

Admiral of the Fleet and then First Sea Lord, Andrew Cunningham, was presented with the Order of Merit in 1946 and had a bronze bust erected in his honour in Trafalgar Square in 1967. Admiral Chester Nimitz, of the United States, despite freely admitting to committing the same crimes the Germans had been accused of, received a gallery of medals from all over the world. To this day, his image adorns an American postage stamp. There is surely little else that would so perfectly define the phrase 'victor's justice'.

---

[601] Taylor, p.570
[602] Nuremberg Trial Proceedings, Vol.5, 34th day, Tuesday 15th January 1946, p.268
[603] Judgement of the International Military Tribunal for the Trial of the Major War Criminals: Raeder
[604] The Treaty restricted the German Navy to 16,500 men and maximum of 36 vessels. Submarines were prohibited.
[605] The United States never signed the treaty and the British co-operated with Germany in breaking it.
[606] Taylor, p.602

16

Befehl ist befehl
(an order is an order)

General Alfried Jodl and Field Marshall Wilhelm Keitel

If the treatment of Dönitz and Raeder was an obvious miscarriage of justice, then by comparison, the cases of Jodl and Keitel were far less clear-cut. In addition to the primary allegation of aggressive war making, the invasion of Russia, codenamed 'Barbarossa' was the umbrella under which many of the worst crimes against humanity had apparently been committed. From the outset, the court's position was that the Generals had to have known. There was no way the SS could have followed behind their men, cleaning up the rear areas by killing civilians without their knowledge and approval.

General Alfred Jodl was born into a family of soldiers in Würzberg and upon completing military school he fulfilled his destiny by joining the army as an artilleryman. He fought on both fronts in the First World War and was wounded twice. From then on he ascended smoothly through the ranks, eventually becoming Chief of Operations Staff in August 1939. His colleague, Field Marshall Wilhelm Keitel, had a similar background. Born in Helmscherode in Brunswick, he also served as an artilleryman in World War One, predominately on the western front and was also seriously wounded by shrapnel. Like Jodl, he remained in the *Wehrmacht* despite the restrictions placed upon it by Versailles, eventually becoming a General in 1937. In 1940, after the staggering success of the French campaign, which was arguably the most impressive military victory by any nation in world history, he received his final promotion to Field Marshall.[607]

The evidence presented against the Army came in drips and drabs throughout the prosecution presenta- tions. Telford Taylor made the main disposition against the *Wehrmacht*, followed by the British lawyer G.D. Roberts who applied what Taylor had said specifically to Jodl and Keitel. However as the aggressive war charge was in many ways the focus of the trial, points relevant to Keitel and Jodl came up in a number of the other presentations also.

---

[607] Biographical details taken from the defendants own testimonies at the trial; Keitel – Nuremberg Trial Proceedings Vol 10, 98th day, Wednesday 3rd April 1946, p.467 & Jodl – Vol. 15, 145th day, Monday 3rd June 1946, p.284

Taylor spoke on January 4th, with the American emphasis on Conspiracy framing his words. His intention appeared to be to delineate the criminality of the German high command and to this end he described them as one of the 'chief tools by means of which the Nazi conspirators sought to achieve their aims,'[608] going on to describe the restrictions placed upon the German armed forces by Versailles and how they 'did not destroy or even seriously undermine German militarism.'[609] Despite relying on national stereotypes, as the prosecution tended to do throughout, he made a point of stating that being a soldier was not, in itself criminal. 'The profession of arms is an honorable one and can be honorably practiced.' He said, before adding, 'but it is too clear for argument that a man who commits crimes cannot plead as a defence that he committed them in uniform.'[610] The key point of his address, soon followed, intended to locate the actions of the German military within the Conspiracy charge. The Wehrmacht high command, he said 'agreed with the truly basic objectives of Hitlerism and Nazism.' His explanation for this was that, 'The generals, like Hitler, wanted to aggrandize Germany at the expense of neighboring countries and were prepared to do so by force or threat of force.'[611]

By this point Taylor had been speaking for five minutes and had outlined the case from the American point of view. It is difficult, however, for the analyst to examine this outline and pick out anything that was of real substance. That the Army had been a tool of the Nazis was a truly redundant allegation, by any standards. The army of any nation is clearly a tool of the government, whoever they may be. His assertion that the Generals had been happy to participate in military actions and were therefore party to the objectives of 'Hitlerism' was similarly resonant with the sound of a barrel-bottom being scraped. One might assume that Taylor was toeing the party line and dancing to Jackson's Conspiracy tune, yet it was a point he was obviously fond of as he later returned to in his memoirs, writing, 'Jodl not only liked war but also thought it good for mankind.'[612] It seems an amazing viewpoint for such a highly qualified individual to put forward. Of course Army generals of any nationality were happy to participate in military activity. It is, by definition, their *raison d'etre*. What sort of Army would they have been if the Generals had refused? Taylor was providing a perfect example of how preconceived notions of Nazi *evil*, coupled with the need to present everything as being part of the great, malignant Nazi conspiracy, shaped the prosecution presentations, causing them to clutch at any straws they felt could be twisted to suit their purposes.

Keitel himself summed it up nicely:

> 'As a soldier, I must say that the term 'War of Aggression' as used here is meaningless as far as I am concerned; we learned how to conduct actions of attack, actions of defence, and actions of retreat. However, according to my own personal feelings as a military man, the concept 'war of aggression' is a purely political concept and not a military one.'[613]

The only part of Taylor's opening that potentially had any real mileage was that which related to war crimes. The fact that this was dressed up with a lot of bluff and waffle was symptomatic of the way much of the prosecution was run. Later, Taylor proceeded to outline the various ranks and layers of the military, the individuals involved in each and the process of rebuilding German military might after Versailles. The implication was that the latter constituted a crime. Again, this is arguable. The Allied opinion was that it was criminal, as the rearming was in defiance of an international treaty. The German view was that Versailles was not a treaty but an illegitimate imposition and therefore they did not feel bound by its terms. The fact that the United States had not ratified the Treaty and that other nations, in particular Britain, had been perfectly happy, at various times, to see it broken when it suited them, lends weight to the German perspective. Regardless of one's views on the matter, however, within the scope of what was being alleged at Nuremberg it was a relatively minor crime. It was not the rearming that the tribunal sought to condemn, but the alleged aggression which resulted.

Matters of German 'aggression' aside, which appear rather subjective and lopsided from a modern per-

---

[608] Nuremberg Trial Proceedings, Vol 4, 27th day, Friday 4th January 1946, p.390
[609] ibid
[610] ibid, p.391
[611] ibid
[612] Taylor, p.436
[613] Nuremberg Trial Proceedings, Vol 10, 98th day, 3rd April 1946, p.474

spective, the most serious accusation for both Keitel and Jodl was that of colluding with the SS *Einsatzgruppen* units in their civilian actions in occupied areas behind lines in the East. As already seen in Kaltenbrunner's case, evidence relating to the *Einsatzgruppen* was presented early in the trial, however this evidence would have no bearing on the cases of Keitel and Jodl unless it could be demonstrated that the Army had collaborated with them.

On this score, the calling of General Erwin Lahousen, by Colonel John Amen, during the American presentation on the charge of Aggressive War, on the ninth day of the trial, November 30th, was crucial. La- housen discussed the diary of Admiral Canaris, in which he was frequently asked to write entries, where there was recorded a meeting on September 12th 1939, at which both Ribbentrop and Keitel had been present. During this meeting a conversation had taken place regarding the resistance movement in Poland. Talk had been about: 'the proposed shootings and extermination measures directed particularly against the Polish in- telligentsia, the nobility, the clergy and in fact all elements which could be regarded as leaders of a national resistance…the Führer…had let it be known that, should the Armed Forces be unwilling to carry through these measures…they would have to accept the presence at their side of the SS, the SIPO and similar units who would carry them through.'[614] Lahousen was then asked to clarify who such measures would be aimed at and said, 'Mainly the Polish intelligentsia, the nobility, the clergy and of course, the Jews.'

The implication was therefore made that the leaders of the Army had been fully aware of the SS *Einsatzgruppen*'s mission prior to their beginning it. However, as before, it appears that Jews were being targeted in the context of anti-resistance and anti-partisan measures rather than racial annihilation. Still, the most incriminating witness for the Generals was yet to come. *Gruppenführer* Otto Ohlendorf had been the commander of the *Einsatzgruppe* D unit, which was attached to the 11th Army operating in the Ukraine. He was questioned by Colonel Amen on the 3rd January.

Ohlendorf testified that the *Einsatzgruppen* had been engaged on the basis of a written agreement between the High Command of the Armed Forces, Hitler and the RSHA. He went on to state that although they were officially under the command of the Chief of the SD (initially Heydrich) 'there existed a general agreement that the army was also entitled to issue instructions to the *Einsatzgruppen*, if the operational situation made it necessary.'[615]

He was then asked what his official duties had been with regard to Jews and and Communist Commissars (party fighters). Ohlendorf answered, 'The instructions were that in the Russian operational areas of the *Einsatzgruppen*, the Jews, as well as the Soviet political commissars were to be liquidated.'

'And when you say liquidated do you mean killed?' Amen asked.

'Yes, I mean killed,' replied Ohlendorf.

It soon got worse. Ohlendorf went on to state categorically that the Generals had known about these orders and that from June 1941 to June 1942, 90,000 people were killed by his unit alone. When asked to confirm if this included women and children, he replied 'Yes'.[616]

With regard to the accusations levelled against him, Keitel described his stance by saying, '…I was a soldier by inclination and conviction. For more than 44 years without interruption I served my country and my people as a soldier, and I tried to do my best in the service of my profession…As a German officer, I naturally consider it my duty to answer for what I have done, even if it should have been wrong…I bear that responsibility which arises from my position for all those things which resulted from these orders and which are connected with my name and my signature. Further, I bear the responsibility, insofar as it is based on le- gal and moral principles, for those offices and divisions of the OKW which were subordinate to me.'[617]

It was the noble thing to do, in contrast to Kaltenbrunner, whom the generals despised. In the eyes of the court, such an admission, knowing that many orders bearing his name were pronounced illegal, would utterly condemn him. Keitel seemed to adopt a sense of fatalism about this, saying to Gilbert that he would tell 'the facts as they were' and 'let the chips fall as they may.'[618]

During cross examination several pieces of evidence were brought out which proved damning. Rudenko,

---

[614] Nuremberg Trial Proceedings, Vol. 2, 9th day, Friday 30th November 1945, p.446
[615] Nuremberg Trial Proceedings, Vol. 4, 26th day, Thursday 3rd January 1946, p.314
[616] ibid, p.318
[617] Nuremberg Trial Proceedings, Vol.10, 98th day, Wednesday 3rd April 1946, p.470
[618] Gilbert, p.239

for the Soviet Union, presented a document which stated that 'To atone for the life of one German soldier, 50 to 100 Communists must, as a rule, be sentenced to death. The method of execution should strengthen the measure of deterrent.'[619] It was signed by Keitel and although Keitel attempted to indicate that the order had, in fact, come from Hitler and not from himself, he had already accepted responsibility for all orders bearing his name.

Rudenko then pressed him to accept that he had known of orders to punish the civilian population including, if necessary 'measures even against women and children.'[620] Keitel accepted that he had known of such an order but denied that it meant the killing of women and children. When pressed further, he conceded that 'I cannot say in every individual case, since I do not know and I could not be everywhere and since I received no reports about it.' However he did state, when Rudenko claimed 'millions' of such cases that he did not believe it. 'I have no knowledge of that and I do not believe that it happened in millions of cases.'[621] He said.

Finally after a prolonged cross-examination by Maxwell-Fyfe, in which much sparring produced little, Dodd stepped up for the USA and immediately trapped Keitel in a corner fashioned from his earlier statements, before delivering a knockout blow.

Dodd – I understand you to say you did, with knowledge, carry out and pass on criminal or illegal orders. Is that a fair statement?
Keitel – I did not have any inner conviction of becoming criminal in doing so, since after all it was the head of the state who, as far as we were concerned, held all the legislative power. Consequently I did not consider that I was acting criminally.
Dodd – Well, I do not want to devote any more time to you except to say this, to suggest to you that I think your answer is not responsive. You told us that some of these orders were violations of the existing international law. An order issued in that form and on that basis is a criminal order, is an illegal order, is it not?
Keitel – Yes, that is correct.
Dodd – Well, when you carried them out, you were carrying out criminal orders in violation of one of the basic principles of your professional soldier's code, no matter by whom they were issued.
Keitel – Yes.[622]

With that, Keitel left the stand, having just admitted to passing and carrying out 'criminal' orders. In the final analysis, he had resorted to blaming the *Führer Prinzip* – he claimed to have had no choice but to ratify and follow Hitler's commands no matter what they required of him. As a defendant, he had been well and truly defeated, undone by a combination of flat honesty and his ineffectuality when it came to a verbal duel. Dönitz thought that Keitel had shown himself to be 'an honest man.' Von Papen agreed but added that he was 'an honest man with no mind of his own.'[623] Göring was contemptuous and referred to him as 'the little weakling'[624] When Keitel later returned to the dock, Göring harangued him for not discussing the Allied treatment of saboteurs and prisoners, or defending himself with more valour. Keitel did not answer or even meet his eyes.[625]

During his testimony, Jodl was to offer several more specific and thought provoking explanations than his former colleague. He was first asked about the plan to exterminate the Jews.

> '...I can only say, fully conscious of my responsibility, that I never heard, either by hint or by written or spoken word, of an extermination of Jews. On one single occasion I had doubts, and that was when Himmler spoke about the revolt in the Jewish Ghetto. I did not quite believe in this heroic fight; but Himmler immediately supplied photographs showing the concrete dugouts which had been built

---
[619] Nuremberg Trial Proceedings, 101st day, Saturday 6th April 1946, p. 618
[620] ibid, p.620
[621] ibid
[622] Nuremberg Trial Proceedings, Vol 11, 102nd day, Monday 8th April 1946, p.24
[623] Gilbert, p.237
[624] Gilbert, p.244
[625] ibid

there, and he said, 'Not only the Jews but also Polish Nationalists have taken refuge there and they are offering bitter resistance.' And with that he removed my suspicions...As far as the activities of the Police are concerned, of the so-called action groups, *Einsatzgruppen* and *Einsatzkommandos* – a conception, incidentally, of which I first heard here in detail-there was never any explanation through the Fuehrer himself other than that these police units were necessary to quell uprisings, rebellions, and partisan actions before they grew into a menace. This was not a task for the Armed Forces, but for the Police, and for that reason the Police had to enter the operational areas of the Army. I have never had any private information on the extermination of the Jews; and on my word, as sure as I am sitting here, I heard all these things for the first time after the end of the war.[626]

He was also asked what he knew of concentration camps, to which he replied:

'I can briefly say that I knew there were concentration camps at Dachau and Oranienburg. Some divisional officers visited Oranienburg once in 1937 and gave me very enthusiastic accounts of it. I heard the name of Buchenwald for the first time in the spring of 1945. When the name was mentioned, I thought it was a new troop training camp; and I made inquiries. The inmates were always described as German habitual criminals and certain inveterate political opponents...I never heard a single word about tortures, deported persons, or prisoners of war, crematoriums or gas vans, torments reminiscent of the Inquisition, and medical experiments. I can only say that, even if I had heard of these things, I would not have believed them until I had seen them with my own eyes.'[627]

His lawyer, Dr Exner, continued with the line of questioning by moving on to the linked subject of partisan warfare, whereby Jodl defined what was meant by a partisan: 'A partisan group is a fighting unit formed behind one's own front... it is not or is only partly in uniform...it is not an organic part of the Armed Forces even though it receives its orders from them...' He went on to relay how German intelligence gathering had revealed the methods of the Eastern European partisan groups and quoted a captured document to show how they were under instructions to 'blow up bridges, to destroy roads, et cetera' and that partisans were ordered to 'disguise themselves cleverly; that they will sometimes appear as farmers or will work in the fields as soon as German forces appear in the vicinity.'

A few questions later and Exner asked, 'The Prosecution asserts that the fight against partisans was only a code name under which Jews and Slavs were killed; is that true?'

Jodl replied with:

'The fight against partisans was a horrible reality. In July 1943. to quote some figures, 1,560 instances of railway sabotage occurred in Russia. There were 2,600 in September; that is 90 per day. A book by Ponomarenko was published from which an American paper quoted 500,000 Germans as having been killed by the partisans. [628]If a nought is crossed off from that figure, it is still quite a considerable achievement for a peaceful Soviet population. But the book is also said to have stated that the population became increasingly hostile; that murder and terror became more frequent; and that the peaceful Quisling mayors were being killed. At any rate it was a tremendous fight which was taking place in the East.'[629]

What was highlighted, beautifully here, by Jodl's testimony is how vastly two sides within a war situation can differ in their interpretation of events. Whereas the Allies described the German civilian round-ups in the East as being acts of racist genocide, carried out on purely innocent people, Jodl described them as being part of an ongoing bitter struggle between the Wehrmacht and a very active and violent civilian enemy. Needless

---

[626] Nuremberg Trial Proceedings Vol 15, 146th day, Tuesday 4th June 1946, p.332
[627] ibid
[628] In the original German, Jodl said, "*Auch wenn man eine Null wegstreicht...*" which would translate as 'Even if a nought is crossed off that figure..." The transcript translators missed the word 'even' however and some analysts have used this faulty translation to claim that Jodl was revising the figure downwards to 50,000. August von Knierem, *Nürnberg* (Ernst Klett Verlag, Stuttgart) p.395
[629] Nuremberg Trial Proceedings Vol 15, 146th day, Tuesday 4th June 1946 p.336

to say, history has only tended to repeat one of these interpretations.

Jodl's cross-examination was handled by Roberts. Despite being roundly criticised by the other prosecutors and even some of the judges, Roberts did manage to do something which neither Shawcross, nor Maxwell-Fyfe, nor any of the more vaunted British prosecutors had done, which was shed some further light on the Norway affair. Although he steered clear of any discussion of British plans in that direction, he produced a transcript of a speech made by Jodl in 1943 in which the General had praised the Norway operation because it secured 'free access to the Atlantic.'[630] This demonstrated that the issue was linked to the Allied Naval blockade. If Britain had occupied Norway, Germany would have been virtually shut in, with no naval outlets. Jodl's case petered out from then on, with less damage, but the same overall feeling as Keitel's. 'It is not the task of a soldier to be the judge of his Commander in Chief.' He said, 'May history or the Almighty do that.'[631] The sentiment of this statement was very similar to that put forward by the Field Marshall.

The military cases were initially discussed by the judges on September 10th, but there was too much division to reach a verdict. Lawrence, Nikitchenko and Biddle had voted for guilt on all four counts and death by hanging. De Vabres was forcibly opposed, believing that a distinction had to be made between 'honourable' and 'dishonourable' punishment[632]. He believed that the soldiers deserved to belong to the former category. This would not have radically altered the outcome for Jodl or Keitel, but simply the manner of it. When discussions reconvened on the 12th, they did not revolve around what the sentence should be, only whether it should be carried out by shooting or hanging. Eventually after some indecision from Biddle, enough agreement was reached for sentences of hanging to be passed.[633]

Keitel appealed, asking to be shot, 'a death which is granted to all soldiers in all armies in the world.'[634] Jodl made a similar request, but as mentioned before, all appeals were uniformly rejected. Keitel had lost both his sons during the war and on the gallows his last words were, 'I call on the Almighty to be considerate of the German people, provide tenderness and mercy. Over two million German soldiers went to their death for their Fatherland. I now follow my sons.' And then, after a short pause, *'Alles für Deutschland, Deutschland über alles!'* When his time to die came, Jodl was composed and dignified. He said only, 'I salute you my Germany.'[635]

During the immediate aftermath of Nuremberg, when the acquitted defendants were rounded up, tried again and found guilty by German courts, when the denazification process swept the country, gathering those with even the most tenuous party links and criminalising them, one hearing was held which reversed the trend. On the 28th February 1953, a German denazification court posthumously exonerated Jodl of his crimes, citing De Vabres' reasoning as an influence upon their decision. Germany had one less war criminal on its conscience.

---

[630] Nuremberg Trial Proceedings, Vol. 15, 148th day, Thurs 6th june 1946, p.465-6
[631] ibid, p.509
[632] Taylor, p.559
[633] Taylor, p.570
[634] Taylor, p.602
[635] Taylor, p.610

17

A Thousand Years of Guilt

Hans Frank, Arthur Seyss-Inquart and Fritz Sauckel

Of the remaining five defendants, three rose through the party to hold sway over large chunks of Europe. One of them, Fritz Sauckel has already been discussed during the chapter on Speer. As mentioned there, his main concern in the face of prosecution was not so much activities conducted during his time as *Gauleiter* of Thuringia but more in connection with his position as Plenipotentiary of the forced labour programme, in particular by organising the round-ups and transports. Arthur Seyss-Inquart, a little known figure, had a brief spell as Austrian chancellor, before working as deputy in Poland and then governing the occupied Netherlands.

Probably the most consequential case of the three was that of Hans Frank, a lawyer from Karlsruhe who had joined the German Workers Party in 1919 and affected a steady rise to prominence. His career had really begun to gather momentum in 1927, when he had been appointed to defend some SA men charged with bullying and destruction of property. Success in that case quickly led him to become Hitler's favoured legal adviser. In 1936 he was given the fabulous title of 'Reich Commissioner for the Standardisation of Justice in the Länder and for the Renewal of the Legal Order' in which he brought the German judiciary to heel according to Hitler's wishes and on 24th August 1939 he received his final position as Governor of the General-Government of Poland.[636] The General Government referred to the part of Poland that, unlike Prussia, or the Polish Corridor, Upper Silesia or Pomerania, had not been absorbed into the Reich. It was occupied and under German control, but was not inside Germany.

Despite his apparent position of importance in a key area for the Reich, in a territory which offered a buffer between Germany and the Soviet Union and potential scope for increased *lebensraum*, Frank was viewed as a minor, even a petty figure by Hitler. During his six years in charge of the General-Government he was only called to meet with the Führer on six occasions[637]. He tended his resignation (and was refused) no less than fourteen times.[638] Hitler, who had a preference for soldiers and visionaries, frequently made disparaging remarks about lawyers, whose expertise in arguing over details and settling dispute by negotiation he saw as the very antithesis of the artistic or warrior spirit.

---

[636] Frank's biographical details taken from Neave, p.116-122 and his own testimony at Nuremberg. Nuremberg Trial Proceedings, Vol. 12, 111th day, Thursday 18th April, 1946, p.1-3
[637] ibid, p.5
[638] ibid, p.12

Frank made an immediate impression on most personnel at the trial because of his willingness to admit guilt. As with Speer, whether this was due to genuine shame at his deeds, or whether he had settled on such an attitude as a tactic is debatable. Much opinion of the time tended to the latter. Unfortunately for Frank, he lacked Speer's charm and interpersonal skills. Even the Allies turned their noses up at his snivelling and grovelling. Airey Neave wrote that he found Frank 'a pettifogging lawyer, sickening in his abject confessions of guilt.'[639]

It is not hard to see how Neave reached such conclusions. When Neave arrived in his cell to indict him, he said, 'It is as though I am two people, me, myself, Frank here – and the other Frank, the Nazi leader. And sometimes I wonder how that Frank could have done those things. This Frank looks at the other Frank and says, 'Hmm, what a louse you are, Frank…And then I am such a weak man.'[640]

The view of Frank as a faker, not just at Nuremberg, but in general, is upheld by the majority of histori- ans. Joachim Fest described him as an 'imitation of a man of violence'[641] and in keeping with history's pruri- ent obsession with Nazi gender issues and sexuality, 'a markedly feminine character.'[642]

Due to his long-standing party ties and his role in Poland, which meant that the camps at Treblinka, Lub- lin and Majdanek, among other things, officially fell under his regional jurisdiction, Frank was indicted on all counts except 'Crimes against Peace'. He was clearly not in any way a military man and had no role in plan- ning for aggressive war, but like Kaltenbrunner before him, command responsibility would see him held ac- countable for atrocities committed by those beneath him. Also like Kaltenbrunner, he appeared doomed from the outset. The documents in the court's possession were damning. Having heard and accepted the testimony of Höss, there was no chance that the tribunal would look favourably on the man under whose authority camps similar to the one run by Höss had been operating.

In the early stages of the trial, as the prosecution case was presented, one piece of evidence was to come to light which would impact on several defendants' cases, but particularly on Frank's. Document 1061-PS, 'The Stroop Report' was a leather-bound collection of operational reports written by *Generalleutnant der Waffen-SS und Polizei* Jürgen Stroop, detailing the clearing of the Warsaw Ghetto in April 1943. It explained the process whereby Jews had been contained in the ghetto, within Frank's General Government area, 'with the intention of protecting the Aryan population against the Jews.' Deported Jews from the *Reich* were sent first to Lublin which was used as a sort of 'collecting area.' However, fugitive Jews had been escaping from this collecting area and crossing into other districts where it was feared that they would pose a security threat and potentially spread *Fleckfieber* or 'Spotted Fever'[643], among the rest of the population.

As a result the Jewish ghetto had been hastily established in 1940. To some extent it had been self gov- erning, administered by a Jewish Board of Elders and patrolled by a Jewish police force, who were subordi- nated in a chain of command which led up to Frank. However, by 1942, fears were rekindled that despite be- ing walled into a small section of the city, the Jewish community still posed a security threat by being a cen- tre for partisan and anti-German activity. It was therefore decided to clear the ghetto. Initially, 310,322 Jews were removed between 22nd July and 3rd October 1942 and taken to several destinations, predominately Treb- linka. Another action carried out by Stroop's predecessor, Obergruppenführer Ferdinand von Sammern- Frankenegg, in January 1943 cleared another 6,500. Frankenegg was then asked by Himmler to clear all the factories of importance to the Reich, including those of arms manufacturers, from the ghetto and relocate them, workforce and all, to Lublin. By this time rumours of the extermination of the Jews had begun circulat- ing in the ghetto and the residents began to offer fierce and well organised resistance. Stroop was then brought in by Himmler to complete the task.

On beginning the operation, Stroop noted that,

'When we invaded the Ghetto for the first time, the Jews and the Polish bandits succeeded in repelling the participating units, including tanks and armored cars, by a well-prepared concentration of fire…I

---

[639] Neave, p.121
[640] Neave, p.122
[641] Fest, p.315
[642] Fest, p.316
[643] sometimes referred to as *Judenfieber* or 'Jewish fever' in Nazi documents due to the large numbers of Jewish refugees who caught it through poor living conditions

cannot imagine a greater chaos than in the Ghetto of Warsaw. The Jews had control of everything, from the chemical substances used in manufacturing explosives to clothing and equipment for the Armed Forces. The managers knew so little of their own shops that the Jews were in a position to produce inside these shops arms of every kind, especially hand grenades, Molotov cocktails, and the like...The managers of these enterprises, which were generally also supervised by an officer of the Armed Forces, could in most cases make no specified statements on their stocks and the whereabouts of these stocks. The statements which they made on the number of Jews employed by them were in every case incorrect. Over and over again we discovered that these labyrinths of edifices belonging to the armament concerns as residential blocks, contained rich Jews who had succeeded in finding accommodations for themselves and their families under the name of 'armament workers' and were leading marvelous lives there. Despite all our orders to the managers to make the Jews leave those enterprises, we found out in several cases that managers simply concealed the Jews by shutting them in, because they expected that the action would be finished within a few days and that they then would be able to continue working with the remaining Jews...'

As a result of these issues, Stroop utilized ever more heavy handed tactics in clearing the ghetto, resorting ultimately to burning much of it down. Altogether some 65,000 Jews were captured and shipped out. Thousands more were killed in the fighting. The subtitle for Stroop's report was ominous. 'The Warsaw Ghetto is no more' it said.

On capture, Frank had surrendered his private diaries, which he had studiously kept throughout his governorship in Poland, to the Allies. Quite why he thought this would be a good idea is not clear. It is probable that he suspected the journals would be found anyway and decided to volunteer them as a sign of good will. Altogether, they amounted to 11,367 pages of written words, included in forty-three volumes.[644] Many passages from them were used to incriminate him.

The inculpatory evidence for his case was presented on the morning of January 10th by Major William Baldwin, of the United States, who spent most of the day reading Frank's own words to the court. 'In September of 1941,' Baldwin said, 'defendant Frank's own chief medical officer reported to him the appalling Polish health conditions. I read now from page 46 of the diary. 'The Poles now have about 600 calories allotted to them, while the normal requirement for a human being is 2,200...The number of Poles with communicable diseases has reached forty percent...The situation presents a serious danger for the soldiers of the Reich coming into the Government-General.'

Baldwin here was describing Frank's genuine fear of Typhus, Dysentry and Cholera. The effects of war were such that epidemics of them swept large portions of Europe. For obvious reasons, it was a priority of the German state to protect their troops from infection as far as possible. He proceeded to heap further ignominy on Frank's head by continuing, 'In August 1942, Frank approved a new plan which called for a much larger contribution of foodstuffs to Germany at the expense of the Poles. I quote again from the diary, page 30. 'Before the German people suffer starvation, the occupied territories and their people shall be exposed to starvation. This means a sixfold increase over that of last year's contributions by Poland. The new demand will be fulfilled exclusively at the expense of the foreign population. It must be done cold-bloodedly and without pity.'[645]

Such planning, similar to 'The Hunger Plan' outlined by Adam Tooze in his work 'The Wages of Destruction', which aimed to starve the population of Western Russia during the playing out of Barbarossa is clearly a gross violation of human rights and easily fits within the categories of War Crimes or Crimes against Humanity. However, set within the context of the Total War being waged, by all sides, from 1939-45 seems fairly in keeping with the mood of the time. The net effect of the Nazi occupation of Poland was very similar to the net effect of the American campaign in Japan, for example. Starvation caused by war was rife all over Europe and beyond. That the Nazis used the territory under their control to prioritise the needs of their own people first and occupied peoples second is no surprise either. Most nations, under the circumstances, would have done the same. It must be remembered that the Allied naval blockade meant that Germany had limited options. Food had to be found from somewhere.

---

[644] Siedler, p.150-151
[645] Nuremberg Trial Proceedings, Vol 5, 31st day, Thursday 10th January 1946, p.82-83

Baldwin produced other documents too, one of them containing the followng statement of Frank's, 'Poland shall be treated as a colony; the Poles shall be the slaves of the Greater German world empire.'[646] Another, callously blasé 'Once the war is won, then, for all I care, mincemeat can be made of the Poles and the Ukrainians and all the others who run around here; it doesn't matter what happens.'[647]

An interesting issue was raised when Baldwin produced a report written by Frank for the attention of Hitler in which the deterioration of Polish society was outlined. Economic and agricultural disaster, the dismantling of the education system and the collapse of law and order were all detailed. Baldwin read his chosen section of the document but was quickly countered by Frank's lawyer, Dr Alfred Seidl who stood to address the tribunal. Seidl pointed out that within the broader context of the document, Frank was not boasting of these things or recording his evil achievements, but actually complaining to Hitler about the worsening conditions in Poland and even suggesting ways in which the situation might be ameliorated. Seidl's perceptiveness and familiarity with the document provoked an awkward few minutes for the prosecuting lawyer, who found himself chastised by Judges Lawrence and Biddle.

The President – Now, Lieutenant Colonel Baldwin, I asked you what was the whole content of the document from which you were reading this paragraph. According to counsel for Frank, the document, which is a very long document, shows that Frank was suggesting remedies for the difficulties which he here sets out. Is that so?
Lt Col Baldwin – That is so, Your Honor.
The President – Well, I think the...
Lt Col Baldwin – May it please the Tribunal, I did not cite this portion of that document, as I will later demonstrate, to show that Frank did or did not suggest remedies for these conditions; but only to explain that these conditions existed as of a certain period.
The President – Well, when you cite a small part of the document, you should make sure that what you cite is not misleading as compared to the rest of the document.
Lt Col Baldwin – I see, Your Honor. I had not considered it to be such, in view of the purpose for which I introduced it, which, as I suggested, was only to indicate a set of conditions which existed at a certain time. I naturally assumed that the Defence, as Dr Seidl has indicated, will carry on with the rest of the document as a matter of defence.
The President – Yes, of course, that is all very well, but the Defendant Frank's counsel will speak at some remote date; and it is not a complete answer to say that he will have an opportunity of explain- ing the document at some future date. It is for Counsel for the Prosecution to make sure that no ex- tracts which they read can reasonably make a misleading impression upon the mind of the Tribunal.
Lt Col Baldwin – I shall now state, then, that the extract which was just read was read solely for the purpose of indicating that at a certain period, namely, June 1943, those conditions existed in Poland, as the result of statements by the Governor General of Poland. Would that be satisfactory to the Tribunal?
Judge Biddle – Well, what is not satisfactory to the Tribunal is that you did not give us the real purport of the document.
Lt Col Baldwin – Well, Sir, I don't have the complete document before me now. Therefore, I can't read all of it...[648]

It reflects well on the tribunal that they reacted to Baldwin's dishonesty in this way, but needs to be remembered that they only did so after having the American lawyer's lying by omission pointed out to them by Seidl. If Seidl had not been so astute and had not remembered the full bearing of the forty page document that Baldwin was reading from, Baldwin's selective evidence would simply have passed by unnoticed and been entered into the record with the subjective slant that he had placed upon it. As throughout the trial the prosecution selectively quoted from countless documents, detaching them from their wider context, it raises the question of how many times this kind of deceptive evidence was presented and accepted, without lawyers

---

[646] ibid, p.76
[647] ibid, p.78
[648] ibid, p.80

as sharp as Seidl to challenge it.

Baldwin went on to detail Frank's engagement with the forced labour programme, deporting Poles from the General Government to the Reich and his upscaling of security measures in the face of Polish resistance; 'You see that we do not hesitate at anything,' he quoted Frank as saying, in a speech to a meeting of district leaders in 1942, 'and stand dozens of people up against the wall. This is necessary because a simple reflection tells me that it cannot be our task at this period, when the best German blood is being sacrificed, to show regard for the blood of another race... Therefore, everything revealing itself as a Polish power of leadership must be destroyed again and again with ruthless energy. This does not have to be shouted abroad; it will happen silently.'[649]

In connection to the Holocaust issue, it is worth noting that during the time of Frank's jurisdiction of the General-Government, the number of Jews living there declined from two and a half million to about a hundred thousand. Despite the civilian round-ups for slave labour and the fact that during the initial resettlement programme, in 1939-40, when Jews (along with other Poles) from western areas were shoved into the General Government, during a winter in which temperatures regularly dropped to forty below and many of them eventually died, without the need for bullets or gas, this is usually stated in relation to the Holocaust, with the implication that all of these people were exterminated as part of the anti-Semitic genocidal plan of the Nazis. Yet even allowing for all the damning statements made by Frank in his diary, the prosecution were unable to provide a single one which referred either to a plan to murder all Jews or to gas chambers or any other related issues. Bearing in mind that Treblinka and Majdanek, which Raul Hilberg alleged gassed 850,000 Jews between them,[650] were in the area under his control, it would be safe to assume he would have known something of them, although Frank himself stated that such matters were solely controlled by Himmler and the SS. It is inconceivable that the governor of a region could not have known of an extermination programme going on in such a way under his nose. Bearing this in mind, why then, when he was perfectly happy to write about starving and shooting civilians, did he not write about this in his diary? He had made many anti-Semitic comments, such as a record of a speech he had made on October 7th 1940, to the Nazi assembly in Poland. 'My dear comrades!' he had said, 'I could not eliminate (*vernichtet*) all lice and Jews in only one year. But in the course of time and if you help me, this end will be attained.'[651] Indeed, in another entry in which a recollection of cabinet session in Cracow was recorded, he said, '...Gentlemen, I must ask you to rid yourself of all feeling of pity. We must destroy (*vernichtet*) the Jews.' He went on to say that, it would be difficult 'to shoot or poison the three and a half million Jews in the General Government, but we shall be able to take measures which will lead, somehow, to their destruction.'[652]

Frank therefore was clearly happy to display anti-Semitism in his diary, especially when recording party official functions at which anti-Semitic statements would have been expected, even expressing them in the most extreme terms. Yet still he did not mention a programme of genocide or devices of mass execution, even stating that he did not believe such things would be possible. This means that once again, one is faced with an absence of evidence regarding key elements of the Holocaust.

It must be clarified however, that there can be no doubt that the people of Poland suffered terribly during Frank's regime and that in these circumstances, Jews, who had been marginalised and ghettoised, would have had the worst of it. But still, as before, we find the most notorious claims of the Holocaust utterly unsubstantiated by the available evidence.

Four months later, during questioning by his defence counsel Dr, Alfred Seidl, on the 18th April, Frank provided historians with one of the most repeated sound-bites of the entire trial. Like Speer, Frank went to great lengths to be as contrite as possible. He claimed to have rediscovered Catholicism in prison and made regular comments decrying Nazism and its implementation[653]. Having already expressed regret at the more extreme atrocities (it is important to note that Frank only claimed to have learnt of what went on after he was brought to Nuremberg), he was asked the following question by his lawyer.

---

[649] ibid, p.86
[650] Hilberg, p.1320
[651] William Shirer, The Rise and Fall of the Third Reich (Pan 1960) p.796
[652] ibid, p.797
[653] Tusa, p.235

Dr Seidl – Did you ever participate in the annihilation of Jews?
Frank – I say 'yes;' and the reason why I say 'yes' is because, having lived through the 5 months of this trial, and particularly after having heard the testimony of the witness Höss, my conscience does not allow me to throw the responsibility solely on these minor people. I myself have never installed an extermination camp for Jews, or promoted the existence of such camps; but if Adolf Hitler person- ally has laid that dreadful responsibility on his people, then it is mine too, for we have fought against Jewry for years; and we have indulged in the most horrible utterances-my own diary bears witness against me. Therefore, it is no more than my duty to answer your question in this connection with 'yes.' A thousand years will pass and still this guilt of Germany will not have been erased.[654]

A thousand years – ironically the amount of time that Hitler had envisaged the Third Reich lasting. Several other defendants were shocked at his identification of guilt with Germany as a whole. Göring called him a 'weak-kneed coward.'[655] And again, we see the importance of the Höss affidavit. Not only was it enough to convince the court, it was enough to convince Hans Frank.

Frank went on to candidly admit the establishment of Jewish ghettoes, the Star-of-David badges that Jews were forced to wear, the use of forced labour, the plundering of libraries and the abolition of Polish universities.[656] He was asked about the exploitation of Poland, to which he responded by stating that considerable efforts had been made by Germany to rebuild Polish agriculture, but were constantly thwarted by internal enemies. This led Seidl onto the issue of partisans:

Dr Seidl – Is it correct that your actions as Governor General, and undoubtedly also many excesses by the police and the SD, were due to the guerrilla activities?
Frank – Guerrilla activities? It can be said that it was the resistance movement, which started from the very first day and was supported by our enemies, which presented the most difficult problem I had to cope with during all these years. For this resistance movement perpetually supplied the police and the SS with pretexts and excuses for all those measures which, from the viewpoint of an orderly administration, were very regrettable. In fact, the resistance movement-I will not call it guerrilla activity, because if a people has been conquered during a war and organizes an active resistance move- ment, that is something definitely to be respected-but the methods of the resistance movement went far beyond the limits of an heroic revolt. German women and children were slaughtered under the most atrocious circumstances. German officials were shot; trains were derailed; dairies were destroyed; and all measures taken to bring about the recovery of the country were systematically undermined.
And it is against the background of these incidents, which occurred day after day, incessantly, during practically the entire period of my activity, that the events in that country must be considered. That is all I have to say to that.' [657]

Later, the matter of concentration camps was picked up in cross examination by Smirnov, for the So- viet Union.
Mr Counsellor Smirnov – Well, then, let us pass on to another group of questions. You heard of the existence of Maidanek only in 1944, isn't that so?
Frank – In 1944 the name Maidanek was brought to my knowledge officially for the first time by the Press Chief Gassner.
There followed some confusion over which part of the document in evidence Frank was supposed to be looking at.
Frank – With reference to Maidanek we were talking about the extermination of Jews. The extermination of Jews in Maidanek became known to me during the summer of 1944. Up to now the word 'Maidanek' has always been mentioned in connection with extermination of Jews.
Smirnov – Consequently, we are to understand-I refer to the text submitted to you-that in May 1943

---

[654] Nuremberg Trial Proceedings, Vol. 12, 111th day, Thursday 18th April, 1946, p.12
[655] Gilbert, p.277
[656] Nuremberg Trial Proceedings, Vol. 12, 111th day, Thursday 18th April, 1946, p.14
[657] ibid, p.20

you heard of the mass murder of Poles in Maidanek, and in 1944 you heard of the mass murder of Jews?

Frank – I beg your pardon? I heard about the extermination of the Jews at Maidanek in 1944 from the official documents in the foreign press.

Smirnov- And you heard of the mass killings of the Poles in 1943?

Frank- That is contained in my memorandum, and I protest; these are the facts as I put them before the Fuehrer.[658]

Frank, therefore, like Kaltenbrunner and Streicher before him was stating that he had not known of mass killings of Jews until he had read about them in foreign media. Shortly afterwards Frank left the stand and professed to Gilbert that he was pleased with his performance.

Frank's last hurrah in court, like all the defendants, took place on August 31st, when each of them was allowed to stand and make a brief statement. Many of the speeches were unremarkable, the accused men were jaded and cynical after eleven months of proceedings, leading to lacklustre orations on their ignorance of the more serious allegations. Even Göring was uninspired. Frank, however, was one of the few to say something worth noting. He referred the court to his earlier statement regarding the 'thousand years of guilt' and said,
'Every possible guilt incurred by our nation has already been wiped out today, not only by the conduct of our wartime enemies toward our nation and its soldiers, which has been carefully kept out of this trial, but also by the tremendous mass crimes of the most frightful sort which – as I have now learned – have been and are still being committed against Germans by Russians, Poles and Czechs, especially in East Prussia, Silesia, Pomerania and Sudatenland. Who shall ever judge these crimes against the German people?'[659]

It was a valid question and one which the Tribunal to which it was posed could not answer. Events since have shown that it has never been answered. The crimes to which Frank referred, the same crimes mentioned in chapter two of this book have never been brought to justice. They have barely been spoken about. It is only now, sixty years on that they are beginning to receive any real coverage.

At the deliberation meetings, Frank's case saw Nikitchenko take the hard-line Russian stance into the territory of caricature by finding the defendant guilty of all four counts, even though he had not been indicted on Count Two. De Vabres voted Frank guilty on all three of the counts he had actually been charged with, while Lawrence and Biddle initially abstained. When the final decision was required, the British and American judges both concurred with De Vabres and Frank was sentenced to death by hanging. It is said that Frank, displaying symptoms which today would be described as conforming to the 'Stockholm syndrome' smiled on the way to the gallows and even thanked the belligerent Colonel Andrus, who was standing by, for 'the kindness which I received in this incarceration.'[660]

Fritz Sauckel had embarked upon adulthood as a merchant seaman and like so many others, joined the party after hearing Hitler speak. Through sheer, dogged persistence he worked himself up to become *Gaule- iter* of Thurungia in 1927, which remained his sole responsibility until 1942, when he was called to an audi- ence with Hitler and Speer at the Reich Chancellery in Berlin. There he was told of the crisis of production faced by Germany, in the wake of the war on two fronts and the engagement of America. He was persuaded to reluctantly agree to a position as General Plenipotentiary for the Employment of Labour. His first task as such was to raise 1.6 million new workers within three months.[661]

At first, after recovering from his surprise, he tried to achieve the impossible by using legal means. Many civilians of occupied territories were initially willing to come to the Reich for waged work, but as the war wore on, the German situation became more desperate and resentment towards German occupation grew as harsher and harsher conditions were imposed. This meant that for targets to be met, ever more coercive methods had to be employed. The responsibility began to weigh heavily upon him and Sauckel, who had really never been much more than an able and competent administrator, attempted to escape his new, unwelcome reality by stowing away on a U-boat. When discovered he had begged to be allowed to stay aboard, but

---

[658] ibid, p.35
[659] Nuremberg Trial Proceedings Vol.12 August 31st 1946, p.366-410
[660] Taylor, p.610
[661] Persico, p.163

the astonished Captain radioed Dönitz who instructed him to bring Sauckel back to port.

Sauckel's prosecution was taken on by Dodd, who read several incriminating documents into the record, probably the most telling of which was a report written by Rosenberg. 'You cannot imagine the bestiality. The order came to supply twenty five workers, but no-one reported. Then the German militia came and began to set fire to the houses of those who had fled.' Sauckel squirmed, but it was to get worse. 'People who hurried to the scene were forbidden to extinguish the flames, beaten and arrested. They fell on their knees to kiss the hands of the policemen, but the policemen beat them again with rubber truncheons and threatened to burn down the whole village. During the fire, the militia went through the adjoining village and seized the labourers...The imprisoned workers are locked in the schoolhouse...'[662]

The brutality of some of the round-ups, particularly those made later in the war, was mitigated to some degree, by other evidence. Sauckel had, it seemed, attempted to improve the conditions of forced labourers under his control. He had once written a directive which stated that, 'underfed slaves, diseased, resentful, despairing and filled with hate, will never yield that maximum of output which they can achieve under decent conditions.'[663]

He was to use this line of reasoning constantly in his defence. Over the weekend of December 15th-16th, Gilbert went to visit him in his cell. Typically, Gilbert described Sauckel as 'trembling' (it seems most of the defendants trembled when Gilbert spoke to them). Sauckel said, 'I want to tell you that I know absolutely nothing of these things and I certainly had absolutely nothing to do with it! It was just the opposite. I wanted to make conditions as good as possible for foreign workers...I was like a seaman's agency. If I supply hands for a ship, I am not responsible for any cruelty that may be exercised aboard ship without my knowledge. I just supplied workers to places like the Krupp works at Hitler's orders. I am not to blame if they are later mistreated.'[664]

As mentioned in chapter eleven, his case is most readily analysed through contrast with Speer's because of the common ground in their indictments. Sauckel organised the gathering of labour, Speer organised its use. Yet unlike his charismatic colleague, the Plenipotentiary for Labour, whom Jackson characterised as 'the greatest and cruellest slaver since the Pharaohs of Egypt'[665] in his closing address, was sentenced to hang with 'virtually no discussion.'[666] The judges and most of the prosecutors discussed Sauckel dismissively and disparagingly. He was tearful upon receiving sentence and appealed vigorously against the decision, citing his large family and the *Führer Prinzip* in his defence. As they prepared the noose and pulled the hood over his head, he maintained his opposition, 'I die innocently' he cried, 'the verdict was wrong. God protect Germany...God protect my family.'[667]

Arthur Seyss-Inquart was another lawyer and another Austrian. He had grown up in Vienna and was a devout Catholic. Since the early twenties he had been a member of *die Deutsche Gemeinschaft* (the German Community) a proto-nationalist organisation that campaigned for the liberation of the German people from Jewish influence. He had spent the immediate part of his pre-Nuremberg career as governor of the occupied Netherlands, having also been Frank's assistant in Poland, and Chancellor of Austria for four days after the Anschluss. After the First World War, Seyss-Inquart had felt that a greatly diminished Austria had no hope in world affairs unless it became a part of a Greater Germany and he, along with many others, worked tirelessly to make this happen. The prosecution therefore implicated him as a player in the 'invasion' of Austria, which he undoubtedly was, yet the illegality and aggressive nature of Anschluss had huge question marks hanging over it.

In 1919, for example, the Austrian Provisional National Assembly had declared Austria part of the German Republic, a decision which was later ratified by the Constitutional National Assembly. 98 percent of Austrians had voted in favour of Anschluss in plebiscites held as early as 1921.[668] The act of Anschluss, although defined by the prosecution as 'aggressive' and officially outlawed by the Treaty of Versailles, was

---

[662] Rosenberg to Sauckel, Dec 21st 1942. NCA 018 PS. Library of Congress
[663] Persico, p.164
[664] Gilbert, p.75
[665] Nuremberg Trial Proceedings, Vol 19, 187th day, 26th July 1946, p.415
[666] Taylor, p.562
[667] Taylor, p.563
[668] Davidson, p.447

clearly mandated by the will of the Austrian people.

Seyss-Inquart had other issues to contend with, however. Like Streicher, he was a self-confessed anti-Semite, a fact he openly admitted to the court. 'I will say quite openly that since the First World War and the postwar period, I was an anti-Semite and went to Holland as such...I had the impression, which will be confirmed everywhere, that the Jews, of course had to be against National Socialist Germany...I had to realize that, particularly from the Jewish circles, I had to reckon with resistance, defeatism and so on...'[669]

When questioned about Auschwitz, he confirmed that he had sent Jews there and had enquired as to conditions at the camp. He reported that he had been told that the quality of life there was generally high and that the camp had a variety of leisure and recreation on offer for the inmates to use, including a hundred piece orchestra, a theatre and sports facilities.[670]

Like Sauckel, Seyss-Inquart's case gave the judges 'very little trouble'[671], despite the fact that he had clearly tried to improve the conditions of Dutch civilians and the fact that 'there was unimpeachable testimony that Seyss-Inquart had displayed both skill and courage near the end of the war in preventing further death and destruction, regardless of Hitler's orders.'[672] Telford Taylor stated that none of this 'aroused much interest among the judges' in contrast to similar actions on the part of Speer. He also stated that this was because Seyss-Inquart, 'refused to turn away from his loyalty to Hitler.'[673]

Seyss-Inquart was therefore declared guilty on Counts Two, Three and Four and sentenced to death. In this way and contrary to all normal practice for a court of law, another defendant's fate was not determined solely by what he had or had not done, but by his views and beliefs, his ideology. Seyss-Inquart was executed, unlike Speer, because he remained an unapologetic Nazi. He was the last man to be executed and during the two hour wait in his cell, he marked an 'X' on October 16th on his calendar. His speech on the gallows, moments before his death, is worth recording:

'I hope that this execution is the last act of the tragedy of the Second World War and that a lesson will be learned so that peace and understanding will be realized among the nations. I believe in Germany.'[674]

---

[669] Nuremberg Trial Proceedings, Vol. 15, 151st day, Mon 10th June, 1946, p.666
[670] ibid, p.667
[671] Taylor, p.563
[672] ibid
[673] ibid
[674] Taylor, p.610

18

The Pied Piper and the Voice of Radio Deutschland

Baldur von Schirach, Hans Fritzsche

The remaining two defendants included Hans Fritzsche, whose case will not be discussed here at great length. The idea of putting a newsreader on trial as a war criminal was ridiculous from the beginning and was apparently based on the Soviet desire to include a couple of defendants from the ranks of those whom they had captured (Raeder also) and the wish to have someone to act as a stand-in for Goebbels, in much the same way that Kaltenbrunner was used as Himmler's understudy. He was indicted on all accounts except crimes against peace, on the basis that he aided in the conspiracy, the commission of war crimes and crimes against humanity by disseminating propaganda.

The problem for the prosecution was that whereas there was scope to claim that Nazi soldiers and politicians had exceeded the boundaries of acceptability, even in times of war, when such boundaries are stretched, Fritzsche clearly had not. He had simply performed a role that was carried out in exactly the same way by similar people in all nations. Throughout the trial and in common with Speer and Schacht, Fritzsche frequently made disparaging remarks about Hitler and Nazism. Despite this, Drexel Sprecher (a United States German/American prosecutor) made a valiant attempt to smear him with the same sort of melodramatic language that the prosecution had been using throughout the trial. He began falteringly, 'There are two allegations of the indictment concerning Fritzsche's positions for which we are unable to offer proof,'[675] he said, as if such a statement were perfectly commonplace in a court of law. Before long, however, he had built up a head of rhetorical steam. 'We of the Prosecution' he announced, 'contend that Fritzsche, one of the most eminent of Goebbels' propaganda team, helped substantially to bathe the world in the blood bath of aggressive war.'[676] He also described how the prosecution would, 'show the important and unique position of the German Press Division as an instrument of the Nazi conspirators not only in dominating the minds and the psychology of Germans...but also as an instrument of foreign policy and psychological warfare against other nations.'[677]

During the course of the trial the prosecution singularly failed to do this, however. The allegation that the

---

[675] Nuremberg Trial Proceedings, Vol 6, 41st day, Wednesday 23rd January 1946, p.53
[676] ibid p.64
[677] ibid, p.56

German Propaganda Ministry was in any way 'unique' was utterly unsustainable. All nations had similar official departments, the British Ministry of Information, for example, had a large staff, in which the author George Orwell worked for a time. Like any such organisation, they busied themselves with spreading disinformation, including atrocity propaganda.[678]

The court's official judgement on Fritzsche reflected the paucity of the case against him. It conceded that he 'sometimes spread false news...sometimes made strong statements of a propagandistic nature,' but went on to conclude that he 'had no control of the formulation of these propaganda policies. He was merely a con- duit to the press...' At meetings 'his only function was to transmit Goebbels' directives... Never did he achieve sufficient stature to attend the planning conferences which led to aggressive war; indeed according to his own uncontradicted testimony he never even had a conversation with Hitler.' They stated that he had made speeches in which he said 'the war had been caused by Jews and said their fate had turned out 'as unpleasant as the Führer predicted.' But these speeches did not urge persecution or extermination of Jews. There is no evidence that he was aware of their extermination in the East.'[679]

Despite the fact that the final point regarding his speeches seemed to be very similar to the one used to convict and execute Streicher, with regard to articles in *Der Stürmer*, the tribunal acquitted Fritzsche on all three counts. He left Nuremberg and was immediately rearrested by German authorities, who tried him in a denazification court and sentenced him to nine years hard labour. He was released early in 1950 and died of cancer in 1953.

The last of the defendants to be considered in this book, Baldur von Schirach, was, like several others, a Nazi *Gauleiter*, having governed Vienna from 1940-45, but the case held against him by the IMT revolved more around his role as a prominent figure in and eventual leader of the Hitler Youth, a position he held between 1931 and 1940. He found himself indicted on counts one and four only.

Even more so than some of the other men in the dock, von Schirach did not meet the masculine ideals of his captors. Airey Neave described his appearance as being, 'bi-sexual and soft with thé-dansant eyes,' stating that he had a 'fat eunuch's face' before delivering the all-too obvious coup de grace. 'He looked like a man who might be dangerous to small boys.'[680] In some form and despite his crudity, Neave had summed up the prosecution case against von Schirach. They also thought he was dangerous to small boys. Just not necessarily in the same way that Neave did.

Von Schirach was indicted on counts one and four, with the indictment document suggesting his case was more heavily tilted towards count one. His role in the HJ saw him touted as prime mover behind the conspiracy, particularly in preparing the youth of Germany for participation in aggressive war. His indictment on count four centred around his official position in Vienna, alleging that he had been responsible for the deportation of thousands of Viennese Jews, with the implication that he had done so in the knowledge they would be killed.

Like Fritzsche, Schirach's case was handled by the excitable Captain Sprecher who presented his initial documents with such zealous detail that he had to be reined in by Judge Lawrence. Barely five minutes after starting his presentation and after labouring the point that Schirach was influential in the training of young Germans, Sprecher found himself interrupted by the president of the court, who tersely told him, 'Captain Sprecher, I think you have told us enough now to satisfy us that Von Schirach was in charge of the ideological education of German youth and completely in charge of it...And we don't want to hear any more of it.'[681]

Sprecher, persisted however, only to receive a more stinging rebuke several minutes later. '...I don't think I made it quite clear that the Tribunal is not really interested in these details...' Lawrence said, '...The only thing that seems to me to be material, at the present stage, is whether or not you can show us any direct evidence that the Defendant Schirach was a party to the aggressive aims of the Reich leaders, or to any War Crimes or to any Crimes against Humanity. Unless you can show us that, your address to us is really not useful to us at this stage.'[682]

---

[678] Edward J Rozek, *Allied Wartime Diplomacy, a Pattern in Poland* (John Wiley & Sons, 1958) p.209-210
[679] From Fritzsche's judgement. http://www.yale.edu/lawweb/avalon/imt/proc/judfritz.htm
[680] Neave, p.103
[681] Nuremberg Trial Proceedings, Vol, 5, 34th day, 15th January 1946, p.287
[682] ibid, p.289

Suitably chastised, Sprecher moved on to discuss a book written by the defendant, in which the concept of *Lebensraum* was discussed, how the HJ provided a large body of recruits for the SS and how the HJ had been trained in such arts as rifle shooting, therefore implying that they were some sort of military offshoot. To support this, an agreement signed by von Schirach and Keitel was produced which stated:

> 'While it is exclusively the task of the Hitler Youth to attend to the training of their units in this direction, it is suitable, in the sense of a uniformed training corresponding to the demands of the Wehrmacht, to support the leadership of the Hitler Youth for their responsible task as trainers and educators in all fields of training for defence by special courses.'[683]

Sprecher's accusations were flimsy however, the military links of the HJ had only been strongly forged in the years of war and prior to that it had much in common with youth movements the world over. Indeed, when considering the role of the HJ within Nazi Germany, it is important, as when considering the role of the SS, to try to strip away the layers of propaganda and discover its real purpose, as intended by its creators. It was not, as commonly believed, or as stated by Jackson in his closing address, an invention solely of Hitler's, created in the bowels of the Nazi conspiracy to serve up German youth to the Party as 'fanatic, unquestioning executors of its will,'[684] but had developed organically from pre-existing movements dating from the 19th century.

The '*Wandervogel*' (travelling or migratory bird) movement was formed in 1898 in Berlin, ten years be- fore Lieutenant-General, Robert Baden-Powell published 'Scouting for Boys' in the UK and while the soon- to-be founder of the international scout movement was still fighting in the Boer war. As in the writings of Rosenberg mentioned in chapter fourteen, the *Wandervogel* rejected much of what they saw as the artificial- ity of modern living. They sought an escape from industrialisation and city life by reconnecting with nature. They sought to find a new community among like-minded youngsters to replace the rural communities that were being dismantled. They relished adventure in the open air, taking members on long hiking trips and cooking over campfires.

Ten years after the *Wandervogel*'s beginnings, the Scout movement spread from the UK and also became popular. Scouting shared some ideals with the *Wandervogel*, particularly the emphasis on outdoor activity, but was far more militaristic due to Baden-Powell's background. The *Wandervogel* did not wear uniforms, for example, or carry flags. They read poetry, their leaders tended to be younger and they formed loose groups rather than being divided into units as the Scouts were. For a variety of reasons, none of them particularly relevant to our topic, the German Scouts and the *Wandervogel* underwent a form of merger after the First World War and although each retained something of their own identity, the new, unified *Bündische Jugend* or German Youth Movement, existed until officially replaced with the *Hitler Jugend* in 1933. However, in many ways this 'replacement' did not radically alter the movement's character. Inspired by the intellectualism of leaders like Gustav Wyneken, who were 'devoted to the ideals of Kant, Hegel, Goethe and Nietzsche'[685] and through the blending of *Wandervogel* idealism and environmental consciousness, with Baden-Powell's militarism, the vast majority of what would become the 'Hitler Youth' was already in place.

It was therefore a simple step for members and leaders of the German Youth Movement to slip into the HJ, but that is not to say that all *Bündische Jugend* leaders were happy to play along. Many of the younger, anti-authoritarian, *Wandervogel* devotees rejected the imposition of the government in their world and formed splinter groups. The Edelweiss Pirates are a famous example of this. But for those who stayed, there was little difference in their day to day activities.

As an adolescent, Baldur von Schirach himself had been a member of a youth organisation, a small group called the '*Knappenschaft*', which he joined in 1923, the year of the Beer Hall Putsch in Munich. The story he relayed on the stand at Nuremberg provided a clear narrative as to how young Germans such as himself were attracted by National Socialism. He said that from discussion with his comrades in the *Knappenschaft* he 'came to grasp for the first time the consequences of the Versailles Treaty in their full import…' He also

---

[683] ibid, p.293
[684] Nuremberg Trial Proceedings, Vol 19, 187th day, 26th July 1946, p.416
[685] Anson Rabinbach. *Between Enlightenment and Apocalypse, Benjamin, Block and Modern German Jewish Messianism*, New German Critique, No.34 (1985).

soon saw that '...The school boy had the prospect of struggling through somehow or other as a working student, and then he would in all probability become a member of the academic proletariat for the possibility of an academic career practically did not exist for him at all. The young worker had no prospect of finding an apprenticeship. For him there was nothing other than the grim misery of unemployment. It was a generation nobody would help unless it helped itself.'[686]

Von Schirach then went on to describe how he became a National Socialist in 'quite a natural way' and attended meetings at which he heard Rosenberg, Streicher and Sauckel speak. He listed the books that had shaped his early thinking. Interestingly after mentioning *'The International Jew'* by the famous American industrialist and car manufacturer, Henry Ford, the President of the Tribunal chose to interject.

The President – Dr Sauter, the Tribunal thinks, as I have said twice now, that the educational influences of the defendant are quite irrelevant to us. I do not want to say it again and, unless you can control the defendant and keep him to the point, I shall have to stop his evidence.
Dr Sauter – But, Mr President, is it not of interest to the Tribunal when judging this defendant and his personality that they know how the defendant became a National Socialist and how the defendant became anti-Semitic? I had thought...
The President – No, it is not of interest to the Tribunal.[687]

Having been diverted from any potential in-depth analysis of the international aspect of Von Schirach's intellectual development and specifically its American influence, Sauter's questioning nonetheless elicited another interesting point regarding ideology. '...I did not become a National Socialist because of anti-Semitism,' Schirach said, 'but because of Socialism.'[688] Much like the testimony of Rosenberg, the statement raised questions about the true nature of Nazism and how it was perceived from the inside, by those involved in it, as opposed to how it was perceived from the outside, by those attacking it. Again, this is a point to be rejoined in the final chapters.

Schirach explained how he had met Hitler, heard him speak and found his proposed solutions to Germany's problems to be compatible with ideas he had forged in camp-fire discussions with the *Knappenschaft*. It was an obvious step for him to join the party and he did so in 1925, aged 18. In 1929, whilst at University he became head of the National Socialist German Students League. Then, at a meeting with Hitler in Graz in Austria in 1931, Schirach was asked his opinion on the best way to further develop the National Socialist Youth movement. With a statement of pure *Wandervogel* philosophy, Schirach told Hitler that 'one cannot lead youth organizations as an appendix of a political party; youth has to be led by youth.'[689] This pivotal moment in his life led to him being given the title of Reich Youth Leader of the NSDAP at the tender age of 25.

In his first act in the role he merged the various NSDAP youth organisations already in existence under the banner of the Hitler Youth. This made them the biggest single youth organisation in Germany, outnumbering the *Bündischer Jugend* a year even before the Nazis formed their first government. After the assumption of power, in 1933, Von Schirach then dissolved the *Bündischer Jugend*, under whose banner most of the other youth movements were assembled. Many of them had natural inclinations towards National Socialism anyway and he saw no point in allowing a variety of pan-Germanic organisations to continue a fractured existence. From that day on, then, the Hitler Youth was the only legal option for young Germans. This was further tightened in 1936 when a law was passed making membership compulsory, yet Schirach maintained that the law was not fully enforced until 1939 and that until then, 97 percent of the membership joined voluntarily.[690] Echoing Göring's words from earlier in the trial about the impossibility of ruling with bayonets, von Schirach commented that 'the concept that any youth organisation can be established and carried on, and successfully carried on, by coercing youth, is absolutely false.'[691]

---

[686] Nuremberg Trial Proceedings, Vol.14, 137th day, 23rd May, 1946, p.366
[687] ibid p.367
[688] ibid
[689] ibid, p.371
[690] ibid, p.375
[691] ibid

With regard to the charges levelled at him by Sprecher, Schirach denied assisting in the planning and preparation for aggressive war by refuting the idea that the HJ had been militaristic. Reaffirming his socialist ideals, he stated that the uniforms worn by the HJ were not significant in a military sense, but only in establishing a culture of equality. 'The uniform was the symbol of a community without class distinctions.' He said. 'The worker's boy wore the same garb as the son of the university professor.'[692] In answer to the charge that the HJ had been a pre-military training school for the Wehrmacht and SS, von Schirach denied vigorously, saying that he had purposely excluded military elements like drilling from the HJ regimen as he considered them to be 'not youthful.'[693] In support of this he was able to quote the judgement of the British Board of Education, who had reviewed a Hitler youth training manual in 1938 and drawn the following con- clusions:

'It cannot fairly be said to be in essence a more militaristic work than any thoroughgoing, exhaustive, and comprehensive manual of Boy Scout training would be. Some forty pages are, to be sure, devoted to the theory and practice of shooting small-bore rifle and air gun, but there is nothing in them to which exception can reasonably be taken, and the worst that one can say of them is that they may be confidently recommended to the notice of any Boy Scout wishing to qualify for his marksmanship badge.'[694]

On the stand, Von Schirach emphasized the point that the Hitler Youth only shot air rifles and never military weapons until the desperate, later years of the war when youngsters were trained and HJ units even lined up alongside those of the *Wehrmacht*.

With regard to participation in the great, malignant Nazi conspiracy, Schirach said:

'I did not participate in any conspiracy. I cannot consider it participation in a conspiracy if I joined the National Socialist Party. The program of that party had been approved; it had been published. The Party was authorized to take part in elections. Hitler had not said-neither he nor any of his collaborators- 'I want to assume power by a *coup d'etat*.' Again and again he stated in public, not only once but a hundred times: 'I want to overcome this parliamentary system by legal means…'[695]

As Schirach's defence drew to a close, attention turned to his treatment of the Jews while *Gauleiter* of Vienna. His position on this matter was much the same as the other defendants:

'Dr Colin Ross came to Vienna in 1944 and told me that he had received information, via the foreign press, that mass murders of Jews had been perpetrated on a large scale in the East. I then attempted to find out all I could. What I did discover was that in the Warthegau executions of Jews were carried out in gas vans. These shootings in the East…mentioned in the documents submitted in the course of the cross-examination in the Kaltenbrunner case, were not known to me at that time. But at a later date – it was before 1944 – I heard about shootings in the ghettos of the Russian area and connected this with developments on the front, since I thought of possible armed uprisings in the ghettos. I knew nothing of the organised annihilation which has been described to us in the Trial.'[696]

Here then, as with so many other cases, we get a couple of nods in the direction of the Nazis' greatest crime, but a complete denial of any knowledge of its alleged scope or methodology. We learn that yet another defendant, a high echelon Nazi official, claimed only to have heard of the mass murder of Jews as a result of stories in the foreign press. We do however, get the only direct reference by any of the defendants to one of the alleged murder weapons, the 'gas vans' although even with this, Schirach is not clear on how the information came to him. He said that he 'discovered' this fact, not that it was something he had first-hand

---

[692] ibid, p.377
[693] ibid, p.378
[694] ibid, p.380
[695] ibid, p.377
[696] Nuremberg Trial Proceedings, Vol. 14, 138th day, Friday, May 24th 1946, p.431

knowledge of. Presumably, therefore, this was something he was told by someone else. Like so much of the evidence regarding the major claims, this amounts only to hearsay. Most tellingly of all, like all the other defendants, he makes the point that the planned attempt at the genocide of an entire people was something he only found out about in Nuremberg.

Despite this, when asked for his reaction to the Höss affidavit he embarked on one of the most oft-repeated speeches of the entire trial.

> 'It is the greatest, the most devilish mass murder known to history. But that murder was not commit- ted by Höss; Höss was merely the executioner. The murder was ordered by Adolf Hitler, as is obvi- ous from his last will and testament. The will is genuine. I have held the Photostat copy of that will in my hands. He and Himmler jointly committed that crime which, for all time, will be a stain in the an- nals of our history. It is a crime which fills every German with shame. The youth of Germany is guiltless. Our youth was anti-semitically inclined, but it did not call for the extermination of Jewry. It neither realized nor imagined that Hitler had carried out this extermination by the daily murder of thousands of innocent people. The youth of Germany who, today, stand perplexed among the ruins of their native land, knew nothing of these crimes, nor did they desire them. They are innocent of all that Hitler has done to the Jewish and to the German people. I should like to say the following in connection with Höss' case. I have educated this generation in faith and loyalty to Hitler. The Youth Organization which I built up bore his name. I believed that I was serving a leader who would make our people and the youth of our country great and happy and free. Millions of young people believed this, together with me, and saw their ultimate ideal in National Socialism. Many died for it. Before God, before the German nation, and before my German people I alone bear the guilt of having trained our young people for a man whom I for many long years had considered unimpeachable, both as a leader and as the head of the State, of creating for him a generation who saw him as I did. The guilt is mine in that I educated the youth of Germany for a man who murdered by the millions. I believed in this man. That is all I can say for my excuse and for the characterization of my attitude...The younger generation is guiltless. It grew up in an anti-Semitic state, ruled by anti-Semitic laws. Our youth was bound by these laws and saw nothing criminal in racial politics. But if anti- Semitism and racial laws could lead to an Auschwitz, then Auschwitz must mark the end of racial politics and the death of anti-Semitism. Hitler is dead. I never betrayed him; I never tried to over- throw him; I remained true to my oath as an officer, a youth leader, and an official. I was no blind collaborator of his; neither was I an opportunist. I was a convinced National Socialist from my earli- est days-as such, I was also an anti-Semite. Hitler's racial policy was a crime which led to disaster for 5,000,000 Jews and for all the Germans. The younger generation bears no guilt. But he who, after Auschwitz, still clings to racial politics has rendered himself guilty.'[697]

It is clear that in Von Schirach's mind, the Höss affidavit, with its three million Auschwitz victims, was enough to persuade him of the ultimate immorality of Nazism and like Streicher he seemed convinced by the vague threats in Hitler's will. Whether this speech was sincerely intended or represents another defendant attempting to ingratiate themselves with the prosecutors and judges is irrelevant. What is clear is that it effectively encapsulates the world view of National Socialism in the post war era. Nazism, we believe, is an evil ideology. We believe this, not because of an examination of its fundamental aims and motivations, but because of Auschwitz and the Holocaust. It is this sentiment, so beautifully encapsulated by von Schirach that has prevented a real, objective analysis of National Socialism from taking place. And it is this sentiment which will form an important basis for the discussion in the final chapters of this book.

Von Schirach's cross examination was handled by Thomas Dodd of the United States and began with faint praise for the defendant's words on Auschwitz. 'Mr Witness, we understood you this morning to make a statement in the nature of a confession with respect to, at least, the persecution of the Jews; and while that part of it that you gave was perhaps bravely enough said, I think there is much of it that you neglected to say, perhaps through oversight.'[698]

---

[697] ibid, p.432
[698] Nuremberg Trial Proceedings, Vol.14, 138th day, Friday 24th May 1946, p.453

It is interesting that Dodd seems to have believed that there were things Schirach should have said, which he omitted. Does this suggest that the prosecution had prior information regarding what he would say? Probably, as on May 3rd, three weeks before he would make his famous declaration, Von Schirach had a lengthy conference with Gilbert in his cell. Up to that point, von Schirach had been wavering between siding with Göring and siding with Speer. During this meeting he expressed his conviction that anti-Semitism and racial politics were 'a tragic mistake.'[699] He became 'finally and irrevocably convinced that Hitler was a destructive demon who had deceived German youth.' Gilbert was obviously delighted to hear this and encouraged von Schirach, saying that he should 'come out with his opinions courageously whether it pleased Göring or not, because continued fanaticism on the part of the Nazis would only hurt Germany and world peace in the long run.'[700] Von Schirach was effusive in his agreement. It must be remembered that by this point in the trial, the defendants had all been in captivity for over a year, during which time they had been interrogated constantly using various methods and subjected to a constant barrage of evidence, in the form of the prosecution case. It is not at all surprising that some of them, von Schirach included, internalised and accepted what they were being told and shown. It must be remembered however, that despite accepting this evidence, none of them admitted to knowing of these events at the time they had allegedly taken place.

Dodd's cross-examination was largely inconsequential. He wasted half of his first day asking question after question about Hitler Youth songs and getting snagged in debates with the defendant over whether they were written by him, or were *Wandervogel* songs or had other origins. He wasted further time trying to establish von Schirach's degree of support for German bombing operations in the UK, with the defendant eventually saying that he supported them as revenge for the assassination of Heydrich, which had been carried out by Czechs using British weapons who he assumed were acting under British instruction. Finally Dodd moved on to the Jewish issue, but was unable to elicit from von Schirach an admission that he knew he was sending the Jews from Vienna to their deaths. Von Schirach even said he had enquired of Hitler of their fates and been told: 'the aged were being taken to Theresienstadt and the others to Poland, to the Government General. On one occasion-it was either when I took my oath of office as Governor or when I made a speech about the evacuation of children-I even asked Hitler how these Jews were being employed, and he told me: in accordance with their professions.'[701] Dodd tried to prove otherwise by producing documents showing that Viennese Jews had really been sent to the Minsk and Riga ghettoes, which were later cleared by the SS, but was unable to show that the documents had made their way through the bureaucracy to Schirach, despite being sent to one of the offices under his command. The cross examination as a whole was a damp squib. It fizzled out into nothing after the relative excitement of von Schirach's proclamation during his defence.

During deliberation, the Russians, of course, voted for guilt on both counts and death, while the other judges largely voted for guilt on count four only, for Schirach's part in deporting Jews from Vienna. The general feeling seemed to be that the conspiracy element was inadequately proven. Twenty years in jail appeared the most likely outcome until the British Judge, Lawrence, President of the Tribunal, threw a spanner in the works by joining the Russians in advocating death because of Schirach's support for the Luftwaffe's aerial bombing of Britain. This incredible show of jaundice and partisanship was not quite enough to sway the majority decision and two decades in Spandau was the result.[702]

Schirach was released in 1966 and like Albert Speer became something of a minor personality, although he lacked Speer's easy manner and ability to win people over. Perhaps the highlight of this period of his life was an appearance on 'The Frost Programme' in which, contrary to his famous outpouring at the trial, he told Sir David Frost that if there was one thing he would tell the young people of Germany about Hitler it would be 'the wonderful way he dealt with unemployment in the thirties.' It would seem that twenty years of isola- tion and tending tomato plants in prison had taken the edge off his desire to condemn his former Führer. In 1974 he published an autobiography titled '*Ich glaubte an Hitler*' ('I believed in Hitler') and died shortly afterwards.

---

[699] Gilbert, G, p.319
[700] ibid
[701] Nuremberg Trial Proceedings, Vol 14, 139th day, Monday 27th May 1946, p.509
[702] Taylor, p.569

19

A final word on the trial

"...the records of this Tribunal, which history will some day scrutinise attentively, nevertheless contain many things which, to us Germans, appear to be false and therefore painful...error and truth are mysteriously mixed, probably more so than ever before in any great trial...these testimonies were certainly made within the framework of law, but also within the framework of power..."[703]

-Dr. Kurt Kauffmann, counsel for Kaltenbrunner

It is often stated in response to those who accuse the IMT of being a kangaroo court that the fact that three men were acquitted and others received custodial sentences is evidence it was fair. If the whole thing was a set-up, they say, all the accused would have hanged. This simplistic gambit collapses however, when it is considered that Fritzsche was only a radio presenter and Von Papen and Schacht were never even Nazis. A more interesting question to ask is why such men were there in the first place. Other than those three, the only defendant who could be deemed to have been treated leniently was Speer and there are obvious reasons for that.

In responding to such statements, we must also take account of evidence which suggests that the court was well aware that the eyes of the world were upon it and knew that blanket death sentences for all would not send the right message. Jackson said as much in his opening statement with his 'poisoned chalice' remark. The British Admiralty, when asked to comment on the Dönitz case, after advising that he should *not* be indicted, wrote, '...If, as it has been somewhat facetiously said, we should have some defendants whom we can acquit, then we should be wary lest we afford other defendants the opportunity to profit by such defence evidence as Dönitz undoubtedly can introduce on his own behalf.'[704] As it turned out, the Admiralty's concerns were justified as Dönitz' appearance and conviction was the source of considerable embarrassment for the tribunal. It would also appear, from the Admiralty's comments, that there was discussion prior to trial within the victorious powers, regarding the possibility of having some acquittable defendants for the purposes of PR. It is entirely possible therefore that Fritzsche and Papen were included for this reason. There was little other justification for the indictment of a newsreader, who was never anything more than a second tier official in the Ministry of Propaganda, as a 'Major War Criminal.'

In his book 'The Memory of Judgement', Lawrence Douglas stated that the pre-trial aim of the British, was the 'summary execution of a dozen or so leading members of the Nazi apparatus.'[705] It seems to be a remarkable coincidence that after nearly a year of courtroom proceedings the result of the trial was exactly that. Including Bormann, twelve death sentences were passed and there is nothing in the trial transcripts to suggest that the outcome of the cases of Göring, Kaltenbrunner, Keitel and the rest of the condemned were ever really in contention. And if not, as said near the beginning of the book, what does that mean the real purpose of the trial was? The American historian, Bradley Smith, stated that the trial served to 'provide the victorious peoples with a feeling that their cause was just and their prodigious sacrifices worthwhile.'[706] But such cosy reasoning does not concur with the ideal of what law is supposed to be about, namely truth and justice. The law is meant to be a neutral instrument.

Indeed, in examining the evidence and the way it was handled by the court, it does not seem that the crimes of the Nazi state, as alleged, were ever in question. That statement does not apply only to a macro-level analysis, but also to a micro level one. For example the claims of the plan to exterminate Jews and the six million victims, were completely accepted, as were the claims regarding gas chambers, shrunken heads

---

[703] Nuremberg Trial Proceedings, Vol.18, 174th day, Tues. 9th July, p.41-43
[704] Conot, p.413
[705] Lawrence Douglas, *The Memory Of Judgement, Making Law and History in the Trials of the Holocaust* (Yale University Press 2001) p.38
[706] Bradley Smith *The Road to Nuremberg* (Basic Books, 1977) p.251

and babies being thrown into furnaces. The situation was exactly the same regarding the claims of aggressive war. Not all of these claims featured on the court's judgement, but this, in itself is not evidence that the tribunal saw them as unproven. It must be remembered that ten thousand pieces of documentary evidence were submitted by the prosecution, in addition to their films and witnesses. It was simply not possible for the judgement document to refer to all of these separate claims. What is clear is that at no point was any evidence presented by the prosecution officially abandoned or rejected. The net effect was that all prosecution evidence seemed to be simply presented and received, even, oddly, by the defence. Later large chunks of it would pass into popular myth. It is worth remembering here the Russian judge, Nikitchenko's comments prior to trial that the guilt of the defendants had 'already been proven'.

Nikitchenko's conviction is easier to understand after examining some evidence that was presented and accepted by the IMT, using the principle of judicial notice, but does not feature in the IMT document volumes. The 'Soviet Government Statements on Nazi Atrocities' is a collection of official Russian reports, dating from 1941 onwards, describing the Soviet view of German Activity in Eastern Europe. It is quite a remarkable book and raises many questions regarding the distinctions between objective history, official or state history and what may be seen as simple propaganda. A textual analysis of the language used in the volume give the reader some insight into the Russian approach to the whole matter of Nazi criminality. For example, in a statement issued on December 19th 1942, by the Information Bureau of the People's Commisariat for Foreign Affairs of the USSR on 'The execution by Hitlerite authorities of the plan to exterminate the Jewish population in the occupied territory of Europe' we find statements such as, 'It is not to be doubted that the criminal Hitlerite rulers, wishing to drown in the blood of innocent people their animal fear of approaching doom and retribution...have put into effect a bestial plan for the physical extermination of a considerable part of the German occupied territories...' It goes on in much the same vein for five pages, calling these events 'the cannibal plan', a 'bloody orgy of extermination', an 'orgy of brigandage and murder' and 'insane orgies of terror'. It also describes 'the bloodthirsty bestiality of the Hitlerite perverts', describing Germans as 'the German-fascist pogrom mongers', 'Hitlerite fiends', 'Hitlerite monsters' and states that 'besides machine-gunning men, women and children, people are murdered in specially equipped gas chambers, electrocuted, burnt en masse. The inmates of concentration camps are poisoned with prussic acid.' After this analysis, it states, as its final sentence, 'Heavy will be the punishing hand of the nations, which will cast off the yoke of the German-Fascist invaders. Neither the ruling Hitlerite clique nor the base executors of its criminal, bloody orders shall escape the vengeance of the liberated nations.'[707] The tone of the document is even more bizarre when it is remembered that this is an official government report. One would have expected a dispassionate description of the crimes committed and the persons responsible for them. Yet the Soviets contented themselves with hysterical hyperbole. When faced with such blatant and artless appealing to fear and emotion, any objective historian must doubt the quality of evidence being presented. That is not to say that everything in the reports was fabricated, they clearly describe events which actually happened, with regard to German occupation of particular towns or areas and civilian killings which did occur, but they do so with such theatrical overstatement that they cannot be viewed as a trustworthy source. All wartime evidence has the potential, indeed the probability to be tainted by propaganda, but the Soviet evidence, which like the statements made by their judges and solicitors, is indicative of their approach to the whole trial, is so shamelessly propagandised that it is difficult not to simply dismiss it out of hand.

The defendants themselves, enduring what must have been a considerable test of mental and emotional resilience, adopted various positions. Some, like Göring, Hess, Streicher and Seyss-Inquart never faltered. They took it as a point of honour to maintain a front of loyalty to the former regime and refusal to kowtow to the Allies. Others, like Speer and Schacht took the opposite approach, recognising from an early stage that the safest path to follow was one of denigration of Hitler and Nazism and cooperation with the victors. The rest adopted various positions in between or swayed from one side to the other. At the beginning, most of them appeared to gather behind Göring, but as the trial progressed and the realities of their own cases were brought to bear, as the various tactics of Gilbert and the prosecution were used to divide them, they took their own paths. Many blamed others, like Hitler or Himmler, some expressed remorse. The rest accepted a degree of culpability, although none to the extent of that for which they were indicted.

It is clear also, from looking at the trial, that the two sets of lawyers had very different experiences in re-

---

[707] *Soviet Government Reports on Nazi Atrocities* (Hutchinson and Co, undated)

gard to the effective performance of their task. Whereas the victorious powers had been preparing their case for some time, the Germans were not in a position to do so until they received the indictment. This had given them only a month to prepare. When proceedings began, the whole manner of the trial was alien to German legal practitioners. The idea of a competitive case between prosecution and defence and cross examining the other's witnesses was completely new to them. Although some concessions had been made to continental law regarding rules of evidence, little else about the way the court operated was in the Germans' favour.

The prosecution had the benefit of a team of over a thousand document and evidence gatherers, but the defence had to find their own materials. Often, they were obstructed from doing so by the Allies. The documents were in the charge of the prosecuting powers who had collected 100,000 altogether, of which they eventually used 10,000.[708] Although the official line of the Tribunal was that the German lawyers should be allowed free access, it did not work out that way in practice. When they arrived at the document centre, they had to say precisely what they wanted. The material was not indexed so it was impossible to know what was in a particular document beforehand. They therefore usually left empty handed. The example of Frank's diary illustrates these issues well. Frank handed over forty-three volumes on the basis that all should be considered, in context. The prosecutors used small excerpts from thirty-eight of the volumes and the defence were never granted access to any of them[709]. It is reasonable to assume that there was exculpatory evidence in the diaries, otherwise Frank would not have been so keen to provide them. It seems the Allies ensured that this did not come to light, however. This sort of imbalance led to Allied prosecutors being able to produce surprise evidence for which the defence had not been able to prepare, whereas any document the defence would use was known in advance by the prosecution. In addition, whereas the Allies had free use of any German documents they could find, the defence were not allowed access to Allied documents. The planned British invasion of Norway, for example, would have been easy to prove with access to British materials. On that particular point, when Colonel Sottman of the *Abteilung Fremde Heere West* expressed a willingness to testify to the British plans, he was promptly arrested and imprisoned.[710] Often witnesses requested by the defence were refused. Of the nineteen witnesses Jodl's lawyer asked to call, for example, he was allowed only four.[711]

In addition to the above, the trial was set up in such a way that the prosecution evidence was heard several times before the defence had an opportunity to respond. The first four months were taken up solely with prosecution presentations and witnesses and often the same ground was covered several times. Particular charges of aggressive war, for example were mentioned in the presentation against the OKW, the individual presentations against Keitel and Jodl and the presentation against Ribbentrop. These same claims would then also come up in cross examination.

Otto Dix, the counsel for Schacht, expressed the defence's dismay at the handicaps under which they were forced to toil, in an address to the tribunal during the case of Göring on 22nd March. Jackson had proposed that the defence document book be simply entered into evidence without being read or otherwise examined by the court, to save time. Dix stood to object and began by talking about 'the motives which prompted the authors of the Charter to give Part IV of the Charter a very pronounced heading. It says: 'Fair Trial for Defendants.' He then went on to explain exactly how this end was not being met:

> 'But I cannot consider it just and I cannot consider it fair if the Prosecution had the right, for months, not only once but sometimes repeatedly and often, to bring their evidence to the knowledge of the public and of the world by reading it into the microphone; and in this regard it should be noted that when these documents were presented often only parts of documents were read which, in the opinion of the Prosecution, were incriminating to the defendants while those parts were omitted which, in our opinion, were exonerating for the defendants. It must therefore be considered an injustice that a defen- dant should not also have the opportunity to bring to the knowledge of the world through his defence, those matters which in his opinion and the opinion of his counsel, speak in his favor, when the Prose- cution had previously had the right and the opportunity to apply that procedure to the incriminating

---

[708] Davidson, p.30
[709] Seidler, p.150-151
[710] ibid, p.28
[711] ibid, p.32

documents.

May I draw attention to this fact – and I have pointed it out repeatedly – that certain incriminating points have not only been brought to the knowledge of the world public by reading the documentary evidence, but were repeated in the form of representation to the defendants when they were examined as witnesses, and thereby they have been drilled into the ears of the listening world again and again. I am asking you urgently and implore Your Honors in the interest of just proceedings, which I am sure are desired by you as well as by the authors of the Charter, to give the same opportunity to the defendants.'[712]

It should be pointed out that Judge Lawrence did not accept Jackson's suggestion, due to the anger it aroused among the defence team, but settled rather on a compromise. However Dix' speech still serves as a reminder of the inherently uneven nature of the trial.

Outside of the courtroom, the Allied lawyers and judges socialised together. The boundaries between tribunal and prosecution were therefore completely blurred. Often at their soirees and dinners, the Russians would toast to the death of the defendants. This caused some embarrassment to the British and Americans who realised that legal standards of impartiality were being compromised.

In analysing issues of fairness we also need to venture into territory which is more sensitive than any other. The Jewish influence on the trial is a matter that few historians will discuss, naturally because it is liable to leave the writer open to accusations of anti-Semitism. It has already been noted in this book that Murray Bernays, who virtually wrote Nuremberg Law single-handed, was Jewish and that several key members of the Nuremberg team, in particular Goldensohn and Gilbert were also. Others, like Kempner, were not only Jewish but émigrés from the Reich, with obvious axes to grind. As will be documented in the next chapter, the Zionist organisation, the World Jewish Congress had several meetings with Jackson prior to trial in order to set out their own agenda for the tribunal. On certain key points, Jackson seems to have been happy to adopt their suggestions without alteration. Further to that, in a letter to his wife, dated September 20th 1945, the American prosecutor Thomas Dodd wrote:

'You know better than anyone how I hate race or religious prejudice. You know how I have despised anti-Semitism. You know how strongly I preach about intolerance of any kind. With that knowledge you will understand when I tell you that this staff is about seventy five percent Jewish. Now my point is that Jews should stay away from this trial, for their own sake. For – mark this well – the charge 'a war for the Jews' is still being made and in the post war years it will be made again and again. The too large percentage of Jewish men and women here will be cited as proof of this charge…They are pushing and crowding and competing with each other and everyone else.'[713]

Other primary sources from members of the prosecution team such as Taylor, Neave and Harris do not make the same observation, so Dodd's statement stands alone, uncorroborated, but there is little reason to doubt it. There is nothing in Dodd's career to suggest he was an anti-Semite and it must be borne in mind that his posthumous publication, collated by his son, is a collection of private correspondence between himself and his wife. When Dodd wrote those words, he did not know that they would ever be released to the world and so would have felt complete freedom to be honest. Men like Taylor, Neave and Harris wrote their memoirs of the trial with the sole intention of mass market publication. They would have been far more likely to be aware of editorial restrictions and public sensitivities. Their omission on this difficult area is therefore understandable.

An American staff that was seventy-five percent Jewish presents us with a somewhat worrying picture, particularly when it is borne in mind that the American staff was roughly twice the size of the staff of the three other prosecuting nations combined. The neutrality that is supposed to be a given within a court of law would clearly have been affected. And such a comment is in no way anti-Semitic. If, hypothetically, an international court had been established to try the British and American Air Forces for their bombing atrocities and 75 percent of the prosecutorial team had been comprised of Dresdeners, or relatives of Hiroshima casual-

---

[712] Nuremberg Trial Proceedings, Vol 9, 88th day, Friday 22nd March 1946, p.662
[713] Dodd, p.135-6

ties, the concern would be exactly the same. An American team composed largely of people with an obvious grievance would not have been able to maintain the necessary standards of objectivity and rationality.

This general issue, in fact, goes beyond the Jewish angle. According to Airey Neave, writing of the Allied teams before the trial began, 'nearly all their (the French) staff had been in the resistance and some had suffered in concentration camps. They were pale and unhappy...they restrained their deep loathing of the Nazis with dignity.'[714] The Russians on the other hand, 'drank to the death of the accused Nazis. They sang and danced and sometimes fired revolvers into the night. Their public drunkenness was part of the Nuremberg scene.' adding that, 'one night a shot was heard...a Russian officer staggered into the foyer (of the Grand hotel) and bled to death...orders were given to continue dancing while the corpse was removed.'[715]

Of the four major nations who formed the prosecution, we therefore get a picture, drawn from the writings of members of that prosecution, of individual teams composed disproportionately of those who had suffered, in some way, because of Nazi activities. This led to a prosecutorial culture of vengeance, indiscipline and hatred, which would have nestled comfortably within the 'climate of the time' as evidenced in chapter two of this book. It is assumed that most objective readers would agree that this is not conducive to impartial legal proceedings.

On this matter, Jackson's assertion that the trial had to operate on this basis needs to re-examined. His belief was that there was no choice other than to have victors judge the vanquished. This was obvious nonsense. The fact remains that if genuine thought was given to who should manage the tribunal, in the spirit of fairness, it would have been difficult to select a prosecution and judicial team that were less likely to be objective than the one that appeared. It is clear that objectivity was simply not desired. Faced with that fact, and the lop-sidedness of the proceedings, added to the outcome of the majority of cases never appearing to be in serious doubt, it must be accepted that Nuremberg was not a legal event, but a political exercise.

Aside from discussion of inherent bias at Nuremberg, which is self-evident, and acknowledgement of the fact that the majority of pre-trial aims were carried through, which in itself is indicative of a fixed agenda, there was one stated intention of the prosecutors and tribunal which became altered. As mentioned in the opening chapters of this book, the notion of the Nazi 'conspiracy', conceived by Bernays, was fundamental to the entire process. It is doubtful whether the trial would have proceeded at all in the form that it eventually took, had the idea not been formulated. The general concept was that it stood both as a charge in its own right, but also as a feeder into all the other charges. Thus the defendants were charged with general participation in the Nazi conspiracy, but also with conspiracy to commit crimes against peace, war crimes and crimes against humanity. At the deliberation meetings that followed the IMT hearings, the judges however felt that the conspiracy charge, in all its forms, had not been borne out in any way by the evidence and was unsustainable. They unanimously agreed that there 'had been no conspiracy to commit War Crimes or Crimes against Humanity' by any of the defendants. [716] In a movement proposed by Judge Francis Biddle of the United States, then voted on and ratified by the others, it was agreed to restrict the Conspiracy charge to the waging of aggressive war. Prior to the next chapter, in which the various Genocide claims of the trial will be discussed, this raises an interesting issue. The Nazi actions of genocide, usually referred to as the Holocaust, are believed, certainly by intentionalist historians at least, to have been the result of a premeditated plan, conceived by the highest echelon of the party and then enacted by several layers of the Nazi state. Yet the judges at Nuremberg ruled that there had been no conspiracy to commit war crimes or crimes against humanity. One wonders if it is possible to engage in a process of systematic genocide without conspiring to do so. It would seem that on this particular aspect, there is a branch of history which contradicts the verdict of the court.

Further to that point, the evidence presented at the trial relevant to Crimes against Humanity and War Crimes, saw a repeated pattern of extreme claims evidenced by affidavits, which were obtained from interrogation centres in which it is known that dubious methods were used. It cannot be a coincidence that these shocking claims were never evidenced by official German documents, yet the prosecution was able to produce many such documents to verify their lesser claims. As the defendants generally denied the major claims and admitted the lesser ones, there is clear scope for rational doubt. That has nothing to do with prejudice or bias and everything to do with common sense.

---

[714] Neave p.54
[715] Neave, p.54
[716] Conot p.483

Before moving on to discuss some of Nuremberg's themes and consequences it is worth taking a moment to consider the trial's place in history. World War Two and in particular, Nazi Germany are historical 'pet subjects' for many. There is a greater output of literature and media attention on this period than any other. A quick scan of your local bookshop, or the listings of 'The History Channel' (known, in some quarters as 'The Hitler Channel'), will confirm this. As such, Nuremberg, the final chapter of the story, has an important role to play. However it has been a comparatively underwritten subject. Unlike the nitty-gritty of the Holocaust or military tactics, or the excitement of Nazism's revolutionary rise to power, relatively few analyses have emerged regarding Nuremberg. We have the primary accounts, some of them languishing out-of-print now, largely Allied, of course, such as Airey Neave, Telford Taylor, Whitney Harris, Dodd, Gilbert, Goldensohn. A few of the surviving defendants also wrote memoirs, which included some reportage of the trial. We have Speer's book, for example, or von Papen's. The problem is that the only defendants to survive Nuremberg and publish were either the most apologetic, the most detached from the regime and the party, or the ones who were most ready to denigrate their own nation in exchange for life. What history needs, but doesn't have, is a record of the trial written by a loyal and unswerving Nazi. The closest we have got is von Ribbentrop's brief letter, which is interesting, but too general to be any use. It would be fascinating to have Göring's thoughts detailed in a volume, for example. Why Hess was prevented from writing full memoirs during his four and a half decades of captivity is a point of interest. He had ample time to compose his thoughts, after all and was even given a typewriter with which he wrote out elaborate fantasies about a new German Reich, with himself as Führer. But his writings and letters home were checked for 'references to the Third Reich or its personalities, Nuremberg or contemporary politics'[717] and duly censored. It is a great shame as with something like that in hand, we would have been able to begin the process of constructing a real historical narrative. One in which both sides of the story were considered.

Until now the history of this subject has lacked all sense of balance. Earlier in this book, the following words were quoted from Justice Jackson's opening address, 'I should be the last to deny that the case may well suffer from incomplete researches and quite likely will not be the example of professional work which any of the prosecuting nations would normally wish to sponsor. It is, however, a completely adequate case to the judgment we shall ask you to render and its full development we shall be obliged to leave to historians.'

For the purposes of comparison, it must borne in mind that these are the words of the United States chief prosecutor, an individual whose views could hardly be said to represent an objective analysis. A brief review of some of the more popular existing secondary literature on Nuremberg will see how far this appraisal has been developed by Historians.

Eugene Davidson's 'The Trial of the Germans', written in 1966, stated as a conclusion that, 'In a world of mixed human affairs where a rough justice is done that is better than lynching or being shot out of hand, Nuremberg may be defended as a political event, if not as a court.'[718] He went on to add that, 'for the deeper answers we must look to history and its meaning for ourselves.'[719] Davidson's book is fascinating and detailed. But his conclusion is unworthy of what goes before. He has simply paraphrased Jackson.

Robert Conot's 'Justice at Nuremberg' (1983) whose title is something of a giveaway, swings the pendulum even further in the pro-Allied direction, by decrying 'Holocaust Denial' with a fervour bordering on hysteria, describing the, '...Neo-Nazis and the Ku Klux Klan, demonstrating for Aryan supremacy, urging the deportation of Jews and Blacks, employing Hitlerian euphemisms and manipulating democratic processes and guarantees in the same way as Hitler a half century ago.'[720] He then quotes Horst Pelckmann, counsel for the SS in saying, 'This trial should be the last warning to those who do not heed the demands voiced by the world and its peace loving citizens.'[721] Prior to that, Conot proceeds through seventeen pages of laudatory analysis, lurching from Hitler's 'evil' and 'insanity' to the balance of eighties power regarding Nuclear weapons. It is a book of its time, written during the death-throes of the Cold War. He fears, with typical neo-con anxiety that a tinpot third-world dictator may one day launch an assault on all that is good and American, 'With the spread of nuclear technology' he wrote, 'need such a mental case be master of one of the great na-

---

[717] Padfield, p.320
[718] Davidson, p.592
[719] ibid, p.594
[720] Conot, p.522
[721] ibid, p.523

tions?'[722] During the course of this polemic, he does not even mention Justice Jackson's misgivings regarding the trial, let alone any he may have had himself. Almost forty years after the war ended, Conot's book, although well researched and fluently written, draws conclusions that are little more than a tawdry victory dance.

Joseph Persico, writing in 1994 stated, 'The trial, in the final analysis, raises the distinction between law and justice. No saint or salesman lost his life or freedom at Nuremberg. All the men who went to prison or mounted the gallows were willing, knowing and energetic accomplices in a vast and malignant enterprise. They were all there for valid moral, if not technically perfect reasons...Nuremberg may have been flawed law, but it was satisfying justice.'[723] Academic Historians fare little better. Lawrence Douglas and Donald Bloxham for example, both of whom have written about Nuremberg, although only within a Holocaust focus, mention little or nothing about the issues of bias and subjectivity at the trial, only criticising it for not emphasising the Holocaust more. Douglas, conforming to the expectations of the current academic idiom, with its anti-intellectual emphasis on emotive terms like 'truth' and 'memory', states that the primary outcome of the entire eleven months was imposing 'the duty to remember.'[724]

The clear fact is that on this subject, History simply has not done its job. Historians are supposed to cock an ear into the sea of voices and listen to as diverse a range as they can. We are told that they apply critical reasoning to the evidence and carefully balance opposing views to attempt to find a core of truth. Yet it seems that with regard to Nuremberg, most of them simply repeat Jackson's dogma. More than sixty years later and on this topic, the narrative has not progressed an inch. This is despite the fact that Jackson himself suggested an alternative interpretation of the events at Nuremberg, when during his closing address at the trial he said, 'Germany has unconditionally surrendered, but no peace treaty has been signed or agreed upon. The Allies are still technically in a state of war with Germany, although the enemy's political and military institutions have collapsed. As a military tribunal, this Tribunal is a continuation of the war effort of the Allied nations.'[725] It is worth noting, prior to the final chapters in which the post-Nuremberg world will be examined, that the Peace Treaty Jackson mentioned does not exist to this day. Germany's place among the world's nations still, in 2008, survives purely on a basis of 'unconditional surrender'.

If it can be assumed that political actions are only ever taken for the purposes of expediency and Nuremberg was a political action, it must be asked how exactly it could have been expedient. How could a time-consuming trial have served Allied purposes more neatly than a series of summary executions? The answer lies in its effect on the defeated people. The Allies had learned a lesson from the Versailles treaty after World War One which had explicitly mandated War-Guilt upon Germany in order to extort open-ended reparations payments and German acquiescence. The War-Guilt concept had never been accepted by the German people, regardless of their political persuasions and had led to the resentment and upsurge in Nationalism which had paved the way for Hitler. This time, the trial would not only show Germans that they were defeated, but ingeniously would also show that there was hope for them – hope that if they joined the Allies in denouncing their former rulers, which many were only too happy to do after years of misery, that they could be re- deemed, become *Guttermenschen*, good democrats and be welcomed into the family of nations. It was from this offer of salvation that Germany gave away its soul. Not because its soul was Nazism – Nazism was a project doomed to failure for a number of reasons, but because from that point on Germans gave up their right to be themselves, to self-determine. They had to be what their conquerors wanted them to be. And that, by any standards, is not freedom.

There was a movement for a while, in Germany, campaigning for a *Realgeschichte* (Real History) of the Nazi era, in which the desperation to condemn would be set aside and the facts, events and policies could be examined as rationally as possible. Unfortunately the movement floundered and died, due to outside pressure. It is hoped that in some small way, this book may be the start of something like that again.

Looking now at Nuremberg's place in history, Winston Churchill's famous remark comes to mind. 'History will be kind to me,' he said, 'for I intend to write it.'

---

[722] ibid, p.522
[723] Persico, p.433
[724] Douglas, p.94 Douglas is not referring to the horrors of war or the complexities of war crimes trials but to Jewish suffering. The concept of 'memory' seems to be the latest term to be politicised and co-opted by the academic herd.
[725] From Jackson's closing address. Nuremberg Trial Proceedings, Vol 19, 187th day, Friday 26th July 1946 p.398

20

Genocide at Nuremberg [726]

This is the site of the infamous Belsen Concentration Camp liberated by the British on 15th April 1945. 10,000 unburied dead were found here. Another 13,000 have since died. All of them victims of the German New Order in Europe and an example of Nazi Kultur.[727]

The genocidal underbelly of Nazism, most of which is now called the Holocaust, was outlined before the IMT in three main ways. Firstly, the Euthanasia programme (otherwise known as T4)[728], secondly, the camp system, accompanied by its murder weapons; gas chambers and vans and thirdly through the *Einsatzgruppen*, the teams of SS who followed behind the regular army on Barbarossa, wiping out civilians as they went.

As stated in chapter five of this book, one of the most startling facts, to the modern eye, regarding the treatment of these Genocide claims by the Nuremberg prosecutors, is that in their drawing up of the indictment and indeed in the playing out of the trial in general, they seemed to give them comparatively little coverage. The prosecution case instead seemed to revolve around the charge of Crimes against Peace. This is problematic to explain.

It has been suggested that the Allied commanders felt guilt at their own lack of intervention. Laurence Rees, the British historian, promoted this view, 'If they were exterminating British prisoners of war, do we seriously think that we wouldn't have done all we could to stop it?' He wrote. Rees believes that as the Allies of the time avoided it, we must now address the question of 'why the Allies failed to do more to save the Jews from Nazi persecution.'[729] It would not require an enormous leap of cognition to suggest that such an attitude, if it existed, would have filtered down to the legal team at Nuremberg.

Such an explanation would be entirely unsatisfactory, however. If the Allies had felt in some way complicit in this crime and wished to brush it under the carpet, then surely it would not have been mentioned at all. The fact that the Holocaust did come up, in some form, in the indictment, but was a secondary issue, suggests other possibilities.

One of those is, of course, controversial, namely that the importance placed upon this great crime and perhaps even our view of the scope of it, has grown, for various reasons, since Nuremberg. This seems impossible to those of us below forty, who could be forgiven after switching on 'The History Channel', or reading the plethora of literature still devoted to it, (on the 8th of July 2007, as this book was being written, three of the top-ten bestselling non-fiction books in Britain were about Auschwitz or other aspects of Nazi Jewish Policy) for thinking that the Holocaust was the defining event of the 20th century.

The view that Holocaust history has snowballed, gathering momentum and prominence, rather like a successful PR campaign (and largely for decidedly suspect reasons) was famously described by Norman G. Finkelstein in his provocative work, *The Holocaust Industry*. 'Until fairly recently,' he wrote, 'the Nazi holocaust barely figured in American life. Between the end of World War Two and the late 1960s, only a handful of books and films touched on the subject.'[730] He went on to state that, 'everything changed with the Arab-Israeli war. By virtually all accounts, it was only after this conflict that the Holocaust became a fixture in American Jewish life.'[731] A corresponding view was provided by Donald Bloxham, who wrote '…for dec-

---

[726] The term 'Genocide' was first coined by Raphael Lemkin, a Polish/Jewish lawyer, following the events of World War Two. He proposed a Convention on the prevention and prosecution of genocide, which was accepted by the UN in 1948.
[727] Overy, *Interrogations*, p.183. Sign erected by the British liberators outside Bergen Belsen. They burned the camp down in June.
[728] Strictly speaking, the T4 programme is not usually included as part of the Holocaust, as it was not racially motivated.
[729] Rees, writer and producer of BBC's 'Auschwitz' series quoted in *'Why Didn't the Allies Bomb Auschwitz'* by Matthew Davis http://news.bbc.co.uk/1/hi/world/europe/4175045.stm
[730] Norman Finkelstein, *The Holocaust Industry* (Verso, 2000) p.12
[731] ibid p.16

ades the murder of the Jews impinged hardly at all on the post-war world.'[732]

Michael Marrus, a celebrated academic who has written about Nuremberg, (but only within the greater context of his main career focus of Jewish history)[733], accepts that it did not receive top-billing at the trial. 'The Holocaust was by no means the centre of attention' he wrote, 'Information about it easily could be drowned in the greater flood of crimes and accusations.'[734] He struggled to explain this and settled eventually on an argument based on 'the American leadership's desire to justify the war to the United States public' as a result of which 'officials in Washington accented the first count against the accused, the common plan or conspiracy.'[735] Marrus provided a quote from Jackson to support the USA's backing for the Conspiracy charge above all others, but the quote mentioned nothing about popular support among the American public. As there are no other sources referenced in that section of the article, it would seem to be the case that Marrus is postulating. Unfortunately, as is so often the case with guesswork, this does little other than demonstrate his own subjectivity. He omits the fact that it was the conspiracy charge that had made the trial possible in the first place. Without the astute creativity of Bernays, it is unlikely that the trial would have happened at all, in the form it eventually took. It is only natural therefore for Jackson to emphasise the point of law on which all the others hang. As the leading force behind the trials, he had to demonstrate that his creation was legitimate. Accentuating the conspiracy element was the only way to do this – if the conspiracy charge had no credibility, then neither did the IMT, or himself. If, on the contrary, justifying entry into the war to the American public had, as Marrus supposes, been Jackson et al's prime motivation, surely the publication of the Nazis' genocidal actions would have served the purpose admirably. The between-the-lines sub-plot to Marrus' article is, of course, that this would not have convinced Joe America of the justness of the war because of the prevalence of anti-Semitic views across the Atlantic. The Germans' territorial demands of other Northern Europeans were a far more compelling argument to the average Yankee than six million murdered Jews. Such argumentation forms the basis of a sizeable chunk of what is called 'Holocaust Studies,' a field populated with subjective individuals and that is 'replete with nonsense, if not sheer fraud,'[736] according to Finkelstein.

Conveniently, within the very same article, Marrus readily exposes his personal bias. On page nine he launches into an overtly judgemental description of the leader of the World Jewish Congress, calling the figurehead of early 20th Century Zionism and eventual first President of the State of Israel 'the venerable Chaim Weiszmann'. Either Marrus is very much an individual who knows on which side his bread is buttered or he may just as well have subtitled his article 'I am a Zionist sympathiser'. The fact that such a respected historian as Marrus feels able to display this kind of brazen subjectivity when writing on this topic is testament to everything that is currently wrong about the academic approach to it.

The substantial evidence for genocide before the IMT came from the Soviet government's 'Statements on Nazi Atrocities' and the testimonies and affidavits of five former members of the regime, Erich von dem bach Zelewski, Otto Ohlendorf, Dieter Wisliceny, Wilhelm Hoettl and Rudolf Höss. There were also eyewitness statements from camp survivors and Graebe's affidavit regarding the *Einsatzgruppen*.

From these, two linked claims were established. The first was that the Nazis were generally brutal towards all civilians within their area of occupation. Such claims are common when one country occupies another. In fact, historically, there are few occupations where such claims have not been made (Germany's 'oc- cupation' of Austria being one). The second was that Jews in that area were singled out for treatment even more brutal than everybody else. In this way, the skeleton of the Jewish Holocaust was put together.

The problem that we have at the IMT is that both claims were forcibly promoted by the Allied powers and others prior to trial as part of their propaganda efforts. They could not be said therefore to have emerged through the evidence. They were already prevalent and evidence was produced to substantiate them. Signifi-

---

[732] Donald Bloxham, *Genocide on Trial, War Crimes Trials and the Formation of Holocaust History and Memory* (Oxford University Press 2001) p.xi

[733] He is Professor Emeritus of 'Holocaust Studies' in the Department of History at Toronto University and therefore someone whom Finkelstein would presumably identify as being a part of the 'Industry', as he makes a living from writing and talking about it.

[734] Michael Marrus, *'The Holocaust at Nuremberg'* p.2, published on the Yad Veshem website http://yad-vashem.org.il/download/about_holocaust/studies/marrus_full.pdf

[735] ibid, p.3

[736] Finkelstein, p.55

cant parts of those claims – the existence of homicidal gas chambers,[737] for example – were never questioned by the court. They were regarded, as per the Charter, as 'facts of common knowledge.' We know this because nobody tried to disprove them. When it is remembered that every single defendant denied knowledge of homicidal gas chambers, yet not one lawyer tried a defence gambit based on questioning their existence, despite the fact that no physical evidence was provided for them at all, the reality becomes clear.

The number of victims, usually fudged to six million, which has remained broadly consistent within the dominant narrative ever since, had an interesting genesis. Richard Overy stated that 'the World Jewish Congress supplied the tentative figure of 5.7 million dead and this was used by the prosecuting teams in drawing up the indictment.'[738] Overy referred here to a meeting between the WJC and Jackson in New York on June 12th 1945. By reading the minutes of the meeting we see that not only did the WJC suggest that figure, based on estimates drawn from 'official and semi-official sources', but stated that, 'the indictment should include leaders, agencies, heads of government and high command... Any member of these bodies will be considered guilty and subject to punishment, unless he can prove he was not a member or became a member under duress.' In addition they also emphasised that, 'The Jewish people is the greatest sufferer of this war' and they 'stressed the magnitude of the Jewish tragedy which transcends the sufferings of other peoples.'[739]

What is remarkable is that established, respected historians like Overy can make this connection and then simply pass by without further comment. They do so through fear of being labelled 'anti-Semitic'. It ought to be remembered that during the time with which we are concerned, the World Jewish Congress was the planet's foremost Zionist organisation and was heavily engaged in the process of recruiting Jews from Europe to populate Palestine, which had, by that point, been more-or-less obtained from the British, following prolonged negotiations since the Balfour agreement of 1917. You do not need to be involved in the polemics of 'memory' versus 'denial' to see that the WJC would have had a clear motive to propagandise and over-emphasise the treatment of European Jews at the hands of the Nazis.

Indeed, it is perfectly apparent, to anyone prepared to look at the subject with both eyes open, that the large Jewish organisations had been making exaggerated or even contrived statements of this kind for many years, going back to the time before the Nazis had even existed.

Following the 'World Conference of Jews' in 1933, the American delegate, leading Zionist, Samuel Untermyer, addressed the American nation on WABC radio with regard to Germany and called for 'the nations of the earth' to 'make common cause against the... slaughter, starvation and annihilation, by a country that has reverted to barbarism, of its own innocent and defenceless citizens without rhyme, reason or excuse...' He went on to describe the Nazis' 'cold-bloodedly planned and already partially executed campaign for the extermination of a proud, gentle, law-abiding people' and called for a 'holy war' against a German nation which was, in his words, 'a veritable hell of cruel and savage beasts.'[740] Untermyer's purposely alarmist speech was a continuation of similar propaganda and a follow-up on statements and mass demonstrations made by the World Jewish Congress in the same year, as evidenced by a Daily Express article written by a 'special political correspondent', which began with the following sentence. 'All Israel is uniting in wrath against the Nazi onslaught on the Jews in Germany.' Its headline was 'Judea declares war on Germany!'[741]

Yet 1933, the year when Hitler assumed control, is not as far back as such analysis can be taken. In an article entitled, 'The Crucifixion of Jews must Stop!' which appeared in a magazine called 'American Hebrew', a former governor of the state of New York, Martin H. Glynn described the plight of Eastern European Jews as a 'catastrophe in which 6 million human beings are whirled toward the grave...' He even went

---

[737] It is known and universally accepted that concentration camps had delousing facilities for clothing and bedding which used gas, as did many similar facilities all over Europe. It is important therefore to differentiate between gas chambers for the purposes of delousing and gas chambers for the purposes of murder, hence 'homicidal' gas chambers.

[738] Overy, *Interrogations* p.190

[739] *Minutes, Meeting of World Jewish Congress with Robert H. Jackson*, held at the Federal Court House New York City, Tuesday June 12, 1945, records of the World Jewish Congress, Jacob Rader Marcus Center of the American Jewish Archives, online at the Truman Library,
http://www.trumanlibrary.org/whistlestop/study_collections/nuremberg/documents/index.php?documentdate=1945-06-12&documentid=C106-16-5&studycollectionid=&pagenumber=1

[740] *Text of Untermyer's Address*, New York Times, Monday, August 7th 1933

[741] *Judea declares War on Germany!*, London Daily Express, Friday march 4th 1933

as far as to describe this as a 'threatened holocaust of human life.'[742] His article was written not as a comment on events in Nazi Germany, but about anti-Semitism in Russia, in 1919, just after the end of World War One, thirteen years before Hitler would form any sort of government.

Even before then, references to the suffering of the six million had been made by Zionist figureheads. As early as 1900, while the Zionist movement was still in its youth, statements which sound startlingly similar to those later made about Nazi Germany were already being declared. Rabbi Stephen S. Wise, later to become leader of the American Jewish Congress and at the time chairman of the Provisional Zionist Committee spoke at a Zionist gathering. He talked of the suffering of Jews in and around Russia, describing them as 'six million living, bleeding, suffering arguments in favour of Zionism.'[743]

It is both striking and challenging to the historian to read these kinds of articles and statements. It is not good enough to simply write off such pointed historical evidence as being of interest only to right wing extremists or conspiracy theorists. That is, in layman's language, a cop-out. History has to look openly at *all* the evidence and then attempt to provide a narrative that best fits that evidence.

Two things become clear to anybody prepared to think through the implications. Firstly, Nazi/Jewish propaganda was not a one way street. It is well known and much documented that many National Socialist figureheads made anti-Semitic statements and speeches and the party involved itself in various other forms of anti-semitic propaganda. However, what is far less well known is that this was returned in kind by some Jewish organisations and Zionist groups who distributed disinformative propaganda about the Nazis and Germany. It must also be acknowledged that some of these organisations wielded considerable influence in Allied circles, particularly in the USA and it was these organisations who were responsible for providing the first reports of Nazi anti-Jewish actions. Bearing in mind the anti-Semitism inherent in the Nazi programme, overtly expressed by the party since its emergence on the political scene, the opposition of Jewish organisations to the regime was understandable, but this does not make their propagandistic claims true. History has to apply to them the principles of rational criticism.

Reflecting upon the authors and speakers of these statements, it is plain that they were made to further the cause of Zionism. That is not to suggest that there was no truth in them at all. The Nazis clearly discriminated against Jews from the earliest days of the regime and engaged in anti-semitic rhetoric and intimidation even before achieving power, but it is also clear that this anti-semitic activity did not even approach the extremes that were suggested. Untermeyer's comments and the Daily Express article mentioned above were made nine years before the Wannsee Conference, two years even before the Nuremberg Laws were passed and only months after Hitler had taken control, yet already described a process of extermination and annihilation which history now tells us did not begin until 1942. Would one modern day, establishment historian agree with their claims? Similarly, Glynn's article demonstrates that the figure of six million victims and even the word 'holocaust' were in use in the circles of Zionist and Jewish speech and writing while Nazism was still little more than a notion in the minds of a few ex-soldiers in Munich bars. Not only that, but as the Wise quotation shows, the six million figure had been touted before, going back to the turn of the century.

Simply and plainly stated, this means that the belief in the six million figure and the concept of the 'holocaust' were not formulated, as most people believe, from analysis of events in the Nazi sphere of influence during World War Two, but evolved from Zionist propaganda dating back for half a century. What makes this awkward for historians, is that the logical follow-through from this analysis would then be to doubt the information provided by the Zionists about Nazi Germany. After all, they had been making similarly alarmist claims, without foundation, for many years. This is dangerous territory for history, or at least, establishment history, as it would cast a shadow over several of the major pillars of the Holocaust narrative, whose origin was from the Jewish organisations. Yet rather than confront these inconvenient facts, draw conclusions from them and attempt to place them within the wider context of the issue being discussed, Historians prefer simply not to mention them. If they did, they might upset some influential people. Unfortunately this suggests that Historians, on the most part, are cowards.

Clearly, at the very least, caution should have been exercised in adopting the WJCs version of events. Was it not probable that their interpretation would have been influenced by their preconceptions? And what does it suggest about the partialities of the IMT that they would accept figures and adopt trial strategies sug-

---

[742] *The crucifixion of Jews must stop*, Martin H Glynn, American Hebrew, October 31st 1919
[743] *Rabbi Wise's Address*, New York Times, June 11th, 1900

gested by such an openly subjective party? Not only that, but the entire community of establishment historians since, have been perfectly happy to accept this six million estimate and use it as the base marker for their own work, as if the WJC were the most judicious and unbiased source possible.

At the trial itself the six million number was evidenced by the testimony of Wilhelm Höttl. (Hearsay evidence in Wisliceny's testimony suggested five million). Höttl worked under Kaltenbrunner in the RSHA and provided an affidavit on the 25th November 1945. The affidavit (doc no. 2738-PS) was read to the court on Thursday 13th December. It was a recollection of a conversation Höttl had with Adolf Eichmann, in which he had apparently suggested the number of Jewish dead to be around six million. This piece of hearsay was the main substantiation used for the six million figure at Nuremberg. Many courts, in various parts of the world, would not have accepted such evidence as valid. The IMT, however, in keeping with article twenty-three of their charter deemed the evidence to have 'probative value' and so admitted it. If, during the course of the trial it had been corroborated by some other evidence, in particular a German document from the RSHA or the SS, detailing what they were doing, or a memo from one department to another in which the progress of the Holocaust was discussed, then the decision to admit the item would have been justified. But it was not. The six million claim, first suggested by the World Jewish Congress, was upheld by the IMT and included in their final judgement and is still upheld by popular history today, on the basis of an affidavit, obtained by an American interrogator, (Frederick L. Felten), during a time when many such affidavits were obtained by dubious means. The relevant section of the document is transcribed below.

> 'In the various extermination camps about four million Jews were killed, while a further two million met their deaths in other ways, the greater part through the *Einsatzkommandos*, the SD or through being shot in the fields of Russia.'[744]

Two defence lawyers asked for Höttl's affidavit to be stricken from the record, primarily because like so many other affidavit witnesses, Höttl was held in Nuremberg and therefore available for cross examination but not presented.[745] With the benefit of hindsight, we also see that despite the IMT's willingness to accept Höttl's figures and include them in their judgement, Historians have not been so content to repeat them. Raul Hilberg stated that 2.9 million died in the camps and 2.2 million from other means, thereby lowering the total to 5.1 million. Gerald Reitlinger suggested the total Jewish losses to be around 4 million. Others have provided a variety of differing estimates, some of them higher than the IMTs figures. Clearly therefore it is legitimate to challenge Höttl's, or the WJC's numbers otherwise mainstream history would not have done so.

Finally, on the matter of the victim count, there is an obvious question to be raised regarding the interrogations at Nuremberg and other detention centres. If, as it seems clear that we should, we accept that the six million figure had little to do with an attempt to count the actual numbers of Jewish dead, but stemmed instead from the propagandistic statements of Zionist groups dating back fifty years, why did it show up in this key witness statement? Although, in itself, not definitely further evidence of coercion or at least leading questioning, it is otherwise a remarkable coincidence. How does one explain the fact that Wilhelm Höttl just happened to include in his affidavit the exact same number mentioned first by Rabbi Wise in 1900, then by other Zionist figureheads throughout the first part of the twentieth century, even though that number is not thought to be particularly accurate by many leading Holocaust historians today? As we know that the WJC had already suggested the figure to Jackson, it only requires a modest leap of faith to propose that it may, in turn, have been passed on to the interrogators who would have used it to shape their interrogations.[746]

Another huge issue to be aired for the first time before the IMT was that regarding Nazi genocidal language. We are told, by semantically inclined historians like the extreme intentionalist Jeffrey Herf, that the words *vernichtung*, *liquidierung* and *ausrottung* which often appeared in speeches made by Hitler and other leading Nazis, also in articles in *Der Stürmer* in relation to the Jews, had only one meaning. Herf states that the 'public language of the Nazi regime combined complete suppression of any facts about the Final Solution

---

[744] Library of Congress 2738-PS (my translation)
[745] Nuremberg Trial Proceedings Vol 3, 20th day, Friday 14th December 1945, p.570
[746] There is no evidence for this in the interrogation transcripts hence 'leap of faith'. However, we are naive in the extreme if we believe that all communication between interrogator and prisoner would be recorded in the transcripts. Much else would have been said 'off the record'.

with a brutal, sometimes crude declaration of murderous intent. Two key verbs and nouns in the German language were at the core of the language of mass murder: *vernichten* and *ausrotten*. These translate as 'annihilate, 'exterminate', 'totally destroy' and 'kill,' and the nouns Vernichtung and Ausrottung as 'annihilation', 'extermination', 'total destruction' and 'killing.' Whether taken on their own from the dictionary meaning or placed in the context of the speeches, paragraphs and sentences in which they were uttered, their meaning was clear.'[747]

This issue, of whether or not these words have unequivocal meanings of murder, or not, has gone on and on and formed one of the central points of argument in the Lipstadt v Irving Trial of 2000. It is, however, a matter easily resolved. All one needs is a German dictionary.

The translation website 'Babelfish' provides a useful starting point. On the 18th December 2007, *ausrotten* was translated only as 'exterminate'. '*Ausrottung*' was extermination. '*Vernichtung*' translated as 'destruction' and '*vernichten*' as 'destroy'. Anybody therefore seeking to verify the claims of the Nuremberg prosecutors and current academics like Herf on the internet would doubtless infer that the claims regarding *Ausrottung* were accurate. In the German language it unequivocally equates to killing. *Vernichtung*, as 'destroy', is not as clear – a statement of intent to 'destroy the Jews' does not necessarily mean mass murder.

Modern paper dictionaries are similar. The Collins Pocket German Dictionary (2nd edition), printed in 1996, provides a decent indicator. The translations it lists for *ausrotten* are 'to stamp out' and 'to exterminate'. For *vernichten* we get 'to annihilate', 'to destroy'.

However, older dictionaries, going back to the time when the events were more contemporary, futher muddy the waters. A German/English dictionary printed in Germany in 1955, the Schöffler-Weis *Taschenwörterbuch*, published by the Ernst Klett Company of Stuttgart, provides a slightly different picture. It gives the following translations of *ausrotten*: 'to root out', 'to destroy', 'to extirpate', 'to eradicate' and 'to exterminate'. For *ausrottung* we get two translations, 'uprooting' and 'extermination'.

According therefore to a dictionary published in Germany in 1955, Nazis discussing the *ausrotten* of the Jews or how the Jews were undergoing a process of *ausrottung*, could have been talking about rooting Jews out or uprooting them. Neither of these terms necessarily have genocidal implications. It is interesting that the literal translation of *ausrottung*, which is 'uprooting' as one can tell simply from looking at the word in both languages, seems to have disappeared from the modern dictionaries.

With *vernichten* we get a similar picture. The 1955 German dictionary translates it as 'to annihilate', 'to eradicate', 'to do away with', to wipe out. '*Vernichtung*' is 'destruction', 'annihilation', 'extirpation'. Therefore Nazis using these words could feasibly have been discussing 'doing away with' the Jews (or 'destroying them). Again it is interesting that this most anodyne translation of the term is not to be found in the modern dictionaries.

Before moving on from semantics, it is worth returning to a point made in chapter ten, that even if we accept that these words could only refer to murder, it seems rather contrary to all common sense to be attempting a secret genocidal programme against a specific ethnic group while making speeches and writing articles for public consumption, in which you tell anyone who is listening or reading that you are doing exactly that. This is what Herf and others like him seem to be proposing. We therefore find ourselves confronting a prob- lem. The meaning of these words is not as clear as Herf suggests. They *could* be referring to mass murder, but to determine that their context would have to be carefully examined by somebody with expertise in Ger- man language usage of the period. Furthermore, there would appear to be a choice to make. Either the Nazis were engaged in a genocidal programme against the Jews and were happy to have it known, or they wanted it to be a secret. If the former, then the whole argument regarding *sonderbehandlung* (special treatment) col- lapses, as the narrative presently holds that it was used as a code word on Nazi documents to keep the Holo- caust a secret. If, on the other hand, the Holocaust was meant to be hidden, then the Nazis public use of *ver- nichten* and *ausrotten* in speeches can not have referred to physical extermination. They must either have been intended with Streicher and Rosenberg's interpretation of the annihilation of Jewish power, or one of the alternative meanings from the 1955 dictionary, which Herf does not acknowledge even exist.

Very simply, it's one or the other. The guardians of the Holocaust narrative, like Herf, cannot have it both ways. They need to decide whether to drop *sonderbehandlung* or *ausrotten* and *vernichten*. In the opinion of this author, the evidence from the trial would point to the latter. Although *sonderbehandlung* may have had

---

[747] Jeffrey Herf, *The Jewish Enemy: Nazi Propaganda During World War Two and the Holocaust* (Belknap Press, 2006) p.11

other uses, as Kaltenbrunner explained, several witnesses, including at least two defendants (Keitel and Kaltenbrunner) confirmed that it generally meant killing.

In discussing the Holocaust further, something else must be made clear, which those who have read popular history on the subject will not necessarily have considered. Like the Industrial Revolution or the Renaissance, or the Civil Rights Movement, the Holocaust is a construct. None of these events happened in the sense that the majority of people understand them to have done. Their grandiose titles glibly encompass a multitude of incidents, enacted for complex and conflicting reasons over long periods of time, which in many cases bore little or no relation to each other. Lithuanian partisan fighters killed during a skirmish with the SS near Kaunas in 1942 have very little in common with a Czech forced labourer at the Buna rubber plant in Monowitz or an elderly, bourgeois Austrian sent to Theresienstadt, for example. It is history and history alone that has grouped them all together and titled them.

As a result of this historical treatment, the title itself has become symbolic and invested with meaning through simplification and popular misunderstanding. The Holocaust has come to exist as much as a fable as a scholarly researched and documented occurrence. Authors like Nobel laureate Elie Wiesel do little to help this situation, by writing books which hover between classification as fiction or memoir. Some people read 'Night' and believe in it as an accurate record of life in a concentration camp. Others, who question some of its more bizarre details are told it has been partially fictionalised. In other words, anything goes, all bases are covered. As a fiction, the work is beyond criticism and if some choose to treat it as fact, they are not dissuaded from doing so. From the birth of the narrative, the Holocaust has existed like this – in rational, scientific, historical discourse but also in a feverish, victim obsessed, fantasy world where even the most absurd claims are accepted. The recent example of Misha DeFonseca, who told a sorry tale of surviving the Holocaust as a child by walking five thousand miles across Nazi occupied Europe under the care and protection of a pack of wolves demonstrates this. She was initially supported by several luminaries, including Mr Wiesel, who described her book as 'very moving' and was invited to speak at a number of universities, before finally being outed as a fraud. She was merely the latest in a procession of similar cases. Within the unhealthy, non-critical culture that surrounds the Holocaust, distortions, exaggerations and manipulations are commonplace as historians and writers seek to make that which they are explaining easier for their readers to understand. In choosing to highlight certain aspects of the event and minimalising or even ignoring others, which all writers must do, to avoid their works being exhaustively long, historians usually demonstrate nothing more than their own subjectivity; their own assumptions in approaching the issue formed through their own set of personal biases. Never has this been truer than in relation to the Holocaust at Nuremberg.

It was first presented, in piecemeal form, by the victorious powers as a (minor) part of the prosecution case. Following other trials, throughout the forties, fifties and sixties, it has since been seized upon by academics, often with clearly identifiable agendas, to the point where it has become a field of study in its own right and a welter of media output has developed around it.

The base of evidence on which the obelisk of Holocaust Studies has been constructed is entirely Allied generated. What is more, the primary sources of opinion and analysis regarding that evidence (and how it was gathered) are also entirely Allied generated. As a result the layers of secondary work that have been written since (with very few exceptions) have displayed only the Allied viewpoint, gaining strength with each wave of new 'research' due to its lack of challenge or counter-narrative, until it eventually became a grotesque caricature of itself as academics like Daniel Goldhagen projected their own points of view and refracted them through this giant, constructed prism of the Holocaust. If you could go back through time and approach Telford Taylor or Jackson, or Thomas Dodd at Nuremberg and ask for their thoughts on the Holocaust, they would have little idea what you were talking about. What we must face and accept is that the Holocaust has been fashioned since then.

The 1945-6 reality is that not only was the Holocaust a minor feature at Nuremberg, but with a few notable exceptions, the evidence that was presented for it was largely of insubstantial nature – either contained in affidavits or eyewitness testimony, much of which was in the form of hearsay. That is not to suggest that 'it' (whatever 'it' may be defined as) did not happen, it is clear that terrible civilian atrocities occurred, but simply that anyone who attempts to claim that the modern Holocaust obelisk was erected in any way during this first great trial at Nuremberg is demonstrating little other than their wearing of a large pair of historical blinkers.[748] At the Trial of the Major War Criminals before the International Military Tribunal (where one would have thought it would have had a prominent role to play) it could not be said, in any reasonable way, to have been factually demonstrated through evidence. Despite this it was stated in the IMT judgement in much the same form in which Historians describe it today. Its component parts had been deemed by the tribunal to be 'facts of common knowledge'.

The claim that no Nazis denied the crime, which is a common popular belief, needs also to be emphatically addressed. The stark reality is that in one way or another, all of them did. Richard Overy wrote 'nothing was denied more vehemently in the interrogation rooms at Nuremberg than the persecution of the Jews.'[749] By careful analysis of the trial, a more complete picture emerges. The defendants admitted to anti-Jewish laws, anti-partisan activity (which would have included actions against Jews) and a deportation and resettlement programme, but not one of them admitted to first-hand knowledge of an extermination plan or devices of mass execution. A few Nazi witnesses did, mainly via affidavits. Bearing in mind what has to come to light about Allied interrogation methods, we must adjust our views of such witness statements and affidavits appropriately.

The closest we came to any small admission of knowledge from defendants was Göring with his 'isolated perpetrations' and Kaltenbrunner with his Himmler 'admitted it' statement. Even with these, the latter is still nothing more than a piece of hearsay. As neither of these comments were followed up by probing enough questions (as one might have expected) we shall never know what these two men actually knew to have taken place and this leads us to a very important point – their narrative, which potentially may have challenged the Allied one, has been lost forever. All we are left with is the version provided by the Allies, their carefully selected documents, their eyewitnesses and their confessions stained with the blood of those who signed them. If we are being kind, this can only be described as 'sloppiness'.

The picture that therefore emerges from straightforward analysis of evidence presented at the trial is one whereby suffering, particularly from hunger and disease, was common in Nazi occupied territory, as shown by the report written by Hans Frank, for the attention of Hitler, referenced by Lieutenant Baldwin in his presentation. The debate over how much of this was due to Nazi policy or was simply a symptom of war (or a combination of both) is worthy of discussion, but that will not be joined here. We also know that orders were passed to eliminate those in occupied areas deemed to be dangerous to the Reich, such as intellectuals, political leaders and obviously, partisan fighters. Such policies, when set within the context of the war make sense, despite their callousness. In addition we also know that Jews had been singled out by the regime as the arch enemy. It seems this was for three reasons. Firstly, a long-standing anti-Semitism, whereby the Nazis resented the Jewish domination of German life in certain spheres and wished to depose them from their alleged elite positions. Secondly, because of the repeated agitation of Jewish organisations and the public declarations of leading Zionists and international Jewish figureheads like Untermeyer and Weizman, who called for boycotts and war against Germany from the earliest days of the regime and thirdly, because once hostilities had begun, Nazis believed Jews to be forming a substantial part of the partisan and resistance movements. As a result of these three reasons, a series of policies were enacted, starting in peacetime with discrimination and exclusion from German life. In wartime, with different pressures upon the Reich, the policies became more draconian, resulting in forced deportation and ghettoisation. Most draconian of all and admitted to by several witnesses, was that the *Einsatzgruppen*, during their anti-partisan activities, often targeted Jews, because of their alleged partisan links. The most striking evidence for this was presented in Rosenberg's case with the letter from Kube to Lohse in which it was claimed that 55,000 Jews of White Russia had been shot, or by the testimony of Ohlendorf, in which he claimed his squad had accounted for 90,000 victims. (Ohlendorf did not stipulate that the victims were solely Jewish, mentioning communist 'commissars' also.) Again, despite the brutality of such actions, when placed within the context of the Russian front, the biggest theatre of war in human history, a vast area full of woodland and villages crawling with hostile civilians who constantly attacked German soldiers and supply lines, as stated by Jodl and Frank, one can see the logic. A wartime ethic of kill or be killed saves little room for sentimental ideals of honour.

Further even than this, however, we have the allegations that the Nazis instigated a plan to kill all the Jews of Europe 'The Final Solution' and used homicidal gas chambers to do so. Yet we see that these two

---

[748] The Holocaust may well have been proven more thoroughly during later trials, but that is outside the subject of this book.
[749] Overy, *Interrogations*, p.178

claims were only really evidenced by the affidavits and testimonies of Wisliceny and Höss, (and Ohlendorf to some extent) which have large question marks hanging over them as shall be explained below.

It is worth pausing here for a moment to highlight one of the more puzzling discrepancies at the trial. With regard to the most serious claims, we see a very clear pattern in terms of the responses of Nazis asked to provide evidence. The senior officials and officers - the defendants, all denied knowledge of the Holocaust. However, several more junior Nazis provided very detailed testimony regarding the Holocaust either on the stand or in the form of affidavits. Thus we see that the narrative which Historians developed and used to construct the Holocaust obelisk, did not begin with the words and confessions of Göring, Streicher, von Ribbentrop or Kaltenbrunner, but unknowns and underlings like Wisliceny, von dem Bach-Zelewski, Ohlendorf and Höss. So why should second and third tier Nazi operatives sing their hearts out for their Allied captors, while their superiors maintained a veil of silence? Richard Overy, in a nonsensical piece of reasoning, conjectured that 'it might well be thought that they were keen to make a full confession so that their bosses would not get away with persistent denial.'[750] Why on earth any German in Allied hands would deem it sensible to admit to these things, knowing the effect it would have on their own immediate future, Overy does not care to explain. Is he suggesting we believe that the junior Nazis in interrogation succumbed to an attack of conscience and told the truth, while their superiors did not? Or is it that these young officers vindictively wanted their former leaders hanged, for some reason? Either way, such reasoning can only ever be conjecture. We could just as easily suppose that the defendants knew that to admit to such things would mean imminent death whereas those not actually yet on trial might hope that saying what their interrogators wanted to hear would secure them some form of future leniency.

In addition to this discrepancy there are also issues contained within the statements of these Nazi confessors, which history has never managed to iron out. Ohlendorf, in his testimony, stated that the first order to begin killing the Jews was given by Himmler in May 1941 and that his *Einsatzgruppen* unit began acting upon this in the fields of Eastern Europe. However, Wisliceny claimed to have held the written order in his hand and said that it was dated April 1942. One of them, therefore, has to be wrong. Höss, on the other hand, claimed the order to kill Jews at Auschwitz came some time in the summer of 1941, although most historians now claim he meant 1942, to tie it in with the Wannsee Conference in January of that year. In other words there is a complete lack of consensus among the three with regard to the most fundamental specifics.

It is possible therefore, as argued by some, that there was no one order for the extermination of the Jews and that there were several orders, given at various times, to various organisations. Yet if this were true it would rather cast a shadow over our understanding of the 'Final Solution'. This was meant to be a state-implemented policy of racist genocide, not piecemeal, regional actions instigated in the heat of war. Beyond any different interpretations, what is clear is that the evidence provided by these witnesses, although corroborative as to the general existence of an order, are otherwise completely contradictory, to the extent that it has to be questioned whether they are referring to the same thing. The idea that these witnesses' stories support each other simply does not stand up. What we find therefore, is that on this most important point, a central plank of the Holocaust narrative for all these years, all the Trial of the Century managed to provide were a few contradictory statements, which historians have since rationalised to match their own assumptions.

Despite this, it is undeniable that terrible civilian atrocities occurred. Shootings, starvation, disease, forced labour, loss of property, ejection from homes, separation from loved ones, all of these combine to create a horrific picture. Many non-Jews also suffered these kinds of horrors, but it would certainly be fair to state that the Jewish population got the worst of it. In some of the cases in which death was caused, people were directly killed by Nazi actions (by shooting, for example), in others indirectly. With regard to the latter, deaths were caused by gradual wearing-down, by people having been pushed to the fringes of society and shorn of the ability to support or fend for themselves. A resident of a walled ghetto, for example, cannot go out foraging for mushrooms in the woods if food runs out. When faced with extreme deprivation and crisis, such people simply died. However it is highly debatable whether this can truly be regarded as 'extermination'. If it is, then a case could be made that many, many millions of Europeans were exterminated because of actions of the Allies, as shall be discussed shortly. Indeed, the idea that the Nazis hatched a plan to murder all the Jews of Europe and these various methods, in addition to gas chambers were used to facilitate such a plan is not borne out by the trial. Not one defendant admitted to it. Not one original document, even of the

---

[750] Overy, *Interrogations*, p.187

defendants' private correspondence or diaries was produced to evidence it. In some cases, like Frank's, many volumes of such diaries or correspondence were combed for references to these things, unsuccessfully. To maintain faith in the regular Holocaust narrative therefore requires a belief in a kind of conspiracy. One must assume that these twenty-one defendants, who were captured individually, kept in solitary confinement and interrogated constantly, all somehow colluded to admit to knowledge of the same things and deny knowledge of the same things. This showed itself in both interrogation and questioning in the courtroom and private writings and correspondence written contemporarily. Further to that point is that the only evidence which supported these most serious claims was that purposely produced or gathered by the Allies for the trial, generally through interrogation of more junior Nazis or eyewitness affidavits, not that which was produced contemporarily by those involved in the events. This division is similar to the 'witting' and 'unwitting' evidence[751] described by Arthur Marwick in his influential work 'The Nature of History'. Why the 'witting' evidence gathered by the Allies should provide a different story to the 'unwitting' evidence provided by contemporary documents would perhaps suggest that the witting evidence was tainted. Knowledge of the methods of Allied evidence gathering makes such a suggestion highly plausible.

In addition to that, it is important to note that the gas chamber claims were just one of several similar claims made during the final years of the war and just as we have Höss' affidavit or the Soviet Statements as evidence of gassing, we also have other very similar affidavits or documents as evidence of some of these other claims. For example, IMT volume thirty-two, which contains interrogation and other documents entered in evidence for the trial contains a document entitled 'Charge Number Six of the Polish Government Against Hans Frank' authored by a Dr Cyprian. The document alleges that:

> 'The German authorities acting under the authority of Governor General Hans Frank established in March 1942 the extermination camp at Treblinka, intended for mass killing of Jews by suffocating them in steam-filled chambers…The best known of these death camps are those of Treblinka, Belzec and Sobibor in the Lublin district. In these camps the Jews were put to death in their thousands by hitherto unknown, new methods, gas and steam chambers as well as electrical current employed on a large scale…[752]

It is arguable, of course, that the Polish report simply confused 'gas' with 'steam', however such reason- ing would fail to account for the fact that later on in the same document, it explains the building and opera- tion of these steam chambers in considerable detail. 'The second building consists of three chambers and a boiler room' it says, 'The steam generated in the boilers is led by means of pipes to the chambers…'[753]

The other bizarre claim contained in that report, that of using electricity to murder inmates at the Belzec camp, also made by the Soviets in their 'Statements on Nazi Atrocities', was given enough credence to be referenced by Lieutenant Colonel Griffiths-Jones during his cross-examination of Streicher. 'Many details are also given about the use of poison gas, as at Chelm, of electricity in Belzec…'[754] He said.

By the time the trial had been concluded and the judgements were drawn up, it seems the idea of steam chambers at Treblinka or death by electricity at Belzec had been quietly dropped, in favour of the universal gas story. Yet both were held in evidence by the IMT on Polish and Soviet documents, accepted in toto via the principle of 'judicial notice' in accordance with article 21 of the Nuremberg Charter, on which many of the most infamous claims were so luridly made.

As a final comment on the above analysis, it should be pointed out that it is not possible to prove or disprove the reality of the homicidal gas chambers based solely on the evidence presented before the IMT. There is a great deal of other evidence which exists outside of the subject of this book. As a starting point, each of the camps denoted as extermination centres were later to have trials of their own. Thus there was an Auschwitz trial, a Treblinka trial, a Majdanek trial and so on. It is assumed that evidence presented before

---

[751] Marwick, Arthur, *The Nature of History* 3rd ed. (Macmillan 1989) p.216-220. Witting evidence is that deliberately collected or made solely for the purpose of being evidence. Unwitting evidence refers to documents or artefacts generated during the course of an event, which provide evidence for it without that actually having been their sole purpose.
[752] IMT Vol.32, Doc no. 3311-PS (Library of Congress)
[753] ibid
[754] Nuremberg Trial Proceedings, vol. 12, 116th day, Monday 29th April 1946, p.368

those courts, used for the conviction and execution of the Nazis that staffed those camps, was of a fuller and more convincing nature than that produced at Nuremberg. What is clear, however is that based on the treatment of this issue by the IMT, there is scope for reasonable intellectual curiosity. Big questions are raised.

None of this is intended to belittle the anguish of any civilian communities that suffered during the war. But sympathy with their suffering is not mutually exclusive with a belief that their suffering has been propagandised for political purposes. An interesting exercise, for comparison, is to set the Holocaust to one side and consider the other 60 million or so deaths of World War Two, for a moment. According to various sources,[755] 47 million civilians died in the war. Of these, 20 million died due to war-related famine and disease. This is worth taking a few moments to consider. One is faced with the idea that inmates in concentration camps and other civilians in German-occupied areas, especially Jewish ghettoes, starved, according to the Nuremberg prosecutors, because of a racist plan to exterminate. Yet millions of other Europeans starved at the same time and in similar areas simply because huge wars are a horrible mess and the prevailing conditions were such that destitution, hunger and homelessness were rife. Of course it could be argued that the 'mess' in Nazi occupied areas was the fault of the Nazis themselves, but one cannot help but see a double standard.

When considering the war's other civilian deaths, it must also be considered how many were caused through acts which could reasonably be described as 'atrocities'. More than 200,000 Japanese died in the blasts at Hiroshima and Nagasaki, for example, countless others during the post war period from radiation sickness and other harmful effects. In their own report on the Japanese bombing campaign, the US Air Force stated that 'total civilian casualties in Japan, as a result of 9 months of air attack, including those from the atomic bombs, were approximately 806,000.'[756] They estimated that at least 330,000 of those died and that this was greater than Japan's military death toll. The Allied bombing campaign of Germany, including the White Phosphorous horrors of Dresden and Hamburg yielded similar results. According to AC Grayling, roughly 600,000 German civilians were killed by the deliberate civilian bombing of the RAF and USAF and the value of this tactic to the Allied war effort was questionable.[757]

Bearing in mind what also happened to German civilians and POWs under Allied occupation, post war, and indeed the many other examples of genocide from ancient to recent history, the question to ask is what makes the Nazi treatment of Jews 'unique'? And I am aware that this is not an original question. The 'uniqueness' of the Holocaust is an issue addressed by Marrus, Finkelstein, Davidowicz and virtually every writer who has written about it. Often we are told that its 'uniqueness' lies in the fact that a single group of people were chosen for extermination, based on nothing other than their ethnicity. But such statements are questionable in some aspects and demonstrably false in others. Firstly we are faced with the problem that History is yet to deliver definitive evidence regarding the decision to exterminate. The *Führerbefehl* (Hitler order) simply does not exist.[758] Even extreme intentionalists like Lucy Davidowicz admit so, saying, 'Though the abundant documents of the German dictatorship have yielded no written order by Hitler to murder the Jews, it appears from the events as we know them now, that the decision for the practical implementation of the plan to kill the Jews was probably reached after December 18, 1940 – when Hitler issued the first directive for Operation Barbarossa – and before March 1, 1941.'[759] It is worth noting here that Davidowicz' estimates would perhaps tie in with the date given by Ohlendorf and the one originally provided by Höss (which many historians have since claimed to be a mistake) but not the one provided by Wisliceny.

As a result and as described by Davidowicz above, historians searching for causes and triggers have played connect-the-dots with a whole bunch of documents and trace evidence – 'the events *as we know them now*' – and provided various theories from Hilberg's famous 'mind reading' conclusion, to Daniel Jonah Goldhagen's objectionable thesis of innate German anti-Semitism. Yet also, it must be thrown into the mix

---

[755] Martin Gilbert's *Recent History Atlas* (1966) alleged 6,780,000 civilian casualties in Russia, Poland and Yugoslavia alone, excluding Jewish deaths. Other works like John Ellis' World War Two Databook, (1993) have figures slightly higher than this, others slightly lower. A useful summary of the last 50 years of statistics on the matter can be found on Wikipedia http://en.wikipedia.org/wiki/World_War_II_casualties#fn_RudOver
[756] United States Strategic Survey Summary Report, Pacific War http://www.anesi.com/ussbs01.htm
[757] AC Grayling, *Among the Dead Cities. Is the targeting of civilians in war ever justified?* (Bloomsbury 2007)
[758] Richard Overy states unconvincingly that 'the central role of Hitler in Nazi Jewish policy was disguised by the absence of written orders.' *Interrogations*, p.183
[759] Lucy S. Dawidowicz, *The War Against the Jews 1933-1945* (Bantam Books, 1976), p.162

that Nazi racial policy was not just about Jews. In actuality, it wasn't really about Jews at all. Nazi racial policy (see chapter 14) was focused on the German people and German living space. This was at the exclusion of *all* others. Jews, through their alleged positions of power were seen as a major opponent to be dealt with and also, as a sizeable minority within the 'living space' were an obstacle to Nazi ambitions, yet so were Slavs, so were Poles and so were other Eastern Europeans. Indeed, in chapter thirteen it was shown that the Russian prosecution presented evidence at the trial suggesting a proposed genocide of thirty million Slavs. Perhaps, if a study was made of numbers of Slavs who starved in the Nazi sphere of influence, Slavs in camps, Slavs recruited as slave labourers and numbers of Slavs killed in anti-partisan actions, we could construct a Slav Holocaust from the available evidence. Obviously, we would not have a Führer order for that either, although it seems that for some, that doesn't matter. Perhaps we could use the 'events as we know them now' to construct a Polish one, or even a French.[760]. But being able to construct something does not demonstrate a reality. It demonstrates the human ability to construct things.

In the final analysis then, it must be conceded that what, apparently makes the Jewish Holocaust 'unique' are the aspects of it that, at Nuremberg at least, were the least satisfactorily proven. The plan to rid the world of Jews and the Homicidal Gas Chambers were not evidenced convincingly. When one bears in mind the nature of wartime propaganda and the imbalance and subjectivity of the trial, it is easy to see how such claims were accepted. By categorizing them as 'facts of common knowledge' the court decreed that relatively flimsy evidence would suffice. It is history's job, so far wilfully ignored, to pick the bones out of this.

Further to that point, is that even if one starts with the idea that Nazi racism was predominately anti-Semitic in its character, it does not necessarily follow that anti-Semitism alone is a substantial enough motive for a system of industrialised genocide, the likes of which had never before been seen. Overy states 'if the interrogation transcripts reveal anything, it is the unwritten assumption on the part of the interrogators that anti-Semitic sentiment is a sufficient explanation for mass murder.' He goes on to say that, 'the current debate on the causes of the Holocaust revolves about the validity of this assumption.'[761] However he doesn't go as far as to point out that it is clearly a ridiculous assumption. Anti-Semitic feeling had bubbled up in numerous countries over the centuries and many had indulged in pogroms for one reason or another, but none of them as yet had seen fit to try to kill off the entire Jewish race or to build bizarre, hellish, extermination centres, elements of which seemed to defy possibility. Why should the Germans be any different? The obvious answer, which Overy seems unwilling to state, is that like most other aspects of the trial, the interrogators were starting with a conclusion and then working backwards. The possibility that the camps were not extermination centres, using gas chambers, but normal prison and labour camps in which either prevailing or imposed conditions led to mass starvation and epidemics was not, for the purposes of prosecution, a valid one. This would explain their confusion over camps like Belsen and Dachau, which originally were thought to have been 'death camps' and later downgraded. As far as the Allies were concerned the Nazis were genocidal from the beginning and that was that.

It is difficult today, with the construction of the Holocaust obelisk[762] reaching record heights (we have Holocaust museums in every major city in the western world and educational programmes and documentaries constantly made in the name of 'memory'), to see past its sheer enormity. But the fact that those who seek to ask questions of this obelisk, or at least subject it to proper scrutiny, are often shouted down, reviled and even imprisoned, is as clear a demonstration as could be asked for of what Nuremberg really achieved.

---

[760] The indictment did include the charge of 'systematic genocide' against 'Jews, Poles and Gypsies and others.' But it was alleged that the *Endlösung* meaning 'The Final Solution', which historians have determined to mean extermination, related only to the *Judenfrage* or Jewish question. Therefore we get the confusing picture of genocidal actions against most Eastern European civilians, but a special genocidal action against the Jews.

[761] Overy, *Interrogations*, p.197

[762] In *The Holocaust Industry*, p. 3, Finkelstein refers to the obelisk as 'an ideological representation of the Nazi holocaust.'

22

Freedom, Democracy and 'The Conquering of Evil'.

'Why, of course, the people don't want war... Why would some poor slob on a farm want to risk his life in a war when the best he can get out of it is to come back to his farm in one piece... But after all, it is the leaders of the country who determine the policy and it is always a simple matter to drag the people along... All you have to do is tell them they are being attacked and denounce the pacifists for lack of patriotism... It works the same in any country.'[763]

Hermann Göring, April 18th, 1946

After the messy business of execution and disposal of remains had been concluded, the Trial of the Century presented the world with eleven dead Germans and three major conclusions. First of these was that it had punished aggression. The Nazis were aggressive. The Nazis were expansionist. The Nazis were to blame for World War Two. Secondly, it had punished tyranny. Nazi Germany had been a dictatorship, in which no recourse was made to the views of the people. It had assumed and consolidated power and imprisoned opponents. It had been totalitarian, ruthless and oppressive. Finally, the tribunal had punished 'racism'. The Nazis had subscribed to racial ideology. They wanted to secure a future and land for the Nordic people. And rather than just moaning about it, like many before them, they had actively sought an answer to the 'Jewish question', through increasingly extreme means.

Or at least, those are the conclusions the world was supposed to believe.

The first of these stated aims of the Nuremberg lawmakers – to show that the waging of aggressive war had no place in the modern world, would need someone or something to arbitrate in such matters from that point on.

The United Nations, established in 1942, by Churchill and Roosevelt, officially became this arbiter. It is worth remembering that the organisation's origins were in a collective term for the Allied nations – the 'United Nations' were initially the US, the UK, the USSR and France. Of the fifteen members of the UN Security Council these four, along with China, have remained the only permanent members.

A quick glance at the UN Charter shows some very Jacksonesque rhetoric, as its very first sentence, 'We, the United Nations,' it declares, 'determined to save succeeding generations from the scourge of war, which twice in our lifetime has brought untold sorrow to mankind...'[764]

Just like so much of the posturing at the trial, it gives the impression that everything is being done from a high sense of altruism. Yet when one looks at the history of the last sixty-two years, since Göring *et al*'s ashes were thrown into a river, the UN's influence on this matter is seen to be a dismal failure. It may be true that we have avoided lapsing into conflicts as catastrophic as World Wars One and Two and that Europe (or Central to Western Europe at least) has managed to live in relative peace but this would seem to be some- thing of a smokescreen. We came perilously close to nuclear oblivion several times during the sixties and seventies, yet even setting this to one side, one nation in particular, with certain hangers-on has managed to repeatedly invade, bomb and commit a variety of civilian atrocities, sometimes involving chemical weapons, since the time the United Nations was formed. This leads us to open our eyes – and the perception of rather a grim reality.

With the defeat of Nazi Germany, the British Empire achieved its primary long-term aim, in maintaining the European balance of power. However it did so at enormous cost to itself. Britain has had to stand by, helpless, as its Empire has been dismantled. The UK has been thoroughly usurped as the world's leading power by the United States, to whom it has become nothing more than an irrelevant ally.

Preperata's Russo-German 'Eurasian Embrace' had been prevented from coming to fruition, but it was clear, that for the new western imperial power, more work would be needed to ensure stability at the top of

---

[763] G. Gilbert, p.278
[764] United Nations Charter http://www.un.org/aboutun/charter/index.html

the global hierarchy. Having crushed Germany and criminalised its former regime, placing compliant satraps in charge of the nation, who were eager to please and only too happy to enforce the denazification purges expected of them, (Japan, shattered and demoralised by nuclear attack, was placed in a similar position of on-its-knees contrition) their attention turned to the Soviet Union and its influence. Suddenly, the great evil of Nazism began to fade into memory, only to be revived at such time when it would again become useful. Communism took over as the spectre at the window. 'The Red Menace' was everywhere.[765] In reality, this was nothing more than history repeating itself.

The western Allies, now firmly led by the United States, with the UK in a state of disrepair almost equalling that of the defeated powers, saw their only challenger on the world stage as Soviet Russia, who had been allowed to annexe most of Eastern Europe post war (not quite the Eurasian Embrace, but not far off) and had the potential to spread its influence into Asia and beyond. American foreign policy during the immediate post war years was formed with the sole purpose of limiting the spread of Communism as far as possible. This, of course, had nothing to do with ideology. They cared not a jot for the validity or otherwise of Marx' theories, just as they cared nothing for the pros and cons of National Socialism. It was a simple matter of seeing off dangerous competition – the potential for an empire to challenge theirs.

As a result we saw the occupation of South Korea between 1945 and 1949, following a Communist uprising. During the same period US Marines were garrisoned in China as a protective force, as Communism threatened to take hold there too. From 1950 – 1953 American entanglement in Korea's business evolved into the Korean War, in which, having seen China readily succumb to Mao's cultural revolution, despite their presence, they responded to the attack of Communist North Korea against the South, eventually ensuring that half of Korea at least did not become a possible Soviet ally.

The infamous Vietnam War, which stretched from 1959-75 began, like Korea, as a reaction to attacks on US forces of occupation that had been there since 1955, who were trying to limit the spread of Communism filtering down from the North. Linked to the Vietnam conflict, we also saw the US engage in Laos between '62 and '75, supporting anti-communist forces there. Less well known, but undertaken for the same reason, was the invasion of the Dominican Republic in 1965, in which US troops were sent in to act as a counter-revolutionary force against communist insurgents on the island.

Activity continued in Laos and Cambodia in 1968, with an American bombing campaign along the Ho Chi Minh trail. This tactic, heavily employed by the Allies in World War Two in the Pacific Theatre and against Germany, was to be used time and time again as the century progressed.

The propaganda picture became more complicated in 1967, with the Arab/Israeli Conflict, when the ghost of Fascism, Nazism and the Holocaust was revived having receded into the recesses of the international consciousness. In 1973 this ghost was used to assist in the facilitation of Operation Nickel Grass, in which the United States came to Israel's aid in the 'Yom Kippur' war. According to Norman Finkelstein, this was a key period in the birth of what is described in certain quarters as, 'the new anti-Semitism'. This new anti-Semitism essentially refers to any form of criticism of the Zionist state of Israel, an important ally for the United States, within the volatile, mainly hostile, but oil-rich, Middle-East.[766]

Having stabilised the position with regard to their global superiority and with Soviet strength on the wane, direct economic concerns, never too far down the list of priorities of any great empire, began to take precedence. Oil, which in a very real way had replaced Gold as the trading currency of the world, was soaring in value. America's attention thus turned to the 'Libyan Socialism' (not really Communism, but with some similarities) of Colonel Gadaffi, whose military coup had inconveniently disposed of oil-friendly King Idris. In 1981 there were several small incidents with Libya, as the United States took it upon themselves to enforce Libya's contentious naval boundaries. This attempt at provocation failed, so in 1986, with one of the most transparent excuses in the history of international politics, President Ronald Reagan claimed that Gadaffi was responsible for a terrorist bomb attack at a German disco that killed two U.S. soldiers. Anyone who has followed world events in the last ten years will see familiarities in this story. Here, for the first time was a Muslim nation and accusations of them nurturing and encouraging terrorism, which they may have been doing, but their potential threat to world peace was propagandised out of all proportion. This led to Operation El Dorado Canyon on April 16th, 1986, when U.S. air and naval forces conducted bombing strikes

---

[765] This is the title of a movie made in 1949.
[766] Finkelstein, Norman, *Beyond Chutzpah, On the Misuse of Anti-Semitism and the Abuse of History*, (Verso, 2005), p.24

on alleged 'terrorist facilities' and military installations in the Libyan capital of Tripoli. The action was roundly condemned by most of the world, with its only support coming from the UK, Australia and Israel. Unsurprisingly relations between these nations and Libya were frosty for many years but have recently healed to the point of Gadaffi agreeing to reopen Libyan oil to the west.

After Libya, international incidents of aggression continued unabated. In 1988 the USS Vincennes shot down an Iranian airliner and in 1989 the United States invaded the state of Panama in 'Operation Just Cause' to depose General Noriega who had previously been on the payroll of the CIA, working to advance US inter- ests in Central America. These were to prove to be only the preliminaries for the final aggressive acts of the twentieth century which would spill over into the twenty-first.

1991 saw the first Iraq or Gulf war. This oil-rich region was crucial to a western world thirsting after dwindling reserves. After its climax, US troops were stationed in Iraq with the official reason of counteract- ing 'oppression of Kurdish people'. Yet Saddam Hussein's regime remained in place and oppression contin- ued, while American bombing of the region went on intermittently.

In 1998 President Clinton ordered military strikes against alleged terrorist sites in Afghanistan and in 2003, after the jolt provided by 9/11 in which a small band of mostly Saudi Arabian[767] extremists managed to live up to every line of US/Israeli 'Islamo-fascist' propaganda, the invasion of Afghanistan and then the sec- ond Iraq war were waged on the premise of harbouring terrorists and the possession of weapons of mass de- struction. This happened despite mass protests in both the UK and the USA, strong disagreement within the international community and dissenting views within both national governments. Speaking in 2004, Presi- dent Bush likened the 'War on Terror' to the fight against Nazism, saying, 'Like the US involvement in World War II, the war on terror began with a surprise attack on the US. Like the murderous ideologies of the last century, the ideology of murderers reaches across borders.'

Yet, as is now well-known, weapons of mass destruction were never found and are now believed not to have existed. US and UK leaders blamed this mistake on poor intelligence, but the second conflict in Iraq was still ongoing as this book was being written, four years after its beginning. Estimates as to casualties vary. A report published in the British Medical Journal, 'The Lancet' in October 2006, said that up to that point, 654,965 Iraqis had met violent death as a result of coalition occupation. Over half of these, the study claimed, were women and children. A more recent survey, conducted by the British research group ORB stated that by September 2007, the figure was 1,220,580.[768] Other studies suggest lower figures. As a result of the war, some two million Iraqis have become refugees. Some analysts question the numbers, but even if they are wrong by a factor of two, which few believe, they are still highly significant. Remember also that this is only since 2003. The region has undergone sustained attack, largely through air strikes, while also suf- fering from severe economic sanctions, since 1991. Total deaths are very difficult to calculate. A report by an organization called Medact, led by Beth Daponte, a research professor at Carnegie Mellon University, esti- mated over 150,000 civilian Iraqi deaths[769] either during or caused by the first Gulf War. A total figure for the intermediate period could not be found, although the investigative journalist, John Pilger asserted that a 1999 report by Unicef calculated half a million Iraqi children who had, by that point, met their deaths through starvation or disease as a direct result of sanctions[770].

Even if the statistics can be quibbled with, it is clear that the human cost of the last sixteen years of action in Iraq has been enormous. The only purposes of this tragedy that are readily apparent are the establishment of American bases near the last world sources of easy-to-pump, high quality, surface oil, an attempt to create another oil-friendly regime in the region and the related matter of increased security for the state of Israel as it continues on its path to being the dominant nation of the Middle East.

One wonders, if at any point in the future this may be referred to as an Iraqi Holocaust?[771] What, we might ask, have the ordinary people of Iraq done to deserve this slaughter? To which side of the conflict can we truthfully apply Mr Bush's terminology of the 'ideology of murderers'?

---

[767] It is worth remembering that oil rich Saudi Arabia is an American ally.
[768] Halinan, Colin, *The Casualties of Iraq*, Foreign Policy in Focus, October 17th 2007 http://www.fpif.org/fpiftxt/4649
[769] Medact, Collateral Damage http://www.ippnw.org/ResourceLibrary/CollateralDamage.pdf
[770] Pilger, John, *Iraq, paying the Price* http://www.johnpilger.com/page.asp?partid=11
[771] Selected details of US military action since 1945 taken from Blum, William, *Killing Hope, Military and CIA interventions since World War Two* (Zed books, 2003) and Allman, TD, *Rogue State, America at war with the World*, (Nation books, 2004)

In the face of sixty years of sustained aggression from the USA (the above events are only a small selection of their military endeavours since 1945) the United Nations has become a secondary factor in world affairs. Perhaps not even that. There is little they can do when a powerful nation chooses to pursue its own path.

It is impossible, after seeing what the main player behind Nuremberg has been doing since, to believe in the sincerity of their expressed aims at the trial. A nation which claimed it wanted to save the world from the scourge of war and which gave death sentences to twelve men it deemed to be guilty of starting one has had a foreign policy based on little other than aggression and the rule of force ever since.

Another stark contradiction of Nuremberg and the United Nations' professed yearnings for peace can be found in a state it was instrumental in helping to create. Since its inception in 1948, the State of Israel has provided the 'homeland for the Jewish people' that Wise, Weizmann, Untermeyer and others had been campaigning for many years. Conversely, the time between then and now is referred to by the Palestinian people as the *Naqba* (tragedy). The development of this tragedy has implications when analysed in the wake of Nuremberg. Repeated British statements in both the White Papers on Palestine (1922 and 1939) established initial plans for accommodating Zionist demands.

> 'Unauthorized statements have been made to the effect that the purpose in view is to create a wholly Jewish Palestine. Phrases have been used such as that Palestine is to become 'as Jewish as England is English.' His Majesty's Government regard any such expectation as impracticable and have no such aim in view. Nor have they at any time contemplated, as appears to be feared by the Arab delegation, the disappearance or the subordination of the Arabic population, language, or culture in Palestine. They would draw attention to the fact that the terms of the Declaration referred to do not contemplate that Palestine as a whole should be converted into a Jewish National Home, but that such a Home should be founded 'in Palestine.' In this connection it has been observed with satisfaction that at a meeting of the Zionist Congress, the supreme governing body of the Zionist Organization, held at Carlsbad in September, 1921, a resolution was passed expressing as the official statement of Zionist aims 'the determination of the Jewish people to live with the Arab people on terms of unity and mutual respect, and together with them to make the common home into a flourishing community, the upbuilding of which may assure to each of its peoples an undisturbed national development.'[772]

Initially then, the idea of the British Mandate was for the Jewish population already in the region, together with Jewish immigrants from Europe, to become part of a Palestinian state in which both Arabs and Jews would coexist. This vision met with agreement from both sides. By 1948 however, following the events of the war and repeated agitation from Zionist leaders like Weizmann, who apparently found the idea of living alongside Arabs distasteful, coupled with the withdrawal of the British who were suffering attacks on their troops from both sides, this had become a two state solution. The representatives of the Palestinian people did not agree to this partition of their territory and this resulted in the Israeli war of independence, in which the new state of Israel occupied even more of the region than had been originally proposed. During the occupation of this territory, the Palestinian communities of the area simply disappeared, either killed or forcibly ejected from their homes and turned into refugees. Norman Finkelstein described this process as one of ethnic cleansing and stated that it was not a matter that could be under dispute: 'the scholarly debate now focused on the much narrower, if still highly pertinent question of whether this cleansing was the intentional consequence of Zionist policy or the unintentional by-product of war.'[773] Bearing in mind that what is being described is an occupying power killing and mistreating civilians, it would seem that Finkelstein is outlining something similar to the 'intentionalism v functionalism' debate which for many years dominated academic discourse about the Holocaust. Add to this the numerous allegations of torture, mistreatment of Palestinian prisoners in Israeli hands and Israel's brutal put-downs of Palestinian uprisings, where youths throwing stones are met with machine guns and tanks, and it can be seen that the victims of Nazi *evil*, just like its conquerors, are more than prepared to create their own atrocities, to act aggressively and to commit violations of human rights when it suits them.

---

[772] British White Paper of June 1922 on Palestine http://www.yale.edu/lawweb/avalon/mideast/brwh1922.htm
[773] Finkelstein, *Beyond Chutzpah*, p.3

Nuremberg's other conclusions fare little better. Issues related to the practice of modern, representative democracy will be dealt with in the next chapter. For now it will suffice to say that there is much about it that is very undemocratic. The ideal of rule by the people, for the people is as distant as ever. It is not necessarily a system that the west should be exporting to the rest of the world, especially when such export seems to be largely conducted via guns and bombs. If there is a genuine moral obligation to force other nations to adopt representative democracy through violence, then it is not one that is readily apparent.

Racism too, is a sticky topic for the victorious powers. Although the American Jewish community have thrived, post war, to the point where despite only comprising two percent of the population, nearly fifty percent of the nation's billionaires are Jewish[774], other minorities do not fare so well. Twenty Four percent of blacks live below the poverty line in the States, for example, as opposed to eight percent of whites.[775] Three percent of the black male population of the United States is in prison, as compared to less than half a percent for whites.[776] Tokenistic, yet powerful evidence of America's racial divide was also provided by the pictures of the aftermath of Hurricane Katrina in New Orleans in 2005. The scenes, broadcast worldwide, showed a form of economic apartheid, whereby the black underclass found themselves bereft and stranded, while the rest of the population escaped. As, apparently, race is only skin deep and theories of racial difference are evil and automatically lead to exterminating millions in death camps, we cannot ascribe any of this to racial difference. These kinds of discrepancies can only be the result of an utterly racist American society. It should be remembered too that immediately after Nuremberg and until the 1960s, racial segregation was still official policy in the southern states.

This means that when looking at the aftermath of Nuremberg, we are faced with a situation in which the three great evils of Nazi Germany, for which it was put on trial before the world, were all conducted, for years afterwards, to varying degrees by the main prosecuting power and its closest allies. There is a word for this sort of thing. And it is 'hypocrisy'.

The real result of Nuremberg was a world order built on moral hypocrisy. The victors glossed over their war crimes and socio-political shortcomings and continue to do so, while overplaying those of the enemy. They did this, a la Göring, to sway public opinion in favour of their imperial agenda. And it has worked. A few examples from recent history will suffice to show how readily people have accepted this ethos as their own.

In his State of the Union Address before Congress on Januray 29th 2002, President George W Bush famously described North Korea, Iran and Iraq as an 'Axis of Evil.'[777] 'States like these, and their terrorist allies,' he said 'constitute an axis of evil, arming to threaten the peace of the world. By seeking weapons of mass destruction, these regimes pose a grave and growing danger.' Just over a year later, in March 2003, the war in Iraq began.

On the 24th of September, 2007, one of Bush's Axes of Evil, President Mahmoud Ahmadinejad, of Iran, arrived at Columbia University in New York to speak to the students and faculty. His visit provoked a full day of intense protest from massed crowds who believed that giving a platform to the man who denied the Holocaust and said 'Israel should be wiped off the map' was to provide him with credibility. It should be pointed out here that these views, falsely attributed to Ahmadinejad by the media, result more from alarmist editing and misquotation than a genuine attempt to engage with his statements. Ahmadinejad's repeated line on the Holocaust is that it should not be regarded as immune to examination and re-interpretation, which is an eminently reasonable standpoint. He has never actually denied it. The Arab news network, Al Jazeera, quoted the Iranian President as saying:

> 'they (the governments of the west) have fabricated a legend under the name of the Massacre of the Jews, and they hold it higher than God himself, religion itself and the prophets themselves...If somebody in their country questions God, nobody says anything, but if somebody denies the myth of

---

[774] Benjamin Ginsberg, *The Fatal Embrace* (University of Chicago Press 1993) p.1
[775] US Census Bureau News, August 26th 2004
http://www.census.gov/Press-Release/www/releases/archives/income_wealth/002484.html
[776] US Department of Justice Prison Statistics, December 31st 2006 http://www.ojp.usdoj.gov/bjs/prisons.htm
[777] The importance of the word 'Axis' here should not be downplayed. Remember that the 'Axis' powers of World War Two were Japan, Italy and of course, Nazi Germany.

the massacre of Jews, the Zionist loudspeakers and the governments in the pay of Zionism will start to scream.'[778]

The idea of the Holocaust being a 'myth' or a 'legend' is one that he has often expressed, but this does not necessarily mean he believes the whole narrative is pure invention. After all, most 'myths' or 'legends' contain a core of fact. In a 2006 interview with the German newspaper *Der Spiegel*, he further defined his position:

> 'If the Holocaust took place in Europe, one also has to find the answer to it in Europe. On the other hand, if the Holocaust didn't take place, why then did this regime of occupation (Israel) come about? Why do the European countries commit themselves to defending this regime? Permit me to make one more point. We are of the opinion that if a historical occurrence conforms to the truth, this truth will be revealed all the more clearly if there is more research into it and more discussion about it....We don't want to confirm or deny the Holocaust. We oppose every type of crime against any people. But we want to know whether this crime actually took place or not. If it did, then those who bear the responsibility for it have to be punished, and not the Palestinians. Why isn't research into a deed that occurred 60 years ago permitted? After all, other historical occurrences, some of which lie several thousand years in the past, are open to research...'[779]

It is clear that Ahmadinejad is not making statements of Holocaust denial, but rather is expressing doubts and asking questions of the obelisk which has been constructed around it, in particular its effect on the people of Palestine. This leads on to his line on Israel, which has been similarly misrepresented. According to Juan Cole, the Professor of Modern Middle East and South Asian History at the University of Michigan, Ahmadinejad really said, in Farsi, that 'the regime occupying Jerusalem must vanish from the page of time,'[780] still an anti-Israel statement, which should surprise no-one, but hardly as exciting as 'wiping Israel off the map' with its obvious whiff of (nuclear?) obliteration. It obviously has occurred to few commentators that if Iran launched a nuclear attack on Israel, they would also be killing the Palestinian people there, whom they are seeking to defend. There is therefore no logical basis for this belief, at all. Yet this faulty translation has been repeated ad nauseam around the world and used by Israelis and American neo-Conservatives to justify the escalation of hostile rhetoric towards Iran. When it is borne in mind that Iran has huge oil reserves, confirmed at 135 billion barrels[781], as well as one of the world's largest supplies of natural gas, this antagonistic process takes on an eerily familiar air.

Based on this misrepresentation of his public statements, the crowd at Columbia shouted slogans and waved placards. One student handed out flyers of the Saudi Arabian terrorist leader, Osama Bin Laden, with the caption 'Too bad Bin Laden is not available.'[782] In response to these protests, the Columbia University President, Lee C. Bollinger decided to play to the gallery by taking to the lectern just before Ahmadinejad and saying, 'Mr President, you exhibit all the signs of a petty and cruel dictator,' adding, to cheers from the audience, 'You are either brazenly provocative or astonishingly uneducated.'

Ahmadinejad responded with considerable dignity, saying, 'In Iran, tradition requires when you invite a person to be a speaker, we actually respect our students enough to allow them to make their own judgment, and don't think it's necessary before the speech is even given, to come in with a series of complaints to provide vaccination to the students and faculty...Nonetheless, I shall not begin by being affected by this un-

---

[778] *Ahmadinejad: Holocaust a Myth*, Al Jazeera, English section, Dec. 15th 2005, http://english.aljazeera.net/English/archive/archive?ArchiveId=17019
[779] Spiegel Interview with President Ahmadinejad, Der Spiegel, May 30th 2006 http://www.spiegel.de/international/spiegel/0,1518,418660,00.html
[780] Cole, Juan (May 03, 2006). *Hitchens the Hacker; And, Hitchens the Orientalist And, 'We don't Want Your Stinking War!*. http://www.juancole.com/2006/05/hitchens-hacker-and-hitchens.html
[781] *Ancient Soul of Iran, the glories of Persia inspire the modern nation*, Marguerite del Giudice, (National Geographic, August 2008), p.64
[782] *Ahmadinejad at Columbia Parries and Puzzles*, Helene Cooper, New York Times, 25th September 2007 http://www.nytimes.com/2007/09/25/world/middleeast/25iran.html?ex=1348372800&en=1855db4aa3b90a29&ei=5088&partner=rssnyt&emc=rss

friendly treatment.'

This episode has not been reported here as an attempt to offer support to Ahmadinejad or the Iranian regime but to demonstrate how the Nuremberg-created culture of political correctness and our childish reactions to what we regard as political evil are stifling the breadth of discourse in western society. Another recent example of this took place at Oxford University on November 27th 2007, when the historian, David Irving and the leader of the British National Party, Nick Griffin, were scheduled to appear in debate at the Union Building. The level of protest at their appearance was such that the debate could not proceed as planned and the two speakers had to be diverted into separate rooms to conduct isolated 'mini debates'.

In an article in which Irving was nonsensically described as 'a historian who denied the Holocaust ever happened'[783], the BBC confirmed that hundreds of protestors blocked the entrance to the Union building and at one point fifty gained entry and prevented whatever debate was taking place from continuing.[784] Comments from some of the protestors indicated the reasons for their anger. They chanted 'Go home Nazi scum!' and 'BNP – off our streets!' 'This has nothing to do with free speech,' said one, bizarrely, 'it's about giving credibility to fascists, making them appear to be part of the mainstream.' For such illogic to work, we would need to infer that those responsible for organising the chamber debates at the Oxford Union have some kind of pro-fascist agenda.

When reading about these occurrences, one has to force oneself to remember that this is not starving mobs, rallying against oppressors in some desperate third world dictatorship we are talking about, but crowds, mostly comprised of young academics, at two of the foremost seats of learning in the world. Yet these individuals, rather than investigating the people they are attacking, rather than engaging them in discussion and countering their arguments with their own views, would prefer to simply see them silenced. The irony, lost on most of them, is that they feel able to do this in one breath and decry 'fascism' in the next. What is silencing of political opponents and stifling of controversial views if not fascistic?

What is even more worrying is that these people, comprising what could be described as our future intellectual elite, are happy to shout and scream and denounce from a position of ignorance. They have simply bought into the image of the evil enemy painted for them by the media.

Such knee-jerk condemnation is also evidenced by the attitude of colleagues and students to Arthur Butz, one of the world's most notorious Holocaust deniers, and author of 'The Hoax of the Twentieth Century: The Case Against the Presumed Extermination of European Jewry'. (1974) Butz also happens to be a tenured Professor of Electrical Engineering at Northwestern University in Illinois. As a result of his published work, which obviously has nothing to do with his teaching position, he has been subjected to a sustained campaign to have him sacked. According to a letter printed in the Chicago Tribune, on February 17th 2006, Sixty-one of Butz's colleagues in the Department of Electrical Engineering and Computer Science published a petition in which they called for Butz to 'leave our Department and our University and stop trading on our reputation for academic excellence.' None of them however, were prepared to offer any details regarding Butz' book and where, precisely they felt he was in error or guilty of falsification. Students at the University followed suit by starting the 'Never Again' campaign, which, on the 30th November 2007, had 10,032 signatures. The campaign described Butz as 'offensive and historically inaccurate' and stated, 'The goal of students, faculty, alumni, and others offended by Arthur Butz's denial of the Holocaust should not be to prove him wrong. Debating Mr Butz in any type of forum would dignify his claims. Lending credibility and dignity to Arthur Butz by engaging him in debate would be equally offensive as his views are to begin with.'[785]

Obviously, something about Butz' book makes him worthy of this sort of vilification. But by the kind of specious reasoning outlined above, whereby Butz is claimed to be 'historically inaccurate', yet no specifics are ever mentioned, the campaigners avoid ever having to address any particular claim in the book, in any way. One wonders how many of them have even read it.

The bottom line, as it applies to all three situations described above, regardless of where anybody may

---

[783] The statement is either ignorantly or deliberately misleading. Irving denied the existence of gas chambers at Auschwitz, nothing else. He even accepts the existence of other gas chambers at Treblinka, Sobibor and Majdanek. He is therefore, in no way, a 'denier'. Such repeated inaccuracy of reporting is symptomatic of the sheer tonnage of misinformation that surrounds this subject.
[784] 'Angry Scenes Greet Oxford Debate' BBC News, 27th November 2007 http://news.bbc.co.uk/1/hi/england/oxfordshire/7114343.stm
[785] http://www.neveragaincampaign.org

stand on the memory/denial continuum, is that University is simply not meant to work on that level. It is supposed to be about investigation, honest analysis, intellectual freedom and open debate. That's how we learn.

But political correctness has put an end to that.

Probably the most striking evidence of the hypocritical culture that Nuremberg created is contained within the treatment of those still pursued for their guilt on its charges. The chain of trials triggered by the IMT has continued into the very recent past, with possibilities of more in the near future. Operation Last Chance, a joint project of the Simon Wiesenthal Center and Targum Shlishi Foundation, was launched in July 2002 as 'a campaign to bring remaining Nazi war criminals to justice by offering financial rewards for information leading to their arrest and conviction.'[786] They give an example of the kind of individual they are targeting, by writing, on their home page, in November 2007, 'If he is still alive, former SS medical officer Aribert Heim is 93 years old, but his age will not protect the alleged Nazi war criminal from justice...'

It goes on to relate that a bounty of nearly half a million dollars has been placed on Heim, a Mauthausen doctor who was first indicted in 1962 and fled Germany for South America. There are, obviously, question marks over the legitimacy of trying a 93 year old for alleged crimes committed more than sixty years ago. However, under international law, there is no statute of limitations allowed by *any* state on Crimes against Humanity.[787] Strictly speaking then, although perhaps many might doubt the value of rounding up nonagenarians, it would seem it does have a legal basis and therefore cannot be questioned. The state of Israel has been something of a prime mover on such matters, as one might expect, as shown by the farcical goings on surrounding John Demjanjuk, a Ukrainian/American auto-worker from Cleveland, who was accused of being the sadistic Treblinka guard 'Ivan the Terrible'.

When evidence came their way regarding Demjanjuk's wartime activities, the Israeli government argued forcibly for deportation and Demjanjuk was extradited and tried in Israel, in 1993, where he was positively identified by five former Treblinka inmates, who swore they had seen him in the vicinity of the camp's gas chamber. He was found guilty and sentenced to death by hanging. After spending five years on Israel's death row, he was eventually exonerated when it emerged that the American Justice department had 'fraudulently withheld evidence...to curry favour with Jewish organizations.'[788] The judges concluded that the Office for Special Investigation (a section of the Justice department especially set up to investigate Nazi war criminals) and the prosecutors had 'acted with reckless disregard for the truth.'[789] A Treblinka Nazi identity card, supposedly his, was, quite simply, a forgery. Demjanjuk had never even been to Treblinka. What this says about the quality of eyewitness testimony speaks for itself.

His ordeal looks set to repeat itself however, as continued pressure has seen him indicted again, in 2007, this time not for being 'Ivan the Terrible' but for being a regular guard at several other Nazi camps. (He was actually captured while fighting for the Red Army and conscripted by the Nazis as a camp guard. Perhaps he is doubly evil therefore, having managed to be both a Commie and a Nazi.) At the time this book was being written, Demjanjuk, now 87 and having already served five years in Israel on false charges, was appealing extradition for another trial in the Ukraine.

To gain a full picture of the legal climate created by Nuremberg, however, we probably ought to compare Demjanjuk's case to one that is similar, to see if any conclusions can be drawn.

Salomon Morel is a Polish Jew now living in Israel. During the expulsions that occurred post-war, when twelve million Germans were forced from their homes, via camps, to the newly diminished German state, Morel was the commandant of the Zgoda concentration camp in Świętochłowice, Poland. While in charge there it is alleged that Morel maintained an utterly brutal regime, in which food and medical supplies were provided to him, but purposely withheld from the inmates and conditions were contrived to be as unsanitary as possible. It is also alleged that he personally tortured and murdered prisoners. Estimates vary, but usually range from between one and a half to two thousand people killed by Morel during his time in charge. Several thousand more suffered horribly under his regime. The inmates were predominately civilians, including

---

[786] http://www.operationlastchance.org
[787] Baasiouni, Cherif *'Crimes Against Humanity'* in *'Crimes of War'* edited by Roy Gutman, David Rieff and Antony Dworkin, (W.W Norton, 1999)
[788] *Judges Assail US handling of Demjanjuk*, Stephen Labaton, New York Times, 18th November 1993
[789] ibid

women and children. Like Heim, Morel fled when it became clear that Polish authorities intended to prosecute him, (to Israel in 1992) but at this point, his and the other stories mentioned above diverge.

Astonishingly, Israel has refused to extradite Morel, despite repeated requests from Poland, the last of which was made in 2005.[790] In a bizarre piece of justification, their first refusals were based on a claim that the statute of limitations on War Crimes had run out. Poland then tried again, having redefined Morel's charge as Crimes against Humanity. With complete disregard for international law and the precedent set on many occasions by themselves, Israel refused again. The Polish Institute for National Remembrance then issued a terse statement in which they reminded the Israeli government of the pressure they and the Simon Wiesenthal Centre had applied to other countries to extradite aged Nazis and promised not to let the matter drop. It will be interesting to see if and how the story re-emerges.

The double standard here is clear to any but the most blinkered of observers and is illustrative of Nuremberg's influence on the post war world. The gilded, pseudo-moralistic rhetoric employed by the prosecution, referring time and time again to the defendants' wickedness and depravity in order to justify the actions of their own states, has spawned a culture in which America and its close allies call the shots and are the ethical arbiters.

Good guys and bad guys. White hats and black. And those who have cast themselves as the heroes (or victims) believe they can do no wrong, provided they do so under the guise of 'fighting evil'.

---

[790] *War Crime Suspect Stays in Israel*, BBC News, 7th July 2005 http://news.bbc.co.uk/1/hi/world/europe/4659985.stm

22
An Unseen Tyrant?

'As long as only those with a vested interest in economic liberalism are at the helm in authoritarian democracies – which are not really democracies at all... they will drive their peoples and their youth to the slaughtering block for the sake of their economic power, for their money bags, for their mammon. And the peoples will be stupid enough and will be kept stupid enough, to go to war in the belief that they are fighting for their fatherland. But they are fighting only to maintain the domination of capital over labour and for the interest paid on that capital.' [791]

-Adolf Hitler

The demonisation of Nazi Germany and by extension, Hitler has occurred largely as a result of the issues discussed in the previous three chapters. To make any concession to Nazism or to say or write anything about it which could be perceived as positive is to ally oneself with a demon and thereby to become one. This means that all Nazism ever receives, in both academic and popular writing is blanket condemnation, conducted with almost religious fervour. Hitler is either portrayed as a laughable mental-case or some kind of evil Demigod. Such is the hysteria surrounding the subject, that in many parts of the world, Germany included, anyone who deviates from this condemnatory norm can find themselves prosecuted and gaoled.

Nazism, we are led to believe, was an empty-headed doctrine. It was a smoke-and-mirrors trick, built with hearts and hands, not brains, cemented with hatred on a platform of ritual and symbol. It appealed to people's basest instincts. Western universities find nothing of merit in it and within the typical Social-Science or History faculty, anyone who professed to Nazi or even fascist inclinations would be sacked. Extremism, we believe, has no place in the foreground of a liberal democracy and when it rears its head, it is the duty of the moderate centre to beat it down. Despite this however, it is perfectly commonplace to find lecturers and researchers in our seats of learning who profess to be Marxists of some ilk or other. Following the example set by the Frankfurt School[792], the far left, it seems, is acceptable. This has meant that academia, rather than presenting a centred, balanced perspective has been left-leaning for a very long time.

In reality, however, the far-right movements of the early twentieth century, first in Italy and then in Germany grew from a complicated process of intellectual development. Not only that, but they shared many similarities with leftist ideas. Indeed, their origins lay in the crisis of Marxism in the 1880s and they then evolved through the thinking of Henri Bergson, William James, Gabriel Tarde, Ludwig Gumplowicz and many others. A variety of schools of thought were synthesised along the way. In essence, the ideas and principles which formed the far right were certainly no less sophisticated and arguably more so than those that formed the far left. They represented both an absorbtion and a development of Marxist ideology.[793] Through this they appealed to many intellectuals and thinkers of the day. George Bernard Shaw, for example, was an avowed admirer of Mussolini and Hitler. The former British Prime Minister, David Lloyd George was effusive in his praise after an official visit to Germany. It is true that far right movements engaged in populism to ensnare support, but all political groups do this. To claim this is all they had to offer is dishonest.

It is odd that modern academia deems these movements to be unworthy of deeper study and fit only for caricature and demonisation, while the ideas of Marx and his many leftist offshoots receive so much attention and analysis. This discrepancy is especially problematic to explain when one remembers that the Marxist influenced regimes of the twentieth century, in particular Maoist China and Stalinist Russia committed terrible genocidal atrocities, with official victim counts that far exceeded the Nuremberg numbers for Nazi Germany.

---

[791] Wagener, Otto, *Hitler: Memoirs of a Confidant*. Henry Ashby Turner Jr (ed) Ruth Hein (trans) (Yale University Press 1985) p.58-59

[792] The Frankfurt School developed Marxist theory, partly in reaction to events in Nazi Germany. It refers to a collective of dissident Marxists such as Max Horkheimer, Herbert Marcuse and Jürgen Habermas. During the Nazi period they fled to America, returning after the war. Their ideas are perceived to have been highly influential all over the world.

[793] Steele, David Ramsay, *The Mystery of Fascism* http://www.la-articles.org.uk/fascism.htm

How do we explain this? How do we account for the fact that regimes built on Marxism, which were brutal, oppressive, murderous and nationalistic have not received the same level of demonisation as Nazi Germany or even Fascist Italy, which conducted no programme of genocide[794] and that the doctrine on which these sadistic states were built is still an acceptable one to follow? The answer, of course, has roots in Nuremberg.

China and Russia, unlike Nazi Germany, were not defeated in World War Two. Unlike Nazi Germany they were never tried before the world and unlike Nazi Germany they do not have vociferous and influential minority groups constantly rehashing their crimes in campaigns of remembrance. Equally, as China and Russia were Allied nations, eventually becoming permanent members of the UN Security Council, and despite the polemics of Cold War propaganda, their crimes have not been repeatedly alluded to by Western heads of state seeking to justify their own imperial agendas. If these crimes were highlighted, after all, and received the same level of demonisation as those of Nazi Germany, perhaps also if the crimes of the Anglo/American bombing campaigns and the post-war expulsions of German civilians received the same demonisation, then the moral crusade that World War Two has been portrayed as would become besmirched. It is not so easy to justify your entry into the war on the basis that you were trying to defeat a mass murderer, if you allied with another, far worse mass murderer in order to do so and then became a mass murderer yourself. This is perhaps why it is so important for some to promote the idea that the Holocaust was 'unique'.

The politicised and propagandistic nature of the trial created this dishonest ethos. All the dirt that could be dug on Nazism was uncovered and presented to the world, while anything about it which may have been worthy of consideration was buried. The crimes of the Allies were similarly hidden from view. Photographs of Hiroshima, shortly after the explosion, showing carpets of bodies covering the streets have only recently been declassified and released, for example,[795] whereas the pictures of corpse-piles at Belsen have been ubiquitous since the war's end. And it is this fundamental bias, this victor's narrative, that has become the nature of political correctness – a false, pseudo-moralistic doctrine, built from a false, pseudo-moralistic legal process, that achieves nothing other than restricting freedom of thought and expression.

Having established that The Nuremberg Trial was a politically motivated and not a legally motivated action, the analyst is drawn toward even more challenging questions. The overt politicisation of events, current or historical, does not happen by accident. It is always a contrived process, enacted to serve the interests of some group or other. We must therefore ask who, specifically, in this case, such a group might be. Whose interests did the trial serve? And whose interests does the political climate it created continue to serve?

The easy answer is that it served the purposes of the Allied states, more specifically Britain and America (and to some extent this is true). Readers might then assume that it is in fact the political leaders of such nations, who are forcing the behind-the-scenes agenda. Yet such an assumption would fail to take account of the other layer of the picture.

Another over-simplification (and it is relatively easy to find people who subscribe to this opinion even in the modern world) would be that the trial served the purposes of 'The Jews'. Clearly however, such a statement is ridiculous, if for no other reason than for the fact that it describes millions of people living in a global diaspora with a diverse range of interests. 'The Jews' have no universal agenda just as 'the Muslims' or 'the Christians' do not. Some Jews may indeed have benefited, but it is necessary to focus on specifics, not generalisations.

On an ideological level, and as mentioned on many occasions during this book, the theme of democracy defeating dictatorship was one heavily used by the prosecution at the trial itself, by the Allied leaders when setting up the United Nations and in the years since by the USA in its ongoing conflicts with Communism, terrorism and Islamo-fascism. Much of the crusade against *evil* has this philosophy justifying it.

To many casual observers it may seem to make some sense. The idea that the people of a nation should be allowed to rule themselves through democratic government has the ring of justice and nobility to it. The idea that people should have to bow to the whims of a Führer seems antiquated and abhorrent. Yet we must also accept that nations have the right to choose their own system of government. It is clearly not the respon-

---

[794] Italy passed anti-Semitic laws in 1938 but conducted no deportations of its own. When Germany occupied Italy in 1943, some 7,000 Italian Jews were deported to the Nazi camp system.
[795] The pictures of Hiroshima available for sixty years after WW2 only showed the town after the streets had been cleared.

sibility of the West to impose upon other nations a form of legislature which it deems to be acceptable.

Beyond that also has to lie the acknowledgement that democracy, as practiced throughout the modern west has strayed so far from its original principles as to be unworthy of the name. Plato would barely recognize what goes on in Westminster or Washington. At present, the citizen's role in the democratic process consists merely of participating in a ballot every four to five years and as a result, the vast mass of the populace of western nations are politically disconnected and pay little attention to issues or policies. Election choices, for those who bother to make them, are shaped largely by the media. It can come as no surprise therefore that the people who win elections tend to be those who can afford to run lavish and sophisticated media campaigns. In this culture, presentation rules over content. It is said, for example, that a major stumbling block for Michael Foot, the Labour party leader of the early eighties and arguably the last real Labour leader, was that he was too scruffy. The 'loony left' tag was far easier applied to a scarecrow in a duffle coat than it would have been to a handsome executive in Saville Rowe cloth. Neil Kinnock, Foot's successor, fared only marginally better at the polls, being equally incapable of playing to the camera. It can be no coincidence, aside from a change in party direction, that it was not until Labour appointed Tony Blair, a media-savvy populist, that they finally achieved electoral success again.

Obviously the sub-plot is that these glossy media drives must be funded. Political parties do not have deep enough pockets for this and they therefore seek assistance from corporate interests who sponsor their efforts. In the 2001 General Election, which they eventually won with a landslide, the Labour Party spent £14 million on their campaign. Thirty-three percent of this came from the traditional support of Trade Unions, with the majority of the rest coming from 'corporate and individual donations.'[796] It would be naive in the extreme to believe that such corporate interests do this through an altruistic regard for the democratic process. Very simply, once they have sponsored a political party or figure into office, they can expect a continued close relationship with them during their period of power. As it would be foolish for the party or individual concerned to bite the hand that feeds, they can also expect some influence in the policy decisions of the government and preferential treatment of various kinds, as demonstrated by the 'cash for honours' enquiry of 2007 into the funding activities of the Labour Party during Tony Blair's last years of office. Such behind-the-scenes manipulation suggests that it is these corporate interests that hold the real power in the world, not the general citizenry of any nation, regardless of whether it is nominally a democracy or not.

This helps to shed some light upon the motivations for Britain and America's madcap military dash into the Middle-East. Its basis, when examined in the light of Nuremberg, becomes clearer. It is being done to secure the oil-based, economic interests of the corporate bodies who sponsor the governments. The USA's failure to sign the Kyoto agreement is for the same reason. Some modern analysts choose to describe this hidden influence as a 'conspiracy'. Others, even more unwisely, as the Nazis on trial at Nuremberg did, have referred to it as a 'global Jewish conspiracy' referring to the Jewish led organisations and bodies which form a substantial part of the neo-conservative movement. Of course, it is neither of these. The religious or ethnic composition of the global elite is broadly irrelevant, although it does have a bearing on modern international affairs, particularly in Israel/Palestine. The idea that they form a conspiracy of any kind is foolish. All they have in common is financial clout and the desire to maintain their own position. On a fundamental level, it is clear that this is simply wealthy and powerful people doing what wealthy and powerful people have always done – protecting their own interests, at all costs.

It needs therefore to be recognised that it is not the elite themselves, whoever they are, that are the enemy of real freedom, of mankind coming to terms with its past or accomplishing in the future. The elite are simply human and engage in behaviour commensurate with human nature. The hatred of those who feel oppressed or marginalised should not therefore be directed at any particular group. The enemy, in so far as it exists, is not other people but the system that allows the few to dominate the many and encourages self interest above the greater good. And this is a problem that is simple to rectify. Commentators often decry the apathy of the western public with regard to their elections. Voter turnout, we are told, hits record lows with almost every passing ballot. This should be of no surprise to anybody. The citizens of the west are not being asked to participate in a democracy in any meaningful sense of the word. The parameters within which any government must operate, set by the hidden pressures of the sponsors, are so narrow that differences between parties are

---

[796] *Explained: Labour Party Funding*, Julian Glover, The Guardian, Monday July 22nd 2002, http://www.guardian.co.uk/politics/2002/jul/22/labour.uk1

often negligible. The system is rather a disguised Plutocracy[797]. This is effectively a world system of government, as it holds sway over the world's most powerful countries. By reducing culture to snapshot, image-happy, sound-bitism, and by gathering most of our information from the television, we have reduced ourselves to being irrelevant as far as the democratic process goes. We are too easily manipulated.

This does not have to be the case, although most commonly touted alternatives to representative democ- racy are broadly unconsionsable. The ideal of the 'philospher king', for example, perhaps best embodied by Charlemagne, which Hitler, among others, have since aspired to, seems to always carry with it the unwelcome baggage of violence and oppression. But there is no reason at all why the democratic process cannot be adjusted to make it more compatible with the era in which we now live. The current system of representative democracy was created in a time of horse drawn carriages and town criers, when sending a message from London to Canterbury took two days. In any nation larger than a small village conferring with the public on any kind of regular basis was simply not possible. Centuries ago, before minds were so easily swayed by television, before we became 'information rich,' the five yearly ballot was the only workable system. In the twenty-first century however, we have fibre optic cables, high speed internet and wireless communication systems. The average mobile phone is more powerful than computers were in the eighties. If it is possible to send instant details of every burger restaurant within a quarter-mile to an individual walking along Tottenham Court Road, it is surely possible to engage the population in a more active role in the government of their country. Internet petitions can gather thousands of signatures in a few hours. Why not use this technology for a real purpose?

In short, there is a strong case to be made for the abandonment of representative democracy. In 2008, it is an anachronism. It could be replaced with a system more in line with the Athenian model, in which referenda were offered, via the web, or some similar platform, on all issues. Political apathy would then become irrele- vant. Those interested in any particular issue would vote. The parties could remain, largely as lobbying bod- ies. And issues of worldwide implication, such as waging war, or refusing to take steps to preserve the planet for future generations, could not be smuggled into legislation without the backing of the people.

Rather than hiding in the easy, infantile option of demonology and childish caricature, there are three obvious lessons that should be learnt from the pre and post Nuremberg era. The first, which is undoubtedly the sound-bite that alarmists and tub-thumpers will choose to repeat from this book is this: Nazism was not *evil*. Neither was Adolf Hitler. Hitler was a man. He had considerable abilities in some areas and deficiencies in others. He had lots of ideas. Some of them were perhaps strange, some of them clearly misguided and objectionable, but some of them were also quite insightful and worthy of attention. In other words, within Hitler existed the same mixture of talent and fallibility that exists within most of us. Nazism, far from being some sort of mystical, demonic, cult, was a political doctrine, created by men. Therefore it was flawed, as all creations of men are. However there are certainly elements of it from which we could learn, if only we were prepared to calm down and examine it rationally.

Secondly, what we now refer to as the Holocaust was an immense tragedy for the Jewish people of Europe, within the much greater human tragedy of the war as a whole. And just as in all nations or communities, where one can find rituals of remembrance of historic events that have affected that group, it is entirely justified for Jewish communities to remember the Holocaust. However, the Holocaust's special place in world affairs, in which its memorialisation and protection from desecration is enshrined in international law[798] is an anomaly. Those who wish to remember the Holocaust should be able to do so but it should not be forced upon everyone. This is a form of fascism. No other genocides are accorded this status.

Finally, it should be clear to anyone who studies the sorry tale of death and despair that was and continues to be the story of our recent past, that tyranny is still alive and well. Moreover, tyranny does not have to have a silly moustache, a wardrobe full of rather camp uniforms or a penchant for bombastic speech making. In fact, it usually doesn't. Tyranny may be more subtle than that. To some extent it may be self-imposed. And perhaps, in reality, it is only when the methods and outcomes of tyranny become too overt, that it finally gets overthrown. To fight against your enemy, you first have to recognise it.

---

[797] Plutocracy is rule by a moneyed elite.
[798] In 2005, a United Nations declaration made Holocaust remembrance a national duty for all member states.

Epilogue

The Conceits of Academia

The only thing man learns from history, is that he learns nothing from history.
Winston Churchill.

In as much as this book has investigated the first, great Nuremberg Trial and its consequences, it has also, in one sense, examined History. And History, like all human pursuits, is imperfect.

History is founded on conceits.

The first of these is the conceit of objectivity, the belief that a human being who has been bombarded with imagery, information and ideology since birth can ever be truly objective about anything. Academics argue from points of view of logic and evidence and causes (see below) and think that they have educated themselves beyond bias. By cross-referencing, evaluating sources and accurate record keeping they intend to get at the 'truth'. Yet powerful narratives emerge and these same objective academics all display degrees of conformity to them, even when their evidence suggests other possible conclusions. They are as much subject to the herd instinct as anybody.

The second is the conceit of causation – the idea that phenomena can be explained by three or five[799] interacting factors and tidied into a rational conclusion. It is notable that historical writers never seem to explain anything happening for seventeen reasons, or twenty-three, or a hundred-and-six. Why not? Because it would be boring to read. The majority of readers would persevere for the first few and drift away, having forgotten the original point. Bowing to the needs of their audience, they therefore bow also to the diktats of literary convention and the 'rule of three'.

Finally, and well known to anyone familiar with the deconstructive ideas of postmodernism, we have the conceit of knowledge – the idea that it is possible to know and state anything as 'fact'. Many view such thinking as pointless, as the death of education and an excuse for anything. In regard to history, however it is particularly applicable (more so perhaps than in Physics or Geology, where the controlled experiment will produce verifiable results.)

It can be said that once upon a time, in simpler days, the historian was viewed as sitting on a hilltop, surveying the landscape of years gone by as it stretched out beneath him. He was able to pick out particular areas, examine them from his vantage point and sketch them with accuracy. It was this sort of thinking that gave birth to the Rankean paradigm to which establishment History still clings. *Erzählen, wie es eigentlich gewesen ist.* (To tell how it actually happened.) Challenges to this approach have been numerous, however. Eric Hobsbawm, as just one example, wrote of how the state, respected figures, literature and the media have 'invented history'.[800] Today, as mass media and information technology continue to deluge us with alternative views, forcing us to look outside of the confines of our own tiny worlds[801], it is more sensible to think of the historian as an astronaut, floating in the vast, three-dimensional vacuum of space. Whatever small part of it he manages to map, there will always be things around the periphery he has failed to account for, probably even things in front of his eyes he did not see or recognise and if he flipped the UV filter on his visor, he would be faced with an entirely new (although connected) scene and entirely new (although connected) data. He would have to start again from the beginning.[802] The vastness of the past precludes real answers to the very questions historians are supposed to answer. This means that all historians can really do, in common

---

[799] More often than not it is three, due to the 'rule of three' a basic literary technique. By the way, I am aware of the irony of decrying the rule of three in a list of three items, but the point remains unaltered – it affects all of us, including historians.
[800] Hobsbawm, Eric, *The Invention of Tradition*, (Cambridge University Press, 1983) p.12
[801] For example, during the Iraq war, it has been possible to see the coalition version of an event on the BBC or Sky TV, then log on to the internet and read or view what Al Jazeera had to say. Never before has there been such freedom of information.
[802] When a historian writing about the origins of World War Two chooses to begin his story is a good example of this. He may start in twenties and thirties, as the Nazis rose to power. He could begin in 1919, at Versailles, or in 1904, at the Anglo-French 'entente', or even at the formation of the state of Germany in 1871. Perhaps he might even choose an earlier date. Whichever choice he makes, he will necessarily be excluding an enormous amount of relevant information.

with any writer, is lay their own soul bare upon the page. Their choice of what to write about, of which material to use and what to ignore is simply an expression of human limitations.

Some historians do this better than others. Most demonstrate their lack of courage – it is safer, of course, not to say anything *too* different. Some have been involved in the ultimate conceit of academia, that it is possible to 'know', that persuasively arguing a case proves its truth, for so long, they probably believe it themselves. After all, an academic who did his three years as an undergraduate, then a masters degree, followed by a doctorate and a few professorial or research positions has little experience of anything else. The world, as he knows it, *is* theoretical. Although they might like to think so, therefore, people like Jeffrey Herf, Lucy Davidowicz and Daniel Goldhagen are not fiercely intentionalist, pro-Israel and (in at least one case) viciously anti-German because they have discovered and revealed facts. Not really. They are intentionalist, pro-Israel and anti-German because they have discovered and revealed themselves.

Such reasoning can, of course, also be applied to the contents and author of this book and I am happy to accept that. But it is hoped that if nothing else it has been clearly demonstrated that the narrative we have in regard to Nuremberg and its place in world affairs is not unchallengeable. History *never* is.

It is the duty and the responsibility of history to attend to alternative narratives, to encourage genuine debate and to seek out 'truths' through real, open discourse. It is essential that this begins to happen with regard to World War Two and Nuremberg. The good vs evil polemic served a purpose for a time, but has run its course. None but the most gullible can sustain faith in it. Furthermore, the new narrative is arriving, despite medieval attempts to crush it.

If we want to apply our knowledge of the past to what has happened more recently, in Iraq, in Israel, even in Sudan, Rwanda or East Timor, then we need to be more critical in our analysis of it. The interests and sensitivities of particular interest groups should be considered, but not upheld at all costs. Questioning is always healthy.

By enshrining aspects of history in law and imprisoning or defaming individuals who wish to provide an alternative, the world has demonstrated that it has learnt nothing from the past. After all, such people (even if they are misguided) are simply contributing, in the only way that works, to the development of human understanding.

References

All trial documents and quoted sections are reproduced with permission from The Avalon Project at Yale Law School. http://www.yale.edu/lawweb/avalon/avalon.htm

Selected Bibliography

Allman, TD, *Rogue State, America at war with the World*, (Nation books, 2004)
Ambrose, Stephen and Bischoff, Gunther, *Eisenhower and the German POWs, Facts against Falsehood* (Louisiana State University Press, 1993)
Arendt, Hannah, *Eichmann in Jerusalem, a Report on the Banality of Evil* (Penguin, 1994 new ed.)
Baker, Nicholson, *Human Smoke* (Simon and Schuster 2008)
Bacque, James, *Other Losses*, (Prima 1991)
Beschloss, Michael R, *The Conquerors: Roosevelt, Truman and the Destruction of Hitler's Germany, 1941 – 1945* (Simon & Schuster 2002)
Bloxham, Donald, *Genocide on Trial*, (Oxford University Press, 2001)
Blum, John Morton, *From the Morgenthau Diaries: Years of War, 1941 – 1945* (Houghton-Mifflin, 1967)
Blum, William, *Killing Hope, Military and CIA interventions since World War Two* (Zed books, 2003)
Bosch, W. *Judgment on Nuremberg* (University of North Carolina Press, 1971)
Brenner, Lenny, *51 Documents: Zionist Collaboration with the Nazis* (Barricade 2002)
Butler, Rupert, *Legions of Death*. (Hamlyn, 1983)
Churchill, Winston, *Closing the Ring* (Penguin, 1954)
Churchill, Winston, *The Grand Alliance*, (Penguin 1954)
Churchill, Winston, *The Tide of Victory*, (Penguin, 1954)
Conot, Robert E, *Justice at Nuremberg*, (Carrol & Graf 1983)
Davidowicz, Lucy, S. *The War Against the Jews 1933-1945* (Bantam Books, 1976)
Davidson, Eugene *The Trial of the Germans* (first ed. 1966, reprint University of Missouri Press 1997)
De Zayas, Alfred-Maurice *A Terrible Revenge, the ethnic cleansing of the East European Germans* (St Martins Press 1994)
Dodd, Christopher, J, *Letters from Nuremberg* (Crown 2007)
Douglas, Lawrence, *The Memory of Judgement* (Yale University Press 2001)
Eisenhower, Dwight D, *Crusade in Europe* (1948, reprinted Main Street Books, 1990)
Ellis, John, *The World War Two Databook.* (Aurum Press, 1993)
Fest, Joachim C, *The Face of the Third Reich*, (Pelican 1972)
Finkelstein, Norman, *Beyond Chutzpah, On the Misuse of Anti-Semitism and the Abuse of History*, (Verso, 2005)
Finkelstein, Norman *The Holocaust Industry* (Verso, 2000)
FitzGibbon, Constantine, *Denazification* (W. W. Norton, 1969)
Foreign Office, The, *Instructions for British Servicemen in Germany, 1944* (Bodleian Library, University of Oxford, 2007, first published by the Foreign Office, 1944)
Gall, Lothar, *Krupp. Der Aufstieg eines Industrieimperiums*, (Berlin 2000)
Gilbert, G.M., *Nuremberg Diary* (Da Capo 1995)
Gilbert, Martin, *The Holocaust, the Jewish Tragedy*, (Fontana 1987)
Gilbert, Martin, *Recent History Atlas*, (Weidenfeld and Nicholson, 1966, 3rd ed, 1977)
Ginsberg, Benjamin *The Fatal Embrace* (University of Chicago Press 1993)
Ginsburgs, George & Kudriavtes, *The Nuremberg Trial and International Law*. (Martin Nijhoff, 1990)
Goldensohn, Leon, *The Nuremberg Interviews* (Pimlico 2006)
Grayling, A.C. *Among the Dead Cities. Is the targeting of civilians in war ever justified?* (Bloomsbury 2007)
Gutman, Roy, Rieff, David and Dworkin, Antony (eds) *'Crimes of War'* (W.W Norton, 1999)
Hague, Arnold. *Destroyers for Great Britain: A History of 50 Town Class Ships Transferred from the United States to Great Britain in 1940.* (Annapolis MD, Naval Institute Press, 1990.)
Harris, Whitney R. *Tyranny on Trial: The Evidence at Nuremberg* (SMU Press, 1954)
Herf, Jeffrey, *The Jewish Enemy: Nazi Propaganda During World War Two and the Holocaust* (Belknap Press, 2006)
Hilberg, Raul, *The Destruction of the European Jews*, (Yale University Press, 2003)

Hitler, Adolf, *Mein Kampf* (reprinted Jaico Books 1988)
Hobsbawm, Eric, *The Invention of Tradition*, (Cambridge University Press, 1983)
Hoess, Rudolf, *Commandant of Auschwitz*, (Weidenfeld and Nicholson 1959)
Hughes, Emrys, *Winston Churchill – his career in War and Peace*, (Unity Publishing 1950)
Irving, David, *Nuremberg, The Last Battle*, (Focal Point Publications 1997)
Kelley, Douglas, M. *22 Cells in Nuremberg: A Psychiatrist Examines the Nazi Criminals* (Greenberg, 1947)
Kennan, George F, *Russia And The West, Under Lenin and Stalin* (Signet, 1962)
Knierem, August von, *Nürnberg* (Ernst Klett, Stuttgart, 1953)
Marrus, Michael, R, *The Nuremberg War Crimes Trial, 1945-6, A Documentary History,* (Bedford Books 1997)
Marwick, Arthur, *The Nature Of History* (Macmillan 3rd ed. 1989)
Maser, Werner, *Nuremberg, a Nation on Trial*, (Penguin, 1977)
McDonagh, Giles, *After the Reich, The Brutal History of the Allied Occupation*, (Basic books, 2007)
McMillan, J, *Five Men at Nuremberg* (Harrap 1985)
Murphy, Robert, *Diplomat Among Warriors*, (Collins, 1964)
Neave, Airey, *Nuremberg* (Coronet 1978)
Nietzsche, Friedrich *Beyond Good and Evil* (Dover Publications, 1997)
Overy, Richard, *Interrogations, The Nazi Elite in Allied Hands*, 1945 (Viking, 2001)
Overy, R.J. *The Origins of the Second World war* 2nd ed, (Longman, 1998)
Padfield, Peter, *Hess, The Führer's Disciple* (Papermac 1995)
Persico, Joseph E, *Nuremberg, Infamy on Trial*, (Penguin 1994)
Preperata, Guido, Giacomo, *Conjuring Hitler, How Britain and America made the Third Reich* (Pluto 2005)
Petrov, Vladimir, *Money and conquest; allied occupation currencies in World War II.* (Baltimore, Johns Hopkins Press, 1967)
Richardson, Stewart (ed) *The Secret History of World War Two* (WH Allen 1987)
Roosevelt, Eleanor, edited and assisted by Joseph P Nash, *The Roosevelt Letters being the Personal Correspondance of Franklin Delano Roosevelt – 1928 – 1945, Vol III*, (George Harrap, 1952)
Rozek, Edward, J *Allied Wartime Diplomacy* (John Wiley 1958)
Rushton, JP, *Race, Evolution and Behaviour* (Charles Darwin Research Institute 2000 3rd ed.)
Schopenhauer, Arthur *Parerga and Paralipomena*, (Oxford University Press 2001)
Scrase, David and Mieder, Wolfgang *(eds) The Holocaust, Introductory Essays*, (Center for Holocaust Studies, University of Vermont, 1996)
Shirer, William L. *The Rise and Fall of the Third Reich* (Pan 1960)
Seidler, Franz W. *Das Recht in Siegerhand: Die 13 Nürnberger Prozesse 1945-49* (Pour le Merite 2007)
Speer, Albert, *Inside the Third Reich*, (Book Club Associates London, 1971)
Stone, Harlan Fiske, *Pillar of the Law*, (New York: Viking, 1956)
Taylor, AJP, *Origins of the Second World War* (Simon & Schuster 1961)
Taylor, Telford, *The Anatomy of the Nuremberg Trials* (Bloomsbury 1993)
Thompson, H.K. Jr. and Strutz, Henry *Dönitz at Nuremberg: A Reappraisal* (Torrance, 1983)
Tooze, Adam, *The Wages of Destruction, the making and breaking of the Nazi Economy* (Penguin 2007)
Tusa, A&J, *The Nuremberg Trial*, (MacMillan 1983)
Union of Soviet Socialist Republics, Government of, *Soviet Government Statements on Nazi Atrocities*, (Hutchinson and Co. undated)
Tzu, Sun, *The Art of War*, (Running Press 2003)
Van Pelt, Robert-Jan, *Anatomy of the Auschwitz Death Camp*, edited by Yisrael Gutman and Michael Berenbaum, (Indiana University Press 1994)
Wagener, Otto, *Hitler: Memoirs of a Confidante*. Henry Ashby Turner Jr (ed) Ruth Hein (trans) (Yale University Press 1985)
Wheeler-Bennett, John W and Nicholls, Anthony, *The Semblance of Peace* (Houghton-Mifflin, 1972)

Articles

Ahmadinejad at Columbia Parries and Puzzles, Helene Cooper, New York Times, 25th September 2007

Ahmadinejad: Holocaust a Myth, Al Jazeera, English section, Dec. 15th 2005

Ancient Soul of Iran, Marguerite del Giudice, (National Geographic, August 2008)

Angry Scenes Greet Oxford Debate BBC News, 27th November 2007

Between Enlightenment and Apocalypse, Benjamin, Block and Modern German Jewish Messianism, Anson Rabinbach, New German Critique, No.34 (1985).

Churchill: execute Hitler without trial John Crossland, The Sunday Times, January 1st, 2006

Drexel Sprecher, 92, US Prosecutor at Nuremberg, dies, Douglas Martin, New York Times, May 8th 2006

EU to agree watered-down anti-racism law, Reuters, 18th April, 2007.

Explained: Labour Party Funding, Julian Glover, The Guardian, Monday July 22nd 2002

Ike and the Disappearing Atrocities Stephen Ambrose, New York Times Book Review, Feb. 24, 1991

Gruesome Harvest: The Allies Postwar War Against the German People, Ralph Franklin Greeling (Institute of American Economics, Chicago 1947)

Judea declares War on Germany!, Daily Express, Friday March 4th 1933

Judges Assail US handling of Demjanjuk, Stephen Labaton, New York Times, 18th November 1993

Nuremberg In Retrospect: Legal Answer To International Lawlessness Robert H Jackson, American Bar Association Journal. 35 ABAJ 813 (1949)

Rabbi Wise's Address, New York Times, June 11th, 1900

Race and Nazi Racism and the Latter's Impact on Anthropology, R. Gayre of Gayre, The Mankind Quarterly, Vol. XVIII, No. 4, (April-June 1978).

Spiegel Interview with President Ahmadinejad, Der Spiegel, May 30th 2006

Stiff Ears, Time Magazine, 25th March 1946

The crucifixion of Jews must stop, Martin H Glynn, American Hebrew, October 31st 1919

Text of Untermeyer's Address, New York Times, Monday, August 7th 1933

The Casualties of Iraq, Colin Halinan, Foreign Policy in Focus, October 17th 2007

The Development of the Morgenthau Plan Through the Quebec Conference John L. Chase, The Journal of Politics, Vol. 16, No. 2 (May, 1954)

The Mystery of Fascism, David Ramsay-Steele http://www.la-articles.org.uk/fascism.htm

War Crime Suspect Stays in Israel, BBC News, 7th July 2005

Whose History Is It? Christopher Hitchens, Vanity Fair, Dec 1993.

Archived Materials/Other

British White Paper of June 1922 on Palestine http://www.yale.edu/lawweb/avalon/mideast/brwh1922.htm

Hitler's Political Will, Web Genocide Documentation Centre, University of the West of England, http://www.ess.uwe.ac.uk/documents/poltest.htm

Interrogation Records Prepared for War Crimes Proceedings at Nuernberg 1945-47 http://www.archives.gov/research/captured-german-records/microfilm/m1270.pdf

Library of Congress IMT documents
http://www.loc.gov/rr/frd/Military_Law/NT_major-war-criminals.html

Medact, Collateral Damage http://www.ippnw.org/ResourceLibrary/CollateralDamage.pdf

Minutes, Meeting of World Jewish Congress with Robert H. Jackson
http://www.trumanlibrary.org/whistlestop/study_collections/nuremberg/documents/index.php?documentdate=1945-06-12&documentid=C106-16-5&studycollectionid=&pagenumber=1

United Nations Charter http://www.un.org/aboutun/charter/index.html

US Census Bureau News, August 26th 2004 http://www.census.gov/Press-Release/www/releases/archives/income_wealth/002484.html

US Department of Justice Prison Statistics, December 31st 2006 http://www.ojp.usdoj.gov/bjs/prisons.htm

United States Strategic Survey Summary Report, European War, September 30th, 1945
http://www.anesi.com/ussbs02.htm

United States Strategic Survey Summary Report, Pacific War, July 1st, 1946
http://www.anesi.com/ussbs01.htm

Index

Act of Attainder; p.16
Albrecht, Ralph G; p.43-44
Alderman, Sydney; p.47, 113
Afghanistan, invasion of: p.126, 176
Ahmadinejad, Mahmoud; p.178-179
Amen, Colonel John Harlan; p.94, 96, 100-113, 114, 135
Anglo-German Transfer Agreement; p.110
Anschluss; p.47, 53, 86, 90, 112, 146
Arendt, Hannah; p.9-10
'Ashcan'; see Mondorf
Atlee, Clement; p.22, 104
Auschwitz (camp); p.33, 38, 44, 58-59, 94-95, 97-102, 109, 115, 121, 124, 125, 147, 153, 162, 170, 171
Bach-Zelewski, Erich von dem; 60, 87-88, 92, 95, 170
Belsen (camp); p.10, 48, 162, 173, 184
Bernays, Colonel Murray; p.23, 32, 41, 158-159, 163
Bernburg (sanatorium); p.121
Biddle, Francis; p.44, 52, 55, 56, 74, 82, 83, 128, 130-132, 138, 142, 145, 159
Birkett, Norman; p.45, 52, 55, 60, 61, 84, 90, 106
Bismarck, Otto von; p.17, 22, 42, 107, 113
Bodenschatz, General Karl; p.50-51
Bormann, Martin; p.14, 36, 41, 69, 78, 79, 80, 124, 155
Brandenburg (sanatorium); p.121
Buchenwald (camp); p.34, 48, 137
Bush, George W; p.176, 178, 184
Capeheart, Homer E; p.18-19
Chamberlain, Neville; p.30
Churchill, Winston; p.9, 16-18, 22, 24, 39, 52, 64, 66, 67, 108, 113, 161, 174, 187
Clay, General Lucius; p.19, 20
Dachau (camp); p.33, 48, 49, 94, 99, 104, 105, 127, 137, 173
Dawes Plan; p.107-108
Demjanjuk, John; p.181
Denazification; p.22, 84, 102, 111, 122, 138, 149, 175
Dix, Rudolf; p.43, 44, 61, 105, 151, 157
Dodd, Thomas; p.14, 47, 85, 106, 110, 122-126, 136, 146, 153-154, 158, 160, 168
Dönitz Karl; p.35, 40, 91, 94, 153, 154-157, 161, 185
Douglas, William; p.23
Dresden, bombing of; p.29, 158, 172
Duke of Hamilton; p.63
Eden, Anthony; p.16, 64
Eichmann, Adolf; p.9, 10, 49, 58, 86, 87, 94
Einsatzgruppen; p.45, 57, 58, 80, 86, 87, 94, 98, 166
Eisenhower, Dwight; p.19, 20, 28, 32, 79
Enabling Law; p.43, 120
Eurasian Embrace (Preparata); p.107, 110, 174, 175
Ex Post Facto; p.23, 24, 28, 39
Falco, Robert; p.26
Final Solution, the; p.45, 70-71, 74, 75, 86-87, 91-92, 95, 99, 100, 101, 120-121, 166, 169, 170
Fiske-Stone, Harlan; p.15
Flossenburg (camp); p.104
Frank, Hans; p.33, 36, 48, 86, 139, 140-146, 157, 169, 170-171
Frankfurt School, The; p.183
Frick, Wilhelm; p.36, 50, 65, 117, 119-123, 127, 128

Fritzsche, Hans; p.33, 36, 37, 38, 49, 50, 52, 61, 64, 81, 104, 148-149, 155
Funk, Walther; p.33, 36, 48, 50, 65, 81, 103-106, 111
Gas chambers; p.10, 16, 38, 44, 48, 75, 93-95, 99, 102, 121, 143, 155, 156, 162, 164, 169, 170, 171, 173
Geneva Convention; p.20, 34
Genocide; p.48, 55, 59, 60, 72, 87, 89, 97, 121, 125, 126, 137, 143, 153, 159, 162, 163, 170, 172, 173, 184
Gilbert, Gustave; p.47, 49, 50, 51, 52, 56, 57, 65-69, 79-81, 83, 104-105, 108-109, 115, 121-122, 127, 135, 145-146, 154, 156, 160
Gisevius, Hans Bernd; p.127
Goebbels, Josef; p.9, 14, 18, 32, 37, 64, 77, 78, 79, 80, 119, 148, 149
Göring, Hermann; p.15, 29, 35, 38, 40, 51-70, 72, 73, 74, 79, 89, 90, 91, 92, 93, 123, 148, 151, 153, 161, 171, 172, 185, 187
Göring, Heinrich; p.51, 157, 191
Goldensohn, Leon; p.56, 57, 65, 77, 85, 114, 159, 161, 191
Graebe, Hermann Friedrich; p.88-90, 165
Grafeneck (sanatorium); p.121
Gramsci, Antonio *cultural hegemony*; p.9
Greer incident; p.25
Griffiths Jones, Lieutenant Colonel; p.65, 73-74, 173
Hadamar (sanatorium); p.48, 120-121
Hamburg, bombing of; p.29, 174
Hartheim (sanatorium); p.121
Heim, Aribert; p.183
Hess, Rudolf; p.12, 14, 33, 34, 36, 37, 39, 41, 49, 61, 62-67, 70, 127, 130, 157, 161
Heydrich, Reinhard; p.10, 56, 86, 87, 90, 91, 101, 120, 136, 155
Himmler, Heinrich; p.9, 14, 32, 56, 57, 58, 59, 60, 66, 78, 79, 80, 85, 86, 87, 90, 91, 92, 93, 95, 96-98, 101, 120, 125, 127, 137, 138, 141, 144, 149, 154, 158, 171, 172
Hiroshima, bombing of; p.10, 29, 160, 174, 186
Hitler, Adolf; p.9, 10, 14, 16, 17, 18, 24, 25, 26, 30, 32, 33, 36, 37, 39, 42, 43, 46, 50, 51, 57, 59, 62, 63, 64, 66, 67, 69-72, 75-84, 86, 92, 96, 97, 103, 104, 105, 106, 108-115, 118-120, 122-125, 127, 128, 131, 132, 133, 135, 136, 137, 140, 143, 145, 146-155, 157, 158, 161, 162, 166, 167, 168, 171, 174, 185, 188
Hitler Youth; p.18, 33, 70, 150, 151, 152, 153, 155
Höttl, Wilhelm; p.66, 196, 199
Holocaust; p.10, 15, 16, 34, 38, 39, 49, 57-59, 63, 64, 69, 72-74, 86, 88-90, 92, 93, 95, 96, 100, 109, 115, 117, 118, 121, 125, 126, 144, 154, 160-162, 164, 165, 167-170, 172, 174-175, 177-182, 186
Höss, Rudolf; p.37, 41, 66, 114-119, 143, 171, 196
IG Farben; p.94, 108-109
Intentionalism; p.179
Iraq war; p.34, 58, 126, 178, 180, 190
Israeli war of independence; p.179
Jackson, Robert H; p.14, 15, 20, 23, 24, 26, 28-32, 37-43, 47, 50-61, 68, 73, 76, 82-84, 104, 105, 111, 118, 120, 127, 147, 151, 156, 158-162, 165, 166, 168, 170, 176
Jodl, General Alfred; p.32, 36, 37, 41, 50, 86, 130, 134-139, 158, 171
Kaltenbrunner, Ernst; p.33, 36, 38, 85-102, 136, 141, 146, 149, 153, 156, 168, 169, 171, 172

Keitel, Field Marshall Wilhelm; p.12, 32, 36, 37, 43, 44, 80, 81, 86, 97, 129, 133-138, 150, 155, 157, 167
Kelley, Douglas; p.77
Kempner, Robert; p.50, 120-121, 158
Koch, Ilse; p.34
Korean War; p.175
Kranzbühler, Otto; p.154
Krupp von Bohlen und Halbach, Gustav; p.14, 36-39, 94, 104, 110, 146
Krupp von Bohlen und Halbach, Alfried; p.39
Kube to Lohse (letter); p.125, 169
Lahousen, General Erwin; p.135
Lawrence, Geoffrey (president of tribunal); p.39, 44, 54, 55, 61, 69, 81, 100, 110, 121, 127, 128, 131, 138, 142, 145, 149, 154, 158
Ley, Robert; p.14, 33, 34, 36, 69, 70
London Charter (also Nuremberg Charter); p.22, 23, 24, 26-31, 38, 39, 41, 118, 131, 157, 158, 166, 171
Majdanek (camp); p.140, 143, 171
Mauthausen (camp); p.48, 93, 94, 96, 181
Maxwell-Fyfe, David; p.37, 57, 74, 82, 96, 98, 115, 136, 138
Mein Kampf; p.63, 71, 118
Milch, Erhard; p.51, 54
Mondorf (detention centre, also 'Ashcan'); p.32, 33, 34, 47, 72, 77, 79
Morel, Salomon; p.181-2
Morgan, JP; p.108, 109
Morgen, Konrad; p.34
Morgenthau, Henry Jr; p.17-20, 23, 78
Moscow declaration; p.17
Müller, Heinrich; p.106
Munich Beer Hall Putsch; p.63, 70
Musslolini, Benito; p.57, 183
Nagasaki, bombing of; p.29, 172
Neave, Airey; p.35, 37, 48, 55, 68, 77, 79, 83, 105, 114, 140, 149, 158, 159, 160
Neurath, Baron Konstantin von; p.36, 65, 112-116
Nikitchenko, Iona; p.26, 66, 83, 128, 138, 145, 156
Norman, Sir Montagu; p.108-110
Oberürsel (interrogation centre); p.37
Oder-Neisse Line; p.22
Ohlendorf, Otto; p.80, 87, 92, 135, 163, 169, 170, 172
Ohrdruf (camp); p.49
Papen, Franz von; p.14, 52, 65, 104, 112-113, 115-116, 136, 155, 160
Pokrovsky, Colonel Yuri V; p.39, 71, 88
Potsdam Conference; p.22, 84
Raeder, Admiral Erich; p.12, 33, 36, 37, 81, 105, 129-133, 148
Rajzman, Samuel; p.44
Rankean paradigm; p.187
Ravensbruck (camp); p.104

Ribbentrop, Joachim von; p.12, 30, 32, 36, 37, 44, 81, 83, 112-116, 136, 158, 161, 171
Richthofen, Manfred von (The Red Baron); p.46
Rosenberg, Alfred; p.32, 36, 113, 117-119, 121-126, 128, 129, 146, 150, 151, 169
Roosevelt, Franklin D; p.9, 17, 18, 22, 37, 39, 174
Rotterdam, bombing of; p.29
RSHA (Reich Security Main Office); p.58, 86, 87, 90, 93, 98-100, 135, 166
Rudenko, General Roman Andreevich; p.57, 60, 66, 100, 114, 115, 122, 129, 135, 136
Sauckel, Fritz; p.12, 32, 36, 82-84, 104, 139, 145-147, 151
Schacht, Hjalmar; p.14, 33, 36, 43, 50, 52, 65, 79, 80, 83, 103-105, 108-111, 114, 115, 148, 155-157
Schirach, Baldur von; p.12, 33, 36, 38, 47, 50, 52, 70, 81, 105, 124, 148-154
Seyss-Inquart, Arthur; p.36, 104, 139, 146, 147, 156
Shawcross, Hartley; p.39, 82, 83, 89, 113, 132, 138
Shmaglevskaya, Severina; p.44
Simultaneous translation; p.14
Sonnenstein (sanatorium); p.121
Spandau (prison); p., 66, 67, 111, 116, 132, 154
Speer, Albert; p.32, 33, 36, 50, 51, 52, 53, 76-84, 104, 105, 140, 141, 144, 146-149, 155-157, 161
Stalin, Josef; p.17, 22, 26, 66, 184
Stimson, Henry L; p.17, 23
Storey, Colonel Robert; p.43, 88, 104
Streicher, Julius; p.14, 33, 36-39, 68-75, 83, 84, 86, 91, 114, 118, 123, 128, 129, 145, 147, 149, 151, 153, 156, 170, 171
Stroop, Jürgen (The Stroop Report); p.140-141
Stürmer, Der (newspaper); p.40, 79, 80-81, 200
Taylor, Telford; p.44, 51, 52, 53, 55, 56, 57, 61, 83, 89, 98, 102, 104, 133, 134, 147, 158, 160, 168, 190
Tehran conference; p.17, 22
Treblinka (camp); p.44, 99, 140, 143, 171, 181
Truman, Harry S; p.9, 18, 22, 189
Tu quoque; p.9, 18, 22, 189
Tzu, Sun; p.9
T4 (Euthanasia programme); p.45, 48, 120, 121, 127, 162
Udet, Ernst; p.64
Versailles, Treaty of; p.16, 24, 47, 53, 54, 79, 103, 108, 112, 132, 133, 134, 146, 150, 161, 187
Vietnam War, p.10, 58, 126, 175
Wannsee Conference; p.64, 100, 125, 165, 170
Warsaw ghetto; p.87, 99, 140, 141
White, Harry Dexter; p.17
Wiesel, Elie; p.168
Wilhelm II, Kaiser; p.17, 42, 63, 86
Wisliceny, Dieter; p.86, 87, 92, 163, 166, 169, 170, 172
Yalta Conference; p.22
Zieries, Franz; p.96
Zionism; p.39, 163, 165, 179

About the Author

Mark Turley is a half-British, half-German writer. He lives in North London and teaches at a secondary school. He has published short stories and articles in a variety of magazines and released a novel with a small press in 2004. When not writing or teaching he spends time with his wife and two daughters.

Since childhood Mark has been fascinated by Nazi Germany and World War Two. His grandfather was a pilot in the Luftwaffe and was killed on the Russian front. His great-grandfather, Adolf Stein, was a prolific, conservative author of Weimar and early Nazi Germany. Known popularly as *Rumpelstilzchen* he wrote many books and published several articles in the *Völkischer Beobachter* (the National Socialist newspaper).

Mark's father, on the other hand, served in the British forces during the war, briefly in the RAF before being transferred to the infantry in Palestine, where among other duties he supervised the influx of Jewish refugees from Europe. When the British pulled out, he was sent to Benghazi, in Libya. Mark's upbringing was with him and his English stepmother in South London.

It is perhaps the ongoing attempt to reconcile these two sides to his background that led to this book.

Early in 2008 Mark began a petition against the German national laws which criminalise reinterpretation of the history of Nazi Germany. Mark believes in the marketplace of free ideas and thinks that any nation which presents itself as a democracy should too. At present the law provides that 'whoever publicly or in a meeting approves of, denies or renders harmless an act committed under the rule of National Socialism…shall be punished with imprisonment for not more than five years or a fine.'

The petition can be found at: www.petitiononline.com/hammer72